D1190126

FAIRCHILD *Custom* books **Publication**

BUSINESS OF LICENSING

FM 324

ISBN: 978-1-50131-638-8

Fashion Institute of Technology

Originally published in:

Fashion Law: A Guide for Designers, Fashion Executives, and Attorneys, 2nd Edition

by Guillermo C. Jimenez and Barbara Kolsun

Fashion Branding Unraveled

by Kaled K. Hameide

Guide to Fashion Entrepreneurship

by Melissa G. Carr and Lisa Hopkins Newell

Fairchild Books

An imprint of Bloomsbury Publishing Inc

1385 Broadway   50 Bedford Square
New York   London
NY 10018   WC1B 3DP
USA   UK

www.bloombury.com

First published 2015

© Bloomsbury Publishing Inc, 2015

All rights reserved. No part of this publication may be reproduced or transmitted in any form or by any means, electronic or mechanical, including photocopying, recording, or any information storage or retrieval system, without prior permission in writing from the publishers.

No responsibility for loss caused to any individual or organization acting on or refraining from action as a result of the material in this publication can be accepted by Bloomsbury Publishing Inc or the author.

ISBN: 978-1-50131-638-8

Original Publications

Guide to Fashion Entrepreneurship
By Melissa G. Carr and Lisa Hopkins Newell
Pages 39-54 and 129-134
© 2014, Fairchild Books, an imprint of Bloomsbury Publishing, Inc.
ISBN: 9781609014933

Fashion Branding Unraveled
By Kaled K. Hameide
Pages 108-217 and 221-261
© 2011, Fairchild Books, an imprint of Bloomsbury Publishing, Inc.
ISBN: 9781563678745

Fashion Law: A Guide for Designers, Fashion Executives, and Attorneys, 2nd Edition
By Guillermo C. Jimenez and Barbara Kolsun
Pages 25-166
© 2014, Fairchild Books, an imprint of Bloomsbury Publishing, Inc.
ISBN: 9781609018955

Printed and bound in the United States of America

CONTENTS

Guide to Fashion Entrepreneurship

THREE   Brand Personification   1

            Distribution Factors   17

Fashion Branding Unraveled

FOUR   Luxury Fashion Brands   23

FIVE   Mass-Market Fashion Brands   69

SIX   Retail Brands   89

SEVEN   iBrand: The Age of the Interactive, Wireless, and Virtual Brands   131

Fashion Law: A Guide for Designers, Fashion Executives, and Attorneys, 2nd Edition

TWO   Trademarks and Trade Dress   172

THREE   Copyright   192

FOUR   Design Patents, Utility Patents, and Trade Secrets   202

FIVE   Design Piracy Legislation: Should the United States Protect Fashion Design?   213

SEVEN   Fashion Licensing   225

EIGHT   Counterfeiting   249

3

Brand Personification

To cut through the clutter of product saturation, entrepreneurs utilize branding as an effective way to differentiate their products and to establish credibility with the consumer. One must carefully orchestrate interplay between inspired creativity and analytical rigor. Creating a brand perception requires intrusion—a remapping of a consumer's brand preference. The brand must be authentic and powerful enough to force consumers out of their routines and into newness. Consumers must remember the brand experience and note it for long-standing preferences. Iconic fashion brands begin with a collective synergy to create a first, lasting impression at a glance.

Brand Power

A strong brand has incredible power—not just in how it is perceived in the world, but also in how it redefines the competitive landscape, connects with prospects and influencers, creates memorable experiences, builds lasting relationships, and helps entrepreneurs and corporate organizations better manage people, resources, and profits. The following images evoke the power and presence of internationally recognized brands (Figures 3.1, 3.2, 3.3, 3.4, and 3.5).

From a holistic perspective, a **brand** is a distinct entity with a name, sign, or set of perceptions intended to create an identity and differentiation among likeness. It represents a product, idea, or service. **Branding** is a vital strategy laced within brand development. It is the process of attaching a name, image, or reputation to a product, idea, or service.

Branding is a major force in the fashion industry. Effective entrepreneurs utilize branding as the solidifying precursor to a product. It is the fundamental voice that embodies the product. A relentless product differentiation strategy is needed to build recognition. Emotional engagement has become a dominant tactic to build consumer loyalty. From the idiosyncrasy to the obvious, a product's positioning is often conveyed through layers of reinforcement to establish and secure its identity in the marketplace.

KEY CONCEPTS

+ Identify assessment tools for brand analysis.

+ Understand the components of a brand statement.

+ Explore the fundamentals of brand development.

+ Examine emotional drivers to make a brand connection.

+ Establish tactics to building brand equity.

Figure 3.1 Zac Posen ready-to-wear collection. Model: Liya Kebede. *Source: Fairchild Fashion Media.*

Figure 3.2 Gucci ready-to-wear collection. Model: Eugenia Volodina. *Source: AFP/Getty Images.*

Figure 3.3 Alexander Wang ready-to-wear collection. Model: Shu Pei Qin. *Source: Fairchild Fashion Media.*

Figure 3.4 Burberry Prorsum collection. *Source: Fairchild Fashion Media.*

Brand Analysis

When an entrepreneur enters into a branding arena that is laden with product saturation and heavy competition, it can be intimidating or over-whelming. Conducting brand analysis and setting strategy will eradicate uncertainty and ensure a firm start. **Brand analysis** involves sizing up the industry, evaluating the competition, and creating a strategic plan.

The entrepreneur should assess the market:

1. Market size—the scope of competition
2. Growth rate of their particular industry sector
3. Current growth cycle of the industry sector
4. Number of competitors and their relative size
5. Market saturation—price classifications
6. Number of customers and their relative size
7. Type of distribution channels used to access existing/potential customers

If these crucial market assessments are not executed, an entrepreneur may find that the brand may not fit well with the intended sector of the industry or may not be capable of establishing and maintaining a competitive advantage for the new product. Once the assessments are determined as a prosperous opportunity, the long-term direction, objectives, and strategies can be developed. Designer, Rebecca Minkoff explains her well-devised brand formula to enter into a competitive market in Box 3.1.

As a step in assessing the market and conducting brand analysis, entrepreneurs must determine the appropriate price classification for their niche products.

Price Classifications

In the fashion industry, products are segmented by price classifications. Based on the retail price range of a product, a brand will position into a specific price category. Entrepreneurs must evaluate their products to ascertain the extrinsic value that correlates to quality. In ready-to-wear, fabric, construction, and fit are significant factors that dictate quality and steer the price classification. Ready-to-wear apparel is mass produced and manufactured to standard size specifications generated by the brand entity. Consumers often utilize fit as a fundamental factor to garner a price-to-quality relationship. Traditionally, the brand entity allows tolerances per size specification that directly impact fit. Tolerance is a measurement that varies from the desired size specification. The higher the price classification, the lower the allowable tolerance permitted for each size specification, whereas the lower the price classification, the higher the allowable tolerance for each size specification. Size categories are based upon fit, also referred to as the body type, of the targeted consumer. An example in women's apparel is junior, misses, petite, or plus. Junior is an adolescent or youthful body type indicated by sizes with an odd numerical sequence 00–11. Misses is a fully developed woman's body type indicated by an even numerical sequence 0–12. Specialty sizes are plus, petite, and tall. The fit of the garment caters to average body specifications for the stated category.

There are six major price classifications in the fashion and beauty sector: designer, bridge, contemporary, better, moderate, and budget.

1. *Designer.* This is the highest price point in luxury ready-to-wear, accessories, footwear, and beauty. Prestigious designer brands such as Prada, Yves St. Laurent, Balenciaga, Ralph Lauren, and Christian Louboutin are in this price sector. Designer boutiques, luxury multibrand boutiques, and specialty stores, such as Bergdorf Goodman, Neiman Marcus, and Saks Fifth Avenue, retail these products. This category has the most astute quality in mass-produced goods. The price points range into the thousands from brand to brand.

2. *Bridge.* This price point positions slightly lower than designer. It consists of designer diffusion collections—strong aesthetics but in lower quality, thus lower prices. Notable collections are C by Chloe, D&G by Dolce & Gabbana, Elie Tahari, CH by Carolina Herrera, and Michael Kors. The prices vary by designer or manufacturer.

3. *Contemporary.* Products in this classification market to youthful-spirited consumers. Notable brands are Rag & Bone, Marc by Marc Jacobs, Alice + Olivia, and Elizabeth and James. Retailers such as Barneys, Nordstrom, and multibrand boutiques carry this price point, which varies for each brand and typically ranges from $300 to $1,000.

4. *Better.* This price point caters to the mass market—the largest consumer segment. Manufacturers such as Liz Claiborne and

Figure 3.5 Christian Louboutin footwear. *Source: Corbis.*

BOX 3.1 Rebecca Minkoff

How to Break into a Crowded Industry

Rebecca Minkoff's fast-track growth is particularly notable because she found success in an already crowded and fiercely competitive fashion industry. While the number of fashion-design houses has decreased 2.3 percent annually since 2005, industry revenues have been growing 0.6 percent per year, giving the remaining players an increasingly bigger piece of the market, according to IBISWorld, a market-research firm based in Los Angeles. Here, Minkoff shares her top three tips for launching a business in a competitive industry:

1. **Be unique.** Piggybacking on an existing product or service usually won't get your business noticed in competitive markets, Minkoff says. Yours should fill a need and stand out from the competition. "I created a line for what I wanted to wear—and what I saw there was a lack of in the market—in terms of design and function at an affordable price," she says.

2. **Know your price point.** Regardless of the industry, customers want a quality product for a great price, Minkoff says. Setting an appropriate price for a product or service is crucial. Minkoff learned that lesson after she downgraded the leather for a particular handbag without lowering the retail price. "I didn't put a tag on it saying it was made with this other type of leather, but the bag didn't look the same, and my customers knew it," she says. "We recognized that immediately when sales for the item didn't perform."

3. **Listen and respond.** Establishing communication with customers and making them feel a part of the decision-making process has been important to Minkoff's success.

Source: J. Fell. 2011. Partial interview from "How a Young Fashion Designer Stands Out in a Crowded Market." *Entrepreneur.com,* May 5. http://www.entrepreneur.com/article/219578

Jones New York provide quality products at affordable price points. Department stores such as Macy's and Dillard's carry these lines. Brand retailers such as Ann Taylor, Banana Republic, and J.Crew focus on this price sector. The retail price points are typically under $200.

5. *Moderate.* These are affordable fashion products for the mass-market consumer. Products have a lower quality to maintain their low-price stance. Brand retailers such as Gap and Zara and department stores such as Kohl's and JCPenney cater to this price segment. The price range is typically below $100.

6. *Budget.* This is the lowest price-point class. Fast-fashion goods positioned in this price sector are trend-driven products that are low-quality goods and sold in high volume at low price points. Retailers such as Forever 21 and H&M and big-box stores such as Kmart and Walmart cater to this price segment.

Brand Statement

To plan for brand development there needs to be an overarching focal point. Much like the mission and vision statements for the company, many entrepreneurs create brand statements. A **brand statement** is a touchstone to communicate the intrinsic value of the brand and provides direction for where the brand is going in the market. A brand statement defines the company's brand message and promise. It identifies where the company is and is used as a tool to guide the company in the future. A brand statement also can be used as a consistency test to ensure all brand efforts are promoting the brand, and not confusing consumers.

Questions to examine when developing a brand statement:

- What is the brand message?
- How does the consumer experience the brand?
- What brand concepts are compelling and differentiating?

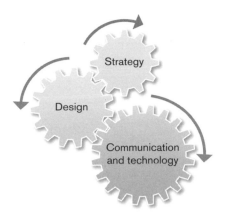

Figure 3.6 Brand synergy. Brands have a unique intersection of strategy, communications, design, and technology.

Brand Building

In today's competitive industry, entrepreneurs must harness traditional communications, digital media, mobile devices, and social networks to make every touch point speak in unison. In every price classification, powerful brands have a unique intersection of strategy, communications, design and technology—the synergy of brand building (Figure 3.6).

CASE STUDY 3.1   The Top Ten Designers

In [2012]'s top ten list of most-recognized designer brands, Calvin Klein, Tommy Hilfiger and Ralph Lauren take the three top spots—and for good reason. Each of these brands stands for a particular genre of Americana that U.S. consumers react to emotionally, and likely identify with. There's no denying the fact that when it comes to brand awareness, American consumers like to keep things close to home.

Calvin Klein, for instance, is a homegrown megabrand with an offering that spans three retail tiers (designer, bridge, and better) and a variety of categories. Tommy Hilfiger's take on preppy-with-a-twist designs offers a novel vision of American East Coast dress codes, and Ralph Lauren, like no other U.S. designer, embodies quintessential luxury rendered through an American lens.

Brand proclivities aside, these three brands are also masters at conveying their messages to consumers. Gucci, in fourth position, knows a hot commodity when it sees one. The Italian fashion company secured Charlotte

Casiraghi, the beautiful yet press-shy daughter of Princess Caroline of Monaco. Coming in at number five, Vera Wang. Besides her high-profile bridal and ready-to-wear collections, Wang has a significant presence at Kohl's with Simply Vera Vera Wang and the Princess Vera Wang junior collection. She also offers more affordably priced bridal gowns through a deal with David's Bridal and the Vera Wang Love collection of wedding bands at Zales.

The Top 10:
1. Calvin Klein
2. Tommy Hilfiger
3. Ralph Lauren
4. Gucci
5. Vera Wang
6. DKNY
7. Louis Vuitton
8. Chanel
9. Dolce & Gabbana
10. Giorgio Armani

Source: Marc Karimzadeh. 2012. "The Top 10 Designers." *Women's Wear Daily,* December 13. http://www.wwd.com/fashion-news/fashion-features/the-top-10-designers-6521785

Brand building is comprised of innovative insights and strategies, brought to life by a product message that engages the consumer.

Core aspects of brand building:

- *Emotion:* Brands drive growth by connecting to emotion and reason in equal measure. For example, Bobbi Brown Cosmetics has redefined beauty to enhance one's unique beauty, not cover it up. The products are formulated to create a natural and healthy appearance. The duality of branding self-esteem and enhancement through product gives an emotional stance to the consumer.
- *Creativity:* Brands are crafted and expressed through inspiration and creativity to generate preference and loyalty. For example, Anna Sui collections are riddled with colorful patterns and prints and the mixing of each. This creative use of texture, color, layering, and mixing is the brand's signature. It has created brand recognition and consumer loyalty. Missoni has masterfully intrigued and maintained consumer loyalty with their iconic pattern, robust color palette, and modern knitwear collections. Both designers have created brand recognition and consumer loyalty with strategic tactics in textiles and design.
- *Longevity:* Brands must retain relevance and appeal over time, using intelligent brand management techniques and metrics. An example, Ralph Lauren collections expand across multiple categories of business and price point. The brands have an aura of timelessness that gives them life beyond the season of purchase. This longevity factor has made the brand a classic.
- *Financial:* Brands, if managed well, enable companies to embody their vision and inspire stakeholders—customers, employees, partners, and the investment community. Brands are economic assets to be invested in and managed for financial returns. For example, lululemon athletica is a publicly traded company that embodies a proven brand strategy with financial stability for the company and its investor.

As a brand owner or creator, entrepreneurs have a unique perspective that builds the brand identity.

Brand Identity

An entrepreneur must create a brand identity that evokes dynamism within its sector of the industry. It must have a point of origin, a storyline, and a concise vantage point to generate consumer interest. Consumers are highly discerning and have myriad choices to satisfy their needs and wants. Brand identity and product consistency ensures a concise vantage point the consumer can rely upon. The repetition and evolution secures and strengthens the identity of the brand in the marketplace.

Brand identity is the personality of a product. It is a set of distinct characteristics that provides identity cues to the consumer. It can be a visual or physical aesthetics or mental association, such as a symbol, of the brand.

- *Color:* Valentino red
- *Graphic:* Target bullseye
- *Logo:* Movado dot (Figure 3.7)
- *Packaging:* Tiffany blue box (Figure 3.8)
- *Typography:* H&M font

Figure 3.7 Brand identification with a symbol: A Movado timepiece with the iconic dot. *Source: Denis Beyeler/Alamy.*

Figure 3.8 Brand identification utilizing color: Tiffany & Co. blue box. *Source: Brendan O'Sullivan/REX.*

Brand Name

What sets the trajectory of a brand's identity often begins with its name: as the adage claims, everything is in a name. The foundation that brings a product to life starts with creating the **brand name.** A brand name is a symbol, word, logo, or set of perceptions intended to identify or represent a product or service. A fundamental goal in developing a brand name is to create a unique identity. The same principle is applicable for an **eponymous brand.** Eponymous brands reflect the name of a person who inspired, designed, or created the idea, product, or service (e.g., Patrick Kelly, Christian Dior, Carolina Herrera, and Marc Jacobs).

Although the formation of a company name is important, it can differ from the product's brand name. The product name, often referred to as the brand name, will permeate the market and establish a relationship with the intended consumer. The brand name can be suggestive or arbitrary rather than descriptive. This approach will allow unlimited flexibility for future brand extension growth.

When a brand name is applied to a product, it should require imagination, thought, or perception to determine the nature of the goods. It should complement the company's positioning and resonate with the target market.

The juxtaposition and dichotomy of the brand name also can evoke emotions of interest and curiosity. For example, the brand name

Figure 3.9 *d*irt, a luxurious natural body scrub collection. *Source: Erthe Beaute, LLC.*

of a luxurious natural body scrub collection is *d*irt (Figure 3.9). The company's name is Erthe Beaute. The product's natural ingredients and earth-inspired essence support the brand name. The name resonates with the contemporary consumer and ecoconscious users because of its earthy, whimsical brand name. Its luxury packaging and suitable product names further define the brand. Furthermore, *d*irt's tagline, "groundbreaking beauty," reinforces the brand's product philosophy of being a niche, underground, natural beauty product. A **tagline** is the verbal or written portion of a message that summarizes the main idea in a few memorable words.

Company Name

Unlike a brand name, a company name provides legal identity to the business entity in a specific trade sector. The company name can be separate and distinct from the brand name of a product or service, or it can be the same. When a company's name is different from their brand name, a

Tip 3.1 **Create-a-minute!**

Remember: Quality is often revealed in the details. In accessories and personal care, packaging is an extension of a product. It often defines the brand image in the mind of the consumer.

term that often is used to describe the brand name is a "DBA," which is the acronym for "doing business as." An example would be the company Erthe Beaute LLC, whose product brand name is *dirt*. The company is legally recognized as the limited liability corporation; however, it conducts business as *dirt*. A core reason to separate the company name from the brand name is for growth or dissolving a brand without interfering with the legal business entity.

Creating a company/business name is a significant task for an entrepreneur. Here are basic guidelines:

- Create a company name that is meaningful and distinct from direct and indirect competition.
- Create a name that resonates with the trade sector and target market.
- Create a name that can be effortlessly pronounced.
- Be mindful of creative name spelling. It can be misinterpreted as erroneous.
- Be mindful that if you use an eponymous name, it will be associated with the success and failure of the company.

Another example of company delineation is subsidiary structuring of secondary business units under a parent company. Louis Vuitton Moët Hennessy (LVMH) has different business entities under its umbrella. Each business is independently operated, yet maintains a relationship with the others through the parent ownership. Examples include LVMH and Donna Karan (Figure 3.10).

As an entrepreneur, one must complete due diligence by researching the availability of the company and brand name. The most common way to ensure name availability is by searching a state's Secretary of State website. Registering a limited liability or corporation business entity/company name is mandatory. In most states, a company will register its name at the county level, but some states require the name to be registered at the state level. It is important to research the law of the state where the business will be formed to see the requirements. A second search option is in the United States Trademark and Patent Office (USTPO) website. Not all companies file claims of ownership of the company or brand mark. Lastly, conduct a name search on all online search engines to see if the name is available. It is critical to conduct thorough name research to avoid trademark infringement.

Figure 3.10 Donna Karan collection. *Source: Victor VIRGILE/Gamma-Rapho/Getty Images.*

Brand Positioning

At the creation of a brand, the product's price classification must be established to position it into a sector of the fashion industry and gain

Tip 3.2 **Create-a-minute!**

Remember: When creating your company name or brand name, research is critical! Be sure the name you choose is available but, equally important, not similar to an existing brand.

identity with the intended consumer. Price classifications are the core determinant of a brand's positioning strategy. The six price classifications for mass produced consumer products are designer, bridge, contemporary, better, moderate, and budget. The highest price classification is designer and descends to budget. The actual price point categories come from the items' industry sector—ready-to-wear is a different price classification than beauty.

Brand positioning is a company's intended posture and image of the brand in the mind of the consumer. It highlights its differentiation among the competition and its advantage in the price classification. Differentiation reflects what is unique or distinctly sets a brand apart from the competition.

In the designer market, Louis Vuitton is positioned as a luxury brand in the designer price sector of the fashion industry (Figure 3.11). The company has successfully personified its consumer as the consummate

Figure 3.11 Louis Vuitton has superior high-quality travel luggage. Product shown was featured at a new store opening celebrating Vuitton's 150th anniversary, February 10, 2004, in New York City. *Source: Peter Kramer/Getty Images Entertainment/Getty Images.*

Tip 3.3 Create-a-minute!

Remember: The psychographics of your customer can easily be identified in their daily routine—from sunrise to sunset.

luxury traveler. Its positioning was created upon introduction of the brand. The brand's point of origin was established in 1854 with its high quality travel luggage that in this modern day is still touted as the Art of Traveling. The company has capitalized on its heritage of superior quality through a succession of brand extensions.

Successful brands have the target customer in mind when creating the product collection. A muse is a personification of the target customer that inspires aesthetics of the brand's image. To capture the essence of the brand persona, entrepreneurs often create a visual board using consumer magazine tear sheets to identify who the muse will be for the brand. This aids in knowing the psychographic matrix for the targeted consumer. Here are questions to consider to aid in harnessing and personifying the brand's positioning:

- What is the targeted consumer demographic—age, education, income, etc.?
- What is the targeted consumer personality type?
- What is the consumer's style—apparel, home décor, etc.?
- What is the consumer's career/lifestyle?
- What are the targeted consumer's hobbies, habits, passions, and pursuits?

By researching the aforementioned questions, an entrepreneur will generate the ideology of the targeted consumer and define the parameters for designing, branding, and selling the product. It's a process of creating a narrative about the consumer in order to identify and ultimately satisfy that consumer's needs or wants: How well do you know your customer and does your brand reflect their interest and mirror their lifestyle? A creative tool that merges technology with fashion is the collaboration between Samsung and Polyvore. With the Samsung GALAXY Note II smartphone, consumers can explore their creativity and put together their own fashion style with the enhanced Easy Clip feature (see Box 3.2 consumer profile and Figure 3.12 GALAXY Note II Smartphone).

Brand extensions are product lines marketed under the same general brand as a previous item or items. Ralph Lauren is touted as the authority on lifestyle branding. His empire ranges from designer to moderate price classifications across apparel product categories. The company stretches its branding strategy into home furnishing collections and his RL restaurants. In apparel, Ralph Lauren has successfully expanded different lines under his varied brands. Another example of brand extension is Louis Vuitton. The distinct brand extension difference from Ralph Lauren is that Louis Vuitton has expanded in a single price classification of prestige to remain solely accessible to their targeted consumer. Louis Vuitton has successfully spread the integrity of its positioning from luxury

BOX 3.2 Consumer Profile

Developing a consumer profile brings the consumer to life in the mind of the entrepreneur. By researching or extracting information about the targeted consumer, you essentially build the "ideal" target customer. This tangible set of demographic, geographic, and behavioral information will help shape the product attributes and benefits. This method of pinpointing a single person from a homogeneous group yields the model consumer for a product or service. This development process is considered idea generation, keeping the entrepreneur sharply focused on its targeted consumer.

Exemplify your target customer using the basic information below.

Name:

Gender:

Age:

Family status:

Annual income:

Geographic location:

Career:

Fashion style:

Brand loyalty:

Buying habits:

Leisure activities:

Travel destinations:

Social media favorites:

Pursuits and passion:

Must-haves:

Figure 3.12 Samsung GALAXY Note II smartphone muse board app. *Source: Samsung.*

travel cases into other product categories such as ready-to-wear, time-pieces, accessories, and footwear (Figure 3.13).

Brand Story

Consumers are intelligent, well-researched, and demanding. Technology has provided a wealth of trade knowledge to the consumer. Increasingly, consumers have fundamental information at their fingertips. They readily seek the story behind the brand and build a relationship with the brand. For many fashion companies, the dominant branding mission has become lifestyle driven. Brands are being introduced within the context of lifestyle utility, while romancing their features and benefits as the ancillary matter.

The entrepreneur must stay ahead of the consumer and create a lure of interest and entertainment that intrigues the target market. Many brands have extended the brand's voice and use a brand story to add meaningful depth and emotional integrity to the product. The core element of a **brand story** is a narrative that communicates the ethos of the brand. It's used to generate brand power through an emotional connection with consumers, whereas the brand is perceived as an extension of consumers' personalities and lifestyle. The most successful fashion brands evoke emotion thorough a series of lifestyle images in their advertisements, websites, and social media platforms. They reflect and confirm the consumer's aspiration, identity, and stature. These visual monologues beckon the consumer to live the brand (Box 3.3).

When a consumer inquires about the derivative of a name, history, or heritage, this is an entrepreneurial opportunity to tell the product or brand story. The story becomes the overarching strategy to engage the consumer and ignite brand loyalty. **Brand loyalty** is when a consumer buys the same manufacturer-originated product or service repeatedly over time rather than buying from competition within the category. Placing consumers outside of a brand story reveals that there are voids in their closets and reinforces the need for relationship with a specific brand by purchasing a product.

A product is a product and a dress is a dress, it seems. One brand story that permeates the industry is the legacy of the little black dress (LBD)

Figure 3.13 Ralph Lauren collection. *Source: Victor VIRGILE/Gamma-Rapho/Getty Images.*

BOX 3.3 *dirt*: Brand Story

Despite its grimy reputation, dirt is literally a natural substance that cleanses, nourishes, and stimulates growth, and produces beauty among other things. Organic in nature, it's the mastermind behind every harvest. We were inspired by its nutrient-rich properties, hence begins the story of our groundbreaking beauty… DIRT.

Created to nurture the body and broaden the landscape of beauty, the DIRT team hit the ground and stayed there. They dug in the garden, rummaged through the pantry and refrigerator to concoct exfoliation recipes from fruits, vegetables, and natural ingredients that could remove dead skin cells while infusing moisture for a healthy, radiant glow. In the laboratory, they refined culinary creations into formulas packed with antioxidants, vitamins, botanical and essential oils and cultivated luxurious body treatments that inspire personal beauty rituals.

Source: Courtesy of Erthe Beaute, LLC. www.dirtbeaute.com

Figure 3.14 Little black dress. Elie Saab ready-to-wear. Model: Drielle Valeretto. *Source: Fairchild Fashion Media.*

that began with Coco Chanel—a story wrapped into a single silhouette. Understanding the story behind the LBD brings interest. The ideology comes to life and creates a relationship with the wearer. It becomes an artistic expression that extends from one fashion generation to the next. It has become a staple in the wardrobe of women across the world. What was once merely a symbol of mourning has become a universal statement for understated elegance and a must-have item for designers and fashionable women across every price classification (Figure 3.14).

Brand Design

Once the company name is established, a brand name is created, the brand positioning is determined, and a story is developed, the brand aesthetics warrant development. The brand design aesthetics are the carriage of the product. They support the packaging of the brand and are the conduit to facilitate visual identity in tandem with the product.

Brand design, the micro level of brand identity, is where the details that settle into the mind of the consumer reside—the logo, the label, the color of the label, the shape of the label, the font, the hangtag, and so on. For a cohesive branding approach, use the same color scheme, fonts, and design for brand labels, marketing materials, business cards, letterhead, and websites and blogs.

At point of sale, there must be a continuum to the brand's dynamism and perception that extends beyond the product to maintain brand positioning and brand loyalty. A brand's logo is just as important as the name. The logo is the first visceral connection the consumer makes with the brand. It triggers the brand perception.

Practical considerations in logo design:

- It must be authentic and easily recognizable.
- Its intention and message should be perfectly clear.
- It must reflect the sensibilities of the targeted consumer.
- It must reproduce well in various sizes and media.

Brand Appeal

To truly captivate an audience, a brand must know itself. Entrepreneurs should be acutely aware of the product's point-of-difference. This will become the brand's competitive advantage.

A **competitive advantage** exists when the factors critical for success within the industry permit the brand to outperform its competitors. Advantages can be gained by having differentiation in terms of providing superior performance or unique attributes that are important to customers. A key to building the brand's image is to be unique within the positioned category.

Each price category has an observed set of aesthetics that reflect the target market. For example, the luxury market has an image of refined exclusivity that conveys simplicity or extravagance. The premium market has a youthful, innovative edge that conveys innovative rebellion with confidence. The better market has a practicality that reads as classic and enduring. The mass and fast-fashion markets have an explicit sense of bold urgency that reads now or never.

Brand Equity

Companies build brand equity through strategic branding execution that happens over time. Brand equity is achieved through brand recognition, brand image, product usage, and customer loyalty. **Brand equity** is the value of a brand. The three common ways brand equity is built:

- *Introduction:* Introduce quality products with the strategic intent to use the brand platform to launch product extensions. Example: Yoga Smoga is high performance, modern yoga clothing company that retains a connection to yoga's ancient Indian roots.
- *Elaboration:* Establish a memorable brand experience that is positive and encourages repeat purchases. Example: Yoga Smoga reiterates their wellness approach through their product and mantra of one breath at a time. Their iconic logo is based on traditional symbology that conveys a balanced and powerful energy center.
- *Fortification:* The brand should carry a consistent message that reinforces its positioning in the mind of the consumer. Example: YogaSmoga supports health, education, and financial support to small cottage industries through its Namaskar Foundation.

To effectively build brand equity, the distribution channels must be parallel in positioning to reach the consumer and solidify the brand message. An entrepreneur must consider the appropriate conduits to market and sell his or her product or service. The channels must mirror the brand personification or image. This is vital to the survival of the brand's identity in the marketplace. A brand must convey a singular brand message from conception to distribution to generated consumer loyalty and build equity.

Summary

Brand personification is a pivotal process that establishes a relationship with the consumer by providing consistent messages about a product or service using multiple platforms. Successful branding involves establishing a clear brand message. The development of a cohesive mixture of elements and strategies creates brand identity. Understanding what makes a product unique provides insight for differentiation and brand image. For branding success, an emotional connection must be made with the consumer. To create brand loyalty, consumers must view the brand as an extension of their personalities and lifestyle.

Online Resources

Entrepreneur.com

A publication that carries news stories about entrepreneurialism, small business management, and business opportunities.
www.entrepreneur.com

Marketing Scoop

A useful website for branding and social media. An Internet marketing expert reveals powerful marketing secrets.
www.marketingscoop.com

Activity 3.1 Brand Identity

1. What is your brand's distinct characteristic or point of difference?
2. Select an established fashion brand with which you've had a positive brand experience. Identify and list the factors about the brand that created the positive experience.
3. List factors that you perceive are pivotal to developing a positive brand experience for your new brand or brand extension.

TRADE TERMS

brand

branding

brand analysis

brand statement

brand identity

brand name

eponymous brand

tagline

brand positioning

brand extensions

brand story

brand loyalty

competitive advantage

brand equity

Activity 3.2 Brand Identity

1. What are three adjectives that describe your product?

2. Define your brand positioning.

3. Write a brand statement for your new product and/or brand extension.

Bibliography

American Marketing Association. "Dictionary." Accessed April 2013. http://www.marketingpower.com/_layouts/Dictionary.aspx.

Bobbibrowncosmetics.com. "Bobbi Buzz: Bobbi's Story." http://www.bobbibrowncosmetics.com/cms/bobbi_buzz/bobbi_story_index.tmpl?cm_sp=Gnav-_-BobbiBuzz-_-BobbisStory

BusinessDictionary.com. s.v. "Branding." http://www.business dictionary.com/definition/marketing.html

Hameide, Kaled. 2011. *Fashion Branding Unraveled.* New York: Fairchild Books.

Marketing Scoop. "Emotional Marketing." Accessed April 2013. http://www.marketingscoop.com/emotional-marketing.htm

Reiss, Craig. 2011. "How to Build a Winning Brand." *Entrepreneur .com.* Accessed April 2013. http://www.entrepreneur.com/article /219314

Tip 8.1 Create-a-minute!

Emerging trends are my friend! I must stay ahead of the curve by researching new opportunities in my business sector.

share projection or forecasting, is to define what business exists or remains within the market and how best to pursue that business with a strategic distribution plan. The approach is subjective and measured by the overall size of the market.

Establish entities, assess the company's current business, quantify the business that remains, and then adopt strategic planning initiatives that increase sales or garner market share from the competition. For instance, JCPenney's 2012 Strategy: With newly appointed executives from Apple and Target came new strategies and a bold overhaul. JCPenney has shifted from a coupon-driven sales-oriented destination in favor of everyday low pricing of "fair and square." The fun advertising campaign is reminiscent of Target, and the new logo has a fresh, clean, modern appeal. The redesigned stores reflect a well-needed update. Although the aesthetics have changed, the challenge is convincing the city-slick, suburban savvy consumer to flee from their tried and true brand-loyal Target commitment to JCPenney's new look. It is apparent that the strategy was developed to increase sales, radically penetrate a new market, and steal market share from the competitors. The strategy has since yielded a negative response (Box 8.2). Consumer readiness is a significant variable that proved the new strategy to be a failed attempt to modernize a fixed strategy employed by the company.

Distribution Factors

Beyond selecting the best distribution channels to reach the consumer, the entrepreneur must be sensitive to balance in the marketplace. To avoid the sporadic approach of random distribution, a distribution plan is also a balancing tool for product dissemination. It is equally important to consider the proximity of channel partners for balanced exposure in the marketplace. If distribution is concentrated, it may cause unnecessary competition between channels and may suppress sales for one or both channel partners.

Entrepreneurs need to know who their potential buyers are, where they buy, when they buy, how they buy, and what they buy. The level of distribution coverage needed to effectively address the customer's needs is measured in terms of the intensity with which the product is made available. The density or number of stores in a particular geographical area and the type of intermediaries used constitute the basics of distribution coverage.

Entrepreneurs are typically conscious of channel **distribution intensity.** This is the availability and the level of saturation of the product in the marketplace in a concentrated geographic area or channel. Market saturation occurs when the product is offered in so many channels that the product is no longer demanded or desired by the targeted consumer. If a brand is distributed in various retail outlets in a concentrated area

BOX 8.2 JCPenney's Strategy Shift

JCPenney: Was Ron Johnson's Strategy Wrong?

JCPenney Co. [JCP] has ousted its CEO, Ron Johnson, the chief executive who reinvented retail at Apple Inc. [AAPL] and who arrived at JCPenney just 17 months ago. Mr. Johnson had a bold vision for JCPenney. On joining the firm, he said, "In the U.S., the department store has a chance to regain its status as the leader in style, the leader in excitement. It will be a period of true innovation for this company."

Mr. Johnson abruptly scrapped JCPenney's dubious pricing policies of marking up prices and then offering discounts with heavy promotions and coupons. He proposed to offer more interesting products, from lines like Martha Stewart and Joe Fresh, at reasonable prices all the time.

The approach didn't fare well with Penney's customer base of bargain hunters. They rebelled, traffic declined, sales fell, and JCPenney slowly returned to the prior era of pricing, with lots of promotions, lots of price-focused ads, and marked-up prices that would be later marked down.

Nor did shoppers respond when Penney started to reintroduce markdowns last year. Sales fell 25 percent in the year that ended Feb. 2 [2013], depriving Penney of $4.3 billion in revenue and causing analysts to ask whether it might run out of cash needed to fund its overhaul.

Above all, Mr. Johnson destroyed his existing business model before the new business model was put in place. As David Cush, Virgin America CEO, said this morning on CNBC's *Squawkbox:* "Don't destroy your old revenue model before you have proved your new revenue model. It was a great idea. But you have this massive structure that you need to support. Revenue supports your structure. You've got to make sure that the new model works before you destroy the old one."

Source: Steve Denning. 2013. "J.C. Penny: Was Ron Johnson's Strategy Wrong?" *Forbes,* April 9. http://www.forbes.com/sites/stevedenning/2013/04/09/j-c-penney-was-ron-johnsons-strategy-wrong/

Figure 8.3 Chloé is a youthful, modern designer collection with very selective distribution channels in the United States market. *Source: Victor VIRGILE/Gamma-Rapho/Getty Images.*

with parallel consumers, the saturation of product will stagnate sales. To avoid market saturation or the cannibalism of sales, entrepreneurs will strategically select channel partners to sell products (Create Tip 8.2). This is referred to as **selective distribution.** Selective distribution is a preferred method of distribution for prestigious brands. For example, Chloé is a youthful, modern, and slightly bohemian designer collection with very selective distribution channels in the United States market (Figure 8.3). The retail partners are noncompeting geographic areas and adhere to image criteria set by the manufacture.

Relative to Chloé, in the contemporary price classification, Free People is a youthful bohemian brand that has **intensive distribution** (Figure 8.4). This distribution approach concentrates product into channels for the targeted consumer to encounter the product at maximum

Tip 8.2 **Create-a-minute!**

I must pick and choose my retail partners and select the preferred geographic locations for distribution to avoid market saturation.

Figure 8.4 Free People is a youthful, bohemian-styled brand that has intensive distribution.
Source: 911 Pictures.

capacity without saturation. In tandem, in the fragrance sector, the long awaited Lady Gaga Fame perfume was introduced to the market with intense distribution (Figure 8.5). On the release date, it was featured in Sephora, Nordstrom, and Macy's stores and online among other outlets.

Another opportunity that can create sales demand is **exclusive distribution.** This is a strategy where as a company will distribute their products to a limited channel or single channel partner. For example, CH by Carolina Herrera employs an exclusive distribution strategy (Figure 8.6). Another example is a private label brand, such as Macy's INC International Concept Brand, or a license agreement, such as Vera Wang's Simply Vera Vera Wang for Kohl's collection. The timeline for exclusivity can vary from a short-term to a permanent commitment. Premium brands will often launch with an exclusive partner and eventually released to the other channel partners.

Distribution Channel Expansion

Distribution assessment is an ongoing process. Entrepreneurs are market opportunists. They seek innovative and insightful ways to boost revenues and maintain profitability. Conducting distribution assessment also enables channel expansion. Companies will often survey the market for new channel opportunities that were not initially considered or are now

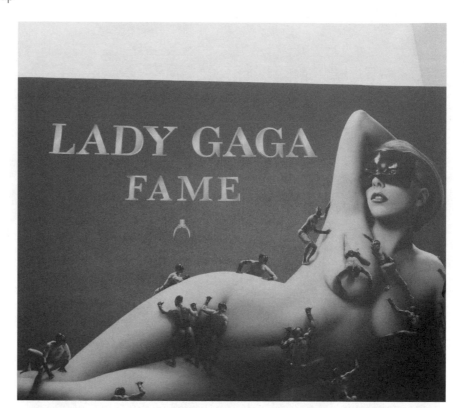

Figure 8.5 The long-awaited Lady Gaga Fame perfume was introduced to the market with intense distribution. *Source: Fairchild Fashion Media.*

Figure 8.6 CH by Carolina Herrera employs an exclusive distribution strategy with its perfume campaign. *Source: Fairchild Fashion Media.*

BOX 8.3 Alexander Wang Interview

"Fashion in some people's eyes is very untouchable and super-indulgent," he said. "For me, it's just clothes to be worn. And at the end of the day, the point is to sell the product."

That sounds pretty hard-nosed, coming as it does from fashion's latest It Child, a lanky, tousled design-school dropout who, in a scant five years, has leapfrogged from toting garment bags for *Vogue* to mapping out the vision behind a $25-million family business that is growing at a gallop. Mr. Wang's aggressively street-inflected collections are as avidly monitored by fashion insiders as they are by the shoppers who snap up his leather leggings, draped jersey dresses, and biker vests.

Mr. Wang's success is partly an outgrowth of his unstudied sexy aesthetic, a tough but sultry look that is as much his stock in trade as his signature filmy T-shirts. But lately this go-to designer for models and assorted urban sylphs has shown signs of growing up. His

sophisticated shapes and wallet-friendly prices are now speaking compellingly to a mature population of bankers, teachers and Botoxed social dragonflies who aspire to his brand of urban cool.

Mr. Wang runs his mini-empire without outside backers or benefit of a family fortune. He works alongside his mother; his sister-in law, Aimie Wang, an accountant; and his brother, Dennis Wang, who brings to the enterprise a background in international business development. "Alexander is the ultimate shopper," Dennis Wang said. "He's very aware of what's out there—the different looks, the different price points. He has a very innate sense, a clarity of vision, of where he sees the company going. Everybody we bring on, from accounting to production, he has an interest in meeting."

Source: R. La Ferla. 2009. "Alexander Wang, For Cool Kids, and Now You." *The New York Times*, Dec. 9. http://www.nytimes.com/2009/12/10/fashion/10WANG.html?pagewanted=all

---

emerging due to a market shift. The strategy has to be an inextricable part of a broader performance management regime that constantly tests and refines the distribution strategy as new information comes to light.

For example, Alexander Wang's women's collection demographic was centered on city-chic, young women who desired an edgy yet effortless look (Box 8.3, Figure 8.7). Distribution channels that cater to that consumer were boutique retailers, such as Jeffery in the meatpacking district of New York. As Wang's collections gained momentum and became more defined, the brand started to appeal to a slightly older, more refined customer who desired the same look. This new demographic triggered a need to broaden channel distribution to reach the new market segment. Products are now positioned into specialty store retailers such as Barneys New York, Bergdorf Goodman, and Fred Segal.

Summary

Entrepreneurs need to define an effective multichannel strategy for selling. Successful companies prioritize the markets they plan to target and outline routes to reach the targeted consumer. The ever-changing business environment allows for a greater need to pursue several sales channels at the same time. Entrepreneurs must develop channel routes that are balanced and used to inform, interact, transact, and deliver. By selecting distribution channels with a parallel brand image and price classification range, the brand integrity remains intact and a unified brand message echoes to the targeted consumer.

Online Resources

U.S. Small Business Administration
www.sba.gov/content/ideas-growing-your-business

Figure 8.7 Alexander Wang's women's collection demographic was centered on city chic, young women who desired an edgy yet effortless look. Alexander Wang, 2012. *Source: Fairchild Fashion Media.*

TRADE TERMS

sales projections

distribution strategy

distribution channel

channel management

market demand

market penetration

market share

distribution intensity

selective distribution

intensive distribution

exclusive distribution

Activity 8.1 Sales Projections

Create a sales projection plan—by unit, by phase of business.

As an entrepreneur, you will build a sales plan to project how you will sell the product inventory across your seasonal selling period. Consider the number of units you will sell per week for each item. Selling should vary to establish best sellers from fringe or secondary selling.

Determine how many units of your inventory will sell across the three phases of business: introductory, maintenance, and clearance. Then determine the estimated duration of each phase of business. A best practice for unit projections is to determine what percentage of sales will occur in each phase.

Will 30 percent of your total inventory sell in the first 2 weeks and 50 percent during the next 3 weeks, then 20 percent the last 2 weeks? Toggle the numbers/units sold on the basis of how you believe your product will sell.

Activity 8.2 Distribution

What is the intended distribution strategy for your product extension? Explain why?

Bibliography

Burns, Leslie Davis, Kathy K. Mullet, and Nancy O. Bryant. 2011. *The Business of Fashion.* 4th Ed. New York: Fairchild Books.

Businessdictionary.com, s.v. "distribution channel." Accessed May 2013. http://www.businessdictionary.com/definition/distribution-channel.html#ixzz1x1s9FQmT

Businessdictionary.com, s.v. "distribution intensity." Accessed May 2013. http://www.businessdictionary.com/definition/distribution-intensity.html#ixzz23ePqRPD2

Businessdictionary.com, s.v. "exclusive distribution." Accessed May 2013. http://www.businessdictionary.com/definition/exclusive-distribution.html#ixzz23eNUT2R3

Businessdictionary.com, s.v. "market demand." Accessed May 2013. http://www.businessdictionary.com/definition/market-demand.html#ixzz24nZsaGxh:

Businessdictionary.com, s.v. "selective distribution." Accessed May 2013. http://www.businessdictionary.com/definition/selective-distribution.html#ixzz23eMx4xg7

Cron.com. "Small Business." Accessed August 31, 2012. http://smallbusiness.chron.com/

Investopedia.com, s.v. "market penetration." Accessed May 2013. http://www.investopedia.com/terms/m/market-penetration.asp#ixzz2548b52un

La Ferla, Ruthe. 2009. "Alexander Wang For Cool Kids and Now For You." *New York Times,* Dec. 10. http://www.nytimes.com/2009/12/10/fashion/10WANG.html?pagewanted=all

Mourdoukoutas, Panos. 2012. "JCPenney's Strategic Mistake. *Forbes,* Aug. 10. Accessed August 31, 2012. http://www.forbes.com/sites/panosmourdoukoutas/2012/08/10/j-c-pennys-strategic-mistake/

4 Luxury Fashion Brands

The quest for luxury is as old as the early days of civilization. Of all segments, luxury seems to have been a good indicator of social and technological changes. Being so closely driven by quality and crafts-manship, it has been an arena for the manifestation of artistry and innovation. At the social level, it's been a good identifier of social status in almost all societies; it defined aristocracy and royalty and eventually attested to the level of democratization in societies as indicated by how fast wealth spread and how far luxury trickled down.

Until the nineteenth century, much of what was considered luxury was custom made. Clothes, jewelry, shoes, even fragrances were custom made for royalty, the aristocracy, and the wealthy. Craftsmanship was the birthplace of luxury, as it embodied all the associations with luxury, such as artistry, scarcity, and uniqueness. In present times, we can still see custom-made suits and shirts for men, dresses and shoes for women, as well as accessories. But machine-produced luxury is now the common trend, and this causes a significant shrinkage of the crafts industry. Today, instead of small independent crafts shops, we now have major luxury groups such as LVMH, Gucci Group, and Richemont dominating the luxury scene (See Figure 4.1.).

In the second half of the twentieth century, luxury brands grew tremendously into global brands that have expanded and extended not only across borders, but across product categories as well. In addition, they expanded their business model both vertically by adding retailing to their manufacturing activities as well as

CHAPTER
OBJECTIVES

- Define what luxury brands are.

- Understand luxury markets and define profiles of luxury customers.

- Appreciate the role and purpose of luxury brands.

- Identify the branding process for luxury brands.

- Examine the possible luxury positioning strategies.

- Highlight the role of the Internet in the luxury segment.

- Examine the relationship between luxury brands and traditional marketing principles.

Figure 4.1

The LVMH group
of luxury brands.
(*Courtesy WWD/
Fairchild Publications*)

horizontally by expanding their range of products to a large range of categories. This growth translated into new marketing strategies and an expansion of the consumers' spectrum, as these brands introduced less expensive standardized products (RTW) as well as accessories and fragrances. As a result, the luxury industry is now estimated to be about a $200 million market.

Why Luxury Brands?

The term **LUXURY** is actually a relative one. What may be luxury to one person or one culture may not be so to another, and what used to be luxury in the past may not be so in the future— in fact, it may even be considered standard. Nevertheless, we all seem to share some common understanding of what luxury ought to be. Just mention the word "luxury" and a mental image is automatically triggered. A few descriptions pop into most people's minds, such as expensive, creative, trendy, exclusive, high quality, and so on. This is how most people envision a luxury brand, and these are their expectations of what the brand promise should be.

Luxury brands have been described as "brands that no one really needs, but everyone desires." If this is so, then what is it about these brands that make them so attractive and coveted? Scholars have concluded a possible set of benefits that motivate us to buy luxury:

- Feel special and stand out in a crowd; feel superior and privileged.
- Demonstrate refinement and connoisseurship.
- Feel of value and importance.
- Exercise ability and freedom ("I can do that").
- Reward ourselves for efforts and achievements; these are symbols of status and success ("I did it," "I can afford that").
- Console oneself and recuperate from a setback or misfortune.
- Command acknowledgement and respect.
- Show feelings of gratitude, love, and affection.
- Feel good, delight the senses, and experience pleasant sensations and feelings.
- Be a part of a certain group and lifestyle; feel a sense of belonging and affiliation.
- Motivate, aspire, and energize.
- Indulge and get pampered.

Luxury brands are designated to fulfill one or more of these aspects. By examining this list, we can conclude some important characteristics of luxury brands and their true relevance to consumers.

- Notions such as feeling special, self-reward, and motivation highlight the strong emotional reward associated with buying a luxury brand and demonstrate how strong a purchase motivator that is. These are brands that highly appeal to the senses.
- Feelings of belonging, admiration, affiliation, even superiority highlight the element of social impact created by luxury brands.

- Feelings of pampering, gratitude, and aspiration imply that these products and services offered under luxury brands are out of normal reach and require an effort to obtain, usually at a premium price.
- Belonging to a group while being apart from the crowd implies elements of elitism and exclusivity.
- Finally, luxury brands seem to have a strong and direct role in defining lifestyles.

These are very important observations that we shall examine in more detail shortly; but with this information on hand, we are now ready to put together a definition that best describes what luxury brands are, a good starting point to our discussion.

Defining Luxury Brands

In chapter 1, we provided the general definition of a brand as an entity with a distinctive idea expressed in a set of functional and experiential features with a promise of a value reward relevant to its end user, and an economic return to its producers (through the building of equity). A successful brand has a strong identity (mentally and physically), is innovative, consistent, competitively positioned, and holds a matching positive image in the consumer's mind.

Being "brands," luxury brands abide by the previously mentioned rules of consistently delivering and adhering to a promise, generating value to their users and (hopefully) profits to their producers, competing through innovation, and establishing a strong and effective identity. As we explore these terms again under the context of luxury, we will notice how most of these conditions are even more relevant and critical to luxury brands than probably most other categories. However, luxury brands possess further unique characteristics that add the "luxury" dimension to the definition. Given what we have illustrated so far about the nature of luxury brands combined with our general understanding of what a brand is, we are now able to put together a definition that attempts to capture the essence of luxury brands.

A **LUXURY BRAND** can be defined as a brand that consistently delivers a unique emotional value and possesses the capacity of creating a lifestyle experience through a strong identity, a high level of creativity, and closely controlled quality, quantity, and distribution, all of which justifies asking for a premium price. Now let us examine the definition more closely and dissect its key words for a closer understanding. A closer examination highlights the following terms or notions about luxury brands.

- High level of creativity and controlled quality
- Controlled quantity and distribution
- Premium price
- Emotional value
- Strong identity

These notions translate into three major characteristics of the luxury brands.

- Heritage and craftsmanship (based on creativity and exclusivity)
- Social element (based on its strong identity and price)
- Luxury brands as lifestyle brands (based on emotional value and strong identity)

Figure 4.2

Gucci founder
Guccio Gucci in
1984 with one
of his craftsman
in a factory
near Florence.

(© David Lees/CORBIS)

The Elements of Heritage and Craftsmanship

Luxury brands are either *designer* brands (such as Chanel and Dior) or brands that were rooted in craftsmanship (such as Gucci and Louis Vuitton) and eventually have transformed into designer brands. (See Figure 4.2.) Most luxury brands are older brands, and most of the older ones have a historic legacy that is rooted in craftsmanship. (See Table 4.1.) This legacy is usually associated with a country's cultural heritage and image, such as French couture and artistry, Italian romanticism and quality materials, English classicism and tailoring, and so on. This sense of heritage and tradition legitimizes the mystique, superiority, uniqueness, and high standard associated with these brands.

These older brands were produced mostly in small workshops by a team of skilled workers, ensuring exclusivity and quality. Many of these brands have transformed in modern times into designer brands known for their creativity and trendsetting, a trademark of this segment along with its strong association with "star" designers. In all cases, talent and heritage seem to be two strong elements that legitimize luxury brands. And because both need time to develop and be tested, most luxury brands take a longer time to get established and accepted.

TABLE 4.1	MOST LUXURY BRANDS ARE OLD BRANDS
BRANDS	**YEAR FOUNDED**
Louis Vuitton	1854
Prada	1913
Coco Chanel	1915
Gucci	1921
Pierre Balmain	1945
Christian Dior	1946
Hubert de Givenchy	1952
Yves Saint Laurent	1962
Emanuel Ungaro	1965
Jean-Paul Gaultier	1976
Christian Lacroix	1987

Figure 4.3

Luxury outer-
wear designer
Moncler has
been crafting
high-quality
down jackets
with care since
the 1950s.

(Courtesy of Moncler)

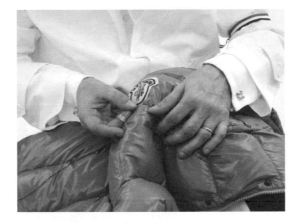

High Quality

Luxury brands' association with high quality is
also rooted in their heritage of craftsmanship.
Interestingly, it is a level of quality that strives on
imperfections. **CRAFTSMANSHIP** is all about
handwork and manual labor, which produces a
high level of quality that is not really perfect but
unique and hard to replicate or reproduce, unlike
machine-produced pieces that are standardized
and identical. It is this imperfection that generates this one-of-a-kind feel that has become an
expected element of luxury. (See Figure 4.3.)

Even apart from couture and hand-made luxury
products, the notion of high quality in the world of
machine-produced luxury remains of the utmost
importance. LVMH, for instance, always bal-
ances the need to ensure creative freedom for its
designers while maintaining the need to impose a
very strict control over the manufacturing process.
It surprises people to learn that the manufacturing
process of any simple garment or purse can go
through around 100 steps (from sample making,
color dips, pattern making, manufacturing, and
so on). The construction of a LV purse or suitcase
may actually go through over 1,000 tasks, including

subjection to torture machines in which it is
opened and closed five times per minute for three
weeks, then thrown, shaken, and crushed to ensure
its resilience and quality. Each of these steps
needs to be closely monitored, of course. In the
same way, Gucci (and other luxury brands as well)
claims to achieve its high level of quality through
its selection of the best materials and strict control
over production, whether in-house or outside.

Creativity

CREATIVITY assures an ongoing flow of newness. (See Figure 4.4.) Fashion houses produce at
least two collections every year, highlighting new

Figure 4.4

Haute couture
is both creative
and trend-setting.
Here is a look
from Dior's
Fall/Winter
2009/2010 Paris
runway show.

(© Stephane Cardinale/

People Avenue/Corbis)

Figure 4.5a, b

(a) Star designer Giorgio Armani embodies the core of the Armani brand identity.

(Getty Images/Bohdan Cap)

(b) Larger-than-life Donatella Versace is another example of a star designer who embodies her brand.

(WireImage/SGranitz)

trends and designs that are meant to surprise, awe, and inspire both customers as well as a trail of factories and manufacturers waiting to copy these trends in every quality and price point possible.

In the world of luxury, designers are usually transformed into superstars and in many ways are seen as *being* the brand themselves. With their talent and character, **STAR DESIGNERS** are a major marketing force behind the brand and in many ways help define the personality of the brand. (See Figures 4.5a–b.) Historically, star luxury designers were the trendsetters and the dictators of what people should wear and when. Today, this power has waned, due to consumers being more informed, empowered, and independent; however, these designers continue to be "celebrities" at the forefront of the brand, and their creativity remains anticipated and influential. It is interesting to see how the industry, consumers, and observers react when a successful star designer leaves a company or retires (such as when Tom Ford left Gucci, Valentino retired, and Alexander McQueen died); questions and speculations are immediately raised about the future of the brand in spite of years of history and tradition behind them. This fact highlights the strong association between luxury and creativity mixed with a strong brand personality. When these masters are gone, it is usually not enough to just bring on board a new creative talent; it has to be someone who is both creative and understands the meaning and personality of the brand. Fresh ideas are always welcomed and surely needed but with a sense of direction, vision, and responsibility.

American Luxury

There is a strong association between luxury brands and heritage, and the fact that most luxury

Figure 4.6

Chairman and
CEO of LVMH,
Bernard Arnault
had proven a
mastermind in
the business
of fashion.

*(© Gaudenti Sergio/
Corbis KIPA)*

brands are old brands explains, among many other reasons, why it is hard to establish new luxury brands.

A great example is the Christian Lacroix brand. Lacroix is admired as a true creative genius and probably one of the few remaining couturiers. Yet to the surprise of many, this brand that adorned fashion magazines around the world never generated any profits. It was acquired by Louis Vuitton, only to be sold later, and it finally filed for bankruptcy in 2009. When asked, Bernard Arnault, CEO of Lacroix's former owner LVMH (see Figure 4.6), explained that it is hard to launch a luxury brand from the ground up today, and that a luxury brand must have a heritage to legitimize its existence.

The power of marketing is always used to compensate for the lack of history or heritage. Marketing creates a myth and a story around the brand that provides a sense of history, tradition, or craftsmanship. A designer who was trained as a

tailor in his youth may use that to imprint that sense of history and craftsmanship on his new brand. For example, while Bontoni is a new label[1] (Italian custom-made men's shoes), the family behind the brand has been creating made-to-measure shoes in a small Italian village for years. Owners Franco Gazzani and his cousin Lewis Cutillo use that story to create a sense of history. (See Figure 4.7.)

American luxury brands, such as Ralph Lauren, Donna Karan, Calvin Klein, and others, are comparatively new, and they lack that history and heritage that most European brands possess (see Figure 4.8). This is why these brands are introduced mainly as lifestyle brands that rely on an enormous marketing machine to establish a convincing story and an identity strong enough to overcome the need for any historical references. Timing is another major factor because most of these brands emerged at a time when there were no recognized international American luxury brands; at the same time, American culture and lifestyle were highly admired around the world, so they benefitted greatly from this association.

Figure 4.7

Luxury shoe
brand Bontoni
plays on a family
heritage of
craftsmanship.

(Courtesy of Bontoni)

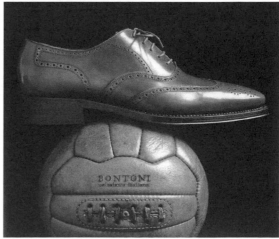

Figure 4.8

Without the
historical
advantage of
many European
luxury brands,
Donna Karan
promotes an
American luxury
lifestyle.
(*Image Courtesy of the
Advertising Archives*)

The Social Element of Luxury Brands

Another strong element of luxury brands is their strong social reference. All brands respond to their social environments; however, luxury brands seem to have an especially strong social association. Luxury brands are aspiring brands that trigger many social signals, such as success, wealth, sophistication, and so on. The level and breadth of their adoption may also indicate the social structure and level of economic maturity of societies. For instance, more people adopt luxury in economically developed and socially stable societies.

The other social dimension has to do with the fact that luxury brands establish a great part of their legitimacy as aspiring brands from the level of social awareness toward them. For instance, a customer may purchase a luxury brand dress for its design and exclusivity, among other reasons. However, if this is the case, then why not go to a

Thus, timing plus effective and intensive marketing plus new unfulfilled lifestyle aspiration helped make American brands succeed (see Figure 4.9). These combined factors may also explain why great American talents from earlier generations, such as Geoffrey Beene and Bill Blass, never reached the international heights of the newer generation.

In comparison to European luxury brands, American brands have been described as "marketing brands" in that they are clearly consumer based, backed by a powerful marketing machine, and driven by American consumer needs. They define an accessible, relaxed, and casual style.

On the other hand, European brands are clearly creative driven in the sense that the creator or designer seems to have full independent authority over the content and personality of the brand. They value aesthetics and products that appeal to the senses. For them, function is secondary to the emotional value created. See Table 4.2 for a comparison of the characteristics of American versus European brands.

Figure 4.9

Calvin Klein is a
master marketer
known for his
controversial,
often massive,
advertising, such
as this billboard
in New York.
(© *Joel Gordon 2009*)

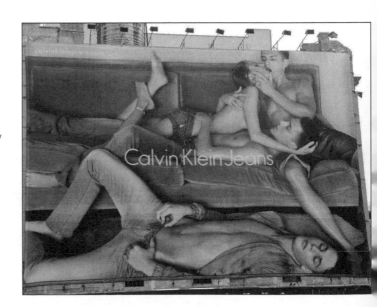

tailor and get a made-to-measure garment that without a doubt will be the most unique and exclusive dress she has?

One of the reasons is that no one will probably know or appreciate the dress the way they would if it was a Dior or a Chanel that they may have seen on the cover of a magazine or on the runway. So part of the significance of acquiring a luxury brand lies in how others perceive and appreciate your purchase. In reality, part of the goals of marketing luxury and its advertising campaigns is to specifically achieve that. Advertising luxury is usually not informative, but rather image focused. It is meant to create awareness and emotional interest. Most regular luxury customers don't really need these advertisements to learn about the brand or where

to buy it. But the image and desire need to stay alive for all to admire and aspire to.

Luxury Brands as Lifestyle Brands

Luxury brands have the potential, more than any other segment, to be lifestyle brands. A **LIFE-STYLE BRAND** successfully identifies itself with a lifestyle and a marketing segment to the point that its name or image is mentally triggered when the segment is mentioned. A brand becomes a lifestyle brand if it succeeds in developing a strong association either through representation or adaptation of a way of life. Thus, a lifestyle brand needs not just to be a part of a lifestyle, but to define that lifestyle. It is common to find almost every manufacturer in the

TABLE 4.2	AMERICAN VS. EUROPEAN LUXURY BRANDS
AMERICAN LUXURY BRANDS	**EUROPEAN LUXURY BRANDS**
MOTIVATIONS: Social · Realization of social dreams and prominence in a group · Fulfill personal ambition · Perfumes are an external, social accessory; they are about the brand	MOTIVATIONS: Individual · Realization of personal dreams · Fulfill emotional desires · Perfumes are about me, my identity, my scent
RELATIONSHIP: Functional · Practicality, utility, functionality · Keywords: wearable, comfortable, informal	RELATIONSHIP: Emotional · Aesthetics, sensory elements, style · Keywords: emotions, vanity, fantasy
POSITIONING: Customer-driven brands · User friendly, casual, simple · Practical needs · Strong marketing, customer service · Lifestyles, modernity, status	POSITIONING: Creativity-driven brands · Eccentric, no constraints · Fantasies · Creativity, imagination, craftsmanship · Culture, heritage, class

Sources: Adapted from Michael Chevalier and Gérald Mazzalovo, *Luxury Brand Management: A World of Privilege* (Singapore: John Wiley & Sons, 2008); and RISC International, *The Luxury Market*, 2003.

Figure 4.10

Harley Davidson
is a classic
example of a
brand directly
linked to a
particular
lifestyle.

(Image Courtesy of the

Advertising Archives)

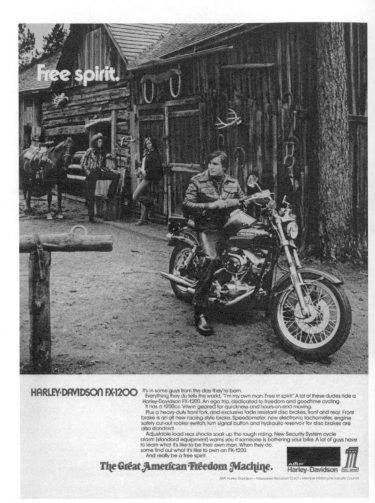

industry claiming that his or her brand is a lifestyle brand; however, they are confusing this with the fact that every brand belongs to or accommodates some lifestyle but does not necessarily define or represent it in the consumer's mind. A true measure of the brand's capacity to represent and define a lifestyle lies in its ability to extend across a wide range of products such as cosmetics, home furnishings, accessories, and even branching out to services such as restaurants and hotels. A lifestyle brand is a brand you want to see at your home, office, in your car and boat, so that its products become integral to a particular lifestyle. However, such extensions need to remain relevant and consistent in portraying the lifestyle, or it may fail and produce negative results.

Lifestyle brands create a sense of belonging to a desired and sought-after subculture by linking the personality traits associated with the brand to the buyers' own sense of identity. Lifestyle brands are mostly luxury brands, but there are successful examples from other segments such as Harley Davidson, which succeeded in establishing itself as the flagship brand for a certain lifestyle and managed to extend the product range into a wide range tailoring to the needs of that lifestyle and that customer (see Figure 4.10). The association between luxury brands and lifestyles is yet another one that highlights the significant role marketing plays in introducing and eventually establishing the brand as a lifestyle brand.

Branding for Luxury: The Luxury Brand Consumer

As mentioned in previous chapters, buying a luxury brand product is more of an emotional than rational decision. It is a decision where the customer may value aesthetics over economic returns. It is a decision where intangibles such as store atmosphere, image, and sophistication play an important role rather than straightforward value for money.

Luxury brands' customers are affluent, sophisticated, and today they are more confident in making fashion decisions and establishing their own personal styles by mixing brands instead of going for a one-brand look.

The first assumption about a typical luxury customer is that he or she is rich. That may be true for the most part; however, in reality, almost anyone could be a luxury brand customer. Therefore, one way to categorize the luxury customer is through the frequency of their purchases. This breaks down into two levels of customers:

- Regular luxury buyers
- Occasional luxury buyers

Regular Buyers

Regular buyers are those who consistently buy the brand's products. Generally they are wealthy customers, but the origins of their wealth may vary from old money (inherited) to new money accumulated through a self-made fortune. The significance of this distinction lies in the way each group reacts to economic changes. In general, luxury brands' customers are less sensitive to economic and price changes. They demonstrate a highly inelastic demand that is not affected that much by these changes.

On the other hand, research shows that "new money" customers, as well as those who belong to the upper-middle class and whose main source of income is their executive salaries or professions, tend to be more sensitive to economic changes because they have earned their money the hard way.

However, consumer behavior studies and research data reveal an interesting observation about luxury brand customers. Studies show that these passionate customers usually develop a strong emotional link to these products, so much so that these products are not necessarily the first things they drop or give up when the going gets tough. For instance, someone may be willing to sell his car and take public transportation to work in hard times but would still prefer to hold on to his Rolex watch.

Or he might take public transportation and make other sacrifices but keep his Porsche safe and sound in his garage for better times.

Whereas these customers' assets may suffer at times of economic recession, their disposable income generally does not drop that much. Nevertheless, statistics show that severe global economic recessions, such as that witnessed at end of 2008, usually hit the luxury industry hard. And for the first time in many years, many of these brands were forced to promote their products through discounts and special offers, which is normally highly uncommon in this segment.

Occasional Buyers

Among buyers of luxury products, about 63 percent of respondents in developed countries said they bought a luxury product in the last 24 months.[2] Occasional buyers can be anyone who every now and then may want to treat themselves or someone they love to a special gift for a significant occasion, such as a wedding, graduation, or an anniversary. These groups are referred to by some as the "outsiders."

An important difference between the two groups of customers is their perception of luxury and their approach to the whole shopping experience. *Regulars* usually take many of the characteristics such as quality and exclusivity for granted; their choice boils down to which brand matches their lifestyle and with which one can they identify. On the other hand, for the *outsiders* it is more of a full experience. When they decide to go to Tiffany's to buy *that* ring or to LV to buy *that* bag they anticipate a complete pleasurable experience from the minute they enter the store. They expect ultimate customer service and an experience that is special and different from any shopping experience they have had before. To them, this is both a financial and emotional investment. They take their notion of value for money to a higher level where they expect a high

Figure 4.11

Occasional buyers of luxury products want a particularly pleasurable shopping experience, such as that enjoyed by shoppers here at the chic new designer shoe department—an entire floor devoted to luxury footwear—at Saks Fifth Ave, New York.

(AFP/Getty Images)

return for their money yet with the understanding that part of this return will be emotional and experiential. (See Figure 4.11.) Thus, they want the product to be beautiful, unique, and scarce. They are also looking for a special shopping experience that speaks to their senses, and although they know it may not make total economic sense, to them treating your senses is worth it once in a while.

Do Luxury Brands' Customers Differ by Nationalities?

A recent report by RISC International comparing customers' responses in three major luxury markets—the United States, Europe, and Japan—in reference to their top "dream" brands, demonstrated how the three markets are quite different and polarized. For example:[3]

- Most brands on the Japanese list are known for their accessories and leather products.
- The top brands in the United States and Japan are not mainly fashion brands (Rolex, Tiffany, and Hermes), whereas in Europe the top three are Armani, Chanel, and Calvin Klein.

- Calvin Klein and Cartier appeared on the U.S. and Europe list and not Japan.
- Rolex and Gucci were the only brands appearing on all three lists.
- The Japanese list was much shorter, including the six brands of Rolex, Hermes, Bulgari, Gucci, Louis Vuitton, and Tiffany. The United States and Europe had eight.
- The American list of preferences is diverse in terms of fashion image. Although it included Gucci and Armani, it also included more casual brands, such as Tommy Hilfiger.
- The American list also included more fashion brands than the other three regions.
- Finally, preferences had an almost equal weight in Japan and the United States, whereas the disparity was noticeable in Europe. For example, Armani got 21.6 percent of the vote, whereas Gucci got 10 percent and Hugo Boss got 16.5 percent.

In addition, the same study showed that even within a market such as Europe, there are significant differences. For example, in France the list included almost all French brands and in Italy almost all Italian brands. On the other hand, the analysis also showed some similarities among luxury customers in all regions.

- They all seek creativity and innovation.
- They all mix styles and appreciate a variety of brands.
- They all are self-conscious, individualistic, achievers, modern, and trendsetters.
- They all care about feeling good as well as looking good (as demonstrated by the products carried by the brands of preferences).

The relationship between luxury brands and their customers is indeed special and interesting.

In the past, luxury brands and celebrity designers were seen as fashion dictators. Trends were born on the catwalks of Paris and other capitals to dictate how and what people should and should not wear. That influence seems to have waned in last decades as customers, especially women, became more socially independent and empowered by career opportunities, education, and new technologies such as the Internet. Customers are more willing to define their own styles and mix and match trends and brands as they please. However, this does not mean that luxury brands have totally lost control. Luxury brands are still trendsetters but not in the old "my way or else" attitude. Indeed luxury brands had always established this interesting relationship with their customers whereby they are not expected to follow their customers all the time (as

marketing theories recommends) as much as they are expected to educate them; after all, this is what trendsetting is all about. This idea is a major departure from marketing principles where brands are supposed to respond to customer needs. Make no mistake, a luxury brand still needs to understand its customers, their habits, and their aspirations to stay focused. However, they also need to be innovative and manage to surprise their customers. They are supposed to be the reference to good taste and new trends and not vice versa.

LVMH conducted a focus study before it launched the Kenzo perfume, Flower (see Figure 4.12). The consensus among respondents and potential buyers was generally negative toward the scent and bottle design. However, the Kenzo team believed that the perfume delivered something new and that it had good potential. They went through with the launch, and the result was an increase in Kenzo's sales of more than 75 percent. The Kenzo team was not just a group of stubborn, egocentric marketers; they were a group who probably understood the potential of their product, its market niche and competitive advantage, and, above all, the role of their brand in the lives of its customers. Luxury is not always meant to offer what people expect. It needs to surprise and innovate.

The Luxury Brand Decision: The Brand Vision

As mentioned in earlier chapters, any new brand idea starts in the mind and imagination of a visionary who sees an opportunity for something new and exciting that will please and satisfy the needs and aspirations of new customers and

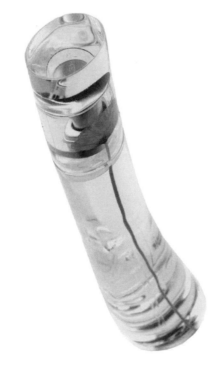

Figure 4.12

Despite negative feedback previous to launch, Kenzo's perfume Flower was a major commercial success.

(© mediablitzimages (uk) Limited / Alamy)

Figure 4.13

Legendary
Coco Chanel,
in her signature
multiple strands
of pearls,
photographed
by Cecil Beaton
in 1938.

(Condé Nast Archive/
CORBIS)

has the potential to strive and grow. In the case
of luxury brands, that visionary has historically
been the creative designer or the craftsman who
possesses the skill, talent, and imagination that
made his or her offering unique and special.
These visionaries include Coco Chanel (see Figure
4.13), Guccio Gucci, Calvin Klein, Christian Dior,
Cristobal Balenciaga (see Figure 4.14), as well as
other legendary figures.

However, as these brands grow and transform
from being a craftsman's workshop- (or atelier-)
based brand into a designer brand and a complex
and extended operation, the business confronts
new market realities and challenges. Thus, it
becomes clear that with the creative vision there is
a need for an entrepreneurial one as well as strong
business acumen. For that reason, the responsibilities of stirring the business are usually delegated

Figure 4.14

Visionary
Spanish designer
Cristobal
Balenciaga
brought his
House of
Balenciaga to
Paris in the
1930s, where he
became known
as the "couturier
of couturiers."

(© Lipnitzki/Roger-
Viollet/The Image
Works)

to business managers and CEOs or a business
partner. All successful luxury brands have this mix
of talents. After all, fashion is serious business.

Bernard Arnault once said

> *true artists . . . do not want the process to end*
> *there (referring to creating new designs), they*
> *want people to wear their dresses, or spray*
> *their perfume, or carry the luggage they have*
> *designed. . . . If you ask them they would say*
> *they don't actually care one way or another if*
> *people buy their products. But they do care, it's*
> *just buried in their DNA, and as a manager you*
> *have to be able to see it there.*

This indeed is the responsibility of the manager
or the business partner. It is no surprise, therefore,
that most successful launches, re-launches, and
repositioning of luxury brands in recent history
have been either orchestrated by a visionary CEO

or businesses managers who teamed up with creative designers to achieve the transformation. Good examples are the teams of Domenico de Sole and Tom Ford for Gucci and Bravo and Bailey for Burberry. Both these cases demonstrate that the brand decision is not just a creative decision, but a marriage between true creativity and a sound business proposal.

LVMH pinpoints five priorities that reflect the fundamental values shared by all group stakeholders.[4]

1. Be creative and innovate.
2. Aim for product excellence.
3. Bolster the image of their brands with passionate determination.
4. Act as entrepreneurs.
5. Strive to be the best in all they do.

are meant to be trendsetters, aggressively bold, and, to borrow from the TV show *Star Trek*, go places where none have gone before. It is through continuous innovation that luxury brands are expected to maintain technical superiority and technological advancement.

Luxury brands do not need just innovation, but leadership in innovation, which some have tagged as "radical innovation," meaning innovation that surprises and awes. This level of innovation is highly expected by luxury customers who traditionally fall into the innovation category on the customer adoption curve. (See Figure 4.15.)

However, whereas innovation can have a strong and positive impact on the functionality of the product and deliver a rational justification for buying it, it is creativity and artistry that delivers the emotional impact that is highly associated with this

The Product Mix

We have determined in previous chapters that a product in its essence is a sum of its features and attributes that we referred to collectively as the product mix, which include: the product itself with its tangible features, the price, the distribution choice, and the relevant service (such as customer service, warranties, etc.). Together this "mix" defines the product.

Product

Luxury brands are driven by high quality, technical superiority, technological advancement, and unique craftsmanship. Creativity and innovation are key factors to the survival of any brand in any category, but it is more so with luxury brands because they

Figure 4.15
Dutch designers Victor & Rolf are masters of innovation who consistently push the boundaries. Here, a look from the Paris runway of their Spring/ Summer 2010 ready-to-wear collection.
(*WireImage/ Dominique Charriau*)

category. As B. Arnault once said, "a new product is not creative if it does not shock. Our whole business is based on giving our artists and designers complete freedom to invent without limits." Thus, it is an essential marriage between innovation and artistry that forms the DNA of luxury brands and their status as trendsetters. (See Figure 4.16.)

Luxury products range from haute couture to RTW. They include various segments such as garments, fur, leather, even jeans, and extend to cosmetics, jewelry, watches, and perfumes. Probably the biggest difference between luxury in today's world and luxury in the past is the relative disappearance of custom or bespoke products.

Another important element of luxury fashion is the concept of the *collection*. A collection is a coherent group of pieces that tell a story. It may sound like a given concept, but in reality it is a common problem among new businesses and young designers who have the tendency to produce beautifully designed *pieces* that do not necessarily work together to form a true collection. The collection concept is important in defining the story and theme behind the designs and highlighting the trends. In collections, individual pieces make more sense than on their own because they are appreciated in relevance to other pieces and a larger concept.

Price

Choosing the right price is still of the utmost importance. Price is a function of many elements, such as cost, competition, and so on. Luxury brands are known for their **PREMIUM PRICES,** in part because a premium price contributes to the exclusivity factor. So in deciding upon price, there is a psychological and marketing element to consider. But obviously there is a financial necessity as well. Luxury brands are expensive to produce, manage, and market. By definition, luxury brands use the best of materials and talents available and are produced in small quantities

They have high costs, and the price needs to cover expenses and generate maximum profit and return on investment while maintaining a healthy cash flow, if possible. As a matter of fact, luxury brands have a lot of limitations and constraints that contribute to their high costs and margins, such as the need to open retail stores in only the best and most expensive locations in every city they enter. (See Figure 4.17.) Their flagship stores, normally

Figure 4.16

A show-stopping piece of luxurious fantasy from John Galliano's 1992 hat collection.

(© Julio Donoso/ Sygma/Corbis)

Figure 4.17

The interior of
Giorgio Armani's
New York
flagship store,
opened in 2009.

(© Stephen Mark

Sullivan)

located in the city of their headquarters, are usually extravagant in order to better showcase the brand and its image. (See Figure 4.18.)

Extensive marketing is another major cost factor; in the case of fashion, luxury brands rely on producing at least two fashion shows annually. Fashion shows cost a lot, with no direct financial return; and many of the couture clothes show-cased are meant for publicity and media coverage rather than for sales. So from a financial perspective, fashion shows seem to be a losing venture; however, it is through these fashion shows and the buzz they generate that the brand is able to sell and market its more saleable items, such as RTW, cosmetics, and perfumes.

From an economic perspective, price is always a function of supply and demand (scarcity), among other factors such as the elasticity of the price in relation to these two elements. By looking at luxury brands, we notice that they are usually in short supply, in high demand, and are price inelastic (demand is not highly affected by price changes), all of which contribute to the premium price strategy.

It is important to remember that just raising the price does not by itself transform the brand into a luxury one. Just as being rich does not make you an aristocrat, so it is with brands: a higher price by itself does not make a brand a luxury brand. There is still the need for some point of reference, such as a heritage or a legacy, to make it legitimate and believable.

One major constraint that luxury brands face with their price strategies is their inability or unwill-ingness to drastically reduce prices as demanded by economic changes. As a matter of fact, many brands would rather kill the product than offer it at a discount price and harm the brand's image.

Given the high costs and constraints, luxury brands actually take much longer to break even, let alone make profit. However, successful brands have the potential for very high profits due to their big margins, product extensions, and global reach. The example of Christian Lacroix given earlier in this chapter is a good demonstration of how a talented designer and a brand that dominated the fashion scene for some time never made a profit and ended up filing for bankruptcy. On the other hand, the Alexander McQueen brand only started to be profitable in 2007 in spite of the celebrated ingenuity of the late designer.

Why do luxury brands take a long time to make money, and why do they still exist if they are losing money?

Figure 4.18

The Louis
Vuitton Paris
flagship store
covered in
a display of
giant luggage.
(*Bloomberg via Getty
Images*)

First, the high costs of distribution, quantity, and production restriction result in luxury brands taking much longer to financially break-even compared to mass-produced brands, which also means that they need higher investment up front in order to start the business. Paired with a long production lead time that is a characteristic of the fashion industry in general, the financial strain on luxury brands is stronger.

Second, although the luxury brand's customer is generally less vulnerable to economic changes, luxury brands may still be forced to deal with unsold merchandise due to severe economic downturns and weakening economies. They have to discount merchandise (a highly unpopular option due to potential negative impact on the brand's image); move the merchandise to their outlets; sell to their employees; or sell to other discount stores that agree to conceal the brand's name and label. In all cases, any unsold amount will represent a higher percentage of total merchandise compared to other mass-produced brands that produce a larger amount of merchandise.

Finally, many investors may shy away from the high cost and long-term financial commitment of developing luxury brands, which could be one of the many reasons why most luxury brands start as family or private operations.

Luxury goods, although sometimes having a utilitarian function such as clothes or shoes, usually do not carry a price tag that reflects their intrinsic cost or the added value they provide, certainly not in comparison to an ordinary pair of shoes or an inexpensive handbag. The markups on some luxury products is sometimes eight to ten fold. Luxury goods are typically of exceptional quality, but the prices charged to consumers are at a huge premium over cost. The price is irrational and justified on the exclusivity and creativity of the products. In recent years, luxury brands have witnessed a dramatic increase in production and occasional reduction in price due to moving many production activities to the Far East. However, the combination of greater availability, affordability, and in some cases diminished quality threatens the luxury status of many brands. If the notion of being extremely expensive is a defining component of being a luxury product, then affordability becomes a measure of reduced luxury. If a brand becomes affordable to a larger market, it brings into questioning its status as a luxury brand.

Whereas these pricing principles may be shared by all luxury brands, pricing strategies may differ from one company to the other. Louis Vuitton, for example, used to adopt a simple strategy of multiplying cost by a fixed gross-margin rate. This strategy is rooted in the old days when LV was made to order, like most luxury crafts-based brands, making one trunk at a time. However, as the company grew and expanded its product range, they kept that policy in place for a long time. Prices were determined simply by multiplying the cost by the fixed margin and then comparing it to the market; if the final price turned out to be too high, they started examining measures to lower cost without compromising quality in order to maintain the desired fixed gross margin. If it could not be achieved, then the product could be easily cancelled. The idea behind this policy was to maintain a certain level of profitability across all products without the need to compromise for the sake of adapting to the market. This attitude is not the norm, and it demonstrates that the craftsman's mentality and artisan attitude somehow remain built in the DNA of many luxury brands no matter how the business model may change.

Distribution

Luxury brands are said to achieve part of their status by being a dream that is only affordable by a few. They are meant to be *exclusive brands* that require some effort to obtain. The exclusivity

factor of luxury brands is achieved in part by a low volume of production and a tightly controlled distribution channel.

Luxury brands are generally smaller operations compared to other segments. Even large luxury groups such as LVMH usually operate through a portfolio of smaller operations (over 50 for LVMH). However, because they are trendsetting brands and at the forefront of innovation and creativity, they possess high awareness, status, and respect that may be much larger than their actual size as a company. This great interest and high exposure does create the illusion that these brands are larger than life.

Exclusivity and the high level of control associated with luxury brands result in minimizing the middleman and franchising arms, while tightly controlling licensing in order to retain control of how and where the products are made and sold. As a matter of fact, this attitude was one of the first strategic decisions adopted by Burberry in the process of repositioning the brand as a luxury one.

In terms of luxury brands' distribution, retailing remains the main channel of distribution. These brands are usually distributed and sold through exclusive or tightly controlled channels: such as:

• *Free-standing or fully owned chains of boutiques:* LV and Hermes sell only in their stores around the world (except for perfumes, which are sold through various chains). For the most part, all the stores are fully owned and controlled from headquarters that enable many activities to be coordinated. In addition, inventory systems are usually very well organized. For instance, classic items are shipped directly to stores, while store managers can selectively decide on seasonal or specific items. It is a highly controlled and efficient system. LV has over 1,000 directly operated stores whereas Bottega Veneta has a network of 83 directly operated stores, which generated 87 percent of the brand's 2005 revenue.[5] These chains usually include a flagship store that is usually the largest of all their stores and the ultimate storefront for displaying the range of products and experiencing the brand's personality. It is the ultimate place to live and experience the brand as it was envisioned. The Ralph Lauren flagship store on Madison Avenue is a great example of an ultimate brand store that reflects the brand's spirit and personality in every detail and product. Flagship stores are usually located in the city of their headquarters and possibly other major fashion capitals of the world such as New York, Paris, Milan, or Tokyo.

- *Exclusive franchise stores:* There are stores that are not owned by the brand, but look and feel like fully owned stores, carrying the brand exclusively and operating under tight guidelines.
- *In-store boutiques:* These are unique areas inside of the world's prestigious department stores (such as Neiman Marcus, Bloomingdale's, and Takashimaya). In most cases, these areas are rented and managed independently from the host store.
- *Catalogs or the Internet:* These are other retailing options that might be employed.

It is possible to have a mixed system of a few exclusive stores headed with a flagship, department store corners or shop-in-shops, as well as counters in case of perfumes and accessories. Cartier and Bulgari are good examples of this mixed system whereby they maintain their own exclusive stores but also sell watches and selected fine jewelry at individual jewelers.

In general, the system must take into consideration the brand's specific strengths and weaknesses in determining the best channels. In some cases, the nature of the market dictates the nature of the distribution channel. Japan, which is one of the top markets for luxury brands, is very hard to penetrate independently due to a tightly closed and complicated retail and distribution system. Because of this, most foreign luxury brands such as LV and Gucci have entered the market through some form of partnership or alliance with a local player.

Location Challenges

The options for luxury brand store locations are much more strictly limited than those of mass-market brands. It is customary to locate luxury brand stores in exclusive neighborhoods and high-end streets around the world to reinforce the brand's image and status. (See Figures 4.19a–b.)

Some of the famous locations where luxury brands are commonly found are:
- Rue du Faubourg Saint-Honoré in Paris
- Via Montenapoleone and Via della Spiga in Milan
- Fifth Avenue and Madison Avenue in New York
- Rodeo Drive in Los Angeles
- Ginza district in Tokyo

Even within these limited choices, more limitations apply. For example, the most desirable part

Figure 4.19a, b
(a) The Christian Lacroix boutique on Paris' tony Foubourg St. Honoré.
(RIM/ARNAUD MONNIER/MAXPPP/ Newscom)
(b) Tokyo's Ginza district, home to luxury boutiques like Chanel and Bulgari.
(AFP/Getty Images/ YOSHIKAZU TSUNO)

of Fifth Avenue is a small section roughly between 54th Street and 57th Street.

The choices are also limited for distribution through hi-end department or specialty stores, which may include Bloomingdale's, Saks, Nordstorm, Neiman Marcus, Bergdorf Goodman, Barneys (United States), Galeries Lafayette, Le Bon Marché (France), Selfridges, Harvey Nichols (England), Seibu, Matsuzakaya (Japan), Grand Palace and Luxury Village (Russia), and Daslu (Brazil). This shallow breadth of choices creates a major challenge for future expansion within the same city. With such limitations, the options for opening a stand-alone store may be minimal, and eventually other options such as in-store boutiques in luxury department stores will be viable.

Luxury Brands on the Internet

Most luxury brands have a presence on the Internet. However, most luxury brand Web sites are designed to offer information, news, and brand updates. For other luxury brands, online shopping options are usually available for standard and lower-priced items. This limited and conservative approach adopted by luxury brands toward the Internet may be due to many factors, such as:

- Shopping luxury products in brick-and-mortar stores and boutiques is an exciting and integral part of the whole experience for many luxury shoppers. The Internet simply can't offer that experience. Shopping in luxury boutiques allows the customer to experience the brand from the moment they enter the door and get pampered by the well-trained sales personnel. This is in addition to fulfilling the obvious need to examine, touch, or feel the product before buying. Also, for many customers, the act of buying a luxury product is an experience in itself. Understandably, all these factors cannot be fully emulated online.

- There is a common belief by luxury brands that the luxury customer is not the typical online shopper; not only because of missing the shopping experience, but because of their lifestyle and working habits.

- The high price tag of most luxury products makes it riskier and less conventional for online shopping.

- The Internet overexposes the brand and denies it one if its main characteristics—exclusivity.

- There are concerns that online customer services may never match the service level and personal factor the customer experiences in stores.

Another factor that may hurt the brand's image if made available online is the tendency for online shoppers to use price comparison sites and software such as kelkoo.com, Net-A-Porter, and so on. The price discrepancies these sites deliver is believed to hurt the brand's image and again limit its exclusivity.

On the other side of the argument:

- Statistics show that wealthy online shoppers spent more per year on luxury goods: $114,632, compared with $23,000 for in-store shoppers, which may indicate that luxury customers are spending more time and money online than believed.[6]
- Fear of lessened exclusivity may be a factor only if the products are sold through various channels, which is usually not the case with luxury brands.
- It is true that the in-store shopping experience is unique; however, research shows that it

may be more relevant for first-time luxury shoppers rather than regular customers who would appreciate an online alternative given their busy schedules. It has also become a common practice for many shoppers to first visit the stores to see and feel the products, then make the actual purchase online at their convenience. Thus, the online experience may actually complement the shopping experience and not necessarily compete with or replace it.

In spite of this cautious attitude toward the Internet by luxury brands, most do have an electronic presence of some form, as discussed in the following sections.

DESIGNER'S ONLINE STORES

A few luxury brands, such as Louis Vuitton, Gucci, Stella McCartney, and Tiffany's, allow customers to shop online. However, most of these Web sites do not offer the complete range of items in their collections, especially high-priced items. (See Figure 4.20.)

SHOPPING PORTERS

These are Web sites that sell different brands and are not exclusively owned by any one brand. Examples are Net-A-Porter and Zappos Couture. They are a one-stop shop for many brands. Their products range from fashion to accessories and shoes. They specifically offer good exposure and marketing opportunities for newer brands and young designers. These sites could offer other services as well. For instance, Net-A-Porter offers an editorial magazine section that covers latest trends and fashion news (see Figure 4.21). These online shopping porters also include discount

Figure 4.20

Oscar de la Renta's Web site allows one to view collections, learn about the house, find retail locations, and make limited purchases.

(Courtesy WWD/ Fairchild Publications)

Figure 4.21

Net-A-Porter's
magazine
portion of the
site covers
fashion news
and trends.

(*Courtesy WWD/
Fairchild Publications*)

Figure 4.22

On the From
Bags to Riches
Web site a one-
month rental of
a Louis Vuitton
bag is available
for $139.95.

(*Courtesy of From Bags
To Riches*)

outlets such as TheOutnet.com, which offers
original designer handbags and apparels with discounts that range from 40 percent to 60 percent.
Ideeli.com is a members-only shopping portal/
blog that offers limited-time discount prices on
sought-after brands. Every day a few brands are
featured for almost 80 percent discounts as a
limited-time event.

INFORMATION AND
EDITORIAL WEB SITES

These Web sites do not have shopping options;
rather, they offer the latest industry trends and
information, including runway videos, photos, and
designers' profiles. Examples are Style.com and
Fashion TV.

LUXURY RENTALS

An interesting group of stores that offer luxury
products for rent on a weekly or monthly basis
(usually with a purchase option). These sites are
seen as yet another step toward the democratization of luxury through the Internet. Examples
are Frombagstoriches.com and Avelle (a.k.a.
bag borrow or steal), which offer customers
a chance to rent expensive designer bags and
accessories at reasonable prices. The bags are
delivered with free shipping within two days and
are to be returned on a specific day in a postage-
prepaid carton provided with the product. They
offer a large selection of brands, such as Betsy
Johnson, Louis Vuitton, Burberry, Fendi, and
others.

With so many options, at the time of this
book's publication, a customer looking for a Louis
Vuitton Totally MM handbag has at least four
online purchase alternatives (see Figure 4.22).

Figure 4.23

Fake luxury bags
of seemingly
every brand.

(© 2007 Condé Nast)

1. *From Louis Vuitton.com:* Around $970
2. *BagBorroworSteal:* For members, $30/week, $90/month; nonmembers, $45/week, $115/month; plus $9.95 shipping, $10 insurance, $5-$9.95 monthly membership fee
3. *FromBagstoRiches:* Small bag: $139.95/month
4. *eBay:* Lightly used bag was recently sold with a Buy Now option for $800

Replicas

The luxury segment is the hardest hit by the counterfeit industry. Fake luxury bags are produced in massive quantities in Asia, making copies available of seemingly every brand (see Figure 4.23). With most of the counterfeit products coming from Asia, the Internet has created a new and convenient outlet for these manufacturers and their replicas or fake products to reach a wider market. What is interesting is that many of these sites do not lie about their products. They clearly state that these are almost identical replicas. The same Louis Vuitton $970 handbag can be bought for a fraction of the price (less than $200) together with easy payment and delivery options, and even a lifetime warranty.

Here is how one site openly describes its services:

> *Nnbag is dedicated to providing the best and newest designer handbags at a fraction of the cost. We start by purchasing original designer handbags and shipping them to our factories in China. We then inspect every nook and cranny and purchase the same materials to ensure that the products we manufacture are virtually indistinguishable from the designer originals in every way.[7]*

Rolex watches, one of the most replicated luxury items, come in about four grades and three major categories, each with its standard of quality and service:

- Chinese manufactured replicas: Watches in the Chinese grade replicas can cost up to $120.
- Japanese manufactured replicas: Watches in the Japanese grade replicas can cost up to $240.
- Swiss manufactured replicas: Watches in the Swiss grade replicas can cost up to $1,000. They claim to be exact matches in material and mechanism to the original style to the point that most people cannot tell the difference.

Parallel Markets (a.k.a. Grey Markets)

Parallel or gray market products are not replicas. They are genuine products that are bought from one market to be sold in another for which it was not intended and usually at higher prices. Parallel markets are common with perfumes, where they are bought at wholesale prices from locations such as Panama and sold at much higher prices in other countries like Japan. The gray market in luxury fashion is a bit limited due to limited quantities of product and short life cycles, but it has more success with accessories. Gray markets also exist because they offer some official distributors a channel (albeit illegal) to get rid of old inventory.

There have been many efforts and legal measures to overcome and counterattack the growth of gray markets. Such efforts include adding laser numbers or barcodes on each perfume box to trace where it is sold. A few luxury brands like Louis Vuitton and Fendi have started stitching holograms into the lining of many of their products, such as handbags, clothes, scarves, and shoes. The

holograms are rectangular, colored stamps with encrypted codes visible only with a special magnifying device. They have a wireless tracking device that is deactivated when the item is sold, allowing the company to track their bags and determine if they have been sold in an unauthorized store.

Service

Luxury customers are known to be among the most loyal group of buyers. However, their loyalty level is in a direct relationship with the level of service they receive. They expect the highest degree of service and an experience that does not just start and end with the purchase of the product. Accordingly, luxury brands are built to pamper their customers in many ways. (See Figure 4.24.)

Four principles are common to nearly all top-performing luxury brand companies[8].

1. *They create a customer-centered culture* that identifies, nurtures, and reinforces service as a primary value.
2. *They use a rigorous selection process* to populate the organization with superior sales and support staff. The impulse to care about accommodating customers cannot be taught to people who are not predisposed to it.
3. *They constantly retrain employees* to perpetuate organizational values and to help them attain greater mastery of products and procedures.
4. *They systematically measure and reward customer-centric behavior* and excellence in sales and service to enforce high standards and reinforce expectations.

Life warranties, flexible return policies, free adjustments and alterations, free delivery, personalization of products, customization, VIP loyalty

Figure 4.24

You can sign up for Nordstrom's personal stylist service directly on its Web site.

(Courtesy of Nordstrom)

programs, personal shopping assistance in stores, special collection viewing and updates, not to mention special in-stores services are but a few examples of the level of service expected from luxury brands. The bottom line is not to just meet customers' expectations, but to exceed them. It's the *Wow* factor.

The tremendous growth and expansion of the luxury market over the past 20 years, however, has diluted the allure of these brands' exclusivity as well as the level of customer service expected. The rise in number of outlet stores where the product is discounted is an indication of these changes. Thus, it seems that luxury brands need to re-examine these traditional strategies, especially in situations similar to the recent economic recession. Still, a high level of customer service will continue to remain a key factor to the success of luxury brands in such conditions. This is something the luxury customer is not willing to compromise, so more luxury brands need to introduce new special programs and services that reward and retain their very best customers. Developing new programs that can be executed in the manner of old-fashioned services is an important differentiating factor between luxury brands.

Brand Identity

The process of creating a brand identity is about developing a personality reinforced by a set of attributes and visual symbols, such as a shape,

Figure 4.25

Currently used on all types of clothing and accessories, the Burberry tartan remains the visual symbol of the brand. (*Getty Images/ Matthew Peyton*)

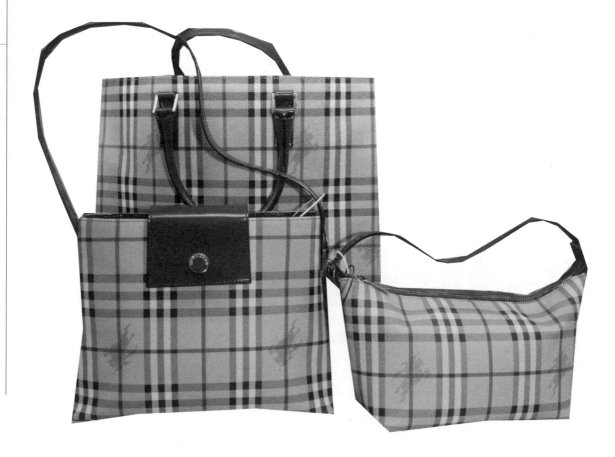

a color, a logo, a package, and so on. (See Figure 4.25.) The personality is developed through the accumulation of activities, decisions, and stories, as well as its products' features and attributes. It's both a process and the development of a culture. Visual symbols play an important role in this process and have great significance for luxury brands because of the strong relevance of their identity to the purchase decision.

When Burberry planned to reposition its brand and relaunch it to a new generation of customers, their goal was to reinforce its status as a luxury brand. In the process, they realized that their biggest asset was their strong visual identity; however, their weakness was a diluted personality that weakened the image and the value perceived by the customers. Thus, in the process of repositioning the brand, they highlighted their signature trench coat with its infamous plaid placed in a new context and modernized the name. Identity symbols are discussed in the following sections.

Iconic Items

These items represent design concepts and signature looks that became iconic for the brand. Usually, it is after the brands establish themselves in these areas that they gain the credibility, status, and stamina needed to extend into other areas such as fashion. Even then, they may choose an iconic product to symbolically identify the brand, such as:

- A Louis Vuitton leather bag
- A Fendi fur coat
- A Hermès silk scarf
- A Kelly bag
- The Burberry tartan
- A Diane von Furstenberg wrap dress

Name

The most visible aspect of a luxury brand's concept is the brand name. Traditionally, luxury fashion brands' names adopted those of their founders or creative designers, whose names in return may reference their country of origin and thus evoke specific mental references about style, craftsmanship, qualities, uniqueness, and so on. Some examples are:

- Gucci, Salvatore Ferragamo (Italy)
- YSL, Dior (France)
- Yamamoto (Japan)

The power of the name is also evident in brands that use a fake name that might indicate different origins but still evokes associations with certain images and cultural references that the creators see appropriate. Examples of this strategy are:

- Comme des Garçons (Japanese brand with a French name)
- Paul & Joe (French brand with English name)
- Jimmy Choo (British brand with Asian name)

In the world of luxury, unlike with mass-marketed brands, there are very few cases of brands with general descriptive names, such as Bottega Veneta (Venetian Workshop), or purely made-up names such as Rolex.

The brand name is the first point of contact between the consumer and the brand, so choosing the right name is very important. No matter which naming strategy is used, the name should evoke positive and relevant associations about the brand. Consumers should be able to decipher some brand connotations from its name, even without necessarily being in contact with its products or advertisements. Thus, it was not a coincidence that designer Rei Kawakubo picked a

French rather than a Japanese name for her brand (Comme des Garçons) in order to associate the brand with a French heritage and generate a specific luxury appeal that is not otherwise achieved with a Japanese name on the label. In the case of luxury brands, which are usually developed with the intentions of global distribution, choosing the name becomes even more challenging, as the name needs to be appreciated in different markets and cultures. The name, therefore, needs to posses an international appeal, be easy to pronounce, and not have any negative connotations in other countries and languages. In addition, it is common with luxury brands to give names to individual products, such as the Kelly bag, the Daytona Rolex watch, and so on. This demonstrates the possible iconic status individual luxury products can acquire.

Initials and/or Logos

In addition to their name, many brands have a logo that could be a word, a graphic symbol, or both (Polo, Lacoste alligator), or letter initials (LV, YSL). (See Figure 4.26.)

Figure 4.26

Logos can be monograms, graphic symbols, or initials.

More than names, logos are easier to modify and develop as times change and the brand grows. Christian Dior has evolved to simply Dior and Burberry's to just Burberry. Initials and logos are particularly relevant for luxury brands, given that they are mostly lifestyles that people are keen to identify with and flaunt.

The use and selection of fonts, typeface style, and colors, as described in chapter 2, is another significant identity choice for luxury brands that can be the design focus of the logo and the vehicle to convey the identity connotation needed. Examples are the signature-like style of Ferragamo, or the whimsical pink typeface of Betsey Johnson. Finally, we can find a logo that is a combination of name and design, such as in the case of Hermes (name + horse carriage).

Slogans

Slogans are another identifiable attribute meant to differentiate one brand from the other and attract the consumer's attention to a specific message and what the brand signifies. However, it is interesting to notice that luxury brands rarely have slogans or tag lines, probably because the message is strongly embedded in the name. In addition, the luxury consumer is usually familiar with the brand prior to purchase.

Personality

A brand's personality is the sum of its culture, vision, and behavior. It translates what the brand is all about and defines the brand promise. A personality also humanizes the brand and allows us to describe it in certain ways such as being hip, sexy, sincere, extravagant, and so on. Luxury brands that are trendy and aspirational as well as lifestyle brands convey, for the most part, personalities

Figure 4.27

Lifestyle brands such as Ralph Lauren possess strong brand personality.

(Image Courtesy of the Advertising Archives)

specific area, which it can use later as a launch pad for other extensions and endeavors. With a set of benefits and values to transfer to the consumer, plus a strong matching identity, the brand is ready and bound for market positioning. It is important to remember that positioning is merely a strategic proposition by the brand, whereas the true position achieved will be decided upon by customers based on the way they interpret and experience the brand.

Luxury brands generally have a very clear positioning strategy in terms of price, market segmentations, and demographics. Yet their biggest differentiator and comparative advantage remains their level of creativity, the creative juices of the celebrity designer that are meant to be unique and trendsetting. This level of creative distinctiveness associated with every luxury brand raises the following question: If, by definition, every luxury brand is creatively different and unique, do they really still need a positioning strategy?

reflecting excitement, sophistication, and sensuality in addition to honesty and sincerity.

Although positioning is heavily built around the product—and in case of luxury, around its creativity—positioning at the brand level is still very relevant because it reflects the emotional core value of the brand translated in its personality. We as consumers are attracted and consumed by the brand's personality. (See Figure 4.27.)

Positioning Strategy

A brand cannot be all things for everyone. It needs to be known and associated with perfection in a

Is Positioning Relevant to Luxury Brands?

Some may believe that the concept of positioning is not relevant to the luxury brands segment, based on the premise that (by definition) a luxury brand is born creatively different and in many ways pre-positioned. This would imply there is no point in comparing it to competition. However, this view is based on the principle that positioning is highly product-based, ignoring the value added by the branding process and its ability to alter the decision outcome. We concluded in chapter 2 that positioning a brand can take place at two levels: at the product level, through any element of the product mix, such as features (creativity), price, distribution, or service; and at the brand level, through the brand's identity (especially personality). It is true that luxury brands are unique as products, that every collection is unique and reflects a vision and design philosophy that is different from one designer to the other. However, what might happen if the same garment is offered to the customer with the label concealed or replaced by a label of a different brand? Is there a chance the buying decision might be affected and altered? The answer is probably *yes*. It is the same garment with the same aesthetics, but it is not the same brand anymore. If a potential buyer changes his or her decision because, under a different label, the garment is now perceived differently, then the garment as a product was not positioned convincingly enough to compete on its own aesthetic values. If the decision was altered because of the label and in spite of the design, then the value produced by the branding process has to be appreciated as a positioning force and a positioning tool. Thus, even a luxury brand may need to draw from the power of a stronger positioning message.

Luxury Brand Communication

Marketing for luxury has always been seen as more reliant on *pull* marketing strategies—strategies meant to entice the potential buyer to seek (and pull) the brand's products and generate sales accordingly.

Being emotionally motivated and lifestyle driven, luxury brands are highly reliant on communication through heavy advertising and marketing campaigns to create and emphasize this aspirational world.

Marketing communication is meant to achieve for luxury brands the following:

- Demonstrate and establish the lifestyle status and proposed image of the brand.
- Compensate for lack of history and heritage in the case of new brands.
- Create social awareness, which makes owning of luxury more meaningful.
- Combat economic downturns.

Communication strategies for luxury brands utilize different media and channels, such as advertising, personal selling, promotions, sponsorships, celebrity endorsements, and PR events (such as fashion shows).

Advertising

Harvard economist John Kenneth Galbraith made the argument that society as a whole has become affluent, enjoying modern conveniences and previously unknown luxuries. As a result, businesses must create consumer wants through advertising to generate an artificial demand for products beyond the individual's basic needs. This theory is particularly relevant in light of the common perception that luxury brands are not necessary or essential brands. One of the interesting realities of marketing luxury goods seems to be the relative ease luxury brands have in convincing consumers to spend vast sums of money on things they simply don't need. No matter how high the price, luxury consumers are typically very happy with their purchases, even though they are completely aware that the cost of the item is usually far too high for its utilitarian worth. Advertising and promotional hype plays a significant role in motivating demand or wants for these products. Thus, advertising becomes essential to creating

Figure 4.28

Some luxury brands have moved beyond traditional channels of advertising and promotion: one can watch an entire Dolce & Gabbana runway show on an iPhone.

(Courtesy WWD/ Fairchild Publications)

the dream and evoking the necessary interest. Indeed, luxury brands rely heavily on fantasy and lifestyle building. Accordingly, luxury brands allocate a comparatively large budget for advertising. The average budget is between $14 million and $50 million, representing about 5 to 15 percent of revenue, which increases to 25 percent with the inclusion of other aspects such as PR events and sponsorship.[9]

Luxury brands' advertisements can be seen in top fashion magazines, such as *Vogue* and *Harpers Bazaar*, business publications, and airline in-flight magazines. Unconventional locations such as on buses and public transportation can be seen in some markets such as Paris, London, and New York but are otherwise not very common. The Internet, iPhones, and other electronic devices and platforms are new channels that have been tapped by luxury brands as well. (See Figure 4.28.)

Choice of advertising options depends on the target market and its size, the circulation and coverage reach of each media, the frequency of exposure needed, cost, and the message and its degree of urgency. One problem with many advertising options such as TV, magazines, and even radio is clutter. These media are so overly crowded with advertising messages that it is very hard for receivers and watchers to recall them long after they are exposed to the ad. Accordingly, many other options have gained a lot of ground, such as PR events (like fashion shows), the Internet, and special promotions (such as VIP previews for loyal customers).

Celebrity Sponsorship

Luxury brands have traditionally had a strong association with celebrities and socialites. Movie and music superstars, top athletes, media personnel, and even politicians are in the public eye at all times. They are trendsetters and the "innovators" among consumer groups. They have a significant influence on their fans and pop culture in general. In addition, celebrities, being brands in their own rights, have various successful collaborations with luxury fashion brands that are effective co-branding efforts. Such collaboration helps both partners draw from the star power of the other brand and emphasize a certain status or image. Another benefit is the global appeal of celebrities, which is extremely essential for luxury brands. Association with celebrities can also be instrumental in repositioning or revamping a brand and appealing to a new generation of customers.

Collaborating with celebrities as part of a communication strategy can take various forms.

- Appearance in TV and printed advertisements
- Endorsement at events, for example, celebrities wearing designer gowns on the red carpet of major events like the Oscars

Sold exclusively in Louis Vuitton stores. 866.VUITTON www.louisvuitton.com

LOUIS VUITTON

Figure 4.29

Uma Thurman
is the type of
A-list movie star
with beauty and
international
recognition a
luxury brand
seeks to feature
in its advertising.
(*Image Courtesy of the
Advertising Archives*)

* Product placement in movies or video clips
* Associating a luxury item with a celebrity (Kelly bag by Hermès)
* Using celebrities as spokespersons of a brand, particularly common in the cosmetics and beauty industry

All of these are good examples, not to mention celebrities using their star status to launch fashion brands of their own (L.A.M.B by Gwen Stefani or Sweet Face by Jennifer Lopez). Luxury brands' expert Uche Okonkwo has identified five rules of celebrity endorsement for luxury brands.[10]

1. *Credibility:* The celebrity must be credible and have a high level of expertise and talent in his or her field; he or she must be a star. It is through this star status that they bring credibility and add value to the brand.

2. *Global appeal:* The celebrity must have international recognition to ensure global appeal. (See Figure 4.29.)

3. *Personality:* The celebrity's personality must match the brand's personality. The association with the celebrity should not just be based on the star's popularity but on his or her relevance to the brand. Ms. Okonkwo highlights the appropriate collaboration between Chanel and Nicole Kidman and between Uma Thurman and Vuitton as good examples.

4. *Uniform power:* The celebrity must not overshadow the brand—especially important for new and up-and-coming luxury brands.

5. *Constancy:* The celebrity must have constancy and lasting appeal.

Okonkwo goes on to add some of the challenges of working with celebrities:

* The image of celebrities can be damaged as a result of professional or personal circumstances, automatically transferring this to the brands they currently represent.
* Celebrities can get into public controversies that can harm the brands they endorse. (Remember

the controversy over Tiger Woods and the speculation over its effect on his relationship with Nike.)

- Celebrities can disappear from the spotlight before or after the advertising campaign is over.
- Celebrities can become overexposed and lose their star appeal as a result of endorsing multiple brands.
- Celebrities can also decide to change their image, which might sometimes be contradictory to the image of the brands they currently endorse.
- Celebrities can decide to intentionally damage a brand that they feel didn't meet their extraneous demands or did not give them the star treatment they desired.

As a result, it is clear that although celebrity endorsement can be a rewarding collaboration, it is a strategy that needs to be well planned, implemented, and monitored in order to succeed.

PR and Fashion Shows

PR stands for public relations, or as it is sometimes called, press relations. It includes activities and events carried out by the organization to boost the brand's image both in the industry as well as in the community. Many of such activities target influential journalists who in return can offer positive publicity and editorial coverage of the brand and its activities. Private PR agencies can play a role in assisting brands with such activities around the world. Fashion shows can be considered a major PR event; they are costly with no direct financial return but are necessary to showcase the brand and its new ideas and trends. In spite of the fact that the fashion

arm of operations for many luxury brands is a losing one, it remains the one that is the most exciting and creates the necessary buzz to grant media coverage and generate interest in its other products. This is one of the reasons why fashion shows usually include impractical, over-the-top designs that are provocative and shocking. It is this eccentricity that gets the coverage and attention needed. A few seasons ago, for example, John Galliano showed dresses made of newspapers in one of his Dior shows. Understandably, this provoked the necessary attention and interest. When it was time to sell the clothes in the stores, B. Arnault was smart enough to reproduce the garments in real fabrics with newspaper prints on them.

Other events of great importance are product launches (such as perfumes) and store openings. All of these events are treated with significant fanfare and media frenzy. Celebrities are invited, lavish parties are held, and every possible member of the media is invited as well.

Sponsorship

Luxury brands have a tradition of sponsoring events of high status and interest in various fields and areas such as art, sports, and movies. Louis Vuitton sponsors the prestigious America's Cup sailing race (see Figure 4.30), whereas Hugo Boss sponsors Formula One. Another example of such a level of collaboration is when designers offer their garments to movie stars to wear at highly visible awards events.

Product Placement

Product placement refers to placing products in productions such as movies and video clips so

Figure 4.30

The winning
team of the
Louis Vuitton–
sponsored
America's cup
celebrates
victory as a crew
member drinks
from the trophy
cup itself.

(Getty Images/ Kos
Picture Source)

that they appear as part of the scripted scenes. James Bond's character wearing Omega watches or riding BMW cars are good examples of product placements where the brand's name and logo are deliberately mentioned or seen on the big screen. Designing for movie characters has also seen a lot of success, as we mentioned in chapter 2 with the example of Giorgio Armani and Richard Gere's *American Gigolo*.

Co-Marketing

Co-marketing can take place in the form of collaboration between a luxury brand manufacturer and a retailer. Announcing exclusive distribution arrangements and/or availability of luxury brands at certain boutiques or specialty stores are good examples of this strategy.

Promotions

Promotional activities are not as common or diverse for luxury brands as they are in the mass-market segment. Luxury brands do not often offer discounts, nor do they compete on such basis. However, luxury brands are extremely keen on customer service and relationship. Their level of service is usually so high that it becomes very personal. Accordingly,

these brands usually work on personalizing the shopping experience for their customers and rewarding their loyalty in different ways. That may include birthday cards or gifts, VIP treatment, catalogs, loyalty programs, invitations to special events, collection previews, and complementary gifts. All of these activities aim to build a stronger and longer-lasting relationship with the consumer rather than a one-time purchase incentive.

Internet and New Media

The relationship between luxury brands and the Internet was discussed earlier in this chapter. And it is clear that the Internet has been more adopted by luxury as a communication channel than as a distribution one. Luxury brands have Web sites that are well designed with exciting media material and information to promote the brand and highlight its products. In addition to corporate Web sites, many luxury brands have ventured into popular social media options such as Facebook and Twitter in order to stay relevant and in touch with fashion enthusiasts. Diane von Furstenberg, Annu Sui, and Karl Lagerfeld are a few examples of this trend. Other attempts include utilizing mobile technology and creating special apps for iPhone whereby users can get the latest news and video clips from fashion shows—this has been used by Chanel and Ralph Lauren, among others. Updates, store locators, and even shopping options are now available on these devices. It is an effective medium for real-time communication, highly personalized content, offers, and news. These new technologies will be examined later in more detail in chapter 7.

The Brand Evaluation and Audit

Any branding strategy needs to be evaluated as it is implemented. A brand's true position is determined by the customer. The customer positions the brand based on the mental image he or she creates as a result of personal experiences with the brand, as well as other external factors such as competitors' behavior. Accordingly, how effective the branding process and positioning strategy has been matching the perceived image with the proposed one is an essential issue to evaluate and measure. The result of the evaluation process may be a decision to continue with the strategy, tweak it, or reconsider it completely. Moreover, most luxury brands are old brands, and in the span of their life cycles, the need may arise to revamp or reposition it to target a different and younger market. In the process, the brand may need to be re-launched and re-introduced in a new form and manner. As a matter of fact, some believe that to prolong a luxury brand's life, it is a marketing necessity to approach it as a series of shorter life cycles during which the brand is continuously re-launched and re-vamped. This seems necessary because of the brand's need to continuously respond to social and other external changes it incurs throughout its lifetime. However, this can be a necessity and a dilemma at the same time. If the brand ignores these changes, it will be out of touch, irrelevant, and may lose its customer's interest; on the other hand, if it responds to every new trend, it will lose focus and identity. Thus, a certain balance needs to be struck that takes into consideration a few important points:

- It is critical to not lose focus of the customer and the brand's core value. Brands should respond only to relevant trends that make sense to their customers. Revamping or revitalizing the brand is a good strategy and may be necessary at times; however, it should not be at the expense of what the brand stands for and means to the customer. Revitalizing the brand is a stage of the brand's evolution, but evolution is not always meant to be a revolution.

- If a brand decides to approach a different customer or focus on a different core value, then it has decided to shift the strategy from revitalizing the brand to repositioning it. Repositioning may be necessary, as mentioned earlier, when the brand ages and its image fades out, or if it has lost focus of its meaning in the process. Repositioning is a serious strategy that needs to be carefully approached and backed with intensive marketing.

- Repositioning a luxury brand is usually more difficult than repositioning a mass-market one. Repositioning mass-market brands upwards such as H&M, Coach) will always be regarded as an improvement and a brand upgrade, which should generally improve the brand's image. However, in the case of luxury brands, it is harder to convince customers of the necessity or rationale behind the shift without raising questions.

In recent years, Gucci and Burberry have been great examples of brands that were re-launched either as part of a revitalizing or repositioning strategy.

Gucci

Gucci's turnaround under the collaboration between Tom Ford and Domenico de Sole is a good example of brand revitalization rather than repositioning. What Tom Ford and his team did was in essence catch up with their customer. Ford managed to re-align the brand's existing image and value as a sensual Italian luxury brand to how these values were defined and perceived in the nineties. He simply met the expectations of the brand's customers and gained new ones in the process. He did not redefine Gucci as much as make it more relevant and modern, while keeping it true to its heritage in an updated way.

We can compare this situation to the recent downturn of the Versace brand. Versace had been known in the eighties and nineties as the ultimate sexy, risqué, luxury brand. It embodied how "sexy" was perceived in the eighties: flamboyant, glamorous, and even what some saw as a bit vulgar. But that was how sexy was perceived then; lately the definition seems to have changed. Today "sexy" has become more subdued and subtle, so when Versace's designs continued to maintain the same attitude as before, they became less relevant, a bit outdated, and out of touch. As a brand, Versace was trying to stay true to its niche and image, but what they did not realize was that they needed to stick to the core value of the brand while innovating and revitalizing the product and its aesthetics. They needed to interpret the new definition of "sexy" into their designs, to remain the sexy brand in a modern and relevant way. They needed to understand the new needs of their customers and find ways to surprise them, something Versace had failed to achieve in recent years. However, in the past few seasons, the House of Versace seems to have realized this conflict and has presented new collections that were calmer and less provocative in an attempt to regain some of their lost market share. Although initial feedback is positive, time will tell how this will work, but unless the move remains true to the core value and the brand's personality in a way that is relevant to our times, the odds are not in their favor, and it may end up distorting the brand's image and confusing the customers instead.

Burberry

Burberry, on the other hand, had slipped through the cracks for some time and was not perceived as a luxury brand. With a lack of originality and control over its trademark tartan design, the brand lost its cachet. When Rose Bravo took over and teamed up with Christopher Bailey, the goal was clear—to move Burberry upwards again and reposition it as a luxury brand. They knew they would alienate many of their current customers, but that was a calculated move toward targeting a new customer and regaining the confidence of some lost ones. This was a clear example of repositioning the brand and not just revitalization.

It is acceptable, therefore, for a brand to revisit its strategies and market positioning throughout its lifetime. However, there is a difference between deciding to polish the image through reinterpreting its values and to completely redefine them.

Brand Growth

Luxury brands can adopt different strategies of growth. Brand extension, licensing, and global expansion are the three common growth strategies discussed in the following sections.

Brand Extension

Brand extension is a common strategy in the luxury brand segment, especially for lifestyle brands. It is through extensions that the brand manages to create a coherent identity that touches every aspect of the customer's life. In general, there are two options for extensions:

- *Product or line extension:* This approach means the extension of products through addition of more items under existing brand categories, offering a wider range of options (more sizes, colors, styles, and so on).
- *Brand extension:* Another approach is extending the brand by introducing a new category of product under the same brand. This approach allows brands to portray themselves as lifestyle brands offering a variety of products with a single coherent and relevant message (for example, extending into perfumes and cosmetics, or when Armani introduced Armani Casa, Armani Jeans, and boutique hotels).

Luxury brands can also expand their operations through brand creation, which is basically the creation of a new sub-brand that allows the mother brand to expand into new markets and segments based on the power of its name and previous successes. Examples are ck by Calvin Klein, DKNY by Donna Karan, and Purple Label by Ralph Lauren.

It is obvious that brand extensions have lucrative financial and marketing potential. In addition to being new sources of revenue, they also solidify the brand's image as a lifestyle brand and attract new customers in the process. However, as with any strategy for brand extensions, there are many challenges as well. The main challenge is achieving a lucrative level of diversification without diluting the brand. Brand dilution occurs when the brand is overextended to products and areas that make no sense to the brand personality and values and thus are irrelevant to the core customer of the brand. Therefore, brand extension is a diversification strategy that may support and boost the brand's performance, but brand dilution can diminish its relevance, erode its image, alienate the customer, and eventually kill the brand.

Brand extension is a growth strategy that should be considered after the brand has established itself with a clear position and identity in the consumer's mind. The more loyal the consumer, the more he or she is willing to adopt other offerings from the brand. This is true even for nonluxury brands, although it is usually harder to achieve this level of loyalty in the mass-market segment because of the fact that the bond between consumers and luxury brands is, for the most part, an emotional one.

We need to remember that if a luxury brand is widely available, it is no longer rare, which is one of the defining components of a luxury brand. In other words, the tremendous success and expansion of some luxury brands may threaten their own luxury status if not handled diligently. Pierre Cardin's case of uncontrolled over-expansion and exposure is always a good example.

Licensing

Licensing is one of the most common channels for product and brand extensions. Subcontracting or giving other manufacturers the right to produce under a specific label is an economically efficient growth strategy. However, if licensing create a discrepancy in prices from one market to the other. This discrepancy occurs, for example, in Japan, where prices tend to be much higher compared with other markets. This situation is not necessarily problematic, but it can create a good opportunity for parallel markets to exist and flourish, as described earlier.

Luxury Brands and Economic Downturns

The economic downturn that started in 2008 has spotlighted the effect of economic recession on the luxury segment. In spite of being generally less sensitive to economic downturns, the recent dip was so severe and global in nature that its impact on luxury brands and their customers has been clear and significant. Under such severe circumstances, the rules of the game changed and a decrease in demand was inevitable. Brands

attempted to counterattack with an increase in promotional activities and adopting strategies of lowering prices, which are traditionally unusual for this segment, in an attempt to turn inventory into cash in every possible way. For the first time in a long period, customers have seen brands such as Gucci and Bottega Veneta being discounted at luxury retail stores. Luxury stores such as Saks Fifth Avenue and Neiman Marcus, among others, offered various promotions such as "friends and family" discounts of 40 percent or more.[13] Hard times did call for drastic measures indeed.

In the recent years of economic prosperity before this downturn, the base of luxury customers (as well as premium ones) had increased more than ever before, which also meant that a higher number of luxury customers became more sensitive to these economic changes than traditionally perceived. Another outcome is a decline in travel and the number of tourists who have been traditionally significant buyers of certain luxury items

Figure 4.31

The Versace boutique in the Kuala Lumpur Airport, Malaysia.

(© Manfred Bail/age

fotostock)

in major tourist destinations and airports. To many people, luxury goods are unnecessary, and for those nontraditional luxury buyers, luxury goods are easier to give up in hard times.

Luxury and Traditional Marketing Principles

By examining our discussion of luxury brands in this chapter, it is easy to understand why luxury brands seem to defy every known marketing principle. It is an observation that we share with other scholars such as J. N. Kapferer and V. Bastien. Many of the points we raised in this chapter seem to support this point of view, which we can summarize in the following points:

- As mentioned earlier, luxury brands are built on high quality, but not perfect quality. In other words, the level of craftsmanship and handwork expected from every luxury product is one of a kind and uniquely flawed, like most handmade products are. Nothing can beat a machine level of perfection and consistency. However, these imperfections are sought after and admired in luxury brands and guarantee its uniqueness.
- Traditionally, luxury brands possessed a level of arrogance, and designers were meant to dictate trends, not follow them. Even today, although luxury designer brands have lost part of that influence, the segment is meant to surprise and awe customers and not respond to their wishes and demands as much as try to shape them. After all, flair of arrogance and elitism is still linked to this segment. Thus, this attitude defies the basic marketing principle of totally responding to and following your customer.

- Luxury brands do not spend a lot of effort changing who they are in order to be more relevant to new customers. The elitism and exclusivity of the brand makes wider availability be perceived as a sign of brand dilution. This is a totally different mentality from a mass-market brand that would be happy to claim relevance to as many market segments as possible.
- If marketing strategies are meant to increase sales volume and market shares and allow for maximization of profit through smaller margins but higher volumes, this is totally the opposite with luxury brands. Luxury brands are keen on deliberate limited production and exclusive distribution, in spite of any rise in demand. Luxury brands are expected (and accepted) to be harder to acquire. Customers understand and appreciate that the product is rare and may require being placed on a waiting list to obtain it. The fact that luxury brands are anti-volume is in itself opposite to simple marketing principles as well.
- Again, luxury brands' rarity and exclusivity mean that they are not easy to access. As we mentioned, it's a brand that customers are expected to exert some effort to obtain, which in a world of mass-market brands can be a call for the brand's demise.
- The role of advertising is totally different. There is usually no sales proposal in luxury advertising. It is usually minimalist with a photo and logo and not much to say. Even more interesting, most of the ads may not be really targeting the luxury customer who is already aware of the brand, its products, and where to find it. In many ways, these ads target the "others" who are meant to be aware of the brand—even if

they cannot afford it. This level of awareness is necessary, as was explained in the discussion of the social dimension and the social status of the brand. Customers need to know about the brand and desire it. If it is currently out of their price range, they should aspire to have it—and the brand will be ready for them if and when they can afford it in future. Moreover, this emotional buildup helps weave the social status and allure of the brand.

- Price for these brands is mostly a function of perceived luxury. Thus, price is determined more by the strength of the brand's identity than actual costs. In mass-market brands, on the other hand, products are created based on possible acceptable prices.

- Another major difference related to price is how luxury defies the simple law of demand. In the case of mass-market products, the lower the price, the higher the demand for it. In the case of luxury, price is not usually an issue nor the basis of positioning; on the contrary, rising prices maintain the brand's prestige status, and while it may lose some of the not so serious luxury customers, it becomes more relevant and attractive to the die-hard ones.

How to Create a "Star" Luxury Brand

Highly profitable luxury brands possess one of the most important credentials to become "star" brands. Of course all luxury brands would love to turn into "star" brands but, according to B. Arnault, a **STAR BRAND** needs to possess four characteristics: timelessness, modernity, fast growth, and high profitability.

Timeless and modernity refer to whether a brand is created with the aim of being around for a long time while staying relevant, current, and desired. In other words, it should have the ability to stay modern and reinvent itself without losing its identity—an interesting mix of being old and new at the same time. Growth is also essential because it confirms the timelessness and relevance of the brand. Growth is achieved through continuous interest in the brand as manifested in its expansion into new products and new markets. As for profitability, the Christian Lacroix example shows that although luxury brands are expected to take longer to generate profits, they cannot survive without sound financial basis. It is very expensive to develop and maintain luxury brands.

Chapter Summary

- Luxury brands have the greatest potential to be lifestyle brands.

- Although there are many reasons for buying luxury, the emotional reward remains the strongest.

- There is a strong social relevance to luxury buying.
- Luxury brands are rooted in craftsmanship, for the most part.

- American luxury brands are relatively new and empowered by powerful marketing.

- Luxury brands can be star brands

- Luxury brands seem to defy traditional marketing principles.

Chapter Questions and Issues for Discussion

1. Explain the social element of luxury brands, and explore how this concept relates to some of the challenges facing luxury brands, such as counterfeiting and parallel markets.

2. What is the meaning of a lifestyle brand? Why are most luxury brands described as such?

3. Explain how luxury brands seem to defy traditional marketing principles.

KEY TERMS

CRAFTSMANSHIP

CREATIVITY

LIFESTYLE BRANDS

LUXURY

LUXURY BRAND

PREMIUM PRICE

STAR BRANDS

STAR DESIGNERS

CASE STUDY: **Louis Vuitton in Japan**

The Japanese Market

Often described as a confusing jigsaw puzzle, the Japanese distribution system has been notoriously complicated and complex. Characterized by extended channels, large numbers and sizes of retailers, as well as domination of manufacturers, the system created a major barrier for market entry. And in spite of some gradual deregulation and liberalization of capital in the retail industry, the changes were not permissive enough for foreign brands to break into the market independently. Thus, most luxury brands such as Gucci and Hermès had to enter the market either through a partner, such as a department store chain that would act as an agent, or through establishing a joint venture with wholesalers, such as in the case of Loewe.

In 1978, Louis Vuitton assigned Japanese consultant Kyojiro Hata to examine the best ways for the brand to enter the Japanese market. Mr. Hata realized at the time that LV did not have the staff nor the funds necessary to enter the market in the traditional ways, so he proposed a new and different strategy that would be based on a two-contract model:

1. A distribution contract between retailers, mainly department stores and Louis Vuitton, whereby department stores would pick up the merchandise directly from the LV warehouse through their Paris offices and ship it themselves to Japan.

2. A management service contract between the LV Japan branch and these department stores, whereby LV would have the right to oversee and take all the necessary measures to maintain the brand's proposed image through quality control, advertising, and management, in addition to charging a franchise and management service fees. In this way, LV managed to build a controlled system with little financial and human resources.

Examples of measures covered in these contracts:

- Department stores would set up in-store LV boutiques at their expense. Eventually LV demanded that these corners would be enclosed spaces and be moved to ground floors, which was a highly uncommon move at the time. As a matter of fact, the idea was initially met with resistance, and it took LV 10 years to completely relocate in department stores.

- Everything from store furnishing, staff uniforms, and supplies such as wrapping paper was to be determined by LV.

- LV controlled advertising and split costs with department stores.

- LV products were not to be sold through discounts for members' loyalty programs, gift catalogs, at events outside the store, nor through the direct marketing practice known in Japan as "Gaisho," which refers to direct sales catered to important customers.

reconsider its distribution strategy. According to the new strategy, LV Japan imported products directly from LV France and distributed them to all other stores. The previously adopted two-contract system was replaced by a one-contract system in which LVJ owned the inventory it had in its stores as well as other departments stores They worked with six department stores at the time, and the move was followed by a leasing system in which LV leased its in-store boutiques in department stores as well as oversaw the staff in order to fully control operations.

After relocating their flagship global store in Paris to the Champs-Elysées, LV started opening a series of what became known as the "global stores." The global store concept meant that customers were to find all the brand offerings under one roof. There were watches, jewelry, leather goods, eyewear, fashion, and shoes for men and women. The Osaka global store opened in 1998. In all its stores, LV always gave special attention to architecture and design, working with world renowned architects to develop modern and original designs.

Figure 4.32

A rendering of the exterior of the elaborate new Louis Vuitton Japan flagship. Due to the economic downturn, the plans for construction were cancelled. *(Courtesy of UNStudio.)*

In a market known for the substantial influence and power of department stores, it was initially challenging to get them to agree to such conditions.

Expansion

In 1982, the LV branch office in Japan was converted into a corporation, and they opened LV's first standalone store in the Ginza district. At the time, Tokyo had no major street known for its luxury brands such as Foubourg Saint-Honoré in Paris or Fifth Avenue in New York, so they picked Namiki Avenue, known for its well-established stores. With the opening of the new store, LV Japan had to

Pricing

LVJ reviewed and adjusted its prices at least once a year, putting into consideration fluctuations in exchange rate. It adopted a simple strategy that was rooted in its early years as a made-to-order business. The price was basically determined by multiplying cost by a fixed gross margin rate. If the price seemed too high to compete, it worked on lowering cost without compromising quality; if it wasn't feasible, the product could be cancelled. That way LV ensured a sustainable level of profitability without venturing into areas where products could be unsuitable or of lower profitability. This strategy, although too simplistic in modern terms, seemed to work well for LV at the time because its business model and products had not dramatically changed through the years. LV also had a strategy for making sure that it offered the same price to all consumers; through contract agreements with retailers, LV products were not included as part of store special promotions or loyalty program rewards as mentioned earlier.

Promotion

In general, LV did not rely heavily on advertising but rather decided to focus on events, such as the LV exhibition that highlighted the brand's heritage and long history. However, LVJ made a strategic decision to target the male consumer in an attempt to change the established image of LV as a woman's brand. It ran a series of interviews and articles in men's lifestyle magazines where they selected famous Japanese men in various fields to share their views about LV products and how these fit in their lifestyles. Eventually, LVJ decided to run advertisements that were produced locally rather than using their universal ad campaigns since brand recognition in Japan was still limited and largely based on its bags.

Figure 4.33

A view of the store's interior.

(*Courtesy of UNStudio.*)

LVMH

When LV became part of LVMH, more men's products were introduced, including watches, scarves, bags, and pens. The merger meant transforming LV from a brand with traditional luxury products to a fashion company offering a ready-to-wear collection. After the appointment of Marc Jacobs, the company witnessed an increase in sales of almost 300 percent. The company also maintained its tradition of quality in establishing a local product repair system and a customer information service. LVMH had plans to open an impressive new flagship store in Japan's Ginza district in 2010, but since being hit by the global economic downturn in 2008, it announced that it is abandoning the plan. (See Figures 4.32 and 4.33.)

CASE STUDY Questions

1. How do LVJ's strategies in Japan demonstrate the challenges of global expansion?

2. LVJ and Mr. Hata have attempted to maintain the integrity of the LV brand in the new market. Discuss some of the measures they adopted.

SOURCE

Hata, Kyojiro. 2004. *Louis Vuitton Japan: The Building of Luxury*. New York: Assouline Publishing.

http://www.gmtmag.com/en/14_atm_vuitton.php

ENDNOTES

1. Lauren Sherman, How and How Not To Sell Luxury. http://www.forbes.com/2009/04/16/luxury-strategy- marketing-opinions-book-review-vuitton-hermes-fendi.html

2. Michael Chevalier and Gerald Mazzalovo, *Luxury Brand Management: A world of Privilege* (Singapore: John Wiley & Sons, 2008), 152.

3. Ibid., 168.

4. http://www.lvmh.com/

5. PPR-Reference Document (2005), 6.

6. http://www.forbes.com/2009/04/16/luxury-strategy-marketing-opinions-book-review-vuitton-hermes-fendi.html

7. http://www.nnbag.com/

8. http://www.strategy-business.com/enews/enewsarticle/enews040307

9. Uche Okonkwo, *Luxury Fashion Branding* (New York: Palgrave Macmillan, 2007), 145.

10. http://www.brandchannel.com/papers_review.asp?sp_id=1234

11. Michael Chevalier and Gerald Mazzalovo, *Luxury Brand Management: A world of Privilege* (Singapore: John Wiley & Sons, 2008), 363.

12. http://www.reuters.com/article/pressRelease/idUS137779+10-Feb-2009+MW20090210

13. Ibid.

5 Mass-Market Fashion Brands

Mass-market brands follow the general guidelines of branding discussed in chapters 2 and 3. Thus, in this chapter, we shall focus on how this broad segment is unique and differs from luxury brands. In the process, we will highlight two categories of significant importance in today's market: premium (or new luxury) brands and private labels.

Mass-Market vs. Luxury Brands

MASS-MARKET brands are ones that are mass produced. They range in price from low-priced budget brands to high-priced premium brands with mid-priced consumer brands in between. Mass-market fashion brands are generally fashion followers and not trendsetters. They may suffer from sameness, indistinguishable differences, or lack of creativity compared to luxury brands; thus, they are rarely positioned on creativity but on values derived from price, and convenience. Accordingly, these brands' values usually stem from price, functionality, and their value for money.

In the first instance, mass-market brands may seem to be anti-luxury in every element we discussed earlier. However, as brands, they still share some common principles, such as the need to generate values and to possess a strong identity. The main difference may be that the core value for most mass-market brands is rational in nature, while for luxury brands, it is emotional.

CHAPTER OBJECTIVES

- Learn how mass-market brands differ from luxury brands.

- Identify the characteristics of mass-market brands.

- Define private and premium brands.

- Examine positioning and branding strategies for private and premium brands.

Figure 5.1

Mass-market
retail shops
are sometimes
located on
small-town
main streets
like this one in
Middleburg,
Virginia.

(© Jeff Greenberg/age

fotostock)

Because mass-market brands are not usually trendsetters, or at the forefront of creativity, the design and creative process is usually different. There is no real purpose for the superstar designer, and designing is usually done by teams of young designers unknown to the public, who in many cases take the role of product developers that are expected to follow and adapt trends rather than create new ones. Accordingly, most design decisions are business and merchandising decisions taken at the executive level and made with price and fashion constraints in mind rather than in partnership with designers—a very different process from the luxury segment. Thus, in the mass-market segment, decision making is highly driven by cost and volume rather than originality and margins.

Price

Mass-market products are highly price driven. At the budget range, for instance, they are quantitative and based on the concept of more for less, so in most cases these brands are positioned primarily based on price. A mass-market brand can adopt any of the pricing strategies mentioned in chapter 2 such as odd pricing, price penetration, price lining, and so on. However, we can identify a couple of major differences between luxury and mass-market brands in relation to price.

- *Attitude toward price premiums:* Mass-market brands do not adopt a premium price strategy.
- *Re-pricing strategies:* Mass-market brands are more susceptible to re-pricing adjustment strategies, such as promotional sales and clearance markdowns, than luxury brands are. Markdowns and price reductions are caused by many factors that can be either internal, such as overbuying of merchandise, broken assortments, or errors in the initial pricing of the product, or external such as an economic slowdown or competition. In all cases, markdowns are meant to stimulate sales, face competition, and entice customers to buy more under the premise of offering a "bargain." Luxury brands have a totally different attitude toward repricing and bargain hunting, of course. They rarely mark down products, and some totally refrain from adopting this strategy, relying on a more controlled production strategy and limited quantities. As an alternative, luxury brands may sell excess merchandise through their own outlets and/or discount stores after taking some measure to conceal the brand, such as removing their labels.

Location

For the mass-market segment, the options are not as limited as they are with luxury brands. (See Figure 5.1.) The options regarding locations may include:

- Central locations, usually downtown where business and shopping activities are mainly centered.
- Main street areas in smaller towns.
- Shopping centers and malls where a cluster of stores are located under one roof or area with an adjacent parking lot and possible food courts.

The choice is made among various options based on accessibility, traffic flow, ease of parking, place and visibility of slot, nearby stores, and competition. (See Figure 5.2.) All these are factors that play a role in the customer's decision-making process. A lot of data are used and analyzed to assist managers in determining the best locations where their target customers are clustered and within easy reach. For example, data obtained from credit card records and mailing lists can be used for creating a demographic profile of certain neighborhoods and areas. Even casual observation of shopping patterns and stores' traffic can produce a lot of information on the activity of the location, such as hours of heavy traffic, ease of parking, customers' profiles, and so on. Stores can also benefit from locating close to competitors because they already attract the same targeted customer. When Steve & Barry was in business, they managed to maintain low prices by lowering their costs through a series of measures, such as operating in underperforming malls where they could get low rents, in addition to manufacturing overseas in countries like China and India. Such a strategy worked for a while; however, it would not have worked as an option for any luxury brand, even if small in size.

Unlike luxury brands, most mass-market brands have a strong presence online. They seem to have utilized the Internet in more effective and innovative ways than luxury brands that are taken aback by the idea of selling their products online for fear of hurting their image by hindering their exclusive appeal, or out of the belief that it is not a suitable environment for their customers.

Service

The difference between luxury and mass-market brands on the level of service is clear. Luxury brands are expected to take extra measures to pamper and please the customer, whereas mass-market brands may only offer the most basic level of services. The level of service within the mass-market spectrum may still differ according to segment and price range. Bargain brands will usually offer the minimum when it comes to complementary services such as extended warranties—and sometimes offer none at all. On the other hand, premium brands' services may be closer to the level of luxury. However, with strong competition at all levels, customer service in general (together with

Figure 5.2

Malls similar to this one in Honolulu, Hawaii, offer the convenience of visiting many stores in one place.

(© Jon Hicks/Corbis)

innovation) has become a major competitive tool in today's markets, especially with the plethora of choices available to the consumer. As a result, levels of service have generally improved and should continue to improve even at the mass-market level in order for brands to compete and survive.

Identity

All brands need to establish a strong visual and emotional identity. After all, this is what branding is all about. However the approach may vary for different segments. Visual symbols such as logos, names, and colors adopted by mass-market brands have fewer restrictions than with luxury brands. They range from made-up names to ones with specific insinuations such as Urban Outfitters or Nautica (see Figure 5.3a). Other mass-market brands like to emulate a luxury attitude toward naming by adopting made-up names that imply the existence of a designer or country heritage (Alfani or Massimo Dutti, for example) behind the brand. By assuming such names, they imply messages of quality, creative legitimacy, and innovation that are generally attributed to luxury brands. (See Figure 5.3b.)

Personality

As always, an identity is a reflection of the brand's vision and of the five personality groups mentioned in chapter 2. Mass-market brands will most likely build their identities around personality traits that reflect:
- Friendliness, warmth, excitement through being cool, young, outgoing, and contemporary
- Competence through being hard working and efficient

Communication and Promotion

Mass-market brands utilize the full spectrum of media options: TV, radio, Internet, and printed media. These brands need all these channels in order to compete with the tough competition they face as a result of their level of sameness and lower level of creativity. As a result, the major differences between luxury and mass-market brands lie in the focus of their promotional messages and content.
- Mass-market brands usually compete and position themselves on the basis of functionality and product features rather than experience, emotions, or lifestyles. They use various communication channels to inform potential customers of these benefits as well as announce any reduction in prices or special sales that would motivate them to seek the brand and make a purchase.
- Their reliance on promotional activities, such as sales and discounts, require more frequent and regular announcements.
- Because mass-market brands differentiate themselves on the basis of convenience, they have a stronger presence in catalogs and infomercials where ease of shopping and access to special products prevail.

Growth Strategies

Although mass-market brands adopt similar growth strategies to luxury brands, such as brand extensions and globalization, they may adopt different implementation strategies.
- Brand extensions are used as a way to upgrade into higher segments by introducing brands that appeal to higher market segments (such as Gap into Banana Republic or H&M to COS).

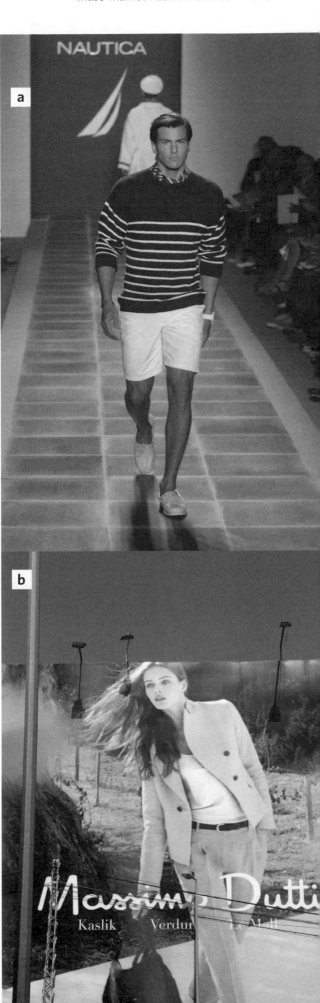

Figure 5.3a

With its lifestyle insinuation, the name Nautica helps to shape the brand's sporty identity.

(Frazer Harrison/Getty Images for IMG)

- Licensing is also a more common mode for global expansion in this segment.
- Franchising is a common distribution strategy, especially as a mode of entry into foreign markets. (See Figure 5.4.) On the other hand, many luxury brands prefer full store ownerships whenever possible.
- Mass-market brands rely heavily on outsourcing for cheaper material and factors of production. Over 60 percent of the world's apparel production is exported from developing countries where cheap labor and low costs of production prevail. On the other hand, many luxury brands still manufacture in workshops or factories located in European fashion capitals.
- Mass-market brands are prone to product adaptations or localization in foreign markets in terms of design, sizing, and marketing. Some level of adaptation can be acceptable for luxury brands, although they are largely built on the universality of their image and products.
- Being cost and price inelastic, mass-market brands face a major pricing challenge as they enter different markets. Transportation costs, taxes, and standards of living may force the brand to change pricing strategies in different markets, causing the brand to be positioned and segmented in a different way. Zara's price in Europe, the United States, or Japan differs greatly from in Spain, where Zara fashions are produced.
- The luxury customer is in general more globally homogeneous than the mass-market customer. Being mainly lifestyle brands, luxury brands represent common values and cultures that are appreciated by their customers everywhere. Many mass-market brands, on the other hand,

Figure 5.3b

Massimo Dutti doubles up on associations, using a brand name that implies the existence of a specific designer (as opposed to a nameless team) as well as one of Italian heritage.

(© char abumansoor / Alamy)

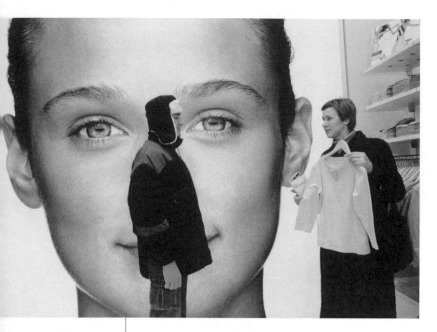

Figure 5.4

Benetton's
franchising
strategy has
proven highly
successful
for entering
foreign markets.
In 1992, this
21,000-square-
foot United
Colors of
Benetton
megastore
opened in
Moscow, Russia.

(© Gerd Ludwig/Corbis)

failed to attract or identify similar segments in foreign markets (such as Gap in Europe).

Premium Brands: The New Luxury or New Luxe

In recent years, the premium segment of brands has emerged with tremendous growth. **PREMIUM BRANDS** are also referred to as "aspirational" or "new luxe" brands and include brands such as Coach, Victoria's Secret, and most RTW labels introduced by luxury brands (see Figure 5.5). By definition, this segment stands at the highest spectrum of mass-market brands; placed just below luxury brands, it shares a few characteristics with them. Some of these characteristics are as follows.

- Whereas premium brands may not be built on exclusivity, they are based on emotions, and consumers have a much stronger emotional engagement with them than with other goods in the mass-market segment.
- Premium brands possess better quality, benefits, and functionality based on a higher level of innovation and creativity. Although most premium products still rely on following trends introduced by luxury brands, it is important to remember that premium brands are not created by simply improving existing products or attempting to reposition them through marketing and advertising. Consumers are sophisticated enough to understand this, and there must be a genuine added value in these products.

- The decision to create a premium brand is primarily a business strategy and as such must be developed and executed by CEOs and divisional leaders of large companies as well as entrepreneurs and innovators of small companies. A premium brand is product centered and also requires keen understanding of consumer motivation and buying behavior.

- Premium brands may have elements of craftsmanship but are not completely handmade or artisan in nature.

- Premium brands are not promoted as elite, the way luxury brands are. Rather, they appeal to a set of values that may be shared by people of many income levels, in many walks of life. As a matter of fact, premium brands are a major culprit in what has been referred to as the democratization of luxury.

In recent decades, the luxury brands segment has witnessed major changes in terms of organizational structure and type of ownership. For instance, this can be seen with the creation of large multibrand luxury groups. Yet it is important to remember that premium brands are more than a marketing exercise or cheap copies of luxury brands. They are legitimate brands created through a strong collaboration of all organizational functions.

Customer

This segment appeals to a category of customers that has grown in number and relevance in recent years as a result of an increase in wealth gained from economic prosperity in many societies such as China. As a result, these customers aspire to trade up to premium brands, motivated by the following:

- Discretionary income has increased among many households due to both parents working. Higher incomes have been matched by an increase in home ownership and equity. In addition, these customers manage to save on basic items through frequently patronizing discount stores.
- Relevant to the previous point, many women have joined the work force and are earning top salaries as well.
- On the other hand, there has been an increase in the number of independent singles with more money to spend on themselves and their desires.
- Demographic profiles have changed; the middle class is better educated, more sophisticated, and better traveled than before.
- The media and celebrities have contributed to the increase in desire for obtaining such brands and other pleasures in life.
- The increased number and spread-out design of shopping centers and malls created opportunities for the new premium group of brands and stores such as Victoria's Secret and Guess to exist and expand through mall-based chains of stores. The rise of these specialty retailers has helped make premium goods more geographically available, while still offering a limited selection of goods and categories at close to premium prices.
- Rapid changes in technology and communications have made it easier to democratize fashion in general and thus made it easier and cheaper to access information and generate interest in these trends.

As for their profile and shopping habits, the premium or new luxury customer has a few notable characteristics, such as:

- Premium-brand customers are generally price and economic sensitive and are willing to trade down if necessary.
- They are very selective and have a tendency to mix brands from different segments. For instance, they might carry a Coach handbag and wear a pair of Levi's jeans at the same time.
- Their selectivity is also motivated by their decision-making process, which can be both rational (involving technical and functional considerations) as well as emotional (aspirational).

Price

Premium brands demand high-end prices that are at the higher end of the mass-market spectrum yet still lower than luxury brands. However, one

Figure 5.5

Coach is considered a premium brand, just below the luxury segment. (© Qi yunfeng— Imaginechina/AP Images)

challenge these brands face is their limited ability to reduce pricing without highly eroding their margins. The fact that they are mass produced in larger quantities than luxury means that they have already received and benefitted from supplier discounts, so they usually have little opportunity to manipulate prices. As a result, where luxury brands are forced to discount their prices in tough times, premium brands may find it even harder to respond and keep their products attractive to their customer. For a premium-brand shopper who may have the choice of purchasing a Coach handbag for around $700 or a Prada on sale for around $900, buying the Prada handbag will most likely make more sense.

Product

New luxury goods cover a wide range of products that can be categorized in three main categories:[1]

1. *Super-premiums:* Products that are priced at or near the top of their category and at a considerable premium to conventional offerings.
2. *Old luxury brand extensions:* Lower-priced versions of products created by companies whose brands have traditionally been affordable only for the rich.
3. *MASSTIGE brands (mass prestige):* Neither at the top of their category in price nor related to other brands. They occupy a sweet spot in the market between mass and class, commanding a premium price over conventional products but priced well below super-premium or old luxury goods (such as Bath & Body Works).

Premium products are more responsive to trends than conventional goods. They may still not be trendsetters but are faster in responding to high-end trends where innovation generally appears first. Therefore, they are able to interpret these trends within a few weeks in less expensive versions. A good example is Zara, which manages through a vertically integrated system to reduce the production cycle, control quantity produced, and minimize inventory so that they can offer new styles in their stores almost every week. However, whereas this system of controlled quantities and shorter cycles allows these brands to respond quickly to trends trickling down from the luxury segment, it also makes it harder to increase their volume of production fast enough if a larger quantity is needed.

Distribution

Many premium brands such as Zara adopt a *fast response* concept of production and distribution. This concept allows them to have better control over the production and development stages as well as better management of inventory by adopting *just-in-time* concepts in operations. (Just-in-time is a strategy whereby raw materials are ordered and delivered only when needed and thus saves in cost and space of warehousing.) As a result, it allows customers to find something fresh and new almost every time they visit the store, raising their level of interest and surprise and motivating them to visit the store more often. However, this also means that most products are produced in small quantities to minimize stock and reduce the need to discount their prices.

Some of the measures these brands take to enhance the distribution process are as follows.
- They use local distribution centers.
- They have real-time communication with stores to respond to each store's need of inventory in a short period of time.

- Whereas these brands, unlike luxury brands, rely on outsourcing in cheaper markets such as Asia, production in some cases may have to be done domestically to ensure a quick response.
- Many of these brands may also rely on workshops or dedicated factories to ensure better control and response.

Premium brands are distributed through a range of distribution channels. In addition to company-owned, stand-alone stores, they can be distributed in other specialty and department stores as well. Premium brands also adopt franchising as a viable channel of expansion, and they are more flexible in being present in locations such as suburban malls and shopping centers than most luxury brands would be.

Communication

The premium brand's communication strategies are similar to the luxury brand's strategies in focusing on high advertisement expenditure in magazine and editorial coverage. As a matter of fact, many believe that the luxury-style communication of premium brands contributed to the changing perceptions that consumers generally have today about mass-market fashion brands versus luxury brands.

Examples of the communication strategies they adopt are:

- Celebrity endorsements.
- Prestige retail locations, though they have a stronger presence outside major cities than luxury brands do.
- Co-branding. H&M for example, has a track record of cooperating with celebrity designers such as Karl Lagerfeld and Roberto Cavalli, and celebrities such as Madonna, in producing specially designed limited-edition collections with great success. Due to this strategy, they may be regarded in some areas as a premium brand.

Growth

Premium brands borrow their global appeal and potential from luxury brands. Aided by their greater flexibility in adopting different modes of entry, such as franchising and through local distributors, premium brands tend to be true global brands. Their fashion appeal and comparative affordability make them more attractive and accessible in different markets while maintaining a certain class status that they may even lack in their home markets (again, H&M is a good example).

Premium brands still face a major challenge of where to go next. They appear to be in a better position than other mass-market brands to enter the luxury market through brand creation; however, they may still suffer from lack of heritage and history. On the other hand, they do have the necessary infrastructure and logistics should they consider downgrading to a lower-priced offering in the mass-market segment.

Private Labels

PRIVATE LABELS are brands owned by a retailer and not a manufacturer. Retailers usually contract these products and have them produced under their own labels.

The definition of private labels has expanded to refer to both private labels sold next to manufacturers brands in multibranded stores (such as Club

Room at Macy's or Target's Isaac Mizrahi collection) as well as private brands sold solely in their exclusive stores (such as Gap and Esprit), which would also fall under the specialty stores category. (See Figure 5.6.)

To avoid confusion in this chapter, we shall focus on the first kind of private labels: those that are produced by retailers such as Macy's and Nordstrom to be exclusively sold side by side with other manufacturers' brands.

Private labels have come a long way since 20 years ago when many consumers preferred national brands because they recognized the names and trusted their reputations. In the past, private labels were generally seen as cheaper products with inferior quality. National brands had the means and legitimacy to attract creative talents as well as the need and capacity to advertise and expand. Today the apparel industry is one of the largest sectors for private labels, which currently account for an estimated 45 percent of sales in the United States, whereas in some categories such as women's wear, skirts, and children's clothing, the share is more than 65 percent.[2] Now these brands compete with established national brands, not just on the basis of price, but of quality and style as well, especially considering that they use the services of the same contractors as national brands. The rise in the transformation of many stores into chain stores and their expansion into global brands have also created the need to be different and compete on the basis of product and service, and not just price.

Today these brands are well positioned as proper brands that possess the same emotional elements generally associated with manufacturers' brands. This is a big transformation from the pure functional role these brands played in earlier years.

One of private labels' core values is creating a sense of "smart shopping" for the customers. Customers feel they are making smarter decisions buying a "designer" creation at Target, JCPenney, Macy's, or H&M, yet at a much more reasonable price. (See Figure 5.7.) This is one of the many reasons why these brands usually become more popular during economic downturns. An interesting research outcome shows how these brands manage to maintain a longer relationship with customers even after economic hard times, demonstrating that these brands have more to offer in values than just price. As a matter of fact, there are some indications that buyers are increasingly shifting their loyalty from manufacturing brands to retailers' private labels.

The rivalry between retailer and manufacturers' brands is also evident in their fight over in-store space and locations dedicated to each brand. Retailers will normally give priority to their own brands.

Figure 5.6

Macy's private label Alfani has become one of the fastest-growing segments of their business. (*Associated Press/ZAK BRIAN/SIPA*)

Figure 5.7

H&M's window display advertises the launch of their special collection by Roberto Cavalli in 2007.

(*Getty Images/Amy Sussman*)

Private labels are generally not trendsetters. They tend to imitate creative and technological innovations of manufacturers' brands and offer their versions at competitive prices. These brands are thus a major source of differentiation and competitiveness for these retailers. Melissa Hopkes, vice president and divisional merchandise manager of INC, Macy's largest private label, said once that "INC has been vital to Macy's success in differentiating the store from its competition. If private labels didn't exist, there would be no reason to shop at Macy's rather than Nordstrom's."[3] As a result INC is given prominent display in the store, where it is usually placed to be seen by customers as they first enter the store.

Product

Private labels are generally created by a team of young designers or product developers, except for those instances where stores decide to work with famous celebrity designers to create exclusive collections. This form of co-branding is seen in collaboration between Target and Isaac Mizrahi, JCPenney and Nicole Miller, and Kmart and Martha Stewart. Target's slogan "Expect more, Pay less" is a good reflection of this strategy.

Categories

In the world of private labels, there are four main categories: generics, copycats, premium store brands, and value innovators.[4]

GENERICS

A dying breed and not very relevant to the fashion industry, **GENERICS** refer to no-name products such as shampoos and soaps that were sold at large discounts next to branded products in supermarkets.

COPYCATS

This used to be the initial rationale behind private labels. In the fashion industry, it is common to find **COPYCAT** private labels that basically imitate the styles, color stories, and details of an established manufacturer brand and offer their alternative at a competitive price. Usually these brands are positioned and marketed on the premise that they offer equal quality and styling with a lower price that they achieve due to their ability to eliminate the middle man from the developing process. Retailers benefit in many ways from such a strategy. By copying trends and styles of manufacturing brands, they indirectly benefit from those brands' proven creative resources and investment. Also, retailers can gain bargaining leverage with manufacturers by competing with their brands, so they can secure better margins and deals with these manufacturers. Finally, they benefit from in-store traffic created by manufacturers' brands to promote their own competing private labels. No wonder that these private labels are usually placed in-store close to the manufacturers brands they imitate.

PREMIUM STORE BRANDS

Retailers began to realize that although the copycat branding strategy helps to generate traffic and compete against manufacturer brands, it may not help differentiate the store from other specialty stores. The alternative was to introduce private labels that offer superior quality at lower prices and high creativity. It's the retailers' way of participating in the premium brand segment that has been gaining an increasing popularity in recent years.

Macy's, JCPenney, Target, and Nordstrom are among the many department and specialty stores that offer a range of private labels that have been successful and instrumental in positioning their store brand. Indeed Macy's has a wide range of private labels with proven successes and history. Terry Lundgren, CEO of Macy's Inc. (formerly known as Federated), said that the "objective is to have more merchandise that is unique to our stores," acknowledging the fact that most department stores sell almost the same manufacturing brands and range of products. Macy's private labels, most notably INC and Alfani, have proven to be the fastest-growing part of their business. Other brands include Style & Co, Charter Club, Tahari by Elie Tahari, and an exclusive collection for the home by Martha Stewart, among others. Lundgren expressed hopes that this strategy will attract the customers' attention away from sales and coupon promotions. As a matter of fact, in recent years, Macy's has reduced the number of promotions by about 20 percent and focused on fewer but better sales.[5] It is interesting to note that at Macy's, sales of private-label apparel, accessories, and other items have outperformed other merchandise categories for years, accounting for 19 percent of Macy's sales in fiscal 2007. In fact, Macy's derives 35 percent of its annual sales from its private-label goods and designer items exclusive to Macy's by celebrities, such as Martha Stewart and Tommy Hilfiger.[6]

VALUE INNOVATORS

The value innovators are an interesting group of retailers that manage to balance low-priced value-driven private labels with a high level of innovation and style. Examples could be Target's collaboration with big name designers like Isaac Mizrahi as well as H&M with Lagerfeld, McCartney, and Cavalli. These brands offer fashion at attractive prices through a series of efforts that focus on consistently lowering and controlling costs, such as:

- Sourcing from low-cost developing countries, mainly in Asia
- Having fewer middlemen
- Buying in large volumes
- Controlling costs at every level and stage
- Using an efficient distribution system that secures quick delivery
- Employing effective marketing campaigns that are in tune with their target market (mainly hip and young) and successfully create the necessary buzz around these collections

Accordingly, these brands differentiate and position themselves on the basis of delivering good quality and design at a very reasonable and competitive price. It is a successful mix of value for money and innovation that has been traditionally hard to achieve.

However, one challenge these brands face is that they obviously cannot rely on price to achieve growth or higher margins. They rely heavily on volume, which means that they either need to target new segments or expand globally. Each option is lucrative but also challenging. Targeting new segments might risk alienating customers of existing ones and thus repositioning the brand, whereas international expansions incur other cost and logistic challenges, requiring extra effort and time to succeed. Nevertheless, these labels' success with shoppers will definitely attract more bands to follow suit.

The strategy seems to also have a positive impact on the store's image. Target has been repositioned as more hip than it used to be in the past and has been nicknamed by many of its customers "Tar-jay," a French-flavored pronunciation to reflect its new trendy fashionable image. However, time will tell if this strategy will backfire in times of economic turndowns if Target chooses to remain positioned as a low-priced discount store.

Price

Most of the previously mentioned private label categories demonstrate that pricing is a major factor in their success. Offering equal or better quality than their competitors' manufacturer brands at a lower price has been instrumental to their positioning strategy and success. One strategy some retailers adopt in promoting their private labels is to inflate the price gap between the retailer's private label and the competing manufacturer brand. The big difference in price makes customers feel that the extra money they pay for manufacturer brands is not proportionate to the perceived extra benefit they may receive. As a result, retail labels make more economic sense to them and appear to be more attractive. Although effective, this strategy may be counterproductive if mishandled. Too much of a difference may reduce the retailers' margin and revenue. Thus, in deciding on this price gap, retailers need to put into consideration the nature of the product and the price sensitivity and elasticity for both competing brands. Elasticity simply

measures how strongly customers respond to these changes and how it would affect their demand for the brand. The other challenge is that if customers focus on the lower-priced private labels and totally ignore the manufacturers' brands, the result may be a decrease in the store's total dollar revenue.

In the case of premium private labels, they usually adopt a different strategy. These brands are not necessarily significantly cheaper than their manufacturers' competitors and in some instances may even be more expensive. Thus, their profitability is driven by other factors such as their exclusivity, lower costs creating higher margins by as much as 25 to 30 percent, and an increase in brand loyalty as a result of private labels in general. In addition, they benefit financially from the leverage bargaining power they gain in negotiating with manufacturers as a result of the threat their private labels impose on the manufacturers' brands.

From an economic perspective, consumers will switch if the benefit they perceive in quality or image is less than the price they pay. Thus, private labels must be able to compete not just on the basis of price but on quality and creativity as well in order to create the right incentive for the consumer. However, these elements do come with their own challenges.

- Measures such as dollar/square foot cannot be ignored. These can be in favor of manufacturers' brands because of their higher prices and turnover. Also, manufacturers offer many services that stores are now forced to provide themselves, such as transportation or warehousing, therefore imposing an added cost burden.

- Manufacturers, in many cases, share costs of promotion and marketing activities, which will be totally handled by the stores in case of private labels.
- Although private labels give retailers a negotiation leverage with manufacturers, they can also alienate manufacturers and force them to take their brands somewhere else. The result is a narrow and less diverse merchandise mix.
- Retailers are selective of what they offer in their stores, and they never buy the full collection of a manufacturer. As a result, many designers have decided to open their own boutiques to showcase their full lines in a space and atmosphere that reflects the image and lifestyle they represent. An increasing tension between retailers and manufacturers has therefore surfaced, and retailers have decided to fight back with various measures including more private labels.
- One other major challenge is that private labels will never be able to compete at the same level of innovation with manufacturers because they do not have the dedicated resources. And the more manufacturers' brands hit the market, the less the share of private labels will be.
- Private labels' success is dependent in a way on the power of the retailer brand, even if they have different names, especially those that are sold exclusively at these stores.
- They also suffer from a general lack of advertising, at least at a level below that of manufacturers' brands.

Communication

Private labels generally advertise less than manufacturers do. However, private labels rely heavily on in-store and point of sales communication. It is an effective and cost-efficient strategy. Products strategically placed in-store where they are visible and can effectively compete with manufacturer brands, signs, sales promotions, and discounts are other examples of how the brands are internally marketed.

Stores also use catalogs and direct marketing to promote their brands. New media such as the Internet and digital devices have allowed retailers to personalize their messages and special offers at a fast rate and in a cost-effective manner.

Global Private Labels

Private labels are global phenomena. Their success is evident in many markets around the world. The United Kingdom, for instance, is generally considered a pioneer in private labels and in various industries: Marks and Spencer, the leading British retailer, launched its highly popular apparel brand St. Michael in 1928. In this chapter, we decided to focus on private labels manufactured by retailers and sold alongside other manufacturers' brands they carry, as opposed to private brands sold solely in exclusive stores, such as H&M and Gap. The latter group's expansion into the global scene is evident through a mix of store ownership and franchises. As for the former group (our focus), their geographic expansion is evidently highly reliant on the retailer's own expansion. However, the Internet and online shopping have opened the doors for global reach to these brands. In addition, private labels have a strong connection with global markets through overseas manufacturing and outsourcing.

Chapter Summary

- Mass-market brands are not usually trendsetters or at the forefront of creativity.

- Buying a mass-market brand is a rational decision for the most part.

- Mass-market brands are still expected to deliver value.

- Compared to luxury brands, mass-market brands generally adopt different distribution and pricing strategies.

- Premium brands gained big growth recently as they respond to new socioeconomic changes.

- Private labels have come a long way and play an important and competitive role in the face of manufacturers' brands.

Chapter Questions and Issues for Discussion

1. How do mass-market brands compare to luxury brands in terms of brand value, pricing attitude, and location choices?

2. Briefly compare premium brands to luxury brands.

3. Name a few of the challenges private labels face to compete with manufacturing brands.

KEY TERMS

COPYCATS

GENERICS

MASS-MARKET

MASSTIGE

PREMIUM BRANDS

PRIVATE LABELS

CASE STUDY: Zara

Zara opened its first store 1975 in La Coruña, Spain, as a store selling medium-quality fashion apparel at affordable prices. By the end of the eighties, the brand was located in most major Spanish cities including Madrid, and in the nineties it began to expand overseas as well. Since 2002, Inditex, the parent company of Zara, now comprises several brands: Massimo Dutti (sophisticated urban fashion), Pull and Bear (casual laid-back fashion), Bershka (street fashion), Stradivarius (young cutting-edge fashion), Oysho (lingerie), Zara Home, and Uterqüe (accessories), with Zara still the largest of its brands.

Inditex

Inditex is a vertically integrated company where most products, especially fashion-sensitive items, are designed and manufactured internally, then distributed to stores. Its design strategy is not to be a trendsetter but rather a fashion follower, responding to customers' preferences and new trends seen on fashion runways, trade shows, and magazines. Zara's competitive edge lies in how fast and efficiently it is able to transform these ideas and trends into quality products that are available in its stores with a short lead time. As a result, both internal and external production channels direct to a central distribution center from where merchandise is shipped directly to stores twice a week. The system is based on the concepts of quick response, a set of policies meant to improve coordination between retailing and manufacturing to ensure more flexibility and better response to market changes such as just-in-time manufacturing (a strategy based on orders, not inventory built-up) and the use of bar codes and electronic devices to share information, thus eliminating the need for warehousing by keeping inventory as low as possible. This system allows the company to shorten its cycle from design to store placement to about five weeks for new designs and almost two weeks for modifications or restocked products. Compared to an industry standard of an average six-month cycle, it manages to beat the system and stay fresh and competitive. The shorter cycle also means reduced working capital and the ability to continue supplying the stores with new merchandise, as well as having the capacity to commit resources to new seasons' merchandise later than most competitors.

Merchandise

Zara produces three lines—women's, men's, and children's—through a team of designers who follow fashion trends and base their new collections on them. Zara has adopted a philosophy of quick response rather than prediction of trends. Fabrics and trims are picked, samples prepared, and prices are determined, followed by production. Zara's designers produce two basic collections each year for Fall/Winter and Spring/Summer. The whole process of product development is done with close consideration for and link to the stores. On many occasions, they will produce limited quantities of new items and place them in a few stores for testing. The brand produces large quantities based only on consumers' reaction. In general, 89 to 90 percent of basic designs are common in all stores, while 10 to 15 percent

Figure 5.8

Spending little on traditional advertising, Zara uses its store windows to promote the brand.

(© uk retail Alan King/ Alamy)

vary according to country. Items that are slow are swiftly cancelled, and returns are either shipped to and sold at other Zara stores or disposed of through a small, separate chain of close-out stores near their distribution center. The target is to minimize the inventory that has to be sold at marked-down prices in stores during the sales period that usually ends each season.

Retailing and Distribution

The company designed a centralized distribution system based in Arteixo, Spain, with a network of satellite centers in other countries. Warehouses are regarded as centers of distribution for moving merchandise to stores rather than storing it as inventory for a long time, and shipments are generally made twice a week to their stores. Zara owns and operates many of its own stores. In 2001, it operated over 200 stores in 18 countries other than Spain. Its vertical integration is more backward oriented, focusing on responding to fashion trends quickly, so in retailing, they also rely on franchising as well as joint ventures in areas where there are market barriers to direct entries, such as in Japan.

The vertically integrated model built on the concept of quick response has generally proven to be effective and profitable for Inditex by reducing merchandising cycles and errors as well as inventory risks.

Promotion

The stores play a major role in promoting the brand because Zara spends very little on traditional media advertising—approximately 0.3 percent of its revenue compared with 3 to 4 percent for most other specialty retailers. Its advertising is generally limited to the start of the sales period at the end of the season. Accordingly, the brand relies heavily on its store front to market the brand (see Figure 5.8). As a result, their stores are usually large in size and located in central locations. The company always prefers to enter a market with a flagship store and considers expansion based on results after they gain local experience. Thus, compared to H&M, for instance, it will usually be running fewer stores in countries where both these brands exist. It also historically has preferred new markets that resembled the Spanish one with a lower level of economic development and easier entry. Store windows are also of great importance because they are meant to showcase the brand. Store window prototypes are usually set up at headquarters to indicate design themes and direction, which are later carried to stores around the world through a team of visual merchandisers and window designers with some allowance for adaptation. In-store music and employees' uniforms are also determined to achieve a consistent look and atmosphere throughout the stores. Store managers decide on which merchandise to carry, then transmit their orders electronically to headquarters, and manufacturing is planned accordingly.

Pricing

A major aspect of Zara's global expansion is its pricing strategy. It adopts a strategy whereby it passes the extra cost of distributing overseas to its customers. This creates a large price discrepancy compared to prices in Spain. For example, prices would be 70 percent higher in the United States and 100 percent higher in Japan than in Spain due to this policy. As a result, the brand is positioned differently in each of these markets. (See Figure 5.9.) In Latin America, for instance, it is positioned with a high-end status emphasizing its "Made in Europe" image (as opposed to being made in Spain), while it is still positioned and priced at the middle market in Spain. Such discrepancies may be among the reasons why the company was late in offering online shopping at their Web site.

Recent Growth

In recent years, Inditex celebrated a few growth milestones, for example:

- In 2009, Inditex signed a joint venture to open stores in India starting in early 2010. Massimo Dutti, Bershka, and Pull and Bear have opened for the first time in China.
- In 2008, Inditex launched Uterqüe, a retailer specializing in accessories. Inditex achieved a new milestone by reaching 4,000 stores in 73 countries.
- In 2007, Zara Home introduced Inditex's first online store. Zara also celebrated the launch of shop number 1,000 in Florence, Italy.

CASE STUDY Questions

1. What are the main challenges in the business model adopted by Zara?

2. Evaluate Zara's marketing and distribution strategies, and compare them to those of another brand you are familiar with. Decide how these strategies would work if Zara decided to enter your local market.

Figure 5.9

With stores in so many countries, Zara prints its hang tags with international sizes.

(*Bloomberg via Getty Images/ Markel Redondo*)

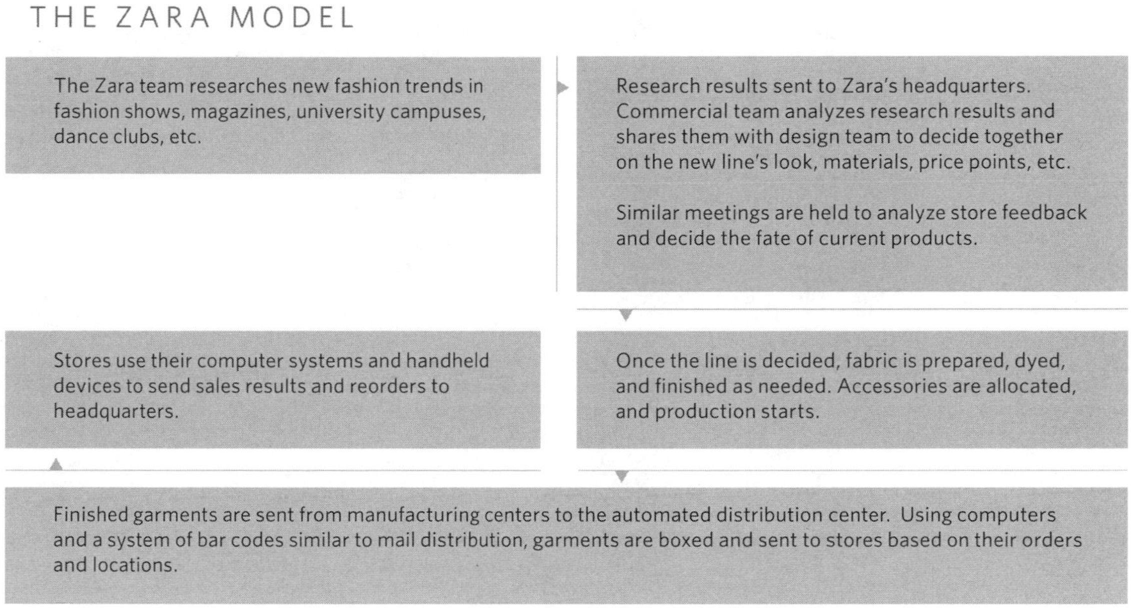

Figure 5.10

This diagram takes us through the stages of the design, production, distribution, and retailing cycle that represent the Zara model.

(Illustration by Andrea Lau)

THE ZARA MODEL

The Zara team researches new fashion trends in fashion shows, magazines, university campuses, dance clubs, etc.

Research results sent to Zara's headquarters. Commercial team analyzes research results and shares them with design team to decide together on the new line's look, materials, price points, etc.

Similar meetings are held to analyze store feedback and decide the fate of current products.

Stores use their computer systems and handheld devices to send sales results and reorders to headquarters.

Once the line is decided, fabric is prepared, dyed, and finished as needed. Accessories are allocated, and production starts.

Finished garments are sent from manufacturing centers to the automated distribution center. Using computers and a system of bar codes similar to mail distribution, garments are boxed and sent to stores based on their orders and locations.

SOURCES

Dutta, Devangshu. 2002. *Retail @ The Speed of Fashion.* Gurgaon, India: Third Eyesight.

Ghemawat, Pankaj, and Nueno, Jose Luis. 2003. *Zara: Fast Fast.* Boston: Harvard Business School Press.

www.inditex.es

www.Zara.com

ENDNOTES

1. Michael Silverstein and Neil Fiske, *Trading Up: The New American Luxury* (New York: The Penguin Group), 7.

2. Nirmalya Kumar and Jan-Benedict Streenkamp, *Private Label Strategy* (Boston: Harvard Business School Press), 7.

3. Pia Sarkar, "Stores Boost Sales with Own Labels," SF Gate, May 5, 2006, http://www.sfgate.com/cgi-bin/article.cgi?f=/c/a/2006/05/05/BUG82IL0QR1.DTL#ixzz0NWTSoWSg

4. Kumar and Streenkamp, *Private Label Strategy*, 26.

5. Jayne O'Donnell, "Beloved Stores Get a Lot More than a New Name," *USA Today*, June 8, 2006, http://www.usatoday.com/money/industries/retail/2006-06-08-macys-shopping_x.htm

6. Kathryn Kroll, "Low-cost Private Label Brands Growing More Popular with Stores, Customers," Cleveland.com, January 20, 2009, http://blog.cleveland.com/business/2009/01/lowcost_private_label_brands_g.html

6 Retail Brands

RETAILING is the major service side of fashion. In general, products and services follow the same principles and rules of marketing and branding. However, there are some obvious differences, such as the intangibility of a service and the human element, where individuals delivering the service, such as sales personnel, are at the core of the brand.

The twentieth century witnessed how stores have grown in number, size, shape, and specialization. Unlike in the past, where shoppers had limited choices of outlets to buy their necessary goods, stores today cater to every need and lifestyle. And in order to compete, a store needs to be more than just a space with a collection of merchandise. It needs to be an experience that is unique, engaging, and fulfilling—both emotionally and functionally. Thus, just as with products, stores need to be branded in order to stand out and simplify the choices for their customers, while ensuring a higher level of emotional satisfaction as well. After all, shopping is indeed an emotional experience.

According to freedictionary.com, a retail store is simply defined as "A place where merchandise is offered for sale."[1] As simple as this definition may seem, it actually highlights the three major components or attributes of any store. They are:

1. *Place:* The need for a space and a location.
2. *Merchandise:* The need for a product to be transacted and sold at a suitable price.
3. *A platform:* The need for a business model or a selling concept that makes this transaction possible.

CHAPTER
OBJECTIVES

- **Differentiate between a product and a service.**

- **Examine the concept of fashion retail branding.**

- **Identify the positioning strategies for a retail operation.**

- **Determine the components of the retail concept.**

- **Highlight the importance of the store experience and the role of sales personnel in shaping the store identity.**

- **Examine the role of internal and external communication in retailing.**

- **Explore the significance and challenges of e-tailing.**

- **Identify retail growth options.**

These three elements formulate the base core of any retailer, which combined with a strong identity and store experience, transform the store into a brand with a unique experiential proposal and **PERSONALITY**.

Adopting the same branding roadmap we used earlier for product brands, our adapted steps for fashion retail branding will be as illustrated in Figure 6.1.

Product vs. Service

In spite of the common grounds among them, there are a few important differences between a product and a service that should impact the branding decisions and process:

• The obvious difference is that products, for the most part, are a sum of tangible features meant to satisfy a functional purpose and need,

Figure 6.1

**The retail
branding
process.**

(*Illustration by*

Andrea Lau)

RETAIL BRANDING PROCESS

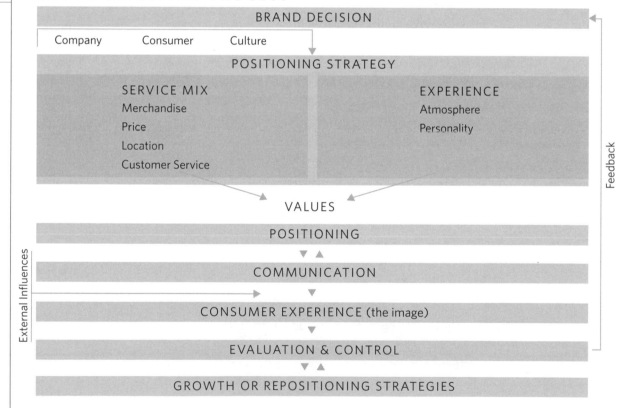

whereas a service, though meant to satisfy a need as well, is intangible, emotional, and generally experiential.

- A product is usually fully experienced by the consumer after the purchase decision has been made; in the case of retail shopping, a major part of the experience is consumed and evaluated before the purchase decision is made.

- Same products are expected to be identical and perform the same way for all users. They may not be appreciated equally yet are expected to be functionally identical. This is hard to achieve with services. The human element and experiential nature of services makes it difficult to duplicate the same experience and circumstances for all customers.

Accordingly, many believe that a service possesses a higher level of risk than a product, so branding becomes even more relevant. Therefore, in this chapter, we shall approach the retail store as a brand in its own right and not just as the distribution component of the product mix.

The Retail Brand Decision

Like any other brand, retailers need to have a clear vision that drives the branding strategy and all other activities. A retail store plays various roles in the life of any product brand. Retailing is the core of any distribution channel; it is also a communication tool. In addition, it is instrumental in monitoring consumer trends and behavior as well as gathering market data. There are many types of stores, each with a different market focus and strategy, so it is essential for every retail venture to

determine the suitable retail concept and business model that fits its philosophy and strategic goals. However, all models share the basic principle of creating the right experience with the right merchandise and service, at the right price, and for the right consumer.

Fashion retailers can be categorized based on different criteria. For example, as a distribution channel, fashion retailing can take various forms:

- *FREE-STANDING STORES*: Available in major streets, malls, or shopping centers.
- *FLAGSHIP STORES*: Usually the biggest and most impressive of the chain and mainly located at the brand's headquarters or in major centers of the world.
- *IN-STORE BOUTIQUES (shops-in-shops):* Fully individualized stores located inside department stores; can be either a space rented by the brand or run and managed by the department store itself while employees are picked and trained by the brand.
- *STORE CORNERS*: More open spaces or boutiques within a department store, compared to in-stores boutiques where the space is enclosed and the brand is the focus of display.
- *DEPARTMENT STORES*: Brands and their products are ordered and managed by the store and are among other brands displayed.
- *CHAINS of specialty stores:* These may sell one or multiple brands, yet the focus is on a segment or a category such as women's ready to wear, lingerie, and so on.
- *Online shopping:* E-tailing offers various models and formats that either complement the physical store's operations or stand on its own.

The Retail Consumer

Similar to products, retailers fall into the three major segments—luxury, mass-market, and premium. Within these categories are various business models that exist in response to the characteristics and shopping habits of each segment's customers.

To satisfy customers, it is essential to understand their shopping habits. In general, shoppers' shopping habits could be categorized as:

- *Routine shopping for basic and daily purchases:* These items usually do not require major decisions and are expected to be conveniently available and affordable. It is a shopping situation where either the product and brand choices are familiar or not very critical. It is a situation where clothing is just a utilitarian commodity and not necessarily "fashion."
- *Shopping to fulfill lifestyle needs:* This is where shopping gets more specific and more about satisfying emotional rather than functional needs. Products sought are usually fashion items where the brand choice is relevant and the decision requires more searching with a willingness to pay higher prices.
- *Shopping on an impulse:* This is where the decision is made in response to external factors and influences that directly appeal to the senses, not necessarily based on recurring or urgent needs.
- *Shopping for solutions rather than for specific products:* This is where the shopper's decision is based on specific items, such as the right gear for their next skiing vacation. Customers may not necessarily be aware of this segment nor have a previous experience with such products, so they mainly look for brands providing confidence and assurance.

These habits are clearly affected by needs as well as the socioeconomic environment that influence them. Accordingly, retailers have always attempted to monitor such social, demographic, psychographic, technological, and economic trends in order to have a better understanding of their customer's behavior and segment their markets accordingly. Examples of such relevant trends are as follows.

- *Population growth:* As population growth slows down, retailers consider shifting their strategies from expansion through opening new stores, to increasing productivity of existing stores, or complementing their operation with online services. Generational differences are also important. The aging baby boomers are at an age where they would prefer saving for retirement than shopping. A decline in the number of child births and the smaller size of new generations, such as generations X, Y, Z (also known as the Google Generation), respectively, who also have different needs and aspirations, has a strong impact on every decision made. In addition, a rise in the number of single professionals and women in higher job ranks all promise a wave of new shopping trends.
- *Economic environment:* Changes in income levels, disposable income, credit, and personal savings level are all examples of economic factors that directly affect the purchasing power of buyers and redefine their priorities. In times of economic downturns, for instance, buyers look for bargains and greater values for their

money as opposed to leisure spending in times of prosperity.

- *Lifestyle trends:* Recent decades have witnessed many changes in lifestyles as a result of the economic and social changes. Moving out to the suburbs, interest in exercising and healthy living, and ease of travel costs have transformed how many people live or spend their leisure time. And with the changes in lifestyles come changes in buying habits and interests. Accordingly, retailers must respond to these new factors and work on fulfilling them when and where needed.

The Retail Concept

The **RETAIL CONCEPT** is the business model and retail philosophy adopted by the brand. The **SERVICE MIX** is the mix of attributes that formulate the concept or define the business model, including:

- The **MERCHANDISE**: The product mix that is offered for sale.
- The **PRICE RANGE**: The price range that defines the segment of focus.
- The **LOCATION**: The retail location signifies the level of shopping convenience and availability.
- The **SERVICE**: Mainly customer service policies that are adopted both at the time of purchase and after.

In many ways, this is similar to what is sometimes referred to as the retailing mix, or the Seven Ps of retailing: place, product, price, promotion, people, process, and physical

environment. However, in our model, we prefer to separate them based on their role and stage in the branding process. Any of these attributes (or a mix of them) can be the base of a retail-positioning strategy, just like the product is for a product-based brand.

Retail brands face similar challenges to those faced by product brands. For instance, the service mix is at the core of the retail brand and faces the same challenge of being easily copied and imitated by other stores competing in the same segment and adopting a similar business model. Therefore, like any brand, a retail brand needs to compete by establishing an emotional value for its customers built on a strong identity (or experience) so that although two stores may have a similar business model or concept and carry similar merchandise, they may not necessarily create the same level of experience and value to the same customer.

Retail Channels
The different types of **RETAIL CHANNELS** mentioned earlier in this chapter can exist under various retail concepts or business models. The range of concepts or business models is designed to target various segments, incomes, and shopping habits. These concepts may include:

- *Specialty stores:* Specialty stores are retailers that focus on one category of products, such as men's sportswear, lingerie, and so on. Although these stores carry a narrow range, they are usually deep in color and size options. Specialty stores range from one of a kind, independent, stand-alone stores or boutiques to a chain of stores (such as Ann Taylor, Talbots, Hollister, Banana Republic).

Figure 6.2

Guess is a brand
with a chain of
specialty stores,
this one in
Venice, Italy.
(© Jeff Greenberg/
Alamy)

well as capable of offering a more personal and attentive service to their clients. In return, they are usually in the higher price range of their segment.

This concept of an exclusive retail space with a trendy image has paved the way for the creation of in-store boutiques (shop in shop) in department stores by many designer brands, such as Ralph Lauren, Tommy Hilfiger, and Tommy Bahama, among many others. Apart from in-store boutiques, many branded specialty stores grow and expand through a franchising network. The growth has also been attributed to the rise of suburban malls and shopping centers where most of them exist and expand.

- *Department stores:* Technically, a department store is a retailer that sells both soft goods (such as apparel) and hard goods (such as appliances and furniture). Thus, whereas Macy's is a department store, Neiman Marcus would be classified as a specialty store. However, there has been a tendency to refer to any large store with many departments and large number of employees as a department store, so Neiman Marcus or Nordstrom can be commonly referred to as specialty department stores. Most department stores are chain stores: they all offer a wide range of products, yet compete on the segment focus. For example, JCPenny and Sears are known for their moderate prices, whereas Macy's offers value through trendier merchandise at a mid to high price range (see Figure 6.3).

Department stores have played a major role in the American retailing scene since the late nineteenth century. In the 1980s, a major wave of mergers and consolidation took place that made

(See Figure 6.2.) In all cases, they tend to be trendier and fashion oriented, carrying designer brands and/or exclusive lines. Some specialty stores are superspecialized (such as Tie Rack), with an even narrower but deeper line of products; others, such as boutiques, are usually small stores with a niche market clientele and a trendy, avant-garde image and merchandise. Whether in the mass-market or luxury segments, specialty stores tend to complement their trendy merchandise with a higher level of service and price range. Their generally smaller size and focused merchandise allows them to be more specialized and knowledgeable, as

Federated acquire some of the nation's prominent department stores such as Marshall Field's and Rich's, among many others. Today Federated is known as Macy's Inc., and it operates Macy's and Bloomingdale's. Recently, there has been a lot of cynicism about the future of department stores. In the past few years, department stores seem to have continuously lost a lot of ground to both higher- and lower-price-range competitors. Lower-price discounters such as Walmart and Target have had much better performance, as have luxury chain specialty stores such as Nordstrom and Neiman Marcus. On the other hand, mid-price department stores like Sears and JCPenney have demonstrated less comparable gains. One major factor is that department stores do not carry many of the categories they did in the past (from fashion to stationary); and when they do, it is never as wide and deep a range as customers now find at category killers, outlets, and specialty stores. Actually, some experts believe that the main factor that may have kept department stores going is Christmas gift shopping. Another factor is the decline in the status of the mall, which has been rapid and dramatic. Mall-based stores' share of retail sales has been halved since 1995, accounting for only 19 percent of total retail sales in recent years. Many of these malls have witnessed a wave of acquisitions and consolidations led by weak sales and low interest rates. In addition, most of these locations have been redeveloped into different retail formats, such as upscale shopping centers with specialty stores, category killers, or discounters like Walmart. Those sectors now command some 80 percent of total retail sales.[2] Indeed, specialty stores have increased their size and scope in cities and suburbs; on the other hand, some believe that the day may come when the majority of currently existing department stores will be acquired by none other than Walmart!

Experts believe that the survival of department stores lies in their ability to provide exceptional customer service, including loyalty programs that are customizable and truly rewarding. Distinctive products and new initiatives are also necessary. In 2002, Sears purchased Lands' End for $1.9 billion; with Lands' End's established customer base, the integration of its merchandise into Sears stores along with the introduction of the new private label, Covington, seem to have helped Sears revive its sales numbers. Another initiative taken by stores such as Nordstrom and Kohl's is to open outside

Figure 6.3

Macy's flagship store in Herald Square, New York City.

(*© Lee Snider/The Image Works*)

traditional malls. In the case of Macy's, internal restructuring and operational streamlining, as well as its strategy to tailor its merchandise to local markets, seem to have helped the company as well.

- *Category killers:* Another form of specialty stores that offers the largest range of a specific category and at competitive prices. These offer both breadth and depth of merchandise assortment, including stores such as Bed, Bath & Beyond and The Home Depot (see Figure 6.4). Category killers manage to dominate their segment through a number of factors.

  1. *Price:* Both category killers and discounters are able to compete on the basis of price. They consistently adopt the adage of "everyday low price," which they are able to deliver through volume of merchandise, expanding their sourcing origins to places such as China and other parts of the globe, and a very efficient and sophisticated system of inventory management and logistics. Although these stores offer a higher level of customer service than discounters do, they still rely on centralized checkout points and a self-service environment (including self-service check-outs as well). Similar to many other retailers, several category killers have also introduced private labels, which helps them to achieve a few objectives: a wider selection of products to fill their usually large-sized stores and extended chains; a competitive price with a higher profit margin due to the elimination of the middle man; and an exclusive product range that differentiates them from their competitors and attracts potential shoppers.

  2. *Competition:* In terms of size, volume, and merchandise range, the closest concept to category killers are department stores. However, as we mentioned, there has been a noticeable decline in the role of department stores in recent years. Many department stores have stopped being the one-stop shop they used to be, and with negligible differences in merchandise and the fact that many have transformed from being true department stores into merely large specialty stores, category killers are facing much less competition.

  3. *Location:* On the other hand, their flexibility in terms of location gives them an edge over department stores, which are still stuck for the most part in the "mall anchor" format in terms of growth and expansion.

- **DISCOUNT STORES**: These are stores that sell known brands at discounted, below-market prices. These no-frills stores offer minimal services and in-store experiences in return for cutting their costs and passing part of these savings on to

Figure 6.4

Bed, Bath & Beyond, a nationwide category killer.

(© *James Houck/ Alamy*)

Figure 6.5a, b

(a) Inside
Walmart,
famous for its
discounted
prices. As its
slogan reads,
"Save money.
Live better."

(Latphotos/Newscom)

(b) Marshall's
is an example
of an off-price
discounter.

(© Lana Sundman/
Alamy)

customers by adopting a low-margin/high-volume policy. (See Figure 6.5a.) Discount stores, in return, come in different formats.

1. *Off-price discounters:* Such as Ross, T.J. Maxx, and Marshalls (see Figure 6.5b).
2. *Factory outlets.* Owned and managed by specialty retailers and used as an alternative to selling off-season and broken sizes merchandise at a discount. On some occasions, the retailer may purchase merchandise especially for their outlets. These outlets are usually located in suburban areas where they offer great bargains to shoppers. Examples include: Nordstrom Rack, Off-Saks, Fossil, and Lacoste outlets. (See Figure 6.6.)
3. *Membership clubs:* Examples such as Sam's and Costco offer merchandise at close to wholesale prices for member customers. Popular for large quantity purchases of household merchandise at great discounts, many of these chains offer their own brands as well.
4. *Mass merchants and hyper-stores:* The major distinction between these stores and other department stores is that in addition to a mix of hard and soft merchandise, they sell groceries as well. Too, they are value oriented with a wide range of inexpensive product, centralized checkout points, and self-service.

As mentioned earlier in this chapter, discount stores, especially Target and Walmart, seem to have been performing much better than other department stores. They obviously become even more attractive at times of economic downturns because they attract newer customers with their range of products (including groceries) and low prices. It is important to remember, however, that a store model or format in itself is no guarantee for success or failure.

Positioning Based on a Retail Concept

Can a store position itself based on a retail concept or a business model? After all, these concepts mentioned earlier in this chapter are conceptually common to all retailers adopting that specific model or strategy. How they differ will most likely be in their execution, which is reflected in what we have called the *concept mix*, such as the merchandise selection, price strategy,

Figure 6.6

Another type of
discounter is a
factory outlet.
Several outlets
can be found in
the Las Vegas
Premium Outlets
Shopping Center,
shown above.

(© PCL/Alamy)

location, or service level. In today's environment where technological advances have created new tools and unconventional opportunities for businesses of all natures, especially retailers, **POSITIONING** based on a concept is possible and refreshingly common. It is the same principle of disruptive positioning that we explored in chapter 2 whereby a business positions itself not against a group of traditional competitors but against the whole segment. In chapter 7, we shall examine many new business models that have developed as a result of new technological advances. All of these models are stepping out of the ring of competitors and challenging the retail environment's status quo by offering new experiences to consumers. Even older retailers such as Nike or Sony have transformed their stores from being purely functional to being entertaining and interactive as well. At a Niketown store, shoppers are intrigued by the interactive displays, sports memorabilia, and images of sports icons, all displayed in a large multifloored space of pure entertainment. In the store, visitors do not just shop, but play and learn as well. They experience the brand and its philosophy (and personality) hands-on. What Nike did (in addition to others such as Sony) was introduce a new store concept that redefined the role of the retail store in our lives.

Thus, positioning based on a concept, if possible, can be highly effective because of its disruptive nature, which allows the business to carve out a niche and be a market leader. However, it is important to remember that a concept is built on its elements or attributes, any of which can be instrumental in a new concept's creation. For example, what has Victoria's Secret really accomplished? Apart from introducing a specialty store with a rich assortment of lingerie, it actually redefined the segment. It took lingerie to a new frontier, from a basic clothing item bought out of necessity, to a fashionable item that might be purchased any time for various reasons and occasions. Having created a new niche and established a new concept, the rest of the attributes followed to shape the model, such as a new distribution channel (a chain of specialized stores) as well as a pricing strategy that reflects the brand's fashion status, and so on.

The Merchandise

As the object of revenue transaction, merchandise is at the core of retailing activity. Selection of merchandise is obviously based on the store concept, which in return responds to the needs of a targeted customer. (See Figure 6.7.) Choosing the right merchandising mix, therefore, is of the utmost importance. It is not just a question of fashion and trends but investment and operations as well. Hence, merchandise management is a series of activities that involve analysis, planning, acquisition, handling, and control of merchandise. Merchandise planning starts with a budget, a sales target, and, accordingly, an inventory forecast. The sales target depends on the pulling power of the brand, the size of the store, and breadth of merchandise offered. Store buyers put together a dollar merchandising plan, which is a six-month or one-year budget that reflects the projected dollar value of the merchandise needed. The dollar merchandise plan is only the starting point. When the retailer has decided how many dollars can be invested in inventory,

other decisions need to be made, such as the assortment of merchandise within each category (menswear, ready-to-wear, accessories, and so on). Choosing the right assortment (or merchandise mix) is influenced by the following elements:

- *Variety:* The number of lines carried in a store.
- *Breadth:* The assortment or the number of brands in a line.
- *Depth:* The number of styles, sizes, and colors within each brand, or what is referred to as the SKUs (stock-keeping units).

These elements in return are affected by other factors, such as:

Figure 6.7

A beautifully displayed selection of merchandise for the 2006 launch of the Ralph Lauren Men's Shop at Saks Fifth Avenue, New York.

(Getty Images/Astrid Stawiarz)

- *Budget constraints and money available:* By definition a budget is a constraint on spending, so retailers need to control their spending and make decisions that maximize the return on their investment. One measure of control is achieved through the concept known as *open to buy* or *OTB*. OTB represents the dollar amount a store buyer can spend on merchandise without exceeding the planned dollar stock.
- *Store space:* The manner of utilizing store space is important because it affects in-store traffic, merchandise exposure, and return on investment. *Sales per square foot* is a tool used to measure the productivity of each department or even section and its contribution to sales.
- *Inventory and turnover consideration;* A deep merchandise mix means more items needed to be stocked and managed, which in turn requires more space and money. In general, managing inventory is equally as important as choosing the inventory. No matter what kind of merchandise you carry, it needs to be available when needed. A customer who is consistently unable to find the item, size, or color he or she needs will be discouraged and eventually take his or her business somewhere else. Obviously customer expectations differ from one business model to the other. A customer shopping at an off-price or a factory outlet store shops with the pre-understanding that not all items or sizes will be available. Actually, the adventure and element of surprise (and possible frustration) becomes part of what defines the bargain-hunting experience at these stores. On the other hand, expectations while shopping at Macy's are totally different: the customer expects to find all offerings available at all times.

Positioning Based on the Merchandise

Using merchandise as a base for positioning is equivalent to using product features in a product brand. Thus, it is an essential positioning tool. Here are few guidelines to consider when positioning on the basis of merchandise.

- Build a merchandise mix that is hard to emulate by competitors. This can be achieved by carrying exclusive lines. H&M's collaboration with designers such as Cavalli and Lagerfeld and celebrities like Madonna produced exclusive and limited collections that proved to be a great success, giving the store's brand an image boost and a competitive edge.
- Distinguish merchandise by its depth as much as its breadth, meaning a store can offer a wider range of sizes (such as full women's sizes) to distinguish itself among competitors. An example of this point is the deep specialization in a specific item or range such as demonstrated by Tie Rack and Victoria's Secret (see Figure 6.8).
- Carry merchandise that caters to a social trend (such as going green and organic), ethnic groups, or specific religious needs. (See Figure 6.9.)

Figure 6.8

Tie Rack is an example of deep specialization in a particular category of product.

(© uk retail Alan King/ Alamy)

(© dbimages/Alamy)

Figure 6.9

This hijab store in Indonesia offers merchandise that caters to religious needs—another type of specialization.

- Determine your brand mix. Carrying a unique mix or exclusive brands is a great differentiator, so choosing your merchandise sources is essential. Barneys New York built its legacy on being the pioneer in introducing new European designers, such as Giorgio Armani who was virtually unknown in the United States at the time.
- Examine your merchandise cycle because this can be an effective differentiator as well. Zara's competitive edge lies in its ability to put merchandise in its stores fast and frequently. The Zara strategy is to have something new in their stores almost every week. This requires smaller quantities, less or no stock, and more flexibility in responding to market demands. It is effective in increasing customers' interest by catering to their anticipation for new products every time they visit.

The Price

Determining the right price is crucial. Too high, and your customers are alienated; too low than expected, and they may doubt the quality of the product offered. Pricing strategies fall into the following categories.

Competitive Pricing Strategies

- *Pricing below competition:* Also known as competition-based pricing, it refers to setting prices based upon prices of similar competitor products.
- *Pricing above competition:* Also known as prestige pricing.
- *Price skimming:* Selling initially at a high price before lowering the price to competitive levels.

- *Price penetration:* Starting with a low price to gain market share and customer base.

Psychological Pricing Strategies

- *Odd pricing:* Setting at a price point implied to be lower than the real price (for example, $1.99, which is perceived as cheaper than $2).
- *Bait and switch pricing:* The practice of advertising the low price of a product to lure shoppers into a store, then attempting to convince them to purchase a higher-priced model. This practice is illegal if the advertised low-priced model is actually unavailable.

Discount Pricing Strategies

- *Multiple pricing:* Selling more than one unit of the same item at a discount for one price, such as three items for $1.00.
- *Bundle pricing:* Here the items bundled are distinctly different.
- *Any other discounts and promotions:* This includes seasonal and occasional discounts such as sales, clearance, or promotions such as buy 1 get one free, and so on.

Other Pricing Strategies

- *Price lining:* Establishing certain price points for a particular merchandise group, such as the case of a $1.00 store.

- *Flexible pricing:* Offering the same products and quantities to different customers at different prices; this occurs in markets dominated by bargaining or personal selling.

Pricing Strategies' Objectives

It is important to remember that any pricing strategy is meant to achieve one or more of the following objectives.

- *Maximize profit:* Targeting as much profit as possible. Suitable policies can include prestige pricing, price skimming, and price penetration (based on volume).
- *Sales and market share:* The economic goal for every business is to maximize profit; however, sometimes the business realizes that its strategic goal at a certain time (as in the case of new businesses) is to increase market share and solidify its market presence, even if it is temporarily at the expense of profit maximization. Thus, achieving a certain level of sales or percentage of market share becomes the goal.
- *Status quo:* Maintaining the current market share or profit levels in the face of strong competition.

Positioning Based on Price

A price is obviously a major differentiator among stores, especially in the mass-market sector. A store will usually offer a range of retail prices that suit their proposed retail concept. However, this price range is bounded by the pricing strategy adopted by the store. In return, the strategy identifies the stores and reflects on its positioning.

Choosing the price as a positioning strategy depends on the retail model, the target market, and type of merchandise. "Offering the lowest price" strategy, for instance, is more suitable for price sensitive items that have marginal differences and are readily available among competitors. Generally speaking, as we move higher on the pricing ladder, quality and fashion become the focal concerns for the shopper. Accordingly, retailers can also be categorized on the basis of their price range, for example:

- *Designer signature price:* The highest price points available at designer boutiques.
- *Bridge price points:* Between designer and better price points, as demonstrated with premium brands.
- *Contemporary price points:* Appealing to a younger fashion-forward market. This mass-market category targets a wide segment of young customers looking for trendy looks at a reasonable price.
- *Better price points:* Aimed at the middle-class market. Many private labels fall into this category.
- *Moderate price points:* Appealing to the less fashion-conscious customers who seek reasonable prices and value for money. JCPenney would be a good example.
- *Budget price points:* Fashion followers and price conscious, these copy fashion trends and offer them at lower quality and prices.

Any of these policies can be adopted as a positioning strategy; however, it is important to remember that offering the lowest price in the market and basing your gains on volume is not an easy strategy. Unless you have the capacity and ability to withstand the pricing war, the time will come when you cannot outbid your competitors or raise your prices to original levels again. Thus, it is usually operations with the size and capabilities of Walmart and Target that can afford such a strategy. Walmart, for instance, is known for its EDLP (everyday low price) policy and adopts the strategy of consistently beating competitors' prices. It even announces that it is willing to offer refunds to customers to maintain that promise. Interestingly, research shows that low-price shoppers are usually not loyal customers. Discounts do attract price-motivated customers, but when they see a lower price somewhere else, they quickly switch.

On the other hand, premium pricing is a strategy common in the luxury segment, whereby a low price might actually raise the suspicion of the consumer regarding the quality and functionality of the merchandise. Premium prices imply high levels of quality and style. In the same manner, by shopping at exclusive boutiques selling exclusive and luxury brands, customers expect a high level of service and quality merchandise. Overall, they expect a shopping experience that is pampering, sensual, and unique.

Most stores fall between these two extremes and compete in their category on the basis of combining a pricing strategy that includes occasional price cuts and promotions with other features such as in-store experience, customer service, or location to offer a unique value to the consumer.

Unconventional pricing strategies, such as allowing shoppers to bid on an item or offer a "best offer" option as seen on ebay.com, attract customers through another form of psychological pricing that totally responds to the market forces of supply and demand. Swoopo.com is an online electronics retailer that adopts an interesting model that may soon find its way to fashion e-tailers. It's

a new model that is somewhere between eBay auctions and gambling. Basically, shoppers pay for every bid they make. Every bid increases the price by small increments as well as delays the auction's countdown. The winning bidder pays the winning price, shipping costs, and the cost of the number of bids he made. In the end the shopper still gets a bargain price compared to the item's original retail price, and the retailer, Swoopo, ends up collecting close to the original price from the sum of what the winning shopper has paid on bids and shipping, plus the amount all other bidders paid for their bids on the same item. A win-win situation for all—except the losing bidders, of course.

Location

In previous chapters we established differences in location choices made by luxury and mass-market brands. Luxury brands have limited options because they are usually located in major city centers and fashion capitals, whereas mass-market brands are more flexible and can be easily located in urban and suburban areas, small towns, malls, resorts, and shopping centers, so their options are certainly wider. However, no matter the choice, choosing a store location remains to be a process that includes the following steps:

1. Identify a target market.
2. Analyze the site.
3. Select the site.

Identifying a Target Market

The retailer must identify the most attractive markets in which to operate. To make that decision, the selected market segment must be:

- *Measurable:* The market can be qualified in terms of objective measures for available data, such as age, gender, income, education, ethnic group, and religion.
- *Accessible:* This is the degree to which the retailer can target its promotional or distribution efforts to a particular market segment.
- *Substantial:* Successful target marketing requires that the segment be significant enough to be profitable for the retailer.

Analyzing the Site

Retailers must evaluate the density of demand and supply within each market and identify the most attractive sites that are available in terms of the buying power index (BPI). BPI is an indicator of a market's overall retail potential and is composed of weighted measures of effective buying income (personal income, including all non-tax payments such as social security, minus all taxes), retail sales, and population size. Other factors include consumers' mobility, size of the trading area (which also has an impact on the merchandise because the more people you attract, the larger the assortment needed), competition, and so on.

Selecting the Site

When the best available sites within each market have been identified, the retailer needs to make the final location decision and select the best site (or sites). When reviewing a site, a retailer must consider:

- nature of site
- traffic characteristics
- types of neighbors

- terms of purchase or lease
- expected profitability

Positioning Based on Location

Positioning based on location ultimately refers to the level of convenience. Earlier in this chapter, we mentioned that luxury brands' customers may be more willing to spend some effort to obtain the brand. However, in all cases a brand should be located where it is expected and needed. Just as price may be a major factor in the decision by the consumer to pick a store, so is the time factor. Easier shopping, including more available parking, less traffic, and longer operating hours are all issues relevant to shopping convenience and are always welcomed, no matter which segment. After all, convenience remains the major differentiator and competitive advantage behind the success of the Internet and online shopping.

Service

Every retail concept comes with certain expectations regarding the level of service it will offer. However, customer service is still important and relevant at every price level because it is a major driver for customer loyalty, which in return is a reasonable measure of success. Customer service and store policies such as operating hours, return policies, alterations, and special services are highly regarded by customers of any segment. Budget and low-price stores generally compete on the basis of convenience and are among the best in offering longer operating hours. They understand that what they offer is easily attainable at other places and that shoppers can easily look for alternatives somewhere else if they don't have easy access to the store. On the other hand, premium and luxury brand stores have more restrictions on location and operating hours. But they offer a greater range of services and benefits. Nordstrom, for instance, is known for its leadership in service and its efforts to please and accommodate customers as much as possible. In addition to free alterations, personal shopper assistance, and relaxed return policy, Nordstrom employees are willing to take unconventional measures to satisfy the customer and gain their loyalty. The following is a true story that took place at a Nordstrom store.

> In Portland, Oregon, a man walked into Nordstrom asking for an Armani tuxedo to wear to his daughter's wedding. The sales representative took his measurements but said she'd need time to work on his request. She called later to say that the tuxedo would be ready the next day. As it turned out, Nordstrom did not carry Armani tuxedos at the time. The sales representative had found the tux through a distributor in New York, then had it rushed to Portland and altered to fit the customer in time for the wedding.[3]

This level of service needs to be deeply embedded in the culture of the store. Retailers are unique in being at the forefront of inter-activity with the final consumer. Where there is personal interaction with the customer, the employee turns into a brand champion and, just like designers who end up embodying the brand, store employees become the brand in many ways as well. Greg Holland, Nordstrom's midwest assistant regional manager, once said, "Great

customer service is not an initiative. It is not the thing of the day. It is part of our culture."

As we've seen so far, one component of what we called *the concept mix* complements the other components, and together they define the type of store and the concept behind the model. The same is true for the level of service expected within the store. The level and mix of services offered is dependent on:

- *The store's physical characteristics:* Customer service can be affected by physical factors, such as location and size.
- *The store concept or business model:* A store outlet by definition will not offer the same level of service as, for example, a full-priced boutique.
- *Competition:* Service is an integral source of differentiation. As a matter of fact, with so many stores offering very similar merchandise, customer service may become the main competitive advantage.
- *Type of merchandise:* This also has an influence because some products may require complementary services such as alterations for suits or for wedding dresses.
- *Price and level of service:* These are directly proportionate: a higher level of service means higher cost, which will reflect on retail price.

All of these points also reflect on the shopper's expectations of service. Stores that exceed expectations and not just meet them achieve a higher level of customer loyalty. The case of Nordstrom and the Giorgio Armani tuxedo is a good example.

Examples of types of customer service are:
- Operating hours; in determining the working hours, many factors need to be considered, such as customers' needs as well as cost and safety.

Figure 6.10a, b

(a) As a shop-
ping incentive,
Nordstrom
offers its
customers
numerous
benefits with
the Nordstrom
Fashion Rewards
Program.
(Courtesy of Nordstrom)

(b) Another
bonus for
Nordstrom
shoppers is
free in-store
alterations.
*(Getty Images/Smith
Collection)*

- Payment and credit options.
- Alterations, gift wrapping, and packing.
- Personal shopping, more common in
  high-end retailers.
- After-purchase support.
- Return policies.
- Shipping and delivery.
- Layaway services.
- Loyalty programs that reward loyal customers
  and entice new customers to join and share
  some real benefits.

   It is important to remember the significance
of after-purchase service, which is the focus of
what has been known as *relationship marketing*.
It is cheaper and probably more rewarding to
maintain older customers than new ones. New
customers cost more because they need to
be lured with promotions and advertising. Old
customers, on the other hand, are more familiar
with the store and its services and are financially
more rewarding in the long run through repeat
purchases. Turning every customer into a loyal
customer is the ultimate goal. It may not be easy,
but is worth trying because loyalty is probably
one of the best measures of a brand's success.
(See Figures 6.10a–b.)

Positioning Based on Service

With so many stores offering almost the same
merchandise, customer service becomes an essential differentiator and competitive advantage. As a
matter of fact, many experts believe that innovation and customer service are the two forces of
success in the twenty-first century. Customers
have many choices and options nowadays, and it
is easier to move and commute than ever before,
not to mention the impact of the Internet in terms

of choices as well as extended customer service. Accordingly, customers' expectations and
demands for service have gotten higher. They need
to be impressed. Thus, retailers need to compete
by exceeding customers' expectations through:

- *Personalized service programs:* The Internet and many existing technologies, such as mobile technologies, allow businesses to communicate with customers on a much more personal and customized level and at a very low cost. A few of these technologies will be discussed in chapter 7, but consider how special promotions, updates, and news can be tailored to each customer's interests and needs and then e-mailed to their computers or mobile phones. Companies that learn how to integrate all these technologies and channels have a better opportunity to attract the customer's attention for a longer time and keep him or her more interested and engaged. One new technology they might consider allows customers to check store inventory availability from a magic screen in the dressing room, make a purchase, or check other customer's review. Customers can use the same screen to take a snapshot of themselves wearing the garment and then upload it to their e-mail or even Facebook to get feedback from friends in real time.

- *Level of convenience:* The more convenient it is to make a purchase transaction or return a garment, the more satisfied the customers are. At a Nordstrom store, you can return any item you purchased online or from a Nordstrom Rack to a regular Nordstrom store, no questions asked.

- *Promise of value:* Remember that like all other brands, retail brands are built on a promise of value to the customer. The aim of the process is to increase the level of loyalty. However, this is not easy nowadays. According to a new study by Adjoined Consulting and SAS Marketing Automation, 77 percent of shoppers in 2006 defined themselves as loyal customers, a drop from the previous year when 84 percent said they met the definition.[4] Customers are more empowered and confident than before, and it takes true value to impress them.

Customer loyalty is built on both rational and emotional grounds. Although incentives such as price discounts, exclusive merchandise, or quality evoke rational values, the sense of recognition and appreciation of being a special customer and not just one in a large group is an emotional incentive that is highly effective. Think of a salesperson remembering your name, a card you receive with special offers on your birthday, or an invitation to a "by invitation only" store event. The emotional reward is priceless.

An emotional reward can also be tied to ethical and socially responsible initiatives adopted by the store. For instance, Target's REDcard rewards shoppers with price discounts, but because Target is an already a low-priced store, the impact of such rewards may not be very significant. Therefore, Target has decided to evoke loyalty through other emotional rewards resulting from its involvements in the community. Through its Take Charge of Education program, shoppers can choose the school they want their money to benefit. Target, in turn, donates 1 percent of customer's in-store and online purchases to the school. This creates a multilevel connection between the store, the customer, and the community. By shopping at Target, these customers feel they truly are making a difference.[5]

Store Experience

Shopping is an emotional experience that has evolved into a favorite pastime where customers experience the brand before making a purchase decision. The store experience is also sensual, is shaped by the physical appearance and feel of the store as defined by its layout, interior design, music, smell, and lighting. All of this combines to create what we may call a store **ATMO-SPHERE**—the equivalent of identity symbols of the product brand. In addition, the store experience is strengthened by the brand's personality. The personality is how the store behaves as a brand. This is highly manifested by its culture, how it is interpreted in policies, and the way its own employees interact with the consumer. Thus, in reality, the shopping **EXPERIENCE** is a manifestation of the store's identity as a whole, as shaped by a mix of store aesthetics (atmosphere) and the store personality, which is demonstrated by its culture, its employees, and the set of rules and policies that are ultimately inspired by its mission and vision statements.

So, based on what we've discussed so far, we can conclude that store branding is about choosing a retail model, defining its concept mix, and creating an emotional and functional experience through a unique atmosphere (look and feel) and personality (together form the store brand identity).

Store Atmosphere

A store atmosphere is created through the aesthetics and feel of the store as expressed in the store design, layout, graphics, colors, lightning, and so on. The store atmosphere plays a pivotal role in attracting customers into the store and influencing them to make a purchase. The whole experience needs to be enjoyable (emotional) and efficient (functional). And hopefully, as a result, the experience will be memorable enough for customers to return.

Layout

A major element of a store's aesthetics is the **LAYOUT**. A store layout needs to achieve the following:

- Minimize material handling costs.
- Increase productivity and profitability through better exposure of merchandise and ease of movement.
- Utilize space efficiently and eliminate bottlenecks.
- Utilize labor efficiently and facilitate communication and interaction among employees and between employees and customers.
- Reduce customer service time.
- Facilitate the browsing experience as well as the entry, exit, and placement of material, products, and people.
- Incorporate safety and security measures.
- Promote merchandise and service quality.
- Provide flexibility to adapt to changing conditions.

The psychological factor in store design and layout is important. Studies in consumer behavior and shopping habits offer a lot of insight on how customers are affected by layout and presentation details. For instance, an open layout allows shoppers to quickly scan the store visually and identify locations of interest—it's a welcoming and accommodating layout.

STRAIGHT LAYOUT

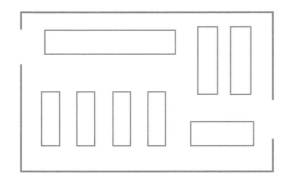

Figure 6.11

Straight layout

(*Illustration by*

Andrea Lau)

DIAGONAL LAYOUT

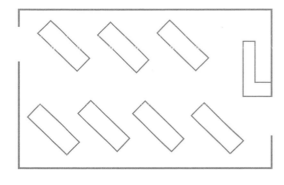

Figure 6.12

Diagonal layout

(*Illustration by*

Andrea Lau)

ANGULAR LAYOUT

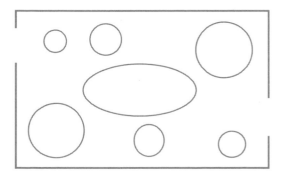

Figure 6.13

Angular layout

(*Illustration by*

Andrea Lau)

There are basically five types of stores plans. [6]

1. *The straight floor plan:* Suitable for any type of retail store. It is economical and utilizes the walls and fixtures to create small spaces within the retail store. (See Figure 6.11.)

2. *The diagonal floor plan:* Suitable for self-service stores. It offers excellent visibility for cashiers and customers and invites movement and traffic flow to the store. (See Figure 6.12.)

3. *The angular floor plan:* Suitable for high-end specialty stores. The curves and angles of fixtures and walls make for a more expensive store design, while the soft angles create better traffic flow throughout the store. (See Figure 6.13.)

4. *The geometric floor plan:* Among the most suitable for apparel shops. It uses racks and fixtures to create an interesting and nontraditional look without high cost. (See Figure 6.14.)

5. *The mixed floor plan:* Incorporates the straight, diagonal, and angular floor plans to create the most functional store design. The layout moves traffic toward the walls and back of the store. (See Figure 6.15.)

Merchandise Presentation

Merchandise presentation utilizes various types of fixtures and shelving in order to effectively expose and promote the product in an attractive and inviting way. Fixtures come in different shapes and forms, such as wall fixtures, tables, bins, or racks. Shelving may be more flexible and easier to maintain. Merchandise display can be done through hanging, folding, stacking, dumping in bins and baskets, and so on.

Merchandise presentations can evoke different mental images and create a different feel to the store, such as a sense of exclusivity or luxury.

GEOMETRIC LAYOUT

Figure 6.14

Geometric
layout

(Illustration by

Andrea Lau)

MIXED LAYOUT

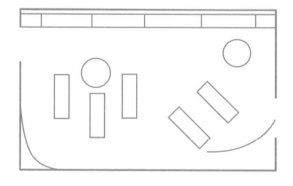

Figure 6.15

Mixed layout

(Illustration by

Andrea Lau)

Store Windows

Store windows are a major communication tool. They promote the store's personality and, in a way, set the mood. As the Zara case study illustrated (see pp. 172–175), the company relies heavily on its store windows to promote the brand, given their lack of traditional marketing budget, which is almost 0.3 percent of sales compared to an industry average of around 10 percent. Instead, they rely heavily on the store windows, in-store experience, and word of mouth to promote their brand. Zara also has a specialized team that travels the world to train store employees on the designs and techniques in order to maintain an effective and consistent message through their stores.

Some store windows have grown to have a strong impact on product brands. In fashion, for a new designer to get his or her design displayed in the windows of Bloomingdale's or Bergdorf Goodman has always been a great achievement. Windows are truly a reflection of the store's personality as much as the designer's.

Figure 6.16

The merchandise
presentation of
the Donna Karan
shop at New
York's Saks Fifth
Avenue is chic
and luxurious.

(Courtesy of WWD/

Robert Mitra)

Figure 6.17

A master of the color red, especially when it comes to sumptuous gowns, this window perfectly captures the personality of the Valentino brand.

(© Atlantide

Phototravel/Corbis)

Figure 6.18

The architecturally impressive building that houses Cartier in New York attracts even more attention during the Christmas season, when it is literally wrapped as a gift with a massive red bow, and oversized jewelry boxes appear to cascade down its façade.

(Getty Images/Thos

Robinson/)

Other Store Design Elements

Store design refers to both the exterior and interior of the store, which combines elements of architecture and interior design. (See Figure 6.16.)

- The exterior store front must be noticeable and inviting. Logo and store name need to be visible, clear, and memorable. (See Figures 6.17 and 6.18.)
- Lighting highlights the store's mood. However, the aesthetic effect should complement the merchandise presentation and visibility.
- Sounds and smells play an integral role in creating a sensory element to the whole store atmosphere. Many retailers distribute sets of music CDs to all their branches, which the stores are then directed to play exclusively.

Store Personality

A store brand personality is the soul of the brand. The personality is an embodiment of the strategic vision and the brand promise, which in return is the force behind every decision made. It, therefore, reflects the concept, aesthetics, functionality, and the way employees behave. As a result, a personality develops over time and is manifested through interaction. It is the brand's soul and attitude.

Positioning Based on Experience (Personality and Atmosphere)

We have explained that a product brand can be positioned at two levels: the product level (in the form of the product mix) and the brand level (in the form of identity). Applying this to retail brands, the two levels of positioning are the store concept level (the business model with the relevant concept mix) and the experience level (created by the branding process). It should now be clear how all elements of atmosphere and personality work together to form a strong store experience, which in return defines the brand identity both physically and emotionally. The functionality and logistics of the retail concept lay the foundations for a store experience that is enhanced and defined by its atmosphere and personality in a way that is meant to complement the merchandise, the price range, location, and all elements of the concept mix.

The store experience can be based on various values.

- *An experience based on entertainment:* One such example is Niketown, highlighted earlier in this chapter (see Figure 6.19).
- *An experience based on expertise:* This is where the store evokes a high level of knowledge, expertise, and specialization. Customers visit the store not just to shop but to learn and be educated. This is common for highly specialized stores in the category killers segment (such as The Home Depot).
- *An experience based on sensual satisfaction:* This is where the "wow" aesthetic factor is manifested in its design and décor.
- *An experience based on a lifestyle:* The store demonstrates the lifestyle of the brand and creates the right environment or world for the shopper to experience the brand as it is intended. Designer flagship stores such as Ralph Lauren's store on Madison Avenue, New York, Louis Vuitton in Paris, or Giorgio Armani in Milan are designed and furnished with every detail that reenacts the brand's dream. The products, the layout, the music—everything creates a picture reflective of the brand's lifestyle.
- *An experience based on a bargain:* Discount stores such as Filene's Basement and Ross with their store layout, centralized checkouts, and most important, their merchandise and prices are a good example of this. (See Figure 6.20.)

For positioning through experience to be effective, it needs to be:

- authentic
- relevant to the merchandise image
- what gets shoppers interested

TABLE 6.1	PRODUCT BRANDS VS. STORE BRANDS
PRODUCT BRANDS	**STORE BRANDS**
=	=
Product Mix	*Concept Mix*
(Features + Price + Location + Service)	(Merchandise + Price + Location + Service)
+	+
Identity	*Experience*
(Symbols + Personality)	(Atmosphere + Personality)
	thus the experience also reflects the store's identity

conclude that there are two platforms of communication for any store.

- *Communication inside the store (internal):* Includes visual communication through store signage and visual merchandising, as well as experiential communication through interaction with employees.
- *Communication outside the store (external):* Includes advertising, direct marketing, PR, publicity, and other channels.

Internal Communication

Consumers are drawn to the store through the brand promise trumpeted in external communications. The brand promise in reality reflects the personality as the brand perceives it. When entering the store, the shopper experiences the brand: in the process of being transformed from a browser to a buyer, the shopper compares what has been promised to what is actually experienced and develops his own image of the brand accordingly (that is, creates his own positioning).

Transforming the customer from a browser to a buyer inside the store is usually achieved with

Figure 6.19

The Niketown experience can be both entertaining and interactive.

(Getty Images/Stuart Franklin/Bongarts)

Finally, it is never sufficient to highlight the important role of employees in shaping the store experience. Employees are at the forefront because they directly interact with the end customer. Employees should be champions of the brand. They need to live it in order to sell it. In many ways they are the brand.

Communication

COMMUNICATION activities play a bi-directional role in the branding process. They communicate and reflect the positioning strategy and brand identity to the outside world and, at the same time, impact the process of identity building—either positively by reinforcing it or negatively by distorting it and reflecting conflicting messages.

The store brand is unique in its ability through its space and physical appearance (such as signs, fixtures, and so on) to become a communication channel in its own right. Internal (in-store) communication activities are an essential component of the communication strategy of any store, and they complement other external activities, such as advertising and publicity. Accordingly, we

Figure 6.20

At Filene's Basement, it's all about the thrill of a bargain.

(© 2007 Richard Nowitz)

Figure 6.21a, b

A comparison of Walmart storefronts displaying its (a) old logo, dividing "Wal" and "mart" with a star, and its (b) new one, which keeps the name undivided.

(© Kathy deWitt/ Alamy)

(Courtesy of Walmart)

and supporting visual elements. The name and logo must be catchy, memorable, and most of all, reflective of the business model and merchandising strategy.

The recent controversy over the new Walmart logo demonstrates the importance of the logo in the brand's life. Some believe it has an organic feel and an eco-friendly connotation; others think it is too generic and undistinguishable. From their side, Walmart describes the new logo as follows: "This update to the logo is simply a reflection of the refresh taking place inside our stores and our renewed sense of purpose to help people save money so they can live better."[7] (See Figures 6.21a–b.)

In-store signage: In-store signage covers many usages. (See Figure 6.22.) For example:

- *Institutional signage:* Describes the store policies, mission statement, and other relevant information.
- *Departmental signage:* Guides the shopper though each department.
- *Point-of-Sale (POS) signage:* Usually located on fixtures with information about specific merchandise items. (See Figure 6.23.)
- *Store graphics:* This includes large images and graphic panels that offer a great opportunity to show off merchandise with attention-grabbing images.

Other forms of in-store communication that appeal to the senses are:

- *Sound:* Music can highly complement the intended shopping experience.
- *Touch:* Use of specific materials such as glass, marble, or wood can convey certain feelings of warmth or modernity.

the help of in-store communication. As some data indicates, 80 percent of purchases are decided upon in-store, indicating the impact of the in-store experience on impulse buying. Accordingly, visual and experiential signals need to be clear and consistent with the perceived personality and targeted experience. When carefully balanced with the human element and customer service, visual communications can create an engaging and successful selling environment.

Examples of the tools of store visual communications are:

- *Name and logo (visual identity):* The first and most visible element in a comprehensive visual communications program is the retailer's visual identity, composed of the store name, logo,

Figure 6.22
A striking in-store graphic from Gap.
(Andrew Harrer/
Bloomberg via Getty
Images)

- *Smell:* For example, Victoria's Secret sprays its perfumes in stores.
- *Lighting:* Lighting sets the mood and makes merchandise more appealing.

External Communication

External communication refers to marketing activities done outside the store in traditional and emerging media channels. External communication is utilized to achieve various goals, such as:

- Inform shoppers of events and price changes.
- Inform potential shoppers of a new store or a new location.
- Inform shoppers of new merchandise.
- Increase in-store traffic through promotions.
- Enforce brand positioning though advertising or celebrity sponsorship.
- Interest new customers in the store and retain old ones.
- Respond to competition pressures.
- Create buzz and interest in the store: Benetton's provocative campaigns are a good example,

as well as H&M's association with famous celebrities and models.

Types of external communication include:

1. *Advertising:* A nonpersonal form of communication through different media channels. Advertising is useful for any of the three purposes of communication: persuade, inform, or remind.

Figure 6.23
In-store displays can inform the customer about special promotions, such as this offer for 50 percent off the price of a top when you buy a bottom.
(© Ilene MacDonald/
Alamy)

2. *Promotions:* Utilizes media or nonmedia channels. Direct marketing is often used as a more personal approach to delivering promotional material to customers.
3. *Publicity:* Nonpaid coverage such as magazine's editorial. Publicity can be positive or negative; however, it is effective, as it seems impartial coming from a third party.
4. *Public relations:* Events and activities that are meant to enhance the retailer's image and champion its role in its community.

Advertising

Retailers don't usually spend as much on advertising as manufacturers do because the store itself plays a major role in communicating the brand. Nevertheless, advertising is still utilized by stores who foresee economic viability of the expense.

The approach to the advertising message can have different focuses.

- Reinforces how the store reflects a specific lifestyle.
- Builds a dream to which the customers aspire.
- Builds a mood around a product.
- Creates interest through humor.
- Demonstrates how the products relate to the consumer's everyday life.
- Demonstrates usage or functionality of a product.

ADVERTISING OPTIONS

The retailer has many different advertising options that include:

- *Newspapers:* Probably the most frequently used in retailing to either announce special promotional events or include promotional inserts such as coupons.
- *Television:* Advertising on national channels makes more financial sense to department and specialty chains with a national network of stores because of its cost and range of coverage. On the other hand, cable and local channels reach a more focused and segmented audience. TV advertising can be effective in generating higher traffic and sales due to its entertaining and demonstrative capabilities and qualities.
- *Radio:* Usually used to address selected customer groups to announce events with a relatively short lead time.
- *Magazines:* Major fashion magazines usually aim for large national circulation. Thus, advertising in magazines such as *Vogue* and *Harper's Bazaar* is more suitable for national chains or co-branding campaigns shared between retailers and manufacturers.

Promotion

There are many possible types of sales promotions such as:

- *Premiums:* Extra items offered with the purchase of a product.
- *Contests and sweepstakes:* Generate interest and excitement.
- *Loyalty programs:* Encourage repeat sales.
- *Coupons:* Encourage sales through price discounts.
- *Samples:* Generate interest through trial, such as perfume inserts in magazines or in-store samples.
- *In-store display:* Generate traffic and benefits from impulse buying.

Direct Marketing

DIRECT MARKETING (DM) allows for a more differentiated and segmented communication. As such, it is more personal and effective in building relationships with customers because they are treated as individuals, not as a bulk group. It is also easier to monitor and control. Another advantage to DM is that, unlike advertising, there is a lack of external noise effect from competitors, which can highly distort the effectiveness of the message.

Retailers use DM to send catalogs, coupons, e-mails, and newsletters. DM relies heavily on a large database of shoppers' details and an effective distribution system. It can also be used as a step toward future targeted advertising. There is always a common-sense belief that if a customer orders tennis shoes from a catalog, he or she might generally be interested in tennis supplies as well.

Personal selling is another example of DM. It is the most direct and personal of any retail activity, and the role of employees in building the store's brand image has been highlighted before and cannot be emphasized strongly enough.

Co-Marketing

CO-MARKETING refers to when manufacturers and other retailers market a brand together and share the cost of the advertising campaign. It is commonly used when certain brands or products are sold exclusively through certain retailers. This case is known as *vertical co-marketing*. On the other hand, *horizontal co-marketing* takes place when two or more retailers collaborate together in a campaign, such as promoting a new shopping center. (See Figure 6.24.)

Choosing the right communication mix depends on the goals and objectives the store hopes to achieve, such as:

- *Creating store traffic:* For which advertising, direct marketing, and internal visual communication can be effective.
- *Transforming store browsers into buyers:* For which in-store visual communication, employees, promotions can be effective.
- *Responding to competition:* Either or both of the previous bullet points can be effective.

Other Options

Stores can try to use unconventional methods of promotion that may create a buzz or attract attentions. For example, the Las Vegas Nordstrom

Figure 6.24

In teaming up with the RED campaign to fight AIDS, tuberculosis, and malaria in underdeveloped countries, Gap offers an example of vertical co-marketing. (*Image Courtesy of the Advertising Archives*)

realized that the city lacks a major influential newspaper publication typical of other major cities, which they could use for running an advertising campaign. As a result, Nordstrom came up with a new campaign that they believed would be more effective. In a city that is a major tourist destination, taxi cabs are something that almost every visitor needs or sees along The Strip and are, therefore, an excellent channel of communication. With this in mind, they came up with a campaign that repainted city taxis with the store name and products.

Growth

Growth in retail operations can be achieved through:
- Opening of new stores
- Horizontal integration and acquiring of existing stores
- Online growth on the Internet (e-tailing)
- Growth through franchising
- Growth into global markets

Franchising

FRANCHISING simply refers to a retailer (the franchisor) offering a store owner (the franchisee) the rights to emulate the retailer's business model or system of conducting his business. Thus, a series of stores can be opened with a consistent concept, look, and feel throughout all franchised stores. Franchisees will usually pay a royalty fee, which is usually a percentage of sales or a combination of a percentage and a guaranteed minimum. In return, they also get training, marketing, and management support from the franchisor. As with

any business arrangement, there are a few advantages as well as challenges in franchising.

Advantages

From the franchisor's perspective, advantages include:
- An opportunity to expand the retail brand into new markets with minimal investment while maintaining the brand's image.
- A source of revenue. The structure of fees can differ, but in general it is a combination of a one-time fee and a percentage of sales that can be around 5 percent. Sometimes a minimum monthly payment is guaranteed even if monthly sales did not cover the royalty fee.
- Exposure and increase in brand awareness.

From the franchisee's perspective, advantages include:
- The freedom of being self-employed.
- A good way to start a business for entrepreneurs who want to own their retail business but lack the expertise and are not sure what to do.
- Support from the franchisor in the form of employee training, marketing material, and possible share of the cost of certain events or advertising campaigns.
- Benefits from opening a store with an already established brand name, image, and customers' interest.
- An opportunity to learn the business model and eventually go out on their own.

Disadvantages

From the franchisor's perspective, disadvantages include:

- Lack of control and possible difficulty in monitoring a large chain.
- Damage to the brand by any malpractice of any one of the franchisees. (Usually customers are not aware that these stores are independently owned, and the blame is directed to the brand as a whole.)
- Legal headaches in cases of disputes.

From the franchisee's perspective, the disadvantages include:

- Lack of freedom and constraints over new ideas.
- Some sense of insecurity, as franchise agreements are usually designed in such a way that a franchisee can be easily dropped if a conflict arises.
- Other franchisees' mistakes and mishaps that can affect store performance.
- Financial burden. All costs of preparing the store are the franchisee's responsibility. In some agreements, for instance, franchisees cannot return unsold merchandise to the franchisor. In addition, in some cases, minimum fees are still expected to be paid even if sales are down.

There are many brands that adopt the franchise model or a mix of franchising and other models (for example, private ownership) such as Esprit, Benetton, and Stefanel, just to name a few.

Global Growth

International geographic expansion is adopted by retailers for various reasons related to growth strategies and competition.

- It presents new growth opportunities in new markets. This opportunity is specifically important if the domestic market is already saturated with limited growth opportunities.
- Businesses with a unique business model or product may find lucrative opportunities overseas. H&M's concept proved successful in the different international markets it entered.
- Economic conditions can be a major factor as well, either to escape a domestic economic downturn or to benefit from an economic boom overseas. The recent rush by retailers and manufacturers alike to enter and be present in the lucrative and large Chinese market is a good example.
- Businesses can benefit from diversification of investment and resources as well as economies of scale in the case of retailers who produce their own private brands.
- In some situations, international markets are a good outlet for certain items that have not sold well locally.
- Strong local competition can be another driving factor for locating in various overseas markets.

However, global expansion for retailers comes with many of the same challenges we discussed in a previous chapter, such as foreign exchange fluctuations, taxes, regulations, and political instabilities, as well as shipping risks such as lead time and cost.

Important Issues to Consider

Retailers may be forced to rethink their pricing strategy overseas due to the previously mentioned differences and end up with price discrepancies that may create different positioning spots to the brand in different parts of the world.

Issues related to product adaptations are also important. Customers' size charts differ from one place to the other. The United States has a large population of oversized customers, while Japan requires mainly smaller sizes. A size "medium" in one country will be a "small" or a "large" in another. These differences create many challenges in production and inventory management.

Distribution and delivery is another issue to consider. The need for a fast and reliable distribution network is essential to meet different stores' needs in different locations. With differences in the levels of infrastructure development, transportation costs, and time zones, the challenges become quite apparent. Many store chains create various local distribution centers servicing specific market zones to facilitate the distribution process and cut down on time and cost.

Modes of Entry into an International Market

Entering and expanding into a global market can be done through different modes.

- *Wholly owned subsidiaries:* Most luxury brands own their boutiques. Although this is helpful from an image perspective, it is a costly venture. Experts estimate that in general, it may not be a feasible venture with sales less than $10 million. On the other hand, some laws in foreign countries may not allow full ownership by foreign entities.
- *Joint ventures:* Necessary in markets where the regulations or distribution system is too intricate to allow for independent market penetration and entry. The Japanese market used to be a good example. Giorgio Armani and Christian Dior were among the many brands that had to join forces with an established Japanese partner to secure a competitive presence in Japan.
- *Franchising:* Selling the business model in return for royalty fees. This minimizes investment and reduces direct control and risks in unfamiliar and foreign markets.
- *Unconventional locations:* Such as airports and duty-free stores. Through duty-free stores, brands gain access to multitudes of customers as they pass through airports around the world. (see Figure 6.25).

E-tailing

The Internet or "click-and-shop" model as a retail concept—commonly known as **E-TAILING**— covers all the previously discussed range of

Figure 6.25
John Couri, president and founder of Duty Free International.
(© Louie Psihoyos/ CORBIS)

models in addition to new ones that only exist online. In the next chapter, we will examine a few of the exciting new models that have emerged online by means of new technological advances. We have established earlier that positioning strategies need to be flexible to remain relevant. As shoppers' lifestyles change, so do their shopping needs and habits. Even in the world of brick and mortar, new models have developed to accommodate customers' new expectations. Niketown stores and Prada Epicenters, for instance, have created new shopping environments and experiences that respond to those new needs and transform shopping into a full sensual experience and a fun leisure activity.

When the Internet exploded in the nineties, it was a good example of a new retailing concept that utilized technological advances to respond to socioeconomic changes. The Internet presented a new retailing channel and shopping opportunity for retailers and shoppers respectively. However, it may seem that Internet shopping is more suitable for some products than others. In general, the greater the degree of variance in the product, the more difficult the online shopping experience will be. In spite of this, one of the greatest advantages of online shopping remains convenience. It is a shopping outlet that is open 24/7 and with global reach. This is not to say that going online is enough to transform the business into an international global operation; to make that claim, the online global presence needs to be supported by marketing and distribution strategies that understand the challenges and demands entailed. There are many decisions and measures that need to be taken into account to successfully run a global retail operation online. These include:

- Packing requirements and costs for overseas shipping.
- Shipping couriers options and costs.
- Taxation and tariffs.
- Delivery times.
- Languages of communication and service. For example, will you need to create mirrors of the site in different languages for different countries?
- Arrangements with suppliers, if necessary.
- Warehousing and inventory control.
- Payment options and constraints.
- Privacy and security measures.
- Updates and maintenance frequency.
- Integration of the online store with the physical brick-and-mortar store. For example, can customers order online and pick up or return an item in a store? (You can with Nordstrom, but not with Victoria's Secret.)
- Laws and regulations in different countries.

The implications of these decisions and measures on cost, price, and store margins are obvious.

Advantages of E-tailing

The Internet also solves a major problem of space restriction and shelf limitations. Your cyber real estate is cheaper and expandable. However, many customers may still prefer to physically visit the store first to get familiar with products before they decide to shop online; others may prefer to get informed about the range of products, prices, and store availability online before physically visiting the store. The former scenario demonstrates the existing challenges of shopping online, while the latter indicates how the Internet can be a convenient and time-saving alternative.

Online challenges include security challenges as well as the inability to physically try, touch, and feel products. Software developers are continuously developing new and more advanced security and data encryption solutions, and e-tailers have attempted to address the other issues of delivery and product trial. Today many e-tailers offer free and fast shipping options and flexible return policies, making it easier for shoppers to buy and try products with minimal risk. The amount of information generated by shoppers as a result of these interactions allows e-tailers to create databases that are valuable in creating high levels of personalized customer service, addressing each customer's or group of customers' specific need. The Internet is also an effective component of after-purchase service and relationship marketing through personalized e-mails, special offers, coupons, newsletters, and so on.

In addition, the possibility of integrating online marketing with offline activities creates an unprecedented opportunity for capturing the customer's attention at all times with an engaging, interactive, and personalized message that is focused, inexpensive, and much more effective. If handled wisely, it can improve brand awareness and loyalty tremendously.

By examining the success of the Zappos.com brand, we realize that it is attributed to a number of factors.

- Free, quick shipping demonstrated an enlightened understanding of the online shopper and the challenges of Internet shopping.
- Zappos.com possesses a clear understanding of the nature of the product.
- They understand that branding, especially nowadays in an environment where the customer is empowered and well-informed, is based on trust (remember the promise) and the experience (remember the identity). They focused not just on the product and prices but on the experience itself and the relationship they wanted to develop with their customer. This experience was backed by a well-designed infrastructure that included a state-of-the-art warehouse and logistics of delivery.
- They adopted a great customer service approach. For instance, "If someone calls for an item that Zappos does not carry, the customer service rep is encouraged to help the person find somewhere online that does carry it. Zappos may not make any money of the sale, but the person goes away with a positive experience."[8] With a trademarked logo that reads "Zappos powered by service," the emphasis on service is highly evident as their core brand value and the heart of the company culture.
- Needless to say, Zappos also has a presence on Facebook and Twitter. They simply want to be where their customers are.
- Zappos.com works on maintaining a fun, young spirit that is strongly present on their site and appreciated by their customers.

There have been many initiatives to make the online customer service experience more personal and fulfilling; for example, the use of live chat with a customer service representative or visual communication through real-time streaming services, such as Skype.

Loyalty is not just about promotions or price bargains; it is, at the minimum level, about getting what is expected whenever and wherever the

BOX 6.1   ZAPPOS.COM

Figure 6.26

Zappos began
as an e-tailer
specializing
in shoes.

(Courtesy of Zappos)

Zappos began as a shoe e-tailer in 1999 (see Figure 6.26) after its founder, Nick Swinmurn, became frustrated while shopping for shoes in traditional stores. The initial success of Zappos was not attributed to its collection of shoes and prices but mainly to its service. According to Zappos.com, the company perceives itself as "a service company that happens to sell shoes." Zappos.com realized early on that with items such as shoes, customers prefer to touch and try the products first before making any purchase. It also realized that buying online, while rewarding in many ways, is hampered by shipping costs and time. Thus, it offered customers free overnight shipping both ways, allowing buyers to try on the shoes in the convenience of their home. And although nowadays it does not ship overnight (three to four business days instead) customers are still offered a 365-day return policy and 24/7 customer service with live online assistance, which is intelligently referred to as "customer loyalty service." Its strong approach to customer service has gained Zappos.com a great following based on word of mouth. On its Web site Zappos declares that its culture and value is based on "best" service, as well as being adventurous, creative, and passionate. Today Zappos.com is more than a shoe e-tailer; the merchandise mix has been extended to include clothes, bags, and accessories such as eyewear and watches. In addition, Zappos has introduced a new site called "Zappos Couture," (see Figure 6.27) which sells brands such as Juicy Couture, Elie Tahari, Adidas by Stella McCartney, Donna Karan, Missoni, and many others.

In July 2009 Amazon.com purchased Zappos for nearly $900 million.

Source: http://www.zappos.com

Figure 6.27

Zappos has
added the
broader Zappos
Couture, offering
a full range of
clothing brands
for both men
and women.

(Courtesy of Zappos)

customer interacts with the brand. However, better service, whether online or offline, is achieved by exceeding expectations. It's about the wow factor—giving the customer something to talk about for a long time and creating the desire to come back for more. Meeting expectations is the first step in loyalty, but exceeding them is the real deal maker. No brand can exceed expectations without understanding where it stands in the consumers' minds and what value they perceive, so wavering too far from the core values and personality of the brand is a major cause for losing loyalty. Unwavering does not mean inflexibility or stubbornness toward new growth opportunities; it simply reflects the need to remain true to the brand's promise and consistent with its values, which remains true online as well.

E-tailing, Merchandising, and Branding

Great merchandise is the key to success for most retailers, online and offline. Great retail brands are not built around advertising but on store experience and having the right merchandise available at the right price and time. If you want to create a successful e-tailer, you must create real value either through a well-conceived, broad selection of products along with better pieces and/or through a rich shopping experience built

around a narrower product selection. This is the core of good merchandising. An example of successful online merchandising strategies is offering consumers "solution selling." Solution selling refers to grouping and selling various products as solutions to needs related to an occasion, a hobby, or a lifestyle. This can be done much easier and more efficiently online than in a retail store because of the ability to link different sites together (it is like shopping at a few stores at the same time). These solution centers bring together cross-category selling opportunities, creating a new and profitable tool to retailers. Moreover, these solutions can eventually be customized to specific customer needs. By introducing new brands online, companies can take advantage of seeding, or building early awareness by offering new brands for trial online before they are available for purchase more broadly in stores. Thus, brands can initiate customers' interests early on and use the process as part of a market testing program.

Finally, it is important to remember that the basic elements of a brand's identity do not need to change on the Web, but the manner in which this identity is communicated will most likely change often. Therefore, the brand's relevance needs to be maintained in conjunction with the technology adopted.

Chapter Summary

- In spite of their differences, products and services share some similarities in their branding process.

- The service mix is the mix of attributes that define the retail store concept. They are: merchandise, price, location, and service.

- Retail store brands can be positioned at different levels and on different components of their service mix.

- Shopping is an emotional and sensual experience.

- Store personalities define how the store brand behaves.

- Store atmosphere is a mix of aesthetics that attracts customers and manifests its visual and sensual identity.

- Internal communication is an integral part of the brand communication strategy.

- Sales personnel play an important role in the branding process. They should be brand advocates.

- Franchising is a common policy for growth in the fashion retail industry.

Chapter Questions and Issues for Discussion

1. Compare services to products, and examine the difference and/or similarities in their branding process.

2. Define *retail concept*, and briefly discuss its role in the positioning strategy of a retail brand.

3. What are the advantages and disadvantages of franchising as a global growth strategy?

KEY TERMS

ATMOSPHERE

CHAINS

CO-MARKETING

COMMUNICATION

DEPARTMENT STORES

DIRECT MARKETING

DISCOUNT STORES

E-TAILING

EXPERIENCE

FLAGSHIP STORES

FRANCHISING

FREE-STANDING STORES

IN-STORE BOUTIQUES

LAYOUT

LOCATION

MERCHANDISE

PERSONALITY

POSITIONING

PRICE RANGE

RETAIL CHANNELS

RETAIL CONCEPT

RETAILING

SERVICE

SERVICE MIX

STORE CORNERS

CASE STUDY: Barneys

Barney Pressman opened Barneys in 1923 in the neighborhood of Chelsea, New York, on Seventh Avenue and 17th Street, a neighborhood at the time with almost no notable stores or interest (see Figure 6.28). In the beginning, Barneys had a hard time getting manufacturers excited about the new store and found it harder to obtain merchandise. As a result, it started with merchandise obtained from closeouts, bankruptcy sales, or merchandise that manufacturers wanted to get off their hands. Barneys managed to survive with its used clothes and cheap merchandise in spite of margins being lower than industry standards (around 30 percent instead of 50 to 60 percent) because of its location and low rent.

Figure 6.28

Barney
Pressman in
front of the
original Barneys
in the 1920s.
(*Courtesy of Barneys
New York*)

The unconventional location meant that Barneys did not get much walk-in traffic but had to rely on loyal customers. Under the leadership of Barney's son Fred, the store took a different direction, buying merchandise more selectively, and by 1965 the store expanded to around 100,000 square feet while changing the look and feel of the store tremendously. Sales people were also chosen carefully for looks, not just skills. Fred started to look toward Europe for new merchandise and designers, and in 1970 Barneys opened its Barneys International House where it embraced European designers, such as Pierre Cardin.

In later years, times got tough and many specialty stores were forced to close down. That is when Barneys came up with the idea to hold a five-day warehouse sale with high discounts that could reach up to 50 percent. The event turned out to be a huge success and has become a kind of New York tradition. With the clout Barneys now had with suppliers, it managed to get specially discounted merchandise for this event and sell it with high margins, even at sale prices. Barneys seemed to always be a step ahead of the competition. Soon it realized how much quality mattered to its customers, and as the Italian industry had a turnaround in production quality, it decided to give up many of the French designers that were by now carried by most department stores in town and turn toward Italy. It was Barneys who discovered a then-young designer named Giorgio Armani and introduced him to the American market. Barneys gained the exclusive rights for Armani's name and design in New York and a say in the future licensing plans of the brand. This marriage between Armani and Barneys proved to be a success for both sides and established Barneys as one of New York's high-end retail destinations. By the mid-seventies, Barneys was performing better than many competitors with inventory of more than $50 million a year.

The Women's Store

In the mid-eighties, Fred's son Gene decided to open a Barneys women's store and embarked on promotional activities, such as a Chanel-sponsored event, in an attempt to attract uptown shoppers to the store. The store was meant to be fun and daring and continue the trend of discovering up-and-coming new talents, such as Azzedine Alaia, as well as embracing the hottest designers of the moment, such as J. P. Gaultier, Yohji Yamamoto, Thierry Mugler, and Romeo Gigli. Although other stores carried most of these brands, Barneys' store identity and image remained unique and distinguished through its special events, merchandise, and infamous iconic and sometimes shocking window displays designed by Simon Doonan (currently Barneys' creative director). In the mid-eighties, Barneys was making over $90 million in sales in its 170,000-square-foot store, or about $530 per square foot, and a gross margin of around 50 percent. However, although the women's wear store was extravagant and attractive, it remained a financial strain, so the Barneys family started looking for strategic business partners and turned to Japan, which in the eighties was seen as a strong flourishing economy eager to invest in America.

The Japan Years

In 1989, Barneys and the Japanese department store Isetan formed a joint venture. According to the deal, Barneys Inc. was formed, and Barneys was to open a chain of stores in the United States. Barneys Japan was also formed through Isetan, which held a license to use the Barneys trademark in Asia, including building stores in Japan, as well as having Barneys USA train Isetan employees on the Barneys method of retail operations with the hope of improving their stores' margins. The financial details of the deal seemed very favorable to Barneys, which would grow without relinquishing full control to Isetan. In a few years, Barneys opened about 14 stores, including locations in Chicago and Beverly Hills, as well as some less successful choices such as Houston and Troy, Michigan, where the stores shortly closed.

With the cheap long-term lease of its Chelsea store coming to an end 1996, and the failed attempts to buy the location, a decision was made to relocate the store to midtown. Finally, and very discretely, a choice was made for the location at 660 Madison Avenue (see Figure 6.29).

The Madison Avenue Store

Designing the new Madison Avenue store started lavishly with no limits or budget constraints. Marble, mosaics, mother-of-pearl-finished wooden shelves made in Indonesia, goatskin-laid woodwork—the list goes on. With problems of its own in the Japanese market and a strained relationship with the Barneys management, Isetan decided to go its own way. Meanwhile, the lavish spending on the Madison Avenue store continued, and by the time the store opened in 1993, Barneys was unable to pay its bills of about $40 million. Designers were not being paid, and many young designers stopped shipping their lines. In addition, many established designers struggled with the choice of the new location, given that they either already had their boutiques a few blocks away or already had their collection in nearby stores, such as Bergdorf Goodman, Saks Fifth Avenue, and Bloomingdale's.

Although the first day's sales were about $1.3 million, many mistakes snowballed, leading the store to file for bankruptcy in 1996. Some of the problems included:

- Lavish interiors (such as floor treatment at $300/square foot)
- The 600-square-foot restaurant entrance on first floor that deprived the store's potential sales of items such as perfumes and accessories that are traditionally known for their high markups of around 75 percent
- Last-minute expensive changes up to minutes before doors opened for the first time
- High employee theft: a porter reportedly walked away with a total of $100,000 worth of suits, and a $1,500 baccarat crystal leopard figurine was stolen four times
- Inability to make payments to vendors and designers

Figure 6.29

Today one of Madison Avenue's high-style destinations, Barneys' controversial new store opened in 1993.

(Getty Images/ Spencer Platt)

For the casual observer, Barneys' financial results may have seemed acceptable. For example, Barneys announced that its gross margin was a healthy 52 percent; however, its undisclosed expenses were 60 percent (over by $10 million). And although the Madison Avenue store was generating $140 million in sales, or about $655 per square foot, it was much less than projected and far less than nearby Bergdorf Goodman's $1000 to $1200 per square foot.

Merchandise

Another important factor was the store's decision to focus on high-priced designer clothes and stop carrying the traditionally more profitable moderate ranges such as Linea Rossi and San Remo, which were selling very well. The result was that Barneys focused on a very narrow market of rich men and stopped being the authority in menswear it once was. (See Figure 6.30.) Barneys also launched its CO-OP concept to offer casual apparel and accessories targeting a younger market. CO-OP originally started within its New York flagship store and eventually branched out into a chain of freestanding stores.

Bankruptcy and Beyond

Many of Barneys U.S. stores closed down, and by 1995 Barneys filed for bankruptcy. In 1997, the original iconic store in Chelsea closed for good. Barneys was first purchased by Jones Apparel and then in 2007 by Istithmar, a Dubai investment company. In 2009, rumors spread of a possible sale; however, Istithmar confirmed that it has no current plans to sell Barneys and that it is standing behind the brand.

CASE STUDY **Questions**

1. Evaluate the decision to relocate on Madison Avenue and how Barneys today compares to that of the early days in terms of strategy and brand image.

2. How would you compare Barneys' international growth strategy discussed here to that of Louis Vuitton's in Japan, as discussed in the chapter 3 case study?

Figure 6.30

Barneys'
Creative Director
Simon Doonan
poses with
his Donatella
Versace in his
Versace window
display.
*(© Diane Cohen/Everett
Collection)*

SOURCES

Doonan, Simon. 2007. "Barney's Green Grass." *New York Observer.* November 27. http://www.observer.com/2007/barneys-green-glass

Levine, Joshua. 1999. *The Rise and Fall of the House of Barneys.* New York: William Morrow and Company.

Steinhauer, Jennifer. 1997. "After Dressing Men for 74 Years, Original Barney's is Closing." June 18. *New York Times.* http://www.nytimes.com/1997/06/18/nyregion/after-dressing-men-for-74-years-original-barneys-is-closing.html

www.barneys.com

www.istithmarworld.com

ENDNOTES

   1. www.thefreedictionary.com/retail+store

   2. "Retail: What Future for Malls, Department Stores?" BNET (August 2003). http://findarticles.com/p/articles/mi_qa3908/is_200308/ai_n9300933/

   3. Robert Reppa and Evan Hirsh, "The Luxury Touch," *Strategy + Business.* (February 29, 2007/Spring 2007, Issue 46). http://www.strategy-business.com/press/enewsarticle/enews040307?pg=all

   4. "Does loyalty really exist?" Customer Insight Group, Inc. (2007), 2.

   5. Ibid., 4.

   6. Shari Waters, "Types of Store Layouts." About.com: Retailing. http://retail.about.com/od/storedesign/ss/store_layouts.htm

   7. Business Week. "What Does Wal-Mart's New Logo Mean?" MSN Money (July 4, 2008). http://articles.moneycentral.msn.com/Investing/Extra/WhatDoesWalMartsNewLogoMean.aspx

   8. Soren Gordhamer, "The New Social Engagement: A Visit to Zappos." Mashable (April 2009). http://mashable.com/2009/04/26/zappos/

7

iBRAND:

The Age of
Interactive, Wireless,
and Virtual Brands

The previous two sections of the text examined a few new technologies that are changing many of our daily habits and the way we interact with each other. This section continues that discussion. We will start in this chapter by explaining some of these new technologies and models and exploring their significance. Then in the next chapter we will examine their direct impact on the general concept of branding.

The iBrand name we created for this chapter is inspired by the trend of terms prefixed with the letter "i" that was initiated by computer guru Apple and adopted by others (Apple's iPod, iPhone, Imagine Publishing's iCreate, and CNN's iReport, among others; see Figure 7.1). With its implication of user empowerment and consumer control, it seemed appropriate and rather inevitable to name this chapter **IBRAND**. Every technology examined and discussed in this chapter focuses on the concept of consumer empowerment one way or the other. As we will discover together in this journey, technology is reshaping our lives and the sociocultural environment in more ways than we ever imagined. And the truth remains that in spite of everything the Internet has brought to our lives, its potential has not been fully utilized, and the best is yet to come.

CHAPTER
OBJECTIVES

- **Introduce the reader to new technologies and models such as mass customization and M-branding among others.**

- **Examine the fashion-related applications under these new technologies.**

- **Examine the new role of the consumer under the new technology environments.**

- **Explore the implication of these technologies on the branding process.**

Figure 7.1

New technology is changing the face of fashion branding in a way that involves the customer as never before. Elie Tahari's iPhone app, for example, offers virtual viewing of its runway shows.

(*Courtesy WWD/ Fairchild Publications*)

The Interactive Brand: Mass Customization

Interactive branding refers to a situation whereby the consumer interacts directly with the brand or the process of creating and developing it. It is through the help of new technologies that it has become possible for consumers to play a direct and interactive role in shaping a brand as he or she likes. A good example of this trend is the concept of mass customization (or MC). In this chapter we focus on mass customization, explain the concept, give examples of various applications, and then examine how this technology relates to the branding process. Let us start by understanding the concept.

Mass Customization vs. Mass Production, Pure Customization, and Personalization

It is essential that we start by defining the concept of "mass customization" and how it relates to and differs from concepts such as pure customization, mass production, and personalization.

Mass customization

MASS CUSTOMIZATION refers to the concept of allowing each consumer to customize or adapt products' features according to his or her needs within a standardized platform with an acceptable price premium.

According to this definition, mass customization gives consumers an option to customize features of a product, given that it is based on a mass-produced structure or frame.

Mass Production

The introduction of the machine and assembly lines during the Industrial Revolution allowed producers to supply large volumes of standardized products with lower costs. The result was a sea of sameness that was best summed up in the famous quote by Henry Ford, founder of the Henry Ford Group, when referring to the infamous Model T car: "Any customer can have a car painted any color that he wants so long as it is black."[1]

The apparel industry was equally affected by the Industrial Revolution and the wave of standardization as evident in the rise and growth of ready-to-wear (RTW) apparel. Although RTW was initially slow to grow, it eventually flourished as urbanism and a new class of professionals grew in the first half of the twentieth century. RTW was modern, suitable for the new lifestyle, and also affordable because it was produced in standardized patterns and sizes. It was under the pressures of standardization that a strong need for differentiation among products existed. As a result, the need for marketing strategies, advertising, and branding grew as necessary tools to achieve differentiation and competitive advantage among brands products.

Made-to-Measure or Pure Customization

Made-to-measure (MTM)—also referred to as bespoke or one-offs—and tailored garments have been the norm in the fashion world throughout history and up to the Industrial Revolution. In the past, most garments, if not sewn at home, were obtained from specialty neighborhood stores where customers were known by name and shopped for in-house or made-to-measure products. It was a pure case of customization whereby every piece could have been totally different and totally customized from beginning to end. It is a trend that still existed with the rise of ready-to-wear in the form of tailored menswear and women's wear clothes and, to some extent, in the grand houses of haute couture.

Personalization

Although this sometimes also refers to made-to-measure or bespoke commissioned products, it refers more accurately to the practice of personalizing a standardized product by adding monograms, initials, or emblems to products such as shirts, bags, wallets, and so on. In this manner, it is not pure customization because it is not a fully tailored or commissioned product, and not mass customization either because it does not involve inherent alteration of product's features. Personalization can also refer to personalizing the shopping experience or choice offerings, as in the case of recommending a few store items based on the personal data and preferences of the consumer (such as personalizing the product offering). This process does not refer to the production of the product as mass customization would, but rather to limiting the customer's choices to what better suits his or her style and personality from an otherwise large range of products. Clearly mass customization is a larger concept in which personalization can be just one element.

Lately we have seen how technology is playing a big role in taking personalization to a higher level. For example, a new range of body scanners is offering customers a uniquely personalized shopping experience by using their personal data and preferences to recommend selective and targeted choices from a large line of products.

Mass Customization in Fashion Products

There are examples of mass customization from various industries, which range from customizing your computer (such as Dell, in electronics) to customizing a novel with your own characters,

Figure 7.2

In an example
of mass
customization,
a customer
gets his
measurements
taken in the
Intellifit booth.
(*Associated Press/ WILL
POWERS*)

scanners to produce what they call the FitPrint—the printout the system produces with the user's exact measurements—only now it is not just used to help the customer select the best fitting jeans from the items already available in the store, but the data is transferred electronically from the retail location to the jeans manufacturer, where the garment pieces are custom cut by computer control. The customer can also choose from a selection of styles and washes and add details such as a pocket shape and design, stitching, and other personalization options. The completed custom jeans are shipped directly to the customer in three to four weeks.

including their names, personal characteristics, and romantic environment (for example, personalnovel.de, in publishing). In the fashion industry, there are various examples that adopted the model with different levels of customer integration. The following are a notable few.

Intellifit

Intellifit is an American company based in Pennsylvania, which introduced the Intellifit Booth. As a customer steps into the booth, fully dressed, the machine collects over 200 body measurements through safe radio waves in as quickly as 10 seconds (see Figure 7.2). The customer then receives a confidential computer printout listing his or her exact measurements and recommendations of all the brands and sizes that fit him or her and are available in the store.

The company has taken the concept a step further by introducing the Custom Jeans Center in its Philadelphia retail store. The concept utilizes the body measurement technology used in their

Ollyfit

Olly is a children's shoe company that introduced the Ollyfit in its stores. The process starts by taking the exact measurements of every shoe and linking it to its computer system. After a child's foot is scanned, the system superimposes the child's foot onto the desired shoe and recommends a perfect fit that even puts into consideration room for future growth.

In addition to being attractive and fun services for customers, both of the Intellifit and Ollyfit examples also deal with one of the great fallacies of standardization—that one size fits all and that same sizes are truly standardized.

Mi Adidas

Adidas first introduced its new Mi Adidas concept in its Paris store. By visiting the store, customers can jog on a computerized catwalk where sensors embedded in the track record the exact pressure of their footfall and gauge their running posture. This data, combined with the customers' accurately measured shoe size is used to create a perfect fit.[2]

Figure 7.3

The interactive miCoach Core Skills area at the Adidas Brand Center in Beijing.

(*Adidas via Getty Images*)

Figure 7.4

The Virtual Mirror for Augmented Reality from Adidas scans a person's feet and presents them with images of how they would look wearing different sneaker styles and colors.

(*JOHN MACDOUGALL/ AFP/Getty Images*)

After the measurements are taken, customers choose the look of the shoe by pointing to a massive interactive screen (see Figure 7.3). By simply pointing at images on the screen, radio frequency identification (RFID) technology (highlighted later in this chapter) interprets their gestures, converting them to commands giving detailed information on the Adidas product. When the choices are made, the customer can see how the new shoe will look on him or her by using a three-dimensional virtual mirror, which allows the customer to "virtually" try on his or her own creations, checking out the shape, color, and cut from every angle even before the shoe has been produced (see Figure 7.4). Mi Adidas orders are produced in the same factories as the brand's mass production orders but are manufactured by small, multiskilled teams capable of producing the entire shoe. Total time for delivery to the customer from receipt of order is less than 21 days. The measuring and fitting process is free, but the ordered shoe costs from $40 to $65 extra depending upon the style. A similar example of such technology is used by Nike I.D.

Threadless.com

Threadless.com is a community-centered, online-based company headquartered in Chicago. The concept of the company is allowing members of the threadless.com community, aspiring T-shirt designers, to submit T-shirt designs online; the designs are then put to a public vote. A small percentage of submitted designs is selected for printing based on the votes' results, then sold through an online store and lately a new brick-and-mortar outlet in Chicago as well. Creators of the winning designs receive a prize of cash and store credit. (See Figure 7.5.) Like all mass-customized processes, this flexible and open-to-creativity environment is controlled by a set of measures such as predefined basic silhouettes and sizes that form the basic canvas for customers' designs and the standardized platform as defined by the model.

The threadless.com model is interesting in the fact that it allows users to share their customized product with everyone else and have it up for sale. This way they manage to keep T-shirt prices low and affordable. It also creates a very inviting environment for users to continuously submit new ideas, make some money, and be a part of a growing community. Some other examples comparable to threadless.com are Look-Zippy.com and Spreadshirt.com.

Figure 7.5

Aspiring T-shirt designers and their designs on threadless.com.

(Courtesy of Threadless. com)

We can conclude that mass customization is a middle-of-the-road solution between mass production and pure customization or made-to-measure. Under mass customization, manufacturers use a common, fixed platform (an element of mass production), allowing them to produce the basic platform or structure of the product in large quantities and with relatively controlled costs, while still being flexible enough to allow the customer to interact and participate in the development process and customize specific features of the final product (an element of made-to-measure).

What to Customize?

In previous chapters we have categorized the fashion industry into various segments ranging from luxury products to mass-market brands. The remaining question is which of these industry segments is more suitable or ready for a process of mass customization?

Luxury Brands

It is important to remember that in this chapter we have distinguished between the concepts of mass customization and pure customization (or made-to-measure), as well as personalization. A good example to demonstrate these differences comes from Louis Vuitton, the leading luxury brand. Louis Vuitton offers its customers three different options and services that range from personalizing to fully customizing their line of bags and luggage:

- *Personalization:* LV offers personalization services on ready-to-purchase luggage and other products. Services include painting monograms on hard-sided luggage as well as hot stamping on tags, smaller leather goods, or soft-sided bags. Customers can choose from different font styles and colors. All these services are complimentary. (See Figure 7.6.)
- *Made-to-order products* (LV's equivalent application to MC): This service is available for both hard sided and soft bags. Customers are allowed to "choose from models available in several materials, and variations can be made to the lining, external material, and metallic pieces."[3] Customers are then given a price and time frame for the completion of the bag. After a 50 percent deposit has been paid, work on the bag will start, which might take four to nine months for completion, based on the type of bag ordered. The bag is then sent to the customer's store for pick up.

- *Made-to-measure products:* This service differs from the previous two services by including a designing stage that takes two to four weeks to create a design based on the customer's requests. It also comes with a much higher cost and could take up to 12 months for completion.

Luxury products and the whole experience that comes with owning one has always been about exclusivity and the feeling of being unique, special, and different from the crowd. And if you desire an exclusive made-to-measure item (or service), you expect it to come with a large price premium. The premium is usually so high that it shifts this item or service into a different segment both in terms of price as well as target customer. For example, a Louis Vuitton customer may expect to pay over five times the price of a ready-made bag for a made-to-measure customized one. This point is crucial to our argument because, as highlighted under the challenges section of this chapter, one of the main criteria of mass customization is that although it comes with a price premium, it should

never be too high to shift the product into a different segment, targeting a different market or hindering current customers from obtaining it if they are willing to pay a reasonable extra amount.

ISSUES TO CONSIDER

- Exclusivity, personalization, or pure customization attainable with luxury goods are not the same as offering a mass-customized luxury product.
- The issue of the effect of MC on risking a brand's image as a result of a mismanaged process will be more relevant for luxury brands than any other fashion category. Accordingly, MC for luxury goods will probably be available under a more controlled environment and with more constraints on what can be customized and how far customization can go.
- MC offers consumers an additive level of exclusivity. Exclusivity is probably the main driver for purchasing luxury goods (in addition of course to the anticipation of quality) and will be so for customizing a luxury brand. It remains to be seen, however, why a traditional luxury brand customer who can afford a fully customized made-to-measure item would settle for a somewhat lesser exclusive option.
- Some argue that luxury products' customers are not our common e-shoppers. And that given the general nature of luxury products, their cost, and exclusivity, the distant Internet environment does not seem very suitable. Looking at the Louis Vuitton examples, we will notice that although the customization options are referenced on their Web site, the process itself takes place in their stores on a one-to-one basis. It is just the personalization option of

Figure 7.6

Louis Vuitton allows you to personalize your purchase by adding your initials.

(Courtesy George Chinsee/WWD/ Fairchild Publications)

adding your initials or monograms (the simpler and less exclusive of all options) that is available online and for free.

- The rise of the new luxury brands referred to in an earlier chapter and the new breed of luxury consumers might be the biggest drive behind the mass customization trend in the luxury segment. Rising from the middle-segment market, these new up traders are younger, hipper, technology savvy, selective, and practical.

  F. Piller highlighted an interesting observation made by Claudia Kieserling, founder and president of Selve, a leading shoe brand in the area of mass customization, when she said, "Luxury is a key characteristic of mass customization. No matter what price you ask, consumers see it as pure luxury," or we can add, at least as something special.

Mass-Market Brands

Mass-market brands and consumer goods should be generally comfortable with adapting MC and inviting customers to participate in shaping and designing the product. In this segment, products are more accessible and affordable; the customer base is more diverse and more value-for-money driven. A customer of a mass-customized pair of Levis or Adidas sneakers is willing to pay the premium for a product that has a better fit and value. Of course the pleasure of exclusivity is a plus. This is usually a customer who shops around before making a purchase decision and is more accustomed to window shopping, online browsing, and e-commerce.

ISSUES TO CONSIDER

- Once again, MC should not shift the price of the brand to a higher segment.

- Mass-market brands may benefit more from new technologies, such as the Internet and virtual communities, than luxury brands probably would, as well as a younger and hipper customer base that is more Internet savvy.
- More value for money and a better product are among the main drivers for choosing a mass-customized product in this category.
- MC also offers customers of such products the opportunity to trade up to a more exclusive brand.
- MC can be a major differentiation strategy in a very competitive market segment that suffers from sameness and copycats. A MC option can actually help prolong the life of an initially less-exclusive brand and in a way create an attractive brand extension that is supported and harnessed by its users.
- When proven beneficial, we should expect a bigger shift toward online mass-customization options in the nonluxury segment. An increase in adopting online solutions and new technologies will be inevitable. Brands will want to stay competitive and be the first to lure customers into engaging in a fun and addictive process of brand manipulation. It might be their only alternative for long-term survival.
- The fact that nonluxury fashion brands are generally of a low to medium price point might be of a great advantage as far as mass customization is concerned. A more affordable cost eliminates an entry barrier for users. Think of the T-shirt customization example explored in this chapter. Because the process is affordable and financially low risk, customers might give it a try for fun, as a venue to express

their creativity, or to fulfill a hobby. Of course, in the case of threadless.com, there is also the incentive of making money as well by having the customized T-shirt available for public purchase.

Mass Customization in Fashion Retailing

The examples of Adidas and Intellifit demonstrate good applications of mass customization in products, which in return impacts the retailing environment and increases the level of personalizing the shopping experience. Yet the possibilities are actually much bigger. Until today a totally personalized shopping experience has been an elite, high-priced service offered by exclusive boutiques or high-end specialty stores, such as Bergdorf Goodman or Neiman Marcus. Yet we have seen how new technologies such as RFID can make a personalized and customized experience available to each and every one of us. Consumers can interact with dressing room windows and TV screens plotted around the stores to decide when and what to try on, make purchase orders, get advice on styles and trends, and seek assistance if needed. These features, coupled with an alternative to shop virtually or online if desired, create a new level of consumer control and a myriad of choices and solutions that can be totally customized to your taste, time, and character.

Secondlife.com

In 2007, Italian fashion designer Giorgio Armani opened a virtual store on Secondlife.com, the 3D virtual community Web site. He modeled the virtual store on his flagship location in Milan. He even created an avatar of himself. Although the store is in a virtual world, it demonstrates the growing popularity of such environments among consumers and Internet users; such an approach allows the brand to relate to its customers and emotionally connect with them as it shares their interests and speaks their language. It shows that the brand is hip, modern, and relevant. And of course it is a gateway to Giorgio Armani's official e-shopping Web site. In addition to Giorgio Armani, Christian Dior chose secondlife.com to display an exclusive collection of jewelry on the virtual community's islands (virtual locations that are visited by users), demonstrating how the marketing potential of these environments can be quite important in the future.

There are estimated over 2 million users (or residents) of Second Life (SL). Thus, it is obvious that apart from their entertainment appeal these virtual worlds can have a serious business impact on developing and marketing brands. For instance, Mary Ellen Gordon from Market Truths, an online research agency, demonstrated that certain products such as athletic shoes have a very high level of brand awareness on Second Life. Gordon also presented relevant consumer behavior statistics[4] that showed:

- 57 percent of Second Life users (or residents) consider buying a real-life product as a result of a recommendation they received from someone in Second Life.
- 55 percent recommended a real-life product to someone they chatted with in SL.
- 25 percent have checked a product in real life after seeing it in SL.
- 9 percent have purchased a product in real life after seeing it in SL.
- 8 percent have bought a real life product in SL.

This data demonstrates the great marketing potential and branding relevance of these virtual worlds in real life and on real products. Another example of an interactive and collaborative online community that offers users the tools to create virtual worlds is SceneCaster.com.

iStorez.com

iStorez.com is a Web site that allows users to create their own customized shopping mall. It is the online equivalent of window shopping,[5] where users can browse thousands of storefronts (a storefront is an extension of a retail store's Web site) from hundreds of stores while iStorez presents the most updated and relevant storefronts based on the users' preferences and criteria. The iStorez storefront creation engine is based on the Web 2.0 technology. iStorez differentiates itself from other comparison shopping sites in delivering a customized shopping experience that dynamically changes based on what a visitor is looking for or a seasonal theme. In addition, shopping comparison sites are usually visited when users have narrowed down what they want to buy and are comparing prices and features, while iStorez allows them to browse around and "window" shop in a virtual mall they have created themselves. iStorez is clearly a good example of mass customization through creation of your own shopping environment or mall, as well as personalization of the shopping offerings.

Stylefeeder.com and Stylepath.com

These are two similar models that create virtual window shopping experiences and learn from your habits and preferences to make suitable recommendations. Stylepath also allows you to virtually decorate rooms from a selection of real furniture.

Your Own CyberSelf

Compucloz and My Virtual Model (Public Technologies Media) offer a similar concept and allow the users to create their own CyberSelf, a 3D virtual model based on their physique and body features. (See Figure 7.7.) The model is an application that, when used by the host Web site, allows shoppers to input their measurements to create their own model and use it to try on various products to see how they would fit on their bodies. Lands' End is a brand that has utilized the Public Technologies Media technology on their Web site.

It is important to note that in the area of retailing, the distinction between personalization and mass customization may be a bit blurred. A simple way of looking at it is that personalization mainly tries to answer the question of what to buy, whereas customization answers the question of how to buy.

Figure 7.7

Myvirtualmodel. com creates a digital mannequin of yourself to let you see how you will appear in clothes before you decide to purchase them.

(My Virtual Model Inc./ Newscom)

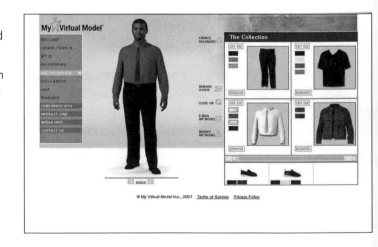

Mass Customization and Technology

In reality, mass customization is not a new concept; the term *mass customization* was introduced in 1987 in Stanley M. Davis's book *Future Perfect*. Yet it owes its current rise to more recent technological advances, such as the Internet, software development, Web-based applications, and telecommunication innovations that are enabling customers to interact and integrate with the developing process and thus complete the circle for the model to function.

The Internet has proven to be a great platform for linking consumers and producers. And the development of what became known as Web 2.0—the newest generation of the Internet—has made it easier to create Web based communities, blogs, wikis, and virtual environments in a manner that makes the process attainable and effective. In addition, technologies such as radio-frequency identification (RFID) promise a new era of data gathering and the creation of a new mass-customized shopping environment that could redefine the retailing experience of the future.

Issues to Consider

- As just mentioned, the Internet has been a great platform for applying mass customization by allowing customers to interact with the brand and its producer. However, not all kinds and segments of fashion brands have embraced the technology in the same manner or with the same level of integration. This is discussed later in this chapter.
- If mass customization is a manifestation of the increasing power of the consumer in the twenty-first century, then the Internet and other technological advances have been instrumental in such a change of power in the branding game together with other social and economic developments, including general increase of wealth, globalization, and economic growth in various parts of the world such as China.
- Not all consumer segments respond to technology advances and embrace them in the same manner or with the same degree. This point will be discussed later as we examine the application of mass customization in the luxury segment.

Mass Customization and the Fashion Branding Process

Based on our discussion of branding in chapters 2 and 3, we developed a branding process that can be summarized in the following four major stages:

1. The brand decision (involves the 3Cs: company; customer; culture)
2. The positioning strategy (incorporates the VIP model: value-identity-product mix)
3. The brand communication
4. Growth (or other) strategies

Let us examine how mass customization relates to these branding stages.

The Brand Decision (3Cs)

- From a consumer's perspective, MC offers users a high level of empowerment and control over the brand they cherish. For the first time, consumers are not just on the receiving end of the branding process but are part of it. They are not just brand users but literally *partners*.

- As a result, mass customization is an instrumental tool in what has been known as *brand democratization*, which is the trend toward more accessible and approachable brands by a wider and newer group of customers.
- The Internet and online applications have proved to be good platforms for customer input and interaction, which diminishes (not necessarily abolishes) the need for other costly channels (such as brick-and-mortar retail outlets), as well as opens the door for a wider integration among parties involved. In a way, it is B2C (business to consumer) meets B2B (business to business) meets C2C (consumer to consumer) meets C2B (consumer to business), all in one virtual environment.

The Positioning Strategy (VIP)

- MC offers a high level of brand differentiation, which in return is a strong element for developing a competitive advantage.
- If well managed, mass customization can offer consumers the right product with the right features and fit, which in return means a higher level of customer satisfaction and diminishes the need to shop somewhere else. The result is customer loyalty, which is the ultimate goal of any marketing strategy.
- Mass customization creates value through economies of scope rather than the economies of scale principles associated with mass production. Economies of scope refer to the economic benefits resulting from producing more than one product. Economies of scope create both revenue opportunities through incremental revenues and the adaptability and flexibility to pursue new and profitable channels.

- The opportunity to outsource certain functions, such as design and creative work, might have a positive economical impact on the manufacturer, as it may reduce the need to possess certain technical or creative skills as well as allowing for the redirecting of resources to other aspects of operations, such as production innovation.
- On the production side, the model is clearly a suitable platform for the concept of just-in-time (whereby raw materials are ordered and delivered when needed) and thus delivers better inventory management and cost reduction benefits.
- In a situation where the product is mass customized through a sourcing community (also known as open innovation) where many users can participate in developing and upgrading the product (think of the threadless.com brand in fashion or the Linux brand in computer operating systems), the product is actually in a continuous state of innovation and development. This is a process that would otherwise cost a great amount of money, time, and research effort on the organization's part. It is interesting that innovation and the future development of the brand in this case is sponsored and crafted by the actual end user who possesses the direct need for the product, a situation that can hardly be imitated with any level of forecasting, market research, or focus groups.

The Brand Communication

- From a marketing perspective, the model delivers a marketer's dream come true, whereby the end product is predetermined, predesigned, and predemanded by the end user, which might hypothetically mean that the producer is making a product that is presold. This impacts the communication and promotion message and the marketing strategies in general.

- Adopting mass customization should impact both the content and mode of brand communication. In terms of content, brands generally highlight their distinctive features that give them their competitive edge as well as emphasize the brand's value. In other words, it promotes their positioning proposal. However, under MC, the features are not as totally predictable because they are altered and finalized by the end users themselves. Accordingly, the focus of the communication message is to remind potential users of the brand value and invite them to participate in a highly gratifying experience of collaborating in developing the product. This gives the message a service focus, not a product one. It's about the experience, not the features; your version of the brand, not ours; how you want the brand to be, more than what we propose. It's all about you, the *customer*. This promotion and communication tone is very strong, personal, and effective in building a strong level of customer loyalty and positive brand image.
- Based on the last point, a mass customized product requires a personalized communication message. Thus under MC, new communication channels such as personalized e-mails, newsletters, text messages, customizable Web pages, and so on are all suitable channels under this model (more new options will be discussed later in the chapter).
- Mass customization of products will inevitably pave the way to the mass customization of

marketing and promotion. In reality, this already takes place in the form of viral marketing. Viral marketing or, as some call it, *buzz marketing*, is based on a C2C (consumer to consumer) environment where the users in a way "hijack " the brand (to be discussed further in chapter 8) and take over the marketing process themselves through message sharing, networking, and word of mouth. The result is a snowballing effect that creates a buzz that is wide reaching, effective, and very low cost. It's a situation whereby the main role of the brand's marketing team is to create the environment, and possibly manipulate the content or initiate an interest, yet the process itself remains in the hands of the users. Just like customization, viral marketing transforms the users from passive receivers to active contributors in the marketing process and in brand ownership. This is not to ignore the role of the brand, though, because viral marketing has to be initiated by something that attracts the users' interest. A strong offer, an important announcement, or exciting news should trigger the interest and get the ball rolling. Let's never forget that any brand, whether it is online or offline, has to be built on true value that is meaningful to the user.

The Internet has witnessed many successful examples of viral marketing in recent years through online communities, blogs, and videos created in support of brand examples such as Barbie, Nike, even British singing sensation Susan Boyle.

Growth Opportunities

- The MC model could very well thrive on a network of workshops to satisfy its low quantity of ever-changing products. Workshops and small business units should flourish under this model, creating new business opportunities for young entrepreneurs and smaller operations. In the Mi Adidas example, the shoes are produced within the same factories by a smaller group of skilled workers, a model reminiscent of the preindustrialization era, borrowing from the customized world of tailoring and haute couture.

- MC allows the brand to grow by offering new options to existing customers and attracting new ones. It's a form of brand extension that expands the brand offering as needed by its end user. In addition, the Internet being a common platform for MC gives the service a global reach that would have been hard to attain in a traditional brick-and-mortar environment.

Challenges under Mass Customization

- The biggest challenge is the mind-set change. The fashion industry is one that has historically strived on secrecy, egoism, and creative dictatorship. Designers and managers who are used to a culture of total control and a highly protective environment may not easily accept an environment of branding democracy, nor comprehend the possibility of letting an outsider take control, manipulate, or hijack a brand they have been building and protecting for years.
- In an open environment such as that created by mass customization, possessing a level of control is not only challenging but necessary to maintaining the brand's integrity. Every brand strives to consistently maintain the image it creates. Yet if customers are allowed to manipulate the brand and reshape the product to their liking without any control measures, the brand image may be vulnerable and easily tarnished.

- Control also refers to measures needed to manage the growing customer database and facilitate smooth feedback channels demonstrating a quick response in order to maintain customer retention and long-term loyalty. In a different environment, special orders are not the norm, and customer feedback is occasional and usually available if and when a customer is asked. Yet under the new environment, every order comes with a unique set of requirements and personal data. This wealth of data has to be well managed and rechanneled in a more dynamic and personal style of service that keeps developing every time the customer returns for a purchase.

- Adopting mass customization is not an immediate guarantee of 100 percent sales. A good example is threadless.com, which as mentioned earlier, bases its T-shirt production on popular vote. Yet popularity did not always reflect actual sales numbers. The same problem encouraged Look-Zippy.com—a French site with a similar model—to develop a measure of control by which they post the selected models online for two weeks where customers can place their orders, followed by production (another example of control measures).

- Mass customization might result in a higher price due to the higher cost brought about by meeting the specific needs of every customer, such as setup cost or skilled labor. Yet these costs are counterbalanced by efficiency in forecasting and product development, postponement of activities until an order is placed, and better customer retention. In addition, customers are usually involved in customization with an expectation and willingness to pay a suitable premium for their new gains, given that it does not imply a switch into an upper market segment[6] (for example, the price premium is not so big as to shift the product to a higher market segment).

The previous examples show that mass customization as a model can be a rewarding branding and competitive strategy in the twenty-first century. As with any model, it has its challenges and limitations. Yet what makes it lucrative is its ability to embrace new technologies and respond to the consumers' growing desire for empowerment over what, when, and how they buy products. The model has also proven to be a flexible one that can be applied in variations, allowing it to quickly react to new challenges as they develop, and transform these challenges into lucrative and profitable options, helping the brand to survive and become profitable.

The Wireless Brand: RFID and Mobile Technologies

Digital and electronic technologies have allowed products and services to be designed, packed, delivered, and experienced in new and different ways like never before. The pace and complexity of options have increased and, with them, the speed of brand success or failure. In the world of wireless technology, the Internet continues to establish new business models that already have and will alter the way we approach marketing in general—and specifically branding—in the near future. The following sections discuss examples of **WIRELESS TECHNOLOGIES.**

RFID

RFID stands for radio frequency identification. The technology is built around the concept of putting cheap and tiny tags that contain a radio transmitter/receiver on physical objects. These tags are then used to allocate the objects. The tag can be attached to anything and can carry different sorts of information about the item. A radio reader device can be mounted anywhere or carried around the store and can read every tag within range, thus monitoring and keeping track of every tagged item while transferring this data to any computer. One of the important features of this system is its reasonable cost. The tags, for instance, can be around 20 cents or higher; however, once prices drop to single digit cents, they would be even more economically feasible to adopt for lower priced products. The advantages and applications are numerous and without any human labor involved. The first obvious application of RFID is inventory control. In addition to placing the devices in stock rooms and warehouses, stores can create what is being dubbed as *smart shelves*. For example, when a customer picks an item off a store shelf to purchase it, the information is immediately transmitted wirelessly to inform the warehouse; before you know it, the item is replenished with no need for phone calls, written forms, or long waiting time. Smart shelves help achieve this through sharing information between the tags on the shelved product, the reader devices, and the computer network. Many stores have already either adopted this system or are in the process of doing so, such as the GAP.

Figure 7.8a

This interactive magic mirror provides a selection of different viewers' garment suggestions as well as their votes on the various pieces. (*Bloomberg via Getty Images*)

Figure 7.8b

Rather than simply showing this woman's reflection, this magic mirror displays an image of a completely different garment from what she is wearing. (*Bloomberg via Getty Images*)

The technology and concept can be taken a step further and be adopted in a multitude of applications and services that will not only streamline the retailer operations but enhance the customers' shopping experience and highly personalize it. Marketing enthusiasts and writers such as Rick Matheson have explored many of the promising and fascinating applications of RFID. Here are a couple of interesting examples.

- TV screens can be placed around the store with RFID readers attached so that after a customer picks an item off the shelf, screen readers close by capture the item's data and initiate a series of special offers and updates relevant to that item or its category. The same experience will be repeated with almost every customer, leading to an unprecedented level of personalization and target marketing. Barnes & Noble is among those exploring this option.

- Imagine smart garment labels that can communicate with your washing machine and transmit the appropriate washing instructions for the garment, such as the right water temperature and drying instructions.

- This wireless technology might eventually lead to similar chips embedded in our credit cards or wallets so that we do not need to check out at store registers anymore. When we leave the store with the items, they are wirelessly intercepted along with our credit card information and automatically charged. Not only will this make it easier and faster for customers to shop, but may eventually reduce rates of store theft as well. Wireless checkout is still in the testing stages, but once again the potential is amazing.

- Nanette Lepore, a New York-based designer, has been at the forefront of experimenting with new technologies that enhance her customer's shopping experience at her SoHo store. For instance, she has been testing what is known as magic mirrors—in-store mirrors that interact with the RFID tags placed on her garments. When you hold or wear a garment in front of the mirror, the magic mirror senses what the item is, then the "transparent video monitor housed within the mirror's glass reveals itself to play animated scenarios featuring the brand's whimsical Lepore Girl mascot upselling accessories and complementary items."[7] (See Figures 7.8a–b.)

- When Prada opened its first epicenter stores in New York and Los Angeles, it adopted RFID to create a highly personalized and unique experience not only for the customer but for the employees as well. Employees held wi-fi-based tablet devices that scanned RFID tags on garments; this way they could check inventory, make recommendations based on previous sales, trace garments, and detect where they had been misplaced. They could also monitor which part of the store had a higher level of traffic. In addition, the tags could trigger nearby screens to display relevant runway clips and make recommendations to buyers based on the items they picked and previous buyers' votes. In the dressing room, shoppers can obtain information on garments using an interactive touch screen display. This information is conveyed to the screen via RFID tags attached to garments throughout the store. While the customer tries the clothes on, the magic mirror takes time delay video and replays the action in slow motion so the shopper can take in the full effect.[8] (See Figure 7.9.)

- Wireless systems can be used to link back-end databases to loyalty programs. So, for instance, when a customer walks into a store, he or she may enter a code that in essence alerts the store that he or she has arrived and is ready to receive special promotions based on their previous purchase history as saved in the database.

- Shopping carts can be equipped with wireless touch screens that provide detailed information about products and where to allocate them in the store.

These amazing examples demonstrate the great potential of the technology and how it can change not only the way customers shop, but how retail operations are run and brands managed in the future. However, like any new technology and application, it comes with a few challenges and concerns.

Figure 7.9

A woman uses a touch screen in a dressing room at the Prada Epicenter in New York.

(Catrina Genovese/Time & Life Pictures/Getty Images)

Challenges under RFID

RFID technology can be utilized in different retailing environments. (See Figure 7.10.) The biggest challenge is the question of privacy. The fact that, through RFID, stores can monitor everything we pick and scan every item that may already be in our pockets and purses as long as it has a built-in tag raises legitimate privacy issues and recalls fears of a Big Brother consistently watching our every move.

Another challenge that stores such as Prada face is the ability and willingness of traditionally trained employees to adopt and learn these new technologies and operate in a totally different retailing environment. The challenge highlights the unquestionable need for intensive training, not only in how to use these new devices but regarding their impact on the whole operation, especially the level of customer service.

M-Branding

M-BRANDING, or mobile branding, refers to the use of mobile technologies and devices such as our cell phones and PDAs. Wireless devices such as cell phones are the most intimate and personal devices any of us has ever acquired, even more

Figure 7.10

At the Tokyo department store Mitsukoshi, RFID technology is used with cosmetics to show virtual before and after faces of their customers.

(*YOSHIKAZU TSUNO/ AFP/Getty Images*)

than a laptop or PC. It is the only device that you carry everywhere and all the time, and it is probably the first thing you check when you wake up every morning. It is a device that has highly penetrated the market; almost every single member of the family probably has a cell phone or PDA of their own. It is also interesting to note how mobile users are generally more willing to pay extra dollars for their mobile services and downloads (such as ring tones) than they are for other online services they would get through their laptops or PCs. Examples of current marketing and branding mobile applications include the following.

Mobile texting is becoming quite a phenomenon all over the world and especially in Europe and Asia. Its effect is comparatively less in America because, for the most part, the American society is based on commuting, which may consume a large amount of time during the day. Nevertheless, a recent study by Forrester Research shows that 85% of U.S. users between the ages of 18 and 30 (also known as Generation Y) frequently use text messages, compared to 57% of all adults. Texting has been effectively used by many organizations in various ways as seen in the following examples.

- When Bravo.com introduced its new fashion program "The Fashion Show," hosted by designer Isaac Mizrahi, it allowed viewers to participate in the voting process online, which they could also do using their cell phone (similar to the "American Idol" format), thus transforming viewers from passive observers into participants and co-owners of the whole competition. In addition, it offered games, show updates, and the ability to view the final collections as well. The same channel offered

Figure 7.11

Nike's fitness
app works with
a sensor that fits
in your shoe.
(*Associated Press/
MARY ALTAFFER*)

photos, ring tones, and wallpaper to subscribers of the Rachel Zoe program, all available for downloading on their mobile cell phones

- Mobile phones are already being used in some parts of the world such as Asia to communicate with vending machines by dialing a number on your phone, making a purchase, and paying at the same time, all through your phone. There might come a day when we do not need to carry wallets or credit cards anymore because our mobile phones will suffice.

The new craze for iPhone apps has created a plethora of applications that can have marketing potential, such as the following.

- *Near to everywhere app:* This is an application that allows users to shop malls and get updates and location of stores.
- *Nike:* Nike introduced its very popular Nike+iPod application for both the iPod and iPhone, which was meant to replicate the online Nikelab experience. You just put the sensor in your Nike + shoe that comes with a built-in pocket. (See Figure 7.11.) No need to connect the device

with the new generation of iPhone 3GS, which includes built-in support. The sensor tracks your run, then sends the data to your iPod. In addition, as you run, the device informs you of your time, distance, pace, and calories burned. Your data is saved on Nikeplus.com where you can monitor your progress as well as access information about products and athletes associated with Nike.

- *Style.com:* This Web site's iPhone application gives the user access to hundreds of designer collection photos and exclusive videos. Style.com reported over 1 million ads served via iPhone in a single month[9] (Fashion Network has a similar app).
- *Ralph Lauren:* An innovative marketing effort was initiated for his 2009 collection by introducing an iPhone app especially for his Fall 2009 and Spring 2009 collections, allowing users to explore the Ralph Lauren collection and view highlight videos, a look book, special video slideshows, as well as use a store locator for the United States and international markets. (See Figure 7.12.)

Figure 7.12

The Ralph
Lauren
iPhone app.
(*Courtesy of WWD/
Fairchild Publications*)

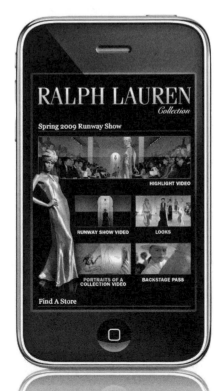

- *Net-A-Porter.com:* The fashion-forward e-tailer launched NET-APP, which allows users to shop using their iPhone or iPod touch. The application is free and updated every Monday and Wednesday. In addition to the shopping, it hosts a number of interesting features:
  - Browse through the latest fashion products and trends with detailed information (such as sizes, fit, prices, and so on) on products with a high-quality customizable photo library.
  - Read the Net-A-Porter weekly fashion magazine.
  - Access product-specific details, including size and fit information.
  - View content that is relevant to the user's location (such as prices in various currencies).
  - E-mail product information to friends.
  - Send an e-mail to a team of fashion advisors offering guidance on sizing, fit, and expert style advice.
  - View and add items to a personalized Net-A-Porter wish list that users can access on their desktops.

ScanLife

ScanLife offers a new software application that allows more interactivity through the mobile phone. After installing the application, users can scan a 2D bar code that is placed on products, hang tags, magazines, or any flat surface using the camera of their cell phone. When scanned, the information triggers actions such as directing the user to a Web page with specific information about the product or where he or she can download materials such as coupons, store location directions, price list, and more. Thus a window shopper, for instance, can target an item he or she sees in a window after closing hours and immediately be directed to information about the item such as availability, sizes, prices, watch video relevant to the garment, read reviews, and eventually have the option to purchase it online from their phone. (See Figures 7.13a–b.)

Presence Application

Presence is an IBM product that allows stores to detect shoppers who have already signed up to the service once they enter the store and accordingly offer them individual coupons and special offers in real time. The application, in addition to offering a highly customized service to shoppers, offers retailers a wealth of information about the shopping habits of their customers and how they respond to special offers and discounts.

Beaming

Beaming refers to a technology that allows companies to use billboards and displays to beam information to PDAs and cell phone devices via infrared or Bluetooth ports. Similar to the RFID examples, you can wave your cell phone or PDA device at an item in a store and view comparison prices of the item online or get different relevant information. This technology is already being used in Japan. Another application for this technology allows billboards placed on highways to intercept FM frequencies of passing cars. Based on your radio station of preference, they start displaying ads relevant to your taste. The system is smart enough to differentiate among cars and not pick up the same signal twice. The same technology can be used in other locations where billboards can send videos, games, and other applications to cell

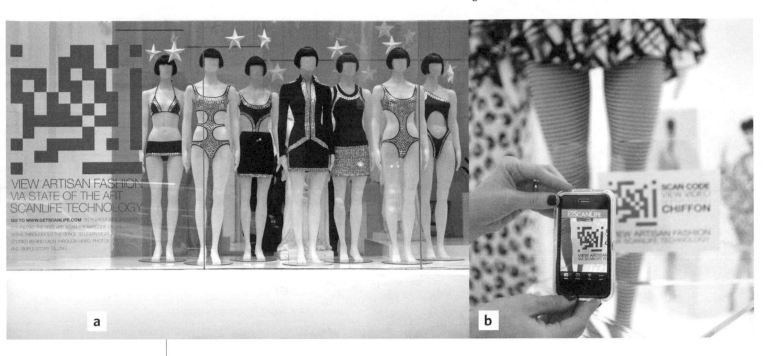

VIEW ARTISAN FASHION
VIA STATE OF THE ART
SCANLIFE TECHNOLOGY

GO TO WWW.GETSCANLIFE.COM ON YOUR MOBILE BROWSER.
DOWNLOAD THE FREE APP. SCAN THE BARCODE ON ANY OF THE
SIGNS THROUGHOUT THE SPACE TO LEARN MORE ABOUT THE
STORIES BEHIND EACH THROUGH VIDEO, PHOTOS, CULTURE,
AND SIMPLE STORY TELLING.

a

SCAN CODE
VIEW VIDEO
CHIFFON

b

Figure 7.13a, b
(a) A shop window promoting the store's use of ScanLife.
(b) All you need is a phone, a camera, and the ScanLife application to access numerous forms of information regarding a product.
(© Michael Falco)

phones through Bluetooth technology. With the users' permission, billboards can complement their displayed messages with these more interactive and fun applications.

Beaming technology is also being tested for use inside stores, beaming interactive content with product and store information on walls, floors, and any other solid surface, adding flexibility to how and where to inform and interact with the customer.

Audio Targeting

Audio targeting refers to directing sound in the same manner that a laser beam directs light. These ultrasonic beams create a sound bubble that can be directed to specific objects or individuals in its path. When the bubble hits a wall or an object, it transmits audible frequencies that are heard only by whoever is passing through these audio bubbles in a very narrow range and targeted frequency, so that it feels like wearing personal headphones. The greatest application for such a technology is the ability to send different audible messages to different targets and create a highly customized message. So in a way, two people can be passing by your store but each receives a different promotional message or offer. Or you can transmit different messages in different aisles or segments of the store that are heard only by whoever is passing there. An example of this technology is the HyperSonic® Sound technology (HSS) from the American Technology Co. The ultrasonic emitters use ultrasonic energy to reflect sounds and voices in very specific areas and remain focused in a narrow column of sound. (See Figure 7.14.) This effect is produced without the conventional speaker's excess baggage—there are no voice coils, cones, crossover networks, or enclosures. Sound does not spread to the sides or rear of an HSS unit, eliminating the problem of uncomfortable and unwanted noise pollution produced by conventional speakers.[10] A listener can stand anywhere within the audio beam range and hear the marketing messages. According to the company, HSS technology can be used to:

- deliver sound to areas that are either physically impossible to access or too costly to install conventional loudspeakers,
- isolate sound to a specific region or person, and
- communicate highly intelligible messages over long distances.

Figure 7.14

Audio targeting allows sound to be directed within an extremely focused area, or sound bubble.

(Courtesy of International Robotics, Inc.)

Wireless Technology and the Fashion Branding Process

Let us examine the impact of wireless technologies on the fashion branding process.

The Brand Decision (3Cs)

- The greatest impact of wireless technologies and all technologies referred to in this chapter lies in their potential for high interactivity and the fact that they establish a two-way channel of communication that is dramatically different from how one-directional traditional marketing has been.
- Because of these technologies, customers are not just on the receiving end anymore; they are partners in a way that will eventually shape and redefine the brand involved.
- Wireless technologies, such as mobile phones, have transformed our personal habits and level of communication as individuals. In return, they help to reshape our culture, expectations, and needs in a manner that affects everything we interact with, including the brand.
- Cultures are dynamic, and through viral marketing and real-time interactivity, wireless technologies do not only shape them, but communicate them and spread them as established values and habits as well.
- From a company perspective, wireless technologies support the virtual organization model and the flat dynamic structure where feedback is crucial and quick. It also offers new income opportunities from new services as well as from lowering costs by introducing new cheaper marketing options. It also offers a great source of consumer data and profiles. But above all it brings the organization closer to the customer and establishes a more intimate relationship built on continuous dialogue and personalized services.

The Positioning Strategy (VIP)

- Just like MC, these communication channels provide more than just communication; they serve as a platform for branding and value generation through their level of personalization.
- One of the biggest advantages of the high level of personalization achieved under this environment as well as MC is their ability to narrow the gap between corporate brand positioning and the brand image as established in the consumer's mind. As consumers get what they want and expect from the brand, and the brand successfully assists them in achieving that, the brand promise is manifested, the image is solidified, and loyalty, which is the best measure of success, becomes more attainable.
- Creation of apps and interactive application are in a way a form of brand extensions. They offer new growth opportunities and exposure for brands where they can not only be promoted but generate income as well (selling ringtones, videos, subscriptions to special services and

updates, new outlets for shopping and placing orders, and so on).

- Wireless applications also have a direct impact on establishing, promoting, and polishing the brand's identity. Co-branding such as that between Samsung Phones and Giorgio Armani, for instance, enables the brand to reinforce its

visual identity in a modern and relevant way that may be more effective than placing the logo on a traditional printed ad.

The Brand Communication

- The intimate relationship we develop with these little wireless devices has a strong impact on

---

BOX 7.1 — THE FUTURE OF CUSTOMER SERVICE?

Figure 7.15

The poster of the film *Minority Report*, a dramatization of a "futuristic" technology about to actually exist. (*20TH CENTURY FOX/ Album*)

In the Tom Cruise/Steven Spielberg sci-fi movie *Minority Report*, Cruise's character has a surgeon replace his eyeballs with someone else's in order to avoid being tracked by police through retinal scanning. In the futuristic world of *Minority Report*, retinal scanning enables everything from collecting subway fares to tracking consumer behavior. At one point when Cruise's character enters a store, the holographic image "reads" his replacement eyes and cheerfully greets him, "Hello Mr. Yakimoto, welcome back to the Gap. How did those assorted tank tops work out?"

The fictional technology of Hollywood is about to exist in the real world through a technology called Human Locator, an interactive visual system developed for advertising and entertainment by Freeset, a Canadian creative technology consulting firm. Human Locator detects when humans are near, tracks their movement, and then broadcasts messages directed at them from a nearby screen.

Drawing on cutting-edge computer visualization techniques to track full body movement in real time, it allows consumers to actively participate in and interact with advertising. It works with most video displays or projectors and

can output video, animations, audio, and motion graphics. At the same time, the system provides advertisers with measurable viewer data.

Sources: www.freeset.com; www.humanlocator.org

Figure 7.16

Armani co-branded with Samsung to produce the Night Effect Soft Bank 830C Emporio Armani mobile phone, released in 2009.

(KAZUHIRO NOGI/AFP/ Getty Images)

marketing and branding strategies. It opens the doors wide open to a world of highly personalized and targeted messages that are not only relevant, instantaneous, and up to date, but a fraction of the cost compared to most traditional marketing channels.

- The mobile environment is capable of delivering information and promotional offers in different ways and formats such as text messages though SMS and e-mails as well as video, audio, ring tones, games, and so on. The messages sent can range from information and announcements, to offers, coupons, or other practical information and news. Another great advantage is the possible seamless integration between mobile technology and the Internet in the form of Internet and e-mail access, tweeting, and more, through the mobile phone.

- Mobile devices can also play a major role in viral marketing through the share of videos and text messages.

- The new environment is more suitable for a pull rather than a push approach, whereby the focus is to address consumers and motivate them to take initiative and be interested in pulling (demanding) the product and starting a viral marketing round. (In a pull marketing strategy, the consumer usually *pulls* the goods they demand for their needs into the market; accordingly, marketing activities target the final consumer. In the push strategy, the suppliers *push* them toward the consumers who may not be aware of it and accordingly, the manufacturer concentrates some of their marketing effort on promoting their product to retailers to convince them to stock the product.)

- Mobile applications such as iPhone apps are being used to broadcast live streaming of fashion shows. Dolce & Gabbana, for instance, have decided to make this move in 2010 as a step to follow their earlier move to go live online and on their Facebook page. It is another example of the democratization of fashion and a manifestation of the role and impact today's ordinary consumer has in the fashion scene.

Growth Opportunities

Wireless technologies and relevant applications (such as iPhone apps) create new brand extension and growth opportunities. They extend the brand's presence in the user's lives in an exciting and interactive manner that in return reinforces the brand image and generates value. What is interesting is that users are also part of this growth and extension strategies because they are capable of developing their own apps and platforms that could support and showcase the brand.

Wireless technologies can be easily integrated with other technologies, such as the Internet as will be discussed later, and accordingly can also play a role in extending the global reach of the brand.

The co-branding example of Armani and Samsung demonstrates the repositioning opportunities such technologies can offer to older brands by making them more hip, current, and relevant to modern users. (See Figure 7.16.)

Challenges of Wireless Technologies

As with any marketing process, the information used needs to be useful, and the value proposed needs to be real and relevant to the consumer. Accordingly, incentives and promotional offers need to be meaningful.

The entertainment value should not be ignored. Interactivity and entertainment can make the message more engaging and exciting in order to encourage the user to respond.

Just like on the Internet, the consumer should not be a victim of spam and unsolicited material or be enticed to subscribe to newsletters without a clear and easy way to opt out and unsubscribe. It is also always advisable to seek their approval and permission before getting them engaged in such activities. This way, the customer feels respected and perceives the promoter as honest and professional. The result is a better chance for building a trusted, long-term relationship.

Always be aware of new trends and technologies. The iPhone apps craze and Twitter mania prove that today's customers get bored easily and are always on the lookout for new cool trends.

As mentioned earlier, one of the biggest benefits of the new media is its ability to microsegment markets and highly personalize marketing messages. Thus, it is essential to clearly identify customers and determine the best ways to customize and personalize messages.

Never ignore the power of real time. Real-time streaming with updated news and information is attractive and can easily capture users' attention and interest.

As with any service, activities need to be backed up with good and effective customer service that offers quick responses and solutions.

Consider integrated mobile campaigns with other activities, such as online activities or in-store promotions. This approach keeps the user engaged, interested, and entertained. An example mentioned earlier about dressing rooms' magic mirrors that can be wirelessly connected to Facebook applications is a concept that could be easily emulated and adapted by a mobile app.

Word-of-text is a term that is quickly replacing *word-of-mouth*. Yet as much as we need to envision the potential of this medium, we also need to understand its limitations and deal with it. Text messages, for instance, are challenging in their focus and length. With a limitation of 160 characters in most languages, you will need to learn how to send a message and make your point across effectively within such constraints.

The Virtual Brand: The World of Social Networking

The Internet differs from many previous technologies in that it is not as centrally controlled as other channels were, such as TV or newspaper. It offers a more open environment because we live in **VIRTUAL COMMUNITIES** that we create with people we choose and trust. Buyers nowadays trust other Internet users' (who are virtually strangers) opinions and feedback regarding a service or a product more than those of real world experts. We now live in virtual social communities and probably interact with each other more through blogs and social networks than we do in the real world. Thus, the impact of such networks cannot be ignored. Even if some models are fads that are destined to be replaced by new ideas, the truth remains that a culture has been shaped and has changed us forever. Here are some examples of virtual environments.

Blogging

Blogging stands for *Web logging*, which is a form of online personal publishing that allows individuals and companies to articulate and broadcast their message in cyberspace.[11] The significance of blogging is that it is personal, fast, casual, and intimate. It also differs from other Internet publishing channels in its frequency and interactivity. Its real-time effect, simplicity, and interactivity have allowed users to express themselves and their opinions in a very casual way. The result has been the rise of the social networking phenomenon that started with a community of blogs referred to as the blogosphere and transformed into the new wave of social networks, such as MySpace, Facebook, and Twitter. Obviously not all blogs are valuable; however, some have becomes sources of debates, serious discussions, and valid critiques. It is estimated that more than 11 percent of Internet users read blogs, making blogs more and more attractive to marketers.

A significant outcome of blogging is the creation of a platform for consumers to group, form communities, and openly share views and comments on different products and brands. Although the challenges are clear, as they may end up criticizing the product or brand, they can also allow users to embrace the brand and take ownership of marketing it and become its champions. It's the same concept again of brand hijacking and viral marketing. What has been amazing is the amount by which users have grown to trust these blogs as their point of reference. For example, Nikeblog.com is a blog that is not affiliated with Nike but was

created by Nike customers (referred to as "sneaker heads") who claim that Nike is their favorite brand. The blog offers product news, discussion, and opinions about Nike and other brands as well. They also offer coupon and shopping links to various sneaker styles in addition to a Facebook and Twitter presence.

On the other hand, businesses have found an opportunity in blogging by participating in a more casual dialogue about the brand that is more trust-building and frank. Guidelines for effective blog marketing may include:

- Write and update interesting and relevant content on a regular basis. There's no substitute for attracting attention than publishing content worth sharing.
- Contact existing customers, marketing partners, and industry peers and let them know you've launched a blog. Profile them in a blog post to give extra meaning and incentive for visitors to pay attention.
- Link to other influential blogs.
- Contribute posts to other blogs. Comments posted on other relevant and influential blogs with a similar target audience may be helpful in building visibility, as these comment forms will usually include the opportunity to link back to your blog.
- Integrate the blog with other social channels such as Facebook, Twitter, and YouTube.
- Include blog links on your Web site as well as everywhere you post your Web site address both online *and* offline.
- Have employees add the blog URL to their e-mail signatures as well as online profiles (on sites like LinkedIn, Facebook, and Twitter).
- Promote your new blog and the value of its content via e-mail to prospective customer lists.

- With PR efforts such as media relations, approach journalists with press releases and other material. Always include a link to your blog in those communications.
- Bloggers can also make money directly by tapping into the money-generating power of affiliate advertising, such as the Amazon's affiliate advertising program, which pays bloggers if a reader buys a book reviewed on a their blog.
- Advertise your blog through links on relevant sites or sponsored links on search engines.
- Remember that although visitors' traffic remains the lifeblood of any blog, not all bloggers make money directly from their blogs. Rather, their blogging may lead to money-making opportunities such as consulting gigs, business connections, or book contracts.

Social Networks

The blogosphere has evolved in recent years into the new phenomenon of social networks such as Facebook, MySpace, and Twitter. These new platforms are redefining the manner in which we communicate and relate to the world. On the business level, they have opened a Pandora's box of marketing tools and options that go beyond the mass-marketing thinking of decades ago. In a recent study by *BtoB* magazine and Business.com,[12] 56% of marketers indicated that they intend to increase their investment into social media, and 44% already reported positive effects for their sites. Respondents also indicated that their top goals for spending on social marketing are to:

- build brand awareness (81%),
- increase traffic (77%),
- generate leads (67%),

- better engage with customers (66%), and
- improve search results (57%).

Other important reasons for a company or a brand to participate in a social network is to be part of their audiences' world and interests, in addition to benefitting from low-cost marketing. However, before a company rushes into being part of this environment, it needs to approach it as seriously as it would any other marketing endeavor. They can always start by asking the following questions:

- *What are my primary goals and objectives? What about my secondary goals?*
- *Does my target audience spend time on these social networks? Which ones? How often? What do they do? And what are their expectations?*
- *What do I need to do to attract my audience and retain their attention?*
- *What resources do I need? How much will it cost? Do I have the technical skills needed to run and maintain my presence?*

To better appreciate the significance of these questions, let's examine two of the most visited of these networks: Facebook and Twitter.

Facebook

Facebook is a free social network where subscribers can create their own blogs and fill them with information and updates about their personal lives and interests. They add and communicate with friends by sharing photos and stories, as well as joining different networks of common interests and locations. Similar to other social networks, Facebook is easy to use and very intimate in nature. In social networking, the most important parameters are the size of your network and the number of people who are part of it.

In addition to individuals, many companies have joined the bandwagon of social networks such as Facebook and utilized it as a marketing channel in various ways, such as:

- Inform readers with updates and latest company news.
- Offer contests and promotions to encourage visitors to link to the blog.
- Participate in groups that interest and attract their target customers.
- Create a database for future e-mails and newsletters.
- Use the entertainment factor with tools such as videos, games, and music to offer fashion updates and generally make the experience exciting and worth revisiting.
- Receive feedback and initiate a dialogue about the brand and its products.
- Use all of these activities to build up interest and confidence in the brand.

Examples of brands that had a strong and early presence on social networks are Nike and Diane von Furstenberg (DVF). The DVF page, for instance, offers news, photos of fans and women in DVF dresses, and a fan-of-the-week application where fans can share ideas and photos of themselves in DVF outfits. (See Figure 7.17.)

In April 2010, Facebook announced a set of new social plugins that were meant to enhance the level of online social interaction and, in return, the level of integration between businesses and online shoppers. For instance, the new open graph protocol introduces a tagging system that allows applications and networks to map users' real preferences and choices. Plugins such as the Like button and the activity stream, among others,

keep track of visitors' preferences and activities in real time, so online users will easily be able to find out their friends' favorite store, music, jeans brand, and so on. Businesses have quickly foreseen the business potential of these new applications. A good example is Levi Strauss & Co., which took measures to use such plugins to integrate its business with Facebook, allowing users to tag products they like, and introducing its Friend Store in which consumers logged into Facebook are able to view their friends' preferred products.[13] This level of integration makes information sharing more accessible, relevant, and dynamic, which will in return create more focused marketing strategies as well as enrich the shopping process in general.

Twitter

Twitter is an example of microblogging. It is a text-based blogging network, but with limitations of 140 characters per entry. It's considered by many to be the next generation of instant messaging. Twitter has gained wide acceptance in a short time due to its capabilities as a real-time platform for self-expression. Twitter is considered a social network because users can add or remove friends as well as attract a group of fans and followers. It is the most "real-time" of all networks and the fastest to spread news and updates. New features are being tested that may allow users to segment fans and group them. The key element to Twitter is to keep the followers interested as you share your news, thoughts, and updates. No wonder that tweets of celebrities are very popular because they give regular individuals the opportunity to get closer to their favorite star's inner thoughts and lives. Designers such as Karl Lagerfeld use Twitter to share their thoughts and views. In one tweet, Karl Lagerfeld described life in the fashion world as a short life where you live six months at a time. As a matter of fact, although this intimate and very personal perspective of Twitter is the most intriguing, it is also the most challenging because users tend to forget that it is still a public platform and that anything said can be used against its user. It also means that it is an extension of our personal lives. People talk on Twitter as they talk in everyday conversations. And the fact that you can access the Internet with your mobile phone and tweet makes it more convenient and accessible at every hour of our lives. For Twitter fans, it is highly addictive and engaging, which means it can also be a very effective marketing channel, especially given the indications showing that most Twitter users are also engaged in other social networks, such as Facebook. As a result, Twitter is used by many to increase traffic and direct visitors to their blogs where they can get more info and details on specific subjects.

Brands are using Twitter in many ways, such as in keeping events' attendees up to date with time, location, delays, and all sort of details and information. It is a great way to document events as well,

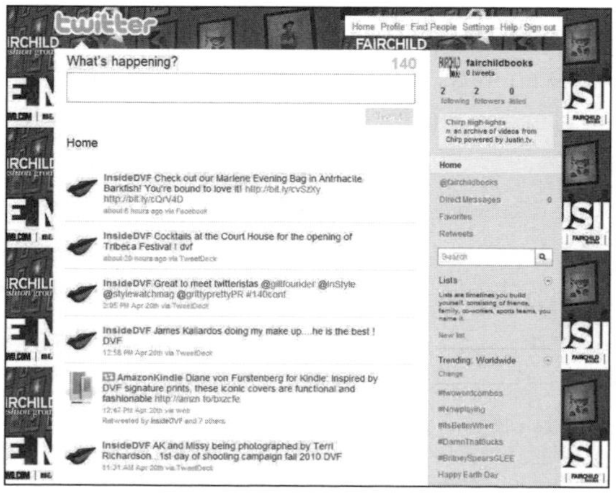

making it a kind of virtual real-time diary.

There have also been various success stories of job hunting through Twitter. Job seekers have used tweets to explain their move, who they are, and what they are looking for; they offer a link to their blogs with details about themselves and get feedback and job leads as a result. Thus, Twitter is more than a one-way stream of information. It can be an effective platform for dialogue and interaction through responding to readers' comments and links to other networks.

Virtual Environments and the Fashion Branding Process

Let us examine the impact of virtual environment on the fashion branding process.

The Brand Decision (3Cs)

- The Internet and its virtual environments have the potential of integrating all previously mentioned technologies and creating a platform of collaboration and shared brand decision making between the brand producer (company) and the customers. Customers are empowered and can easily communicate with the company and the brand at various levels in an engaging environment and on daily basis.
- Activities on virtual worlds and communities are a great source for information about consumer behavior and profiles. This data is precious in guiding companies through critical branding decisions, such as market segmentation, positioning strategies, and relevant communication strategies.

Figure 7.17

Diane von Furstenberg takes advantage of the Twitter craze to update DVF fans on events, new products, and more.
(*Courtesy Fairchild Publications*)

- Similar to mobile technologies, virtual communities reshape our social habits and define our new culture. As culture reshapes, so do our needs and the products and services we seek to satisfy them. Virtual communities (VCs) created an environment of options, variety, a culture of mix and match, and a new sense of community. Consumers today trust and seek the advice of other community members and bloggers more than they do professionals or traditional sources.

The Positioning Strategy (VIP)

- Virtual communities are instrumental in brand positioning. They provide platforms where ideas, suggestions, and support for the brand are initiated and shared. They offer a wealth of information that companies can use to enhance their strategies. However, they are also places where verdicts of the brand are strongly and bluntly shared. Just as favorable, viral marketing through social networks is a fast (and cheap) and effective promotional tool, though negative stories, reviews, and shared bad experiences can hurt the brand with a faster and stronger impact than could have happened before.
- VCs as well as wireless technologies offer the company a great opportunity to reposition the brand if needed by listening and responding to targeted customers' needs as well as integrating their new lifestyle. Older brands can come across as more relevant and part of the current "cool" culture.
- VCs can reinforce the brand's identity in terms of both its personality and visual identity. It presents the brand as modern and fresh, as well as offers opportunities to showcase its visual identity in a clear and attractive way.

The Brand Communication

- Virtual worlds offer a direct and real-time channel of communication between the company and the user as well as between different users, allowing a more effective spread of messages and ideas (once again, showing the importance of viral marketing).
- Related to the previous point, VCs also allow the creation of brand communities that become brand advocates and play an instrumental role promoting the brand or even killing it. The example of Nikeblog.com mentioned earlier is a good one.
- Companies have adopted the brand community concept by creating their own blogs and Facebook/social networking site pages, and made these sites work to promote the brand and support it. For example, Adidas introduced the Your Area tab on its Facebook page. It allows its almost 2 million fans to view content from their local countries where they buy sneakers and other products. The page includes links to photos, videos, news, a store locator, and promotions, making it very interactive and engaging.
- Another interesting impact is that of communities together, with streaming capabilities, on the future of fashion shows. The late Alexander McQueen was a pioneer in bringing high fashion through live streaming to the Internet. The show, done in collaboration with SHOWstudio.com, was broadcasted with six video cameras operated by using motion-control technology that captured the models walking down the catwalk from various angles in order to deliver to the online viewer as close to a real-life watching experience as possible. With many others to follow such as Burberry, Marc Jacobs, Ralph Lauren, and Calvin Klein, each in their own way, many marketing professionals

are starting to question the future of traditional fashion shows as a marketing and communication platform, which may in return have its effect on traditional print advertising and editorial coverage that have always thrived on these shows. The role and look of future fashion shows will change as part of the changing marketing environment. Technology will democratize fashion shows as they target new and different groups of customers. As live technology expands the outreach of fashion shows, it also eliminates the elements of news and exclusive coverage, which other media such as magazines live on. It is just another example of how technology will reshuffle the roles and goals in the world of marketing, and the time may come when virtual fashion shows will totally replace traditional ones.

- In chapter 8, we will discuss in more detail how virtual environments alter the traditional communication model and place these social networks in a strategic position to play a direct role in forming, altering, and delivering the promotional message of the brand in collaboration with the company or on its behalf.

Growth Opportunities

- Similar to other technologies, VCs create new brand extension and global growth opportunities, especially for retail brands as they offer new e-commerce and marketing solutions that are supported and reinforced by the end user and in many cases created by him or her as well.
- VCs could also play an important role in global growth and brand globalization in general. The level of interactivity, information sharing, integration, and entertainment they deliver could easily diminish cultural and geographic

barriers, as well as create an engaging and inviting experience for many to share.

Technology Integration

One of the most fascinating things about all the previously mentioned technologies is the potential for **TECHNOLOGY INTEGRATION**—the possibility of integrating all of them to create a rich, interactive, entertaining, and personalized environment for the user. Everything is so interlinked on the Internet now that among Twitter, Facebook, MySpace, YouTube, and all the other social networking sites on the Web, you have many different vehicles to promote and get your brand and message out there.

For instance, IconNicholson Social Retailing® created (and trademarked) *social retailing*, a technology that integrates in-store shopping with online social networks in order to target young adult shoppers and respond to their new shopping habits. It is basically the technology behind the magic mirrors discussed earlier. With social retailing, interactive mirrors can send live video feed to any cell phone or e-mail account selected by a shopper.

The same feature will allow shoppers to check what may be available on the store's Web site that is not available in-store, with the option of making the purchase right there in the dressing room. Some other examples include:

- *Polyvore.com:* Polyvore is a fashion site that describes itself as a "fashion and social shopping platform that's redefining how people around the world experience, create and shop for fashion on the Internet."[14] It allows users to mix and match images of garments by simply dragging from any Web site online to the fashion sets they create on Polyvore.com. Users can use the images to create sets of outfits that demonstrate their personal style and that they can eventually purchase, promote, or share with friends. The sets are displayed on the site and can also be shared on blogs or social networking sites. (See Figures 7.18 and 7.19.) The site is easily integrated with users' Facebook profiles, for example, and users are able to use personal items they may have uploaded from their cell phones, such as to their Facebook pages and showcase them in their sets. Sets are displayed and shared by users and organized in groups based on themes, allowing people with common tastes to interact. In addition, Polyvore highlights new trends, news, contests, and style advice in a blog-style format. Brand producers and designers can also use the site to showcase their designs by setting up a feed with their products as well as to benefit from the exposure they get by the sets the users create. According to Polyvore, they have an estimated audience of over 3 million "trendsetters and tastemakers," as they call them, with 118 million page views per month. The average user is a 22-year-old female on the cutting edge of fashion. Polyvore's appeal lies

in its ease of use, level of integration with other Web sites and social networks, as well as the community and social networking environment it creates for its users. This model demonstrates a workable level of integration between various platforms and models. It is e-commerce meets blogging meets social networking meets designers' showcase, all in one place.

- *Rivolta Shoes:* Rivolta Shoes is a good example of the integration between mass customization and M-branding. Rivolta produces and sells customized high-quality, tailor-made shoes by replacing the traditional method of tracing customers' feet on paper with a digital scanning device. The store personnel perform a 3D scan of the customer's feet to record their perfect shape. The customer is then able to customize all of the shoes parameters and try them on virtually in front of a special virtual mirror, all in real time. The company also has plans to create an iPhone application where customers can design and purchase their shoes anywhere they are. Being a luxury item, the shoes are quite expensive (close to $2,000), but the experience is also a good example of the new level of service luxury brands can offer in the new environment.

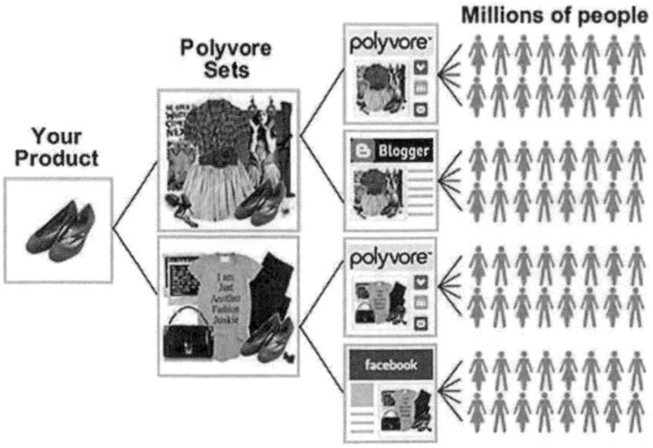

The Impact of Technology Integration on the Branding Experience

One of the biggest impacts of technology integration on the brand is in the way users can experience the brand. A platform of these technologies integrated together creates a richer, more engaging, and interactive environment like never before. Environments where customers can experience the brand, manipulate, evaluate, promote, and utilize it all within a mix of both real and virtual worlds. For example, the previously mentioned Secondlife.com

Figure 7.18

Highlighting the newest trends as well as directing traffic to individual brands' Web sites, Polyvore provides exposure to millions of viewers.

(Published by permission of Polyvore. All other rights reserved.)

Figure 7.19

A sample set—according to Polyvore, 30,000 new sets are created every day.

(Set "No" created by Polyvore Member "this hot person". This set contains the following items from the following retailer websites: Milton Jersey Dress/Diane von Furstenberg/mytheresa. com. Published by permission of Polyvore. All other rights reserved.)

is a demonstration of virtual environments where users move and interact with places and objects through the use of avatars (virtual characters). The prospects of these virtual environments have been the focus of many new studies that aim at integrating various technologies to create more interactive and seamless experiences that may eventually blur the lines between what is real and what is virtual. Advances in animation movement (think of the movie *Avatar*) will soon be brought to these applications, allowing online avatars to not only have a more real-life movement and look but be better integrated among applications. For example, users will eventually be able to move their avatars between virtual worlds so that a visitor to Second Life can walk into another virtual world carrying their possessions with them. It is really like going shopping in a virtual mall, moving from one location to the other while matching and comparing items. This level of seamless integration will open the door for new shopping habits and the ultimate goal of integrating real-life shopping with a virtual one. One of the greatest future developments anticipated in this area is the introduction of "virtual reality touch." A haptic technology (haptic is from the Greek haptesthai, meaning to touch; in technology it refers to the science of the sense of touch) is being tested at Queen's University, Ireland, that will bring the sense of touch to the virtual world. The field of haptic technology will allow a future where shoppers can feel the products they want to buy online. This technology is already being seen in some racquet-based sports games in Nintendo's Wii where players can feel the weight and impact of the ball. Thus, if we revisit our example of the Giorgio Armani store in Second Life, we can imagine a time when you can visit the virtual store, touch and feel the weight and texture of the garment,

carry it (virtually) to another location where you can check a matching accessory, try them all on your avatar, then maybe send a photo to your friends' cell phones to have their opinions before you make the final purchase online or send the info to your local store for you to pick up on your way home—all taking place without leaving your seat.

The Power of the "i"

The technology examples mentioned in this chapter may quickly be replaced by, or developed into, more advanced applications, as is always the case with technology. However, what these new technologies and examples have established are a few important trends that are here to stay, such as the rise of the consumer and user as the true marketer behind the brand. They also demonstrate how market segmentation can be taken to a more microlevel as a result of the need and ease of the personalization of the marketing message. Thus, market structures and segments, consumer habits and roles, and the dynamics of the branding process are all changing. The forces are shifting faster toward empowering the consumer. It's the power of the "i" and the birth of the iBrand.

Chapter Summary

- New technologies and models are empowering and redefining the role of the consumer in the branding process.

- As the role of the consumer changes, so do the dynamics of the branding process.

- New technologies also create new growth and communication opportunities.

- The concept of positioning may need to be revised under the new models.

- Technology integration creates a new environment of interactive shopping experience that may eventually blur the lines between our real and virtual worlds.

Chapter Questions and Issues for Discussion

1. Given the discussion on mass customization, the model seems to hold new opportunities for young entrepreneurs considered to establish a new business. Highlight the advantages and challenges of the model from an entrepreneurial perspective.

2. Compare the way luxury and mass-market brands adopted the new technologies. What are the opportunities and challenges that each segment may encounter?

3. Based on the chapter arguments and your personal analysis, how would you interpret the term *iBrand*?

KEY TERMS

IBRAND

MASS CUSTOMIZATION

M-BRANDING

RFID

TECHNOLOGY INTEGRATION

VIRTUAL COMMUNITIES

WIRELESS TECHNOLOGIES

CASE STUDY: **Boo.com**

"Unless we raise $20 million by midnight, boo.com is dead."
Ernst Malmsten, boo.com CEO, May 17, 2000

Boo.com was the brainchild of Swedish entrepreneurs Ernst Malmsten, founder of Bokus.com, a European online bookseller, and Kajsa Leander, a fashion model. (See Figure 7.20.) They were eventually joined by Patrik Hedelin, an investment banker at HSBC Holdings who had worked with Malmsten earlier on Bokus. com. Together the three founded Boo.com in 1999 with great anticipation, media fanfare, and the financial backing of some of the world's heaviest investors, such as LVMH and JPMorgan, only to pull the plug within six months of the launch.

The Concept

Boo.com was envisioned as the Amazon.com equivalent for fashion and sportswear, a world-loading e-tailer for prestigious brands such as DKNY, Polo Ralph Lauren, Nike, Fila, Lacoste, and Adidas. However, Boo was not just about the products sold, but the shopping experience, global reach, and new technologies. It was meant to be more than just a shopping Web site; it was supposed to represent *a lifestyle*.

The Product

Boo.com was to offer its mix of top and trendy fashion and sportswear products at full retail price in an engaging Web site offered in multiple languages. The site was to enable shoppers to view every product in full color and from various angels on three dimensional models, along with the ability to zoom in and rotate them to examine all details. Items could be searched by color, brand, price, style, and even sport. And with the goal of catering to a global clientele, the site featured a universal sizing system based on size variations among brands and countries. The site also introduced Miss Boo, an animated avatar that interacted with visitors by giving styling advice based on specific activities or geographic location. One of the site's most appealing services was its quick delivery within one week, with free returns from any location through its 24-hour operating service center. To emphasize the lifestyle concept of Boo.com, they launched *Boom* magazine, which was available online in different languages and contained articles about movies, music, fashion, sports, and editorials, all of which reflected the urban lifestyle Boo.com aimed to represent.

The Customer

The Boo.com team did not really do much traditional market research at the early stages of their venture; instead they relied on the vague idea of who their customer might be and the pioneering proposal on hand. The team perceived their target customer to be between the ages of 24 and 40 and saw themselves as the perfect profile. However, in a meeting with Jerry Fiedler, chairman of Leagas Delaney Advertising Agency, Fielder advised them to focus on the 18-to-24-year-old customers. As he explained, this group includes the influential trendsetters in the market—younger customers like to dress like they are 18 and those above 30 who dress like they are 24. He also advised them to visit department stores to learn about their merchandise mix and the power of different brands: to compare which brands were showcased in their windows (mainly expensive and exclusive young designer clothes to gain fashion credibility and entice customers into the store) with those actually filling most racks (the more mainstream brands).

Figure 7.20

Boo.com founders Kajsa Leander and Ernst Malmsten.

(© Lars Tunbjork)

The Identity

Boo.com relied on three elements to create a sensory, exciting quality and modern identity for their brand. These were its name, Web design, and character Miss Boo.

The Site Design

The team spent a lot of time perfecting the aesthetics and visual appeal of the site. They created a modern hip design with a distinctive orange color and soft modern fonts dominating its look. As their only selling outlet, the site was the company's window to the world and therefore perceived by the team as a major marketing tool. However, many believed that so much emphasis on marketing appeal eventually hampered the functionality and practicality of the design.

The Name

The name is probably the most intriguing of all the site's attributes. Choosing the name was not an easy task: Their goal was to pick one that was easy to pronounce globally and would work well in various media. Toying with various options, such as "sneaky.com" among others, the team finally stopped at Bo.com. Bo was a name inspired by movie actress Bo Derek, famous for her role in the movie 10, whom they perceived to portray a retro image. The name was appealing because it was short, easy to remember and pronounce, and meant nothing in particular. However, the domain Bo.com was already taken, so they decided to add another "o," ending up with Boo.com instead.

Miss Boo

Miss Boo was a virtual sales assistant meant to guide visitors through the site, offering advice, and creating a fun interactive experience. Miss Boo was an important identity component because she was the face of the company. Accordingly, the challenge of deciding on her looks and style was neither easy nor cheap. One of the most controversial decisions to make for

Miss Boo was the style and color of her hair. Miss Boo was meant to reflect the site's lifestyle and character while appealing to its international clientele without representing just one race or group. To assist in her styling, therefore, they hired international hair stylist Eugene Soulemain, known for his work with Hollywood stars and fashion houses like Prada. In addition, they hired Glenn O'Brian, a well-known New York style commentator, to make Miss Boo's statements cool and fun and, most important, possess an international appeal rather than one specifically European. For example, when asked "How old are you Miss Boo?" she offers the flip response, "None of your business, but I'm legal." And to the question, "What's your background?" she cleverly threw back, "For somebody two-dimensional, my background is remarkably deep."

Proposed Values

The new venture and business model seemed like a very attractive proposal with promising values and benefits for all its stakeholders, such as its customers, suppliers, and investors.

- *For customers:* Boo.com aimed to offer customers around the world a unique shopping experience. The goal was to be the first global retailer of sportswear and fashion on a customer friendly, cutting-edge site, with 24/7 worldwide access to an unlimited selection of brands that would otherwise be difficult to find in one place. This was to be backed with excellent customer service and a system of quick delivery with free returns.
- *For suppliers:* At a time when e-tailing was in its infancy, Boo.com offered suppliers global reach and an online outlet that was not meant to be a discount site.

- *For investors:* The team managed to secure the financial backing of some of the world's biggest investors, including LVMH from France, the Benetton family from Italy, investors from the Middle East, and financial institutions such as JPMorgan, among others. At a time when everything related to the Internet was attractive, and big investment decisions were being made based on potential rather than accurate and detailed financial analysis and projections, Boo.com was particularly attractive for its aggressive vision, innovative technology, global reach, and growth potential, especially because most online businesses back then were mainly national operations. After all, "e-commerce was supposed to be global," declared a JPMorgan executive. Accordingly, the company was attractive enough to secure $130 million in investments and at one point was valued at $390 million.

Communication

"...the biggest, boldest bet in the short history of electronic shopping."
— Herald Tribune

The team believed that with their business model and an aggressive promotional strategy the company would create what they called its "big bang" rate of growth, achieving an estimated customer base of 500,000 by the end of their first year. They focused on a PR strategy that gained coverage in influential consumer and trade publications, such as *WWD* and the *Financial Times*. And with an estimated $25 million dedicated to advertisements in expensive, trendy fashion magazines such as *Vogue* and *Vanity Fair*, as well as on cable television and the Internet before their Web site had been launched, they managed to attract about 350,000 e-mail preregistrations from people who wanted to be notified of the site's launch date. Boo.com was greatly anticipated and perceived by many as the biggest new thing on the Internet.

The Challenges

Initially, Boo.com was meant to launch in May 1999 with an IPO to follow in six to nine months. However, in spite of all the excitement, Boo was hit by a wave of challenges both at the business model level as well as at the technical, operational, and financial ones, forcing it to postpone the launch date more than once.

Some of these challenges can be summarized as follows:

- Inventory management was challenging, because the model Malmsten had adopted earlier with Bokus.com—in which it purchased items only after they were sold online rather than carrying any inventory in advance—could not work for Boo.com. Most suppliers would not agree to sell their items on an order-to-order basis because this would have required that they always keep these items available in their warehouses. Given the seasonal nature of the fashion product, this system would never have worked. Suppliers prefer advance orders that allow them to manage their inventory accordingly rather than fill their warehouses with old seasons' merchandise.
- Another hurdle with merchandise was that some suppliers such as New Balance did not respond favorably to their initial partnership proposal because they already had an international presence or representation with other partners.

- In order to overcome the anticipated reluctance of online customers to purchase fashion products they hadn't tried on or touched first, Boo.com decided to offer customers free returns from any location. For an international operation with an operational network in various countries, this meant they had to be prepared to cope with a very high level of returns because customers in these cases tend to order different items in different sizes and colors to try them on before making their final decision (which is also a common problem with the catalogue industry).
- Postage paid, free return policy also meant dealing with different mailing systems and costs, which seemed a bit complicated, especially on the European side.

Here is how it worked: All European orders were packed from the warehouse in Cologne, Germany. When a French customer placed an order, French postal service La Poste labels would be put on the box so that it appeared as if it were shipped directly from France. Meanwhile, the package would be transferred with other items from Cologne to a location in France, where it was then sent through regular French mail. In the case of returns, the item was to be sent to a given French address where all returned items were collected and sent back to the warehouse in Germany. This unique approach meant that every sale was, in a way, taxed three times because the company's headquarters and servers were in London with operating offices in France and its distribution center in Germany.

- Some experts questioned the viability of their concept, selling both fashion and sportswear items in one place. To them it was not clear if Boo.com was to be positioned as a fashion company or a sports one. And when the reply was "both," they believed it would never work, given that each industry approaches its market differently. For instance, the sports goods market is known to be particularly specific and focused in its marketing and distribution channels.

- With the large amount of product to sell came the huge task of developing a database that would accommodate around 50 pieces of descriptive information referring to the size, color, and price of each product in more than one language and currency.

- The biggest challenge of all was technology. Although some of the proposed technological applications may seem common and easy to adopt today, in 1999 they created a series of bottlenecks and headaches:

  — For most existing e-tailers at the time, such as Amazon.com, the technology platform was built in-house as they started small and then gradually grew. Yet in the case of a global operation such as Boo.com, it had no choice but to rely on another party to develop the needed infrastructure that would accommodate a multilingual version of the site with a ballooning database to cover different price, tax, and postal options based on each country.

  — As Boo.com's Web site was the only selling outlet for the company, it needed to be attractive, sophisticated, with plans to heavily use 3D, animation, Flash applications, java scripts, photos, and a range of frills. Yet back in 1999, many of these byte-hungry technologies were in their infancy, and most Internet users still connected through dial-up with a maximum speed of

54k. A reporter expressed the frustrating experience in his own words: " . . . 81 minutes to pay too much money for a pair of shoes that I'm still going to have to wait a week to get." Even the constant presence of Miss Boo seemed to be an annoying feature to some. (See Figure 7.21.)

  — Another major access problem and technical embarrassment that haunted the system was the inability of Mac computers' users to complete their orders.

  — The project management was a nightmare, given that at one point they were dealing with about 18 different technology companies from all over the world with no central architect. The result was an unavoidable range of system bugs and glitches.

  — The huge database was not well managed nor synchronized, leading to product mismatches and confusion that eventually meant customers would not be able to buy the right product or obtain the right information.

The End of Boo.com

With many technical issues and frustrations, Malmsten launched PROJECT LAUNCH, an operational plan meant to tackle seven main areas: bug fixing, business testing, technology operations, merchandising operations, order fulfillment, customer operations, and operational resourcing.

Among the measures taken was delaying the launch date, which also meant cancelling many of the planned marketing events and ads. However, the greatest challenge was raising about $60 million to finance the three-month delay. The plan yielded some positive results. When the site finally

Figure 7.21

Boo.com's virtual sales assistant Miss Boo was an important element of the site's identity. Here she entices potential customers to get involved by taking a quiz that "she" has created and potentially win $1,000 worth spending money on the site.

(Boo.com)

launched on November 3, 1999, it hosted around 50,000 visitors on the first day. However, they had only a 0.25% conversion rate, meaning only 4 in every 1,000 visitors placed an order. The low conversion was partly due to the still-existing technical difficulties and confusion in placing orders. The site was buggy, even causing some visitors' computers to freeze, and about 40 percent of the visitors could not even gain access.

Although the company managed to work on and solve many of these glitches, as well as more than double the conversion rate to 0.98 percent before Christmas, the negative publicity buildup was inevitable. The high costs and excess spending did not help either. Boo.com spent lavishly, had a presence in more than 18 countries, and for a company that employed over 350 people when it started with 30, Boo was overstaffed with overpaid employees scattered in its international offices. Accordingly, in its first 18 months, the company had managed to spend $135 million of investors' money.

Sales were lagging badly and the company running out of cash. Their ad agency BMP filed claims and UPS refused to distribute unless paid in full. Boo.com began selling clothing at a 40 percent

discount and laying off employees as well as cancelling Kajsa's baby project, *Boom* magazine.

In a final attempt to salvage the business, Malmsten considered making available to outside companies the spare capacity of Boo.com's technological and logistic platform capable of handling a growing number of orders and shipments in Europe and the United States within five days. The new restructuring plan required an urgent injection of cash, and the new funding target was $20 million to be raised by midnight, May 17. Yet by that deadline, the company had only managed to raise $12 million, which was not enough. Addressing the board members in a phone conference, Christopher Heather, Boo.com's legal council, warned, "I hope everyone understands what this means: if you don't put up more money, the company will go bust." The long silence that followed said it all. The same day, Malmsten hired a liquidating firm. On May 18, the Web site was shut down. The headline in the *Financial Times* article read, "Boo.com collapses as investors refuse funds." The article then declared, "Online sports retailer becomes Europe's first big internet casualty." Boo.com was closed.

CASE STUDY Questions

1. Compare Boo.com to an existing e-tailer (such as Zappos.com) and evaluate their differences and similarities.

2. Using the concepts learned thus far in this book, create a brand profile for Boo.com, highlighting its concept, value, identity, and so on. From a branding perspective, why did it fail?

SOURCES

Chaffey, Dave, and Fiona Ellis-Chadwick, et al. *Internet marketing: Strategy, implementations and practice.* Harlow: Pearson Education Limited, 2009.

Lanxon, Nate. "The greatest defunct Web sites and dotcom disasters," Crave: The Gadget Blog from CNET UK, January 5, 2008. http://crave.cnet.co.uk/gadgets/0,39029552,49296926-3,00.htm (accessed April 5, 2010).

Louis, Tristan. "Boo.com goes bust," tnl.net, May 19, 2000. http://www.tnl.net/blog/2000/05/19/boocom-goes-bust/ (accessed March 24, 2010).

Malmsten, Ernst, and Erik Portanger, et al., *Boo hoo.* London: Random House, 2001.

Slatalla, Michelle. "Boo.com tries again, humbled and retooled." *New York Times*, January 11, 2001. http://www.nytimes.com/2001/01/11/technology/online-shopper-boocom-tries-again-humbled-and-retooled.html?pagewanted=1 (accessed April 2, 2010).

Sorkin, Andrew Ross. "From big idea to big bust: The wild ride of Boo.com." *New York Times*, December 13, 2000. http://www.nytimes.com/2000/12/13/business/from-big-idea-to-big-bust-the-wild-ride-of-boocom.html?pagewanted=1 (accessed June 27, 2009).

ENDNOTES

1. Henry Ford, *My Life and Work* (Whitefish, Montana: Kessinger Publishing, 2003), chapter iv.

2. Marina Kamenev, "Adidas' High Tech Footwear," *BusinessWeek*, November 2006. http://www.businessweek.com/innovate/content/nov2006/id20061103_196323.htm

3. www.louisvuitton.com

4. Alicia De Mesa, *Brand Avatar* (London: Palgrave, 2009), 33.

5. www.istorez.com

6. F. Piller, K. Moeslein, and C. Stoko, "Does Mass Customization Pay? An Economic Approach to Evaluate Customer Integration," *Production Planning & Control*, 15, no. 4 (June 2004): 435–444.

7. Rick Mathieson, *Branding Unbound* (New York: AMACOM, 2005), 147.

8. Ibid.

9. Jason Jobson, "Fashion Apps: The New Wave of Mobile Fashion PR," The Fashion Rag (March 12, 2009). http://www.piercemattiepublicrelations.com/fashionprdivision/2009/03/fashion_apps_the_new_wave_of_m.html

10. Product Overview, LRAD Corporation. http://www.lradx.com/site/content/view/13/104/

11. Tomi Ahonen and Alan Moore, *Communities Dominate Brands* (London: Futuretest, 2005), 101.

12. *PC Today*, November 2010, 9.

13. Ross Tucker. "Memo Pad: First In Line," *WWD*, April 22, 2010, 15.

14. http://www.polyvore.com

Part II

Intellectual Property Issues

	Subject Matter	Scope of Protection (Standard for Infringement)	Advantages/Disadvantages
Trademark/ Trade Dress	**Trademark:** Distinctive logos, names, images, designs that indicate the source of the product. **Trade dress:** The characteristic and distinctive visual presentation of a product; may include packaging and design elements.	**Trademark:** Registered trademarks provide nation-wide protection against confusingly similar marks. **Trade dress:** Unregistered trade dress is protectable for distinctive packaging and for designs that have established secondary meaning by being recognized by the public. **Duration:** Indefinite, but the mark must continue to be used in commerce.	**Trademark:** • **Pros:** Long duration, covers entire product line, rewards branding investments. • **Cons:** International registrations or on multiple style or product lines can become expensive. **Trade dress:** • **Pros:** Can protect the "look" of a brand. • **Cons:** May require establishment of secondary meaning.
Patent	**Utility patent:** New, useful and non-obvious devices, processes, formulae, or compositions, e.g., new fabrics, fasteners, production methods. **Design patent:** New ornamental designs for non-functional features or aspects of manufactured products.	**Utility patent:** Protects against products that make use of the patented process or composition or copy the patented product. **Design patent:** Protects against copies that appear to an ordinary observer to be the same as the patented design. **Duration:** Utility patent—20 years. Design patent—14 years.	**Utility patent:** • **Pros:** Broad protection against infringing products. • **Cons:** Application process is onerous, can be expensive and difficult to obtain. **Design patent:** • **Pros:** Strong protection for design elements of fashion products like shoes, eyewear, bags. • **Cons:** Can take from 8 to 24 months to obtain, slow for fashion cycle.
Copyright	Original, creative works that have been fixed in a tangible medium. In fashion, can apply to fabric prints, jewelry, images on fashion items, photography, sculptural elements of fashion items or accessories, fashion photography.	Protects against copies that are substantially similar to the original. **Duration:** For works created by individuals—70 years after the life of the creator. For works for hire (owned by corporations)—95 years after publication or 120 years after creation, whichever comes first.	**Pros:** Easy and inexpensive to obtain, long-lasting production, good international protection. **Cons:** Does not apply to fashion designs or to elements of products that are dictated by functional rather than purely aesthetic considerations.

2

Trademarks and Trade Dress

Marc Misthal

Trademarks are perhaps the most widely recognized form of IP in the fashion industry. This chapter covers the scope of trademark protection, registration procedures, the issue of trade dress protection for packaging and design, international protection of trademarks, and Internet domain name issues related to trademark. We begin with an overview of IP protection as it applies to fashion and apparel items generally, then move on to a detailed discussion of trademark and trade dress.

2.1. Introduction: IP Protection of Fashion and Apparel

This section introduces the various types of IP rights that apply to fashion. The first key concept to understanding IP as it relates to fashion is that of *multiple protection*: a single garment or product may be covered by several different forms of legal protection at the same time. Consider a dress with a screen print of a photograph, as well as the company logo, on the front and a brand name on its label. The logo and brand name are protected as trademarks, but the photographic image is protected by copyright. If the dress is fabricated from an innovative microfiber that the company developed, this textile could be protected by a utility patent. Thus, this single garment could have three different kinds of potential IP protection. A competitor of the company that produced this dress interested in imitating or knocking off the dress must be very careful not to infringe upon *any* of the first company's valid IP. As we will see in greater detail, a company may be able to produce a legally valid imitative product, but it must first be careful not to imitate a protected logo or brand name, not to use a copyrighted image or photograph, and not to reproduce a patented fabric.

A second key concept in the IP of fashion is that *fashion design* is generally not currently protected under U.S. law, though there are exceptions, which we will explore in this and subsequent chapters. When we refer to a fashion "design" in this regard, we are referring to the way a specific garment is cut and assembled. We are not referring to the drawings and patterns from which the garment was derived but rather to the construction of the garment itself (note that from this perspective a garment still has a design even if it was constructed without an

Allison Tennenbaum, who worked as an intern for Mr. Misthal's law firm, Gottlieb, Rackman & Reisman, P.C., aided in the preparation of this chapter.

Fashion Law *in Court*

Trademark Infringement? You Decide

Most fashion consumers can easily spot a classic Louis Vuitton bag even at a distance. Louis Vuitton has used its famous Toile Monogram trademark on trunks and accessories since 1897. The Toile Monogram consists of the "LV" initials, a curved diamond with a four-point star inset, its negative, and a circle with a four-leafed inset. However, in 2002 Louis Vuitton decided to revamp its image by launching a "new signature series" handbag line designed by Japanese artist Takashi Murakami, which updated the Toile mark by printing it in bright colors on white or black backgrounds. Bags with these new designs were widely advertised and promoted. Shortly thereafter, competitor Dooney & Bourke launched its own series of bags using a "DB" monogram in an array of bright colors set against a white background. The new Dooney & Bourke bags were visually similar to the Louis Vuitton bags, and their design was clearly inspired by Louis Vuitton's, but had Dooney & Bourke crossed the line, committing trademark infringement?

A handbag from the Louis Vuitton line designed by artist Takashi Murakami. (*Courtesy of Fairchild Publications, Inc.*)

Dooney & Bourke's handbag was inspired by the Murakami line but did not constitute trademark infringement. (*Courtesy of Fairchild Publications, Inc.*)

After sending a notice letter, Louis Vuitton sought a preliminary injunction (a court order) in the District Court directing Dooney & Bourke to stop selling the allegedly infringing bags. In the end, Louis Vuitton's case was thrown out of court without a trial. The Court found insufficient evidence to establish a likelihood of confusion between the D&B bags and the LV bags. The Court ruled that a defendant's product may "remind" the public of a plaintiff's product and still not constitute illegal "confusion."

Sources: Louis Vuitton Malletier v. Dooney & Bourke, Inc., 454 F.3d 108 (2d Cir. 2006) and *Louis Vuitton Malletier v. Dooney & Bourke, Inc.*, 561 F. Supp.2d 368 (S.D.N.Y. 2008).

original drawing). Thus, even when a garment possesses an innovative and unusual design, it is usually not illegal to copy the precise construction of the garment, even if in the end the two garments are virtually indistinguishable. It is surprising to many fashion professionals that one of the most creative aspects of their industry, fashion design for garments, does not receive specific legal protection. In contrast, the European Union and certain other countries do provide a specific kind of protection for fashion designs. Similar legislation has recently been proposed in the United States and may one day become law, as discussed in the following chapters. There is always an exception to every rule, and *occasionally* the cut of a garment can be protected by a *design patent* or *trade dress*, discussed later in this chapter and in Chapter 4, "Design Patents, Utility Patents, and Trade Secrets."

2.2. The Scope of Trademark Protection

Trademarks protect consumers and producers by enabling customers to distinguish between products made by different companies. Trademarks can include brand names, slogans, logos, and designs. A "service mark" is a trademark for service providers.

Fashion designers often use their names to identify product lines, as in the cases of Ralph Lauren, Calvin Klein, and Diane von Furstenberg. Personal names may be protected as trademarks only if the designer can establish that the public has come to recognize the designer's name as identifying the source of the designer's products. As a general rule, this takes several years of significant advertising and promotional efforts.

In some cases successful designers may wish to leave a fashion company in order to start their own enterprises. If the company the designer is leaving was using the designer's name (with the designer's permission) for its own line of products, the designer may be surprised to discover that he or she is not entirely free to make use of his or her own name. There is no absolute right to use one's personal name if doing so would create confusion in the marketplace. While courts are generally reluctant to forbid a person from using his or her own name as a trademark,[1] they will do so if such restraint is necessary to avoid marketplace confusion.[2]

Practice Tip: Trademarking a Designer's Name

A fashion company wishing to market apparel under a trademark consisting of a designer's name should do the following:

► File a trademark application to register the designer's name at the U.S. Patent and Trademark Office (PTO).

► Negotiate a clear-cut agreement setting forth the conditions under which the designer may use that name in the event of a departure from the company.

If you are the designer:

► Consider filing your own trademark application to obtain a registration for your name and then license it to the company on a royalty basis.

► Negotiate a clear-cut agreement setting forth the conditions under which you may use your name if you and the company part ways.

Fashion Designers' Personal Names as Trademarks

While courts are generally reluctant to forbid a person from using his or her own name, they will do so if such restraint is necessary to avoid confusion in the marketplace. For example, Paolo Gucci, the former chief designer of Gucci and grandson of its founder, was prohibited by a court from using the name "Gucci" as part of any trademark or trade name. Paolo Gucci was allowed to use his name only to identify himself as the designer of the products sold under a separate name.

Similarly, Paul Frank Industries, Inc. ("PFI") once brought a trademark infringement action against its former namesake designer, Paul Frank Sunich, alleging that Sunich's continued use of his own name in the sale of T-shirts after he had left PFI violated PFI's trademark rights. The court enjoined Sunich from using his name in areas (such as clothing) where the public had come to associate the use of Paul Frank with PFI. The court also ruled that if Sunich identified himself as the designer of products in other areas, those products would still have to bear a disclaimer stating that Sunich is no longer affiliated with PFI.

In 2000, menswear designer Joseph Abboud sold the trademark "Joseph Abboud" to JA Apparel Corp. for $65 million dollars. Abboud was contractually prohibited from competing with the company for a period of two years. Abboud later clashed with JA Apparel's management and chose to part ways with them. After the expiration of the non-compete period, Abboud announced his plans for a new line called "jaz," which would use the tagline "a new composition by designer Joseph Abboud." JA Apparel Corp. sued Aboud, alleging that such usage amounted to trademark infringement and violation of the parties' noncompete agreement. The district court agreed with JA Apparel in virtually all respects, finding that Abboud had sold both the right to use his name as a trademark on clothing and his right to publicize his new jaz line by using his name in a tagline. On appeal, however, the Second Circuit ruled that the contract between Abboud and JA Apparel was far from clear on the issue of "fair use," that is, on whether Abboud could identify himself as the designer of the new jaz line of clothing. The appeals court vacated the injunction granted by the district court and instructed that the case be remanded to the lower court for a ruling on the permissible extent of Abboud's non-trademark use of his own name.

These cases demonstrate the great care with which contracts to buy, sell, and restrict use of names as trademarks must be prepared.

Sources: Paul Frank Industries, Inc. v. Paul Sunich, 502 F.Supp.2d 1094 (S.D. Cal. 2007); *Paolo Gucci v. Gucci Shops, Inc.*, 688 F.Supp. 916 (S.D.N.Y. 1988); Ray A. Smith, "JA Apparel Sues Designer Abboud," *Wall St. Journal*, September 5, 2007, at B3; *JA Apparel Corp. v. Abboud*, 591 F. Supp. 2d 306 (S.D.N.Y 2008), rev'd 568 F.3d 390 (2d Cir. 2009).

2.3. Obtaining Trademark Protection

A certain minimal level of trademark protection can be obtained simply by placing the trademark on products and selling those products to consumers, even if the trademark has not been registered at the state or federal level. In such a case, one is said to possess "common law trademark" rights. However, the scope of protection afforded common law marks is quite narrow: they provide protection only in the geographical area in which the goods are sold. For this and other reasons, most serious business users will seek to register their important trademarks by filing a trademark application in the PTO. A federally registered trademark confers nationwide rights.[3]

2.4. Selecting a Strong Trademark

Not all ideas for trademarks are good ones. A well-chosen trademark will be strong from both the business and legal perspectives. From the business perspective, an ideal trademark will be one that is memorable and striking, and in addition, it may be desirable for the trademark to convey some positive quality or association with the product or service. Many large corporations employ special consultants to develop potential brand names and trademarks. Toyota's selection of the Lexus trademark for its luxury car division was based on such an approach. In today's global marketplace it is also wise to consider the potential international usage of a trademark. There are many famous examples of trademarks that are effective in the home country but not in others. The Danish toilet paper brand Krapp, the French soft drink brand Pschitt, and the Japanese soft drink brand Pocari Sweat are trademarks that work well in their home markets but have limited appeal in the United States and other English-speaking countries.

From a legal perspective as well, some potential trademarks are more advisable than others. First of all, the trademark must be available—it must neither duplicate nor be confusingly similar to an existing trademark for the given type of product. If you would like to name your shoe brand Adidas or your jeans brand Calvin Klein, it is simply too late; those names have been taken—hence the importance of conducting a proper trademark search before deciding on a name. However, even if no one has registered your proposed mark, it still may not be advisable from a legal point of view. In the law, trademarks are classified in a hierarchy from strong to weak, and weak marks may be ineligible for legal protection:

1. Strongest—Arbitrary or fanciful trademarks
2. Next strongest—Suggestive trademarks
3. May be strong or weak depending on circumstances—Descriptive trademarks
4. Weak—Generic trademarks

Let us begin our discussion with the weakest type of mark, which should always be avoided: the *generic* mark. A generic mark is one in which the proposed trademark consists of the same commonly used term by which the product is known to the general public. Thus, you would not be allowed by the PTO to register the Denim Pants trademark for your jeans line, nor could you obtain trademark protection for a sneaker line called Athletic Shoes. The reasoning behind this limitation is that no one should be able to restrict everyday usage of a common term. In some cases, therefore, it is possible for a trademark to be too successful if the mark enters the everyday lexicon as the most common descriptor for a particular type of product or service. In such cases, the trademark is said to have become *generic* and trademark protection will no longer be afforded. Among the most famous examples of this fate are *aspirin* and *escalator*, trademarks that became so widely used that the original trademark owners lost the right to prevent others from using those marks.

Stronger than a generic mark but still potentially questionable is the *descriptive* mark, a mark that describes a characteristic of a good or service, for example, Tough Denim or Sheer Silk. One commonly encountered type of descriptive mark is the geographically descriptive one, as in Brooklyn Brewery. The main problem with descriptive marks is that they are not entitled to strong protection until they acquire "secondary meaning," which refers to the recognition by the public that the mark is used on particular products sold by a specific provider. Such secondary meaning may be obtained only through use of the mark in interstate commerce for a significant period of time—in other words, by selling products bearing the mark.

A *suggestive* mark evokes images and requires an imaginative leap to conclude the nature of the goods or services. An example of a suggestive mark is "Coppertone." Suggestive marks are generally quite strong.

An *arbitrary* mark is a mark that is surprising in the context in which it is used, and a *fanciful* mark is a made-up word. An example of an arbitrary mark is "Apple" for computers, and examples of a fanciful mark are "Exxon" or "Oreo." Arbitrary and fanciful marks are the strongest types of marks from a legal perspective.

2.5. Trademark Searching

After selecting a potential mark, the next step is to check the Trademark Electronic Search System (TESS) on the PTO website to determine whether the mark is already being used in connection with similar goods and/or services. If the mark is to be an important one, such as a "house mark" (the trademark by which the company is known to the public), then a comprehensive search of various additional sources is necessary. If the mark to be adopted is intended for a less important use (such as for a line or style name), the company may decide to skip a comprehensive search and rely instead only on a TESS and an Internet search. Because common law trademark rights may be acquired when a mark is put into use, it is not strictly necessary to register less important marks in all cases, especially if they will not be in use for a long time. However, some kind of search should be conducted for every mark the company adopts.

Evaluating the results of a trademark search is a good example of the value that can be provided by an experienced fashion law practitioner. Frequently a trademark search reveals that similar trademarks are already in use or that the same trademark is used but for a different category of product. In such cases, is it advisable to proceed with a registration? An attorney can provide a formal written opinion stating that the proposed mark does not violate existing trademark rights. Preparation of such opinion letters often requires the company and its attorney to discuss and work through the legal issues involved. If the attorney raises concerns with the mark, the company and attorney may collaborate to rework or revise the mark to reduce or eliminate the likelihood of infringement or of rejection by the PTO. If a desired mark is already registered for the proposed use by another party, the PTO will not allow the second mark to be registered. In such cases, it may be sufficient to make slight changes to the mark, such as by making it a stylized or design mark, or it may be sufficient to identify a more specific good or service to which the mark will apply. In any case, a strong advantage of consulting expert IP counsel is that a company that received a formal opinion letter from an attorney is much less likely to be deemed a willful or intentional infringer by the courts in the event of an infringement suit. Thus, the opinion letter process not only reduces the chances of an infringement lawsuit, it also limits a company's exposure and damages if a suit does occur.

2.6. The Trademark Registration Process

Federal trademark registrations[4] offer benefits not available to common law trademarks. First, federally registered marks receive nationwide protection. Second, federally registered marks can be recorded with the U.S. Customs Service so that Customs can be enlisted in the prevention of importation of infringing or counterfeit goods[5] (note that this benefit is available only to marks registered on the "principal register" as opposed to the "supplemental register"[6]). In addition, federally registered marks are presumed valid in trademark infringement litigation.[7]

2.6.1. Marks That Cannot Be Registered

The Trademark Office will not register "immoral" or "scandalous" marks (a registration was refused for "c**k sucker"[8]). Similarly, deceptive and disparaging marks will not be registered, nor will marks that falsely suggest a connection with a person, institution, or national symbol.[9] Geographic indications cannot be registered if the mark misleadingly identifies a place other than the actual origin of the good.[10] A name, portrait, or signature of a person cannot be registered as a trademark without that individual's consent.[11] A trademark will also be refused if it consists of merely a surname.[12] Any mark that conflicts with an already registered mark cannot be registered.[13]

2.6.2. Preparing and Filing the Trademark Application

It is possible to file a trademark application prior to using a mark in commerce in order to prevent others from filing the same or a similar mark. However, such an "intent to use" application cannot mature into a trademark registration until proof is submitted that the mark is actually being used in commerce. Alternatively, the application can be filed based on actual use of the mark, meaning that the mark has been affixed to goods sold in commerce. With a use-based application, proof of commercial use is filed with the application; with an intent-to-use application, proof of use is filed later in the process.[14]

Trademark applications must contain the following information:

▸ Owner of the mark
▸ Address of the owner
▸ Drawing of the mark

- ▶ The goods or services to which the mark will apply
- ▶ Attorney's name and address, if using one
- ▶ Declaration/signature
- ▶ Payment[15]

It is advisable to include email addresses and other contact information for the applicant.

Use-based applications must include the date on which the mark was first used anywhere and the date on which it was first used in interstate or international commerce.[16] A specimen that shows use of the mark, which must be identical to the drawing in the application,[17] must also accompany the application. For use-based applications, the specimen must be filed with the application. With intent-to-use applications, the specimen is generally filed after the application has been examined and published for opposition. The Trademark Office is very particular as to what it will accept as a specimen, and no trademark registration will issue unless an acceptable specimen has been submitted.[18] Typically, a label, hang tag, or packaging is an acceptable specimen; in some instances a photograph of the product bearing the mark, catalogue, sign, or point-of-sale display may be acceptable.[19]

Int. Cl.: 18

Prior U.S. Cls.: 1, 2, 3, 22 and 41

Reg. No. 2,052,315

United States Patent and Trademark Office   Registered Apr. 15, 1997

TRADEMARK
PRINCIPAL REGISTER

POLO RALPH LAUREN, L.P. (DELAWARE LIMITED PARTNERSHIP)
650 MADISON AVENUE
NEW YORK, NY 10022

FOR: CLUTCHES, SHOULDER BAGS, COSMETIC BAGS SOLD EMPTY, TOTE BAGS, SADDLE BAGS, BACKPACKS, GYM BAGS, DUFFLE BAGS, TRAVEL BAGS, ROLL BAGS, SLING BAGS, GROOMING KITS SOLD EMPTY, SUIT BAGS, TIE CASES, SATCHELS, POLE BAGS, GARMENT BAGS FOR TRAVEL,

COIN PURSES, DRAWSTRING POUCHES, OVERNIGHT BAGS, WALLETS AND KEY CASES, IN CLASS 18 (U.S. CLS. 1, 2, 3, 22 AND 41).

FIRST USE 12–30–1975; IN COMMERCE 12–30–1975.

OWNER OF U.S. REG. NOS. 1,378,247, 1,512,754 AND OTHERS.

SER. NO. 75–057,170, FILED 2–13–1996.

M. E. BODSON, EXAMINING ATTORNEY

Fig. 2.1. The registration for the Polo trademark.

2.6.3. Examination of Trademark Applications

Trademark applications are reviewed by an examining attorney in the Trademark Office. If the application is deficient in some way, the examining attorney will issue an Office Action requesting correction of the application. For example, this could involve further specifying the goods or services on which the mark will be used. Thus, the Trademark Office will not accept "clothes" as a proper specification of goods. Instead, they require specification of the types of clothes that a mark is used on, so a typical specification might say: "clothing, namely shirts, pants, underwear, skirts and dresses."[20]

An Office Action can also be issued explaining why the PTO refuses to register the mark. If similar marks have been found that are registered or pending and used in connection with the same goods or services, registration will be refused based on the likelihood of confusion. Registration will also be refused for marks found to be principally ornamental or decorative in nature and that do not identify the applicant's goods. Marks may also be refused registration if they are found to be the following: generic; descriptive; geographically deceptive; immoral; deceptive; or scandalous. Upon refusal, the trademark applicant is given 6 months to establish why the mark should be registered.[21] If an applicant is able to overcome all objections, the mark is published in the Official Gazette for opposition. Other trademark owners then have the opportunity to oppose the registration of the mark before the Trademark Trial and Appeal Board (TTAB).

2.6.4. Trademarks for Style Names

It is important to conduct a search of possible style names (names for a given item in a fashion line or collection). If the company adopts a style name for a particular product that is the same as or confusingly similar to a name used by a competitor, it may receive a ccase and desist letter demanding that the name be changed, which can be cumbersome and expensive (in some cases, labels might need to be removed and changed, and products might have to be pulled from stores to do so).[22]

2.7. Costs

A professional trademark search and report by an attorney typically will cost approximately $1,500 to $2,000 (this commonly includes a disbursement of $650 to $750 to the company running the search). In addition, attorneys typically charge $1,500 to $2,000 for handling a trademark application and registration (this includes fees for legal services plus the $325 charged by the PTO—but note that such filing fees may increase depending on the range of products listed in the application).

Practice Tip: Best Practice in Trademarks

▶ Select a trademark that is unusual or a made-up word, for example, Kodak or Exxon; simple or descriptive marks such as "Best" or "Supreme" may be difficult to protect.

► Conduct a thorough trademark search for prior common law and/or registered trademarks. Utilize the marking ™ or ® on labels, hang tags, and packaging to give others notice of your rights.

► Promptly notify copiers of your rights; "sitting" on your rights, hoping to collect more in damages, rarely works.

► If funds are really tight (e.g., you are a small startup) file your own trademark application using the forms on the PTO website.

2.8. Marking on Product

Products should be marked "TM" for trademark or "SM" for service mark. The registration symbol, ®, standing for registered trademark, may be used only when a trademark registration has been issued by the PTO.[23]

2.9. Time Is of the Essence

Common law trademarks are effective as soon as they are actually used on a product that is shipped to a customer. A trademark registration will generally be issued by the PTO about 13 months after an application is filed. Once a trademark is in use or has been registered, a company can prevent a competitor from using the same or a similar mark on the same or similar goods by promptly sending that competitor a *cease and desist letter*. If a company does not act promptly to police its trademark, it may lose its rights to the trademark because the delay may be considered harmful to its competitors. Such a delay may be viewed by a court as evidence that the matter is not urgent and may preclude the availability of injunctive relief.[24] For example, to prevent the Chanel mark from becoming generic, Chanel promptly and aggressively polices its rights and regularly runs ads in *Women's Wear Daily* to remind fashion companies that "Chanel" is a registered trademark and that they must not describe a collarless jacket as "Chanel-style" if it is not a Chanel jacket.

2.10. *Advantages and Limitations of Registered Trademarks*

The main advantage of trademark registration is that it affords strong legal protection against infringing activity anywhere in the United States.[25] However, one important limitation is that a competitor's use of a similar trademark can be stopped only when used in connection with similar goods or services. Trademark protection usually extends only to a particular product category or closely related categories. Thus, even if a company registers a particular mark for clothing, it may not be able to stop someone from using the identical mark for bottled water.

In principle, trademark protection can last forever, though proof of continued usage must be periodically filed with the PTO. As compared with copyright and patent protection, which lasts for only a finite number of years, trademarks afford indefinite protection.

2.11. Trade Dress

2.11.1. The Scope of Trade Dress Protection

Trade dress is a form of IP that may protect a product's physical appearance or presentation, including its shape, size, color, color combinations, texture, graphics, packaging, labeling, or other elements of its overall "look." In order to receive legal protection, the trade dress must be inherently distinctive or have achieved secondary meaning (i.e., be widely recognized by the public as identifying the company that is the source of the product).[26] Courts have applied trade dress protection in very diverse cases, including unique shapes for bottles, colors for pills, and characteristic decorative elements of a restaurant or boutique. The blue Tiffany box and Hermès's Birkin bag are notable examples of trade dress in fashion.

An important limitation is that trade dress protects only nonfunctional elements, or those elements of a product design that are primarily aesthetic (when these elements indicate the source of a product or service). A product element is considered functional when the product would not work properly without that element. Trade dress is deemed functional if it is "essential to the use or purpose of the article or if it affects the cost or quality of the article."[27] Determining whether trade dress is functional requires consideration of the following factors: (1) the existence of a utility patent that discloses the utilitarian advantages of the design,[28] (2) advertising by the applicant that touts the utilitarian advantages of the design, (3) whether alternative designs are available, and (4) whether the design results from a comparatively simple or inexpensive method of manufacture.[29]

Practice Tip: Rely on Copyright; Resort to Trade Dress

► Seek copyright protection before considering trade dress; copyright protection is relatively quick and inexpensive to obtain and is very powerful in court. Resort to trade dress protection only if no other form of protection is available.

► Consult with your IP attorney to see whether your trade dress can be registered as a trademark.

2.11.2. Obtaining Trade Dress Protection

A company can acquire common law rights in trade dress, although these are not as desirable as registered trade dress rights. In determining whether trade dress is protectable, the two most significant factors are functionality and distinctiveness. The Supreme Court has distinguished two categories of protectable trade dress: product design and product packaging.[30] Because product design has been held not to be inherently distinctive, it can be protected only if it has acquired secondary meaning. The party seeking protection must show that consumers have come to associate the trade dress with a particular source.[31] Secondary meaning can be created through use in commerce and through advertising. Product packaging, on the other hand, may be protectable without a showing that consumers associate that packaging with a particular source.[32] When it is hard to distinguish whether a trade dress is product design or product packaging, the courts will err on the side of caution and classify the trade dress as product design.[33]

Fashion Law *in Court*

Protecting Originality: Copyright versus Trade Dress

Knitwaves, a domestic manufacturer of children's knitwear, marketed a line of sweaters with a "fall" motif. One was a multicolored striped sweater with puffy leaf appliqués, while another had a squirrel and leaves appliquéd onto its multipaneled front. A design executive at another firm, Lollytogs, told the manager of his design department that he wanted to introduce a similar line. He instructed the Lollytogs designer to come up with sweater sets with the "same feel" as the Knitwaves sweaters. The Lollytogs designer admitted afterward that she used the Knitwaves sweater as her only reference work. However, she claimed that she had substantially changed the type and placement of leaves and added acorns. When the competitive sweaters came on the market, Knitwaves was unable to sell its full inventory and had to reduce its prices. Knitwaves filed suit against Lollytogs, claiming that Lollytogs sweaters had infringed Knitwaves' intellectual property.

Could Knitwaves' sweaters be protected by copyright or trade dress, and was the copying unlawful? A New York–based appeals court found that the leaf and squirrel designs on the Knitwaves' sweaters were protected by copyright, since they were considered to be artwork. Also, these designs had been registered in the Copyright Office before any litigation had begun.

Having decided that Knitwaves' original leaf and squirrel designs were protected by copyright, the court went on to determine whether the copying by Lollytogs was unlawful. In its defense, Lollytogs argued that all the elements in the Knitwaves' sweaters—squirrels, leaves, and stripes—were in the public domain, and therefore not protectable by copyright. However, the Court refused to follow Lollytogs' reasoning. Instead, the Court ruled that the test for copyright infringement is whether the two items are "substantially similar." In other words, the Court asked whether the two items had the same "total concept and feel." The Court found that because the Lollytogs sweaters used substantially the same "fall" symbols (namely squirrels and leaves), an ordinary purchaser would think they came from the same source. Thus, there was copyright infringement.

The Court also considered whether the Knitwaves' line was protected by trade dress, that is, whether that line was recognized by consumers as coming from a single source, even if they could not name that source. The Court found that Knitwaves' primary objective in the sweater designs was "aesthetic," to market to the public children's clothing that looked fashionable and pleasing, and not primarily to identify itself as the source of the product. It therefore found that these sweaters were not protected by trade dress. This case demonstrates how difficult it can be to obtain trade dress protection.

Source: Knitwaves, Inc. v. Lollytogs Ltd., 71 F.3d 996 (2d Cir. 1995).

In light of the above, acquiring trade dress protection usually requires several years of active sales, advertising, and promotion because the public must have come to associate a particular product's trade dress with the company that makes it. Moreover, the trade dress must be used consistently on a product line.

2.11.3. Registration of Trade Dress as Trademark

In some instances, trade dress can be registered with the PTO as a trademark. If the trade dress is not inherently distinctive (as, for example, with design features, as opposed to packaging, which may in appropriate cases be considered inherently distinctive), the rights holder must prove that consumers associate its trade dress with its company. Such proof may consist of copies of articles recognizing the trade dress and associating it with a particular source; evidence of sales success; affidavits from competitors or experts attesting that the trade dress is associated with a single source; and advertising (especially "look for" advertising). Despite these difficulties, trade dress should be registered if at all possible. If trade dress is unregistered, the burden to show that it is protectable is on the person asserting protection.[34] If the trade dress is registerable but elements of the trade dress are not inherently distinctive, those elements must be disclaimed.[35] Where trade dress has been registered, proof that it is in use must be periodically filed with the PTO. Once trade dress is registered, products should be marked "Trademark design of XYZ Co."

2.11.4. Limitations of Trade Dress Protection

Trade dress can be the most difficult form of IP protection to obtain. There is generally no "piece of paper" to demonstrate that unregistered trade dress rights are held. Indeed, the U.S. Supreme Court looks at trade dress rights restrictively. To obtain protection, a company must demonstrate to a court that consumers recognize its products as having been produced by it. This might be an easy standard for the trade dress of very famous companies (e.g., Adidas' three stripes), but it is a very high standard for smaller companies. It may also be necessary to prove that the claimed trade dress is not functional, which is not always easy to do. Thus, trade dress protection should be resorted to only if there is no other form of protection available.

Fig. 2.2a. A Longchamp Pliage handbag registered for trade dress. (*Courtesy of Fairchild Publications, Inc.*)

Fig. 2.2b. The registration for the Longchamp Pliage bag.

2.11.5. Costs

Evaluation of trade dress rights and the initial cease and desist letter sent to infringers will cost approximately $2,500 to $5,000 in legal fees. The cost of registering trade dress with the PTO can range from $5,000 to $10,000, substantially more than the cost of filing an "ordinary" trademark application because, as discussed above, a significant amount of evidence must often be submitted to convince the PTO that consumers associate the trade dress with the source of the product.

Practice Tip: Best Practice in Trade Dress

▸ Conduct a careful trade dress search for prior common law or registered trade dress in order to avoid a conflict with owners of prior rights.

▸ Use your trade dress consistently across multiple products.

▸ Utilize the marking "Trademark design of XYZ Co." to give notice of your rights. If the trade dress is registered, use the ® symbol.

▸ Promptly notify copiers of your rights.

2.12. Recording Marks with U.S. Customs

Federally registered marks may be recorded with U.S. Customs and Border Protection (CBP) for the purposes of detecting and preventing importation of goods that infringe the registered mark (the recordation fee is $190 for each class of goods).

2.13. International Filing

Trademarks rights are territorial, meaning that trademark protection must be obtained on a country-by-country basis (although it is possible to obtain in all 28 EU countries through a single European application for a Community Trademark). However, it is also possible to file applications in many countries simultaneously through a streamlined application process established by an international treaty known as the Madrid Protocol (88 countries are currently signatories), which is administered by the World Intellectual Property Organization (WIPO).

One limitation on international protection is that many countries have trademark "use" requirements. If a company does not use its trademark in that country, it can lose its rights.[36] Furthermore, when licensing trademark rights to a third party in a particular country, local law may require the parties to "record" that license agreement with the national trademark office.[37]

Ideally, trademark protection would be obtained in every country in the world, but this is often not practical for budgetary reasons. At a minimum, however, trademark owners should secure protection in those countries in which the company sells or plans to sell its products and also in countries where the company's products are manufactured.

2.14. Trademark Licensing

One of the most common IP transactions in the fashion field is the trademark license, in which a famous brand or designer (the licensor) contracts with another party (the licensee) to manufacture and market products bearing the licensor's trademark. Fashion licensing is covered in Chapter 7.

2.15. Domain Name Issues

Today it has become essential to register trademarks also as Internet domain names. This is advisable even if there are no plans to operate a website under the given domain name because it can prevent problems associated with third parties registering those domain names. Domain names corresponding to the trademark should be registered in all appropriate general top-level domains (such as .com, .net, .org, .biz, and .info) and all appropriate country code top-level domains (such as .us, .cn, .eu, .it, .uk, br, etc.).

2.15.1. New Domains

A number of new domains are in the process of being launched (e.g., .google, .amazon, .apple, and .walmart), and additional new domains are likely. Trademark owners are well-advised to stay up-to-date with such developments, as it may be to their benefit to file applications for their own domains[38] or object to applications for domains. Thus, Coach applied for the .coach domain, probably in part to prevent a third party from owning the .coach domain. The introduction of new domains will mean increased costs for trademark owners. Trademark owners will have to monitor applications for new domains and object to any that raise the likelihood of abuse or confusion.

2.15.2. The Trademark Clearinghouse

Given the concerns raised by the introduction of new domains, an entity known as the Trademark Clearinghouse is being introduced to facilitate the protection of trademarks in new domains. The Trademark Clearinghouse will serve as a central repository for authenticating and validating trademark information submitted by trademark owners and providing that information to the operators of new domains. To take advantage of its services, trademark owners will need to record their marks with the Trademark Clearinghouse (there is a charge of $150 for one year, $435 for three years, and $725 for five years). Fees will quickly add up for trademark owners with large portfolios and will likely prove too steep for many smaller trademark owners.

2.15.3. Uniform Domain Name Dispute Resolution Policy (UDRP)

If a third party registers a domain name that incorporates another company's trademark (such as buygap.com) to resell the domain name for an exorbitant price or to draw users to a website offering competitive products, relief may be obtained without having to file a court action. The company that holds the trademark may request that the domain name be transferred to it under the Uniform Domain Name Dispute Resolution Policy (UDRP). The UDRP is a nonbinding administrative dispute resolution procedure that may result in the issuance of an order for the transfer of the domain name if it can be shown that (1) the domain name is identical or confusingly similar to the company's common law or registered trademark; (2) the party who registered the domain name lacks rights or a legitimate interest in the domain name; and (3) the domain name was registered and used in bad faith.[39]

2.15.4. Anti-Cybersquatting Consumer Protection Act (ACPA)

The Anti-Cybersquatting Consumer Protection Act (ACPA) also provides trademark owners with a means of dealing with abusive domain name registrations[40] (i.e., as when a domain name registrant has a bad faith intent to profit from the use of another's mark as a domain name). To succeed on an ACPA claim, a trademark owner must establish that (1) that the defendant registered, trafficked in, or used the domain name; (2) the domain name is identical or confusingly similar to a distinctive mark;[41] and (3) the defendant acted with a bad faith intent to profit from the mark.[42] As with the UDRP, the remedies available under the ACPA include cancellation or transfer of the domain name.[43] However, under the ACPA, courts may award damages, including statutory damages that range from $1,000 to $100,000 for each infringing domain name.[44]

2.16. Summary of Key Points

1. A trademark is any device, such as a logo, brand name, or symbol that indicates the source of a product. Common law trademarks are trademarks that are being used in commerce but that have not been registered; these have very limited protection. Trademarks that have been federally registered at the USPTO are afforded nationwide protection. To receive international protection, trademarks must be registered in each foreign country in which one seeks to utilize the mark; the Madrid Protocol is a helpful tool for facilitating multiple registrations.
2. Trademarks are legally classified according to the strength they have as inherently distinctive source indicators, with more-distinctive trademarks considered stronger. The strongest are those termed arbitrary or fanciful, followed by those that are suggestive. Descriptive trademarks can be difficult to protect or are protectable only upon a showing of secondary meaning, and generic trademarks are the weakest and cannot be protected.
3. Before registering a trademark, be sure to conduct a broad trademark search, ideally with the support of an experienced attorney, to detect any possible conflicts with existing trademarks, either domestically or internationally.
4. Suspected trademark infringement should be challenged in a timely fashion so the mark owner does not lose rights against the infringer.
5. Trade dress is a form of IP that covers the characteristic look or overall physical presentation of a product, including such elements as packaging, product configuration, color, color combination, texture, graphics, or labeling. If trade dress is inherently distinctive, as in the case of unique packaging, it may be registered as a trademark. Design elements of trade dress can be registered only upon establishing secondary meaning.

6. Trademark owners may wish to obtain Internet domain names corresponding to their marks and may wish to prevent others from registering domain names that are identical or confusingly similar to the marks. The Uniform Domain Name Dispute Resolution Policy (UDRP) and the Anti-Cybersquatting Consumer Protection Act (ACPA) provide two avenues for dealing with abusive domain name registrations.

Notes

1. See, e.g., *Brennan's Inc. v. Brennan's Restaurant LLC*, 360 F.3d 125 (2d Cir. 2004) (refusing to enjoin use of "Terrance Brennan's Seafood & Chop House" for use as name of New York City restaurant even though plaintiff had incontestable trademark registration for BRENNAN for use in connection with restaurant services).

2. *JA Apparel Corp. v. Abboud*, 682 F. Supp. 2d 294 (S.D.N.Y. 2010).

3. 15 U.S.C. §1115.

4. It is also possible to register trademarks in individual states. State trademark registrations offer protection only in the particular state and do not offer the same benefits as federal trademark registrations. Nevertheless, in certain circumstances a state trademark registration may be appropriate, particularly if a company has no immediate plans to sell out of its home state. Given the reach of Internet commerce, one suspects that such businesses are few and far between.

5. 15 U.S.C. § 1096; 19 C.F.R. §§ 133.0-133.27.

6. In general, the supplemental register is reserved for descriptive marks that have not acquired secondary meaning. 15 U.S.C. § 1091.

7. 15 U.S.C. § 1115.

8. *In re Fox*, 702 F.3d 633 (Fed.Cir. 2012).

9. 15 U.S.C. § 1052(a).

10. *Id.*

11. 15 U.S.C. § 1052(c).

12. 15 U.S.C. § 1052(e)(4).

13. 15 U.S.C. § 1052(d).

14. 15 U.S.C. § 1051.

15. 15 U.S.C. § 1051 (a)-(b); 37 C.F.R. § 2.21.

16. 15 U.S.C. § 1051 (a)(2).

17. 37 C.F.R. §§ 2.51(a) and (b).

18. In certain limited circumstances, registrations will issue without proof of use, but these are limited to situations where registrations based on foreign registrations are issued in accordance with treaties to which the United States is a party. See 15 U.S.C. § 1126, 1141-1141n.

19. 15 U.S.C. § 1127; 37 C.F.R. §2.56.

20. TMEP §§ 705-705.08.

21. TMEP § 711.

22. See *International Star Class Yacht Racing Ass'n v. Tommy Hilfiger, U.S.A., Inc.*, 1999 U.S. Dist. LEXIS 2147 (S.D.N.Y. 1997) (use of knockout search does not indicate bad-faith adoption of mark).

23. 15 U.S.C. § 1111.

24. *Citibank, N.A. v. Citytrust and Citytrust Bancorp, Inc.*, 756 F2d 273 (2d Cir. 1985) (preliminary injunction denied because of 10-week delay in seeking injunction).

25. 15 U.S.C. § 1115.

26. *Two Pesos, Inc. v. Taco Cabana, Inc.*, 505 U.S. 763.

27. *Qualitex Co. v. Jacobson Prods. Co.*, 514 U.S. 159, 165 (1995).

28. *TrafFixDevices, Inc. v. Mktg. Displays, Inc.*, 532 U.S. 23 (2001).

29. *In re Becton, Dickinson & Co.*, 675 F.3d 1368, 1374-75 (2012).

30. *Wal-Mart Stores, Inc. v. Samara Bros.*, 529 U.S. 205 (2000).

31. *Id.*; *Zatarain's Inc. v. Oak Grove Smokehouse Inc.*, 698 F.2d 786 (1983).

32. *Wal-Mart Stores, Inc. v Samara Bros.*, 529 U.S. 205 (2000).

33. *Id.*

34. 15 U.S.C. § 1125(a)(3).

35. 15 U.S.C. § 1056.

36. For example, if a mark is not used in China for three consecutive years, the registration may be canceled for non-use if a third party brings a cancellation proceeding.

37. Mexico has such a requirement.

38. Applications for the first round of new domains were accepted by the Internet Corporation for Assigned Names and Numbers ("ICANN") between January 11, 2012, and May 30, 2012, and cost $185,000 per application. New domains had to consist of at least three distinct characters or letters and be no more than 63 characters long. Applications also had to include financial disclosures and technical disclosures about the applicant's ability to operate a new domain.

39. *Uniform Domain Name Dispute Resolution Policy*, http://www.icann.org/en/help/dndr/udrp/policy (last visited January 26, 2013).

40. 15 U.S.C. §1125(d).

41. Misspellings of marks are regularly found to be confusingly similar. See *Texas International Property Associates v. Hoerbiger Holding AG*, 624 F.Supp.2d 582 (N.D.Tx. 2009) (horbiger.com confusingly similar to HOERBIGER); *Electronics Boutique Holdings Corp. v. Zuccarini*, 56 U.S.P.Q.2d 1705 (E.D.Pa. 2000) (electronicboutique.com; eletronicsboutique.com; electronicbotique.com; ebwold.com; and ebworl.com confusingly similar to EB and ELECTRONICS BOUTIQUE).

42. The statute contains a nonexhaustive list of nine factors to be considered when determining whether a registrant acted in bad faith. See 15 U.S.C. §1125(d)(1)(B)(i)(I)-(IX).

43. 15 U.S.C. §1125(d)(1)(C).

44. 15 U.S.C. §1117 (d).

Appendix

Researching IP Issues: Links and References

Statutes

Trademark Act 15 U.S.C. § 1051 et seq. (also known as the Lanham Act)

U.S. Trademark Law, http://www.uspto.gov/web/offices/tac/tmlaw2

Organizations

American Intellectual Property Law Association (AIPLA), www.aipla.org

International Trademark Association (INTA), www.inta.org

International Intellectual Property Alliance (IIPA), www.iipa.com

International AntiCounterfeiting Coalition (IACC), www.iacc.org

The New York Intellectual Property Law Association (NYIPLA), www.nyipla.org

The Los Angeles Intellectual Property Law Association (LAIPLA), www.laipla.org

Volunteer Lawyers for the Arts (VLA), www.vlany.org

American Apparel and Footwear Association (AAFA), www.wewear.org

Council of Fashion Designers of America (CFDA), www.cfda.com

Websites

United States Patent and Trademark Office (USPTO), http://www.uspto.gov—Offers trademark database search (TESS) for a knockout trademark search, Trademark Electronic Application System (TEAS) for filing a trademark application.

U.S. Customs and Border Protection, www.cbp.gov—Offers ability to record trademarks so that Customs will monitor ports for the importation of infringing and/or counterfeit goods.

World Intellectual Property Organization (WIPO), www.wipo.int—Offers international services for filing trademark applications.

Cornell Legal Information Institute, www.law.cornell.edu—Provides overviews of trademark and trade dress law and legal resources. The text of all decisions cited in this chapter can be found on this website.

Domain Names

Internet Corporation for Assigned Names and Numbers, www.icann.org—Oversees the operation of the domain name system.

Trademark Clearinghouse, www.trademark-clearinghouse.com—Allows recordal of trademark registrations for use in connection with sunrise periods and trademark claims services.

Network Solutions, www.nsi.com—Domain name registrar through which domain names can be registered.

Register.com, www.register.com—Domain name registrar through which domain names can be registered.

Blogs

TTABlog—thettablog.blogspot.com—Reports on and summarizes decisions of the Trademark Trial and Appeal Board regarding the registrability of trademarks.

43(b)log—tushnet.blogspot.com—Covers recent developments in the law relating to false advertising.

3

Copyright

Charles Colman

3.1. Introduction

This chapter explores copyright law in fashion. We review the basic principles of U.S. copyright law, discuss difficulties that fashion designers encounter in attempting to protect their creations using copyright law, review categories of fashion design elements that are copyrightable, and note certain fashion-specific issues that frequently arise in copyright litigation.

3.2. What Is Copyright?

Copyright in the United States is a form of quasi-property authorized by the Intellectual Property Clause of the Constitution.[1] The Copyright Act of 1790, the first U.S. copyright statute, granted 14 years of protection (with a possible 14-year renewal term) to eligible "authors" of "any map, chart, book or books."[2] Over the years, Congress has progressively extended the copyright term (today, most copyrighted works are protected for the life of the author plus 70 years),[3] expanded the scope of eligible subject matter,[4] and removed most of the formalities that once served as barriers to protection and enforcement. Despite this expansion of the law, much of fashion remains outside the scope of copyright protection.

3.3. Fashion Design under U.S. Copyright Law

As a starting point, let us observe that although many elements of fashion are protectable by copyright, fashion designs, strictly speaking, are not. Thus, for example, drawings, photographs, jewelry, editorial content, and design software, are fully protectable by copyright. Copyright may protect an image or drawing on a T-shirt, a fabric pattern, a photograph of a model wearing an article of clothing, or a piece of jewelry. However, three-dimensional articles of fashion apparel (in other words, fashion designs) have never been fully brought into the copyright fold in the United States.[5] Note, however, that such works may nevertheless qualify for other types of intellectual property protection, such as design patent or trade dress.

The copyright law's unfavorable treatment of fashion design derives from the Copyright Act's exclusion of useful articles: "the design of a *useful article* . . . shall be considered a [copyrightable] pictorial, graphic, or sculptural work *only if*, and only to the extent that, such design incorporates pictorial, graphic, or sculptural features that can be identified separately from, and are capable of existing independently of, the utilitarian aspects of the article."[6] To the chagrin of many designers, "[i]t is well settled that articles of clothing are 'useful articles' not protected by the Copyright Act."[7] In other words, only those components of fashion that are separable from clothing or apparel are copyrightable. This leads to the question: Which aspects of fashion design are separable, and thus potentially protected, under U.S. copyright law? The answer: some, but not many.[8]

Sometimes, a component of a useful article can actually be removed from the original item and separately sold, without adversely impacting the article's functionality. In such circumstances, courts have found the removable component to be "physically separable" and thus entitled to copyright protection.[9] More often, however, the artistic and the utilitarian aspects of fashion design are inextricably intertwined. Removal of the "aesthetic" elements could be achieved only by destroying both the aesthetic and the functional parts of the design. The "physical separability" test is of no help in such situations, so the courts have employed other tools—most notably, the so-called "conceptual separability" test.

Unfortunately, as one judge candidly acknowledged in a case involving shoe designs, "[t]he line between protectable separable design elements and unprotectable inseparable functional elements is not always clear."[10] Nevertheless, as plaintiffs have brought one case after another alleging the unlawful copying of fashion creations, a body of law has gradually emerged revealing that certain categories of design components are *generally* protectable while others are *generally* unprotectable.

3.4. Categories of Generally Copyrightable Works

3.4.1. Original Fabric Patterns

Textile patterns displaying a minimal level of "originality" are eligible for copyright protection[11] (this rule has been extended to lace[12] and decorative weaves of sweaters).[13] Under U.S. copyright law, a work may be "original" even if it is not "novel" (the more demanding novelty requirement is applied in patent law) as long as the work (1) originates with the author claiming protection and (2) "possesses at least some minimal degree of creativity."[14]

In *Prince Group v. MTS Prods.*[15] the court upheld the validity of plaintiff's copyright in a shaded polka-dot textile pattern, noting that a standard polka-dot design might not be eligible for protection, but holding that the design at issue revealed the "minimal degree of creativity" required for copyrightability because the shading and color variation of the dots made them "more than average circles."

In *Folio Impressions, Inc. v. Byer California*,[16] the plaintiff's rose-themed fabric pattern consisted of public-domain material—dangerously close to the edge of non-originality. Nonetheless, the court upheld the plaintiff's copyright in the overall work, but only in "narrow" form due to its "slight originality." Since part of plaintiff's pattern came from the public domain, the court carefully scrutinized the patterns involved and found no infringement.

In *Royal Printex, Inc. v. Unicolors, Inc.*[17] the court found insufficient originality to warrant copyright in a "daisy flower design with a polka-dot background." The court ruled that "neither the flowers, nor their repetitive placement, were independently created by Unicolors. [Further, the] deletion of the ticking stripe background from the forties flower design, and the insertion of generic polka-dots, does not constitute the requisite originality required for a design to be copyrightable."

Judicial decisions like *Unicolors* represent a fairly recent development. Between 1960 and the early 2000s, courts rarely found fabric patterns uncopyrightable due to a lack of originality. While this is still unusual, rulings denying copyright protection for very basic patterns are becoming more common. Even apart from the threshold question of copyrightability, rights in fabric patterns can be difficult to enforce. As *Folio Impressions* shows, where a pattern is simple, based on a preexisting design in the public domain, and/or shows little creativity, many courts will grant only "thin" copyright—that is, protection against only close copies. The standard copyright infringement test of "substantial similarity" is applied more stringently.

Despite this trend, copyright litigation over fabric patterns shows no sign of abating; indeed, the opposite appears to be true. While many lawsuits over allegedly infringed textiles might ultimately fail due to the lack of the pattern's originality, insufficient similarity with the accused design, or other reasons, it is so expensive to defend against such suits that many apparel designers and retailers—who might incur liability even for the "innocent" sale or distribution of items incorporating infringing material[18]—find it preferable to settle such disputes. This dynamic has given rise to a phenomenon described by some as "copyright trolling," in which entities bring dozens or even hundreds of nearly identical suits over textiles to which they have (a) purchased the copyright for the sole purpose of suing, or (b) lack any proper title to a textile copyright at all. Some recent court decisions[19] have made it difficult for defendants to dispose of these cases in an efficient, cost-effective way. Thus, it is important for designers and retailers to protect themselves by carefully vetting sources of textiles, requiring "indemnification agreements," and doing business, whenever possible, with established merchants (who are subject to provisions such as Section 2-312 of the Uniform Commercial Code, which imposes obligations on merchants regarding the non-infringing nature of the goods they sell[20]).

3.4.2. Images Placed on Otherwise Unprotected "Useful Articles"

Sufficiently original images placed on otherwise uncopyrightable fashion apparel and accessories are also granted protection. Thus, in *Knitwaves, Inc. v. Lollytogs Ltd.*,[21] for example, puffy leaf appliqués on children's sweaters were accorded copyright protection. Likewise, in *Swatch v. Siu Wong Wholesale*,[22] the court held that artwork on watches was copyrightable.

As with fabric patterns, however, the more commonplace the images, the greater the skepticism of the courts. Thus, in *Samara Bros. v. Wal-Mart Stores*,[23] a panel majority found that copyright protection was appropriate for appliqués of strawberries, daisies, hearts, and tulips. However, the court emphasized the narrowness of its decision by observing that "copyrights depicting familiar objects, such as the hearts, daisies, and strawberries in Samara's copyrights, are entitled to narrow protection [as against the] virtually identical copying present in the instant case."[24]

Fashion Law *in Court*

Jovani Fashion, Ltd. v. Fiesta Fashions

Jovani Fashion, Ltd. ("Jovani") brought a complaint alleging that defendant Fiesta Fashions ("Fiesta") infringed Jovani's registered copyright for the design of a prom dress. The District Court for the Southern District of New York dismissed Jovani's complaint. Jovani appealed to the United States Court of Appeals, Second Circuit.

Jovani argued that its prom dress merited copyright protection because its arrangement of decorative sequins and crystals on the dress bodice, horizontal satin ruching at the dress waist, and layers of tulle on the skirt constituted a combination of features that could be "identified separately from and are capable of existing independently of, the utilitarian aspects of the article."

The design elements of Jovani's prom dress were not physically separable from the garment itself because to be separable, one or more decorative elements must be able to be "actually removed from the original item and separately sold, without adversely impacting the article's functionality." The court observed that design elements of Jovani's prom dress could not be removed from the dress and separately sold, nor could the design elements be removed without adversely affecting the prom dress's functionality.

The design elements of Jovani's prom dress were held not to be conceptually separable because to qualify for conceptual separability, a designer must exercise artistic judgment "independently of functional influences," rather than as "a merger of aesthetic and functional considerations." The artistic judgment exercised in applying sequins and crystals to the dress's bodice and in using ruching at the waist and layers of tulle on the skirt did not, in the court's view, invoke in the viewer a concept other than that of clothing. Such elements are merely used to enhance the functionality of the dress as clothing for a special occasion. This means that there was a merger of aesthetic and functional considerations.

Therefore, the Second Circuit affirmed the judgment of the district court in dismissing Jovani's complaint. This case illustrates the difficulty that fashion companies may have in utilizing the concept of "conceptual separability" to protect creative elements of their fashion items.

Source: Jovani Fashion, Limited v. Fiesta Fashions, Court of Appeals, 2nd Circuit 2012, No. 12-598-cv.

The *Maharishi Hardy Blechman Ltd. v. Abercrombie & Fitch Co.*[25] decision shows that it is often possible for a crafty defendant to avoid infringement simply by reinventing the image that provided "inspiration." As the *Maharishi* court noted, the plaintiff's "particularized expression of the dragon [placed on a pant leg] is protectable, [but] not the idea of the dragon itself or even the idea of putting a dragon on pants." In this case, the presiding judge found that defendant's dragon image was not close enough to plaintiff's to constitute copyright infringement.

In the past decade, a few courts have gone so far as to reject copyright protection altogether in cases involving images on useful articles. Thus, in *Eliya, Inc. v. Kohl's Department*

Stores[26] a shoe designer claimed copyright protection in the stylized, line-based ornamentation on the sides of its shoes. The court ruled that the design at issue was not copyrightable. The court held that the doctrine of "physical separability" did not apply because "[r]emoving the strap, stitching, or sole of a shoe would, to some degree, adversely impact a wearer's ability to locomote by foot" and because "the design elements, once removed, [could not] be separately sold or exist as an independent work of art."[27] The doctrine of conceptual separability was equally inapplicable, because the "design features of [the shoe] do not represent independent artistic expression, as would an image displayed on the shoe's surface."[28] The court cited *Knitwaves, supra*, as a contrasting example.

3.4.3. Sufficiently Original Works of Jewelry (and Related Goods)

Jewelry designs were among the first fashion-related works to be brought under the umbrella of copyright law. As early as the 1950s, New York federal courts affirmed the copyrightability of ornamental jewelry, such as pins, bracelets, earrings, and necklaces.[29] But while jewelry designers do not face a categorical bar to copyright protection, their success in the courts has been inconsistent.

Courts have sometimes upheld the copyrightability of jewelry designs even where the works consisted solely of common motifs or shapes that had been slightly modified. In *Yurman Design, Inc. v. PAJ, Inc.*,[30] for example, the appellate court rejected a defendant's challenge to the copyrightability of bracelets and earrings consisting of "silver, gold, cable twist, and cabochon cut colored stones," declaring that the works' protectability lay in the particular way in which the admittedly common elements were "placed, balanced and harmonized."

On other occasions, however, courts have displayed skepticism that allegedly copyrighted jewelry designs possessed the minimal level of originality required for protection. Alternatively, some courts have construed the scope of protection for jewelry so narrowly that even very similar items escaped a finding of infringement.[31] Some judges, instead of according "thin" copyright to relatively basic works of jewelry, have denied protection to jewelers altogether based on a lack of the requisite originality. In *Todd v. Mont. Silversmiths Inc.*,[32] copyright protection was denied for certain bracelets and earrings on the grounds that the "arrangement [was] visually but not conceptually distinguishable from barbed-wire." In the court's view, such works were "not truly 'original' in the ordinary meaning of the word."[33]

3.4.4. Certain "Sculptural" Components of Apparel and Accessories

In *Kieselstein-Cord v. Accessories by Pearl, Inc.*[34] copyright protection was granted for an ornamental belt buckle that was reminiscent of (and had even been used as) jewelry. Since the buckle "could properly be viewed as a sculptural work with independent aesthetic value, and not as an integral element of the belt's functionality," it qualified for copyright protection as a work of art.[35]

Kieselstein-Cord is often described as a "landmark" case and cited as the archetypal example of copyright protection being accorded to "separable" artistic components of fashion. For a time, the case proved influential.[36] However, recent attempts to invoke *Kieselstein-Cord* in favor of expanded protection have largely failed. Probably the most frequent *successful* invocation of *Kieselstein-Cord*'s sculptural-components-as-art principle has been in the realm of costumes and novelty items.[37] Thus, in *Prima Creations v. Santa's Best Craft*,[38] the court affirmed the copyrightability of a costume "elf hat," either as a conceptually separable costume component or, alternatively, based on the separable components of the hat itself. Such cases, however, represent exceptions. Most recent attempts to invoke the *Kieselstein-Cord* doctrine in favor of copyright protection for fashion have failed.[39]

3.5. Proposed Legislation on Copyright for Fashion Designs

Efforts to secure greater copyright protection for fashion designs than that described above are nothing new; indeed, over 100 bills to this effect have been introduced in Congress since 1914, none of which became law. For an exploration of the legal and policy debates surrounding such legislation, see Chapter 5.

Practice Tips

▶ Set up an in-house program to routinely file copyright applications in the Copyright Office, and do so promptly after the product is shown to the trade or to the public.

▶ Do not rely on anecdotal rules of thumb for avoiding copyright infringement (e.g., the so-called "5 Percent Rule" or the "Seven-Point Rule": e.g., if you change 5 percent of the imitated design or make seven changes to it, you are not infringing the copyright). These "rules" have no basis in the law. The amount by which an imitated design must be altered will vary from case to case; when in doubt, consult expert counsel.

▶ Use the copyright notice in the following style: © 2014 XYZ Co., All Rights Reserved.

▶ Do not delay in sending notice letters to copiers.

▶ Do not try to copyright ideas or concepts; they cannot be protected by copyright.

▶ Do not copy literally or substantially from anyone else's work; it could get you into deep legal trouble. Looking for "inspiration" is fine, but literal or substantial copying may be dangerous to your company's financial health.

3.6. International Protection

In an age of global markets, protecting IP in the United States, while necessary, is not sufficient. IP rights should be protected on a worldwide basis. Thus, it is necessary to both take steps to prevent knockoffs from entering the United States and to prevent others from producing knockoffs elsewhere in the world.

3.6.1. Protecting Copyrights

Very few countries aside from the United States have national copyright offices that issue certificates of registration to copyright owners (Canada and China are two notable exceptions). However, many countries, including the United States, are members of an international treaty on copyright, the Berne Convention. All signatories to the treaty have agreed to recognize the rights of copyright owners in each member country and afford those owners the same protection as national citizens. One of the benefits of obtaining a U.S. copyright registration is that it may help a company take advantage of Berne Convention provisions to enforce its copyright in other countries.

3.6.2. Protecting Registered or "Industrial" Designs

A registered or "industrial" design is similar to, and in some countries equivalent to, a design patent, meaning it protects the "ornamental" design of any product or component of a product, such as handbags, shoes, eyewear, and perfume bottles. Most countries require a company or designer to file an application to register a design *before* the associated product is introduced into the marketplace (some countries like the United States do have a "grace period"). An IP attorney should be consulted in the development stage when working on a product with unique features. Generally, the company should apply for design protection *before* that product is offered to the public.

3.7. Resolving Copyright Disputes

Although fashion IP litigation is covered more fully in Chapter 6, it is useful to consider a few principles relevant to copyright here.

3.7.1. Strategies to Protect Your Company's Rights

First, do not limit yourself to copyright protection if other forms of protection are available. Figure out which and how many of the several types of IP protection can be utilized to protect your company's new product, based upon the discussion in this book (see especially Chapter 2 on trademarks and trade dress and Chapter 4 on design and utility patents). It is generally preferable to obtain as many different types of protection as possible within your company's budget.

As regards copyright, your company should promptly register copyrightable designs in the Copyright Office. One important benefit of filing promptly within three months of the first public showing of the design is the ability to obtain "statutory" damages and an award of your attorney's fees. Moreover, you must have a copyright registration to start a lawsuit against an infringer. Usually, your company's attorney will send a "notice" letter to any copiers stating the nature of your rights, requesting that the infringers stop all infringing activities, and making a monetary demand. Sometimes the dispute can be settled at this stage. If not, your company will have to start a civil action for copyright infringement in a federal court located where the infringer does business (see Chapter 6, "Litigation Strategies in Fashion Law").

3.7.2. The Value of a Legal Opinion: The Opinion Letter

Often a fashion company will desire to follow a fashion trend and even "copy" the product of a fashion leader. The question arises as to whether this copying is legal. Is the "follower" infringing the IP of the fashion "leader"? What the follower-company wants to avoid at all costs is to be deemed a "willful" or "intentional" infringer. An IP owner may be entitled to enhanced damages in the event of a lawsuit when IP has been infringed upon willfully or intentionally ("treble"—or triple—damages are not uncommon when willful infringement has been proved). This is a classic example of an instance in which a fashion company can benefit from the services of an experienced fashion law practitioner who can provide a formal written opinion stating that—in the attorney's professional opinion—the company's products do not or will not violate another company's IP rights. Such "opinion letters" provide a number of advantages. A company that is alerted via an opinion letter that its proposed product may infringe another company's copyright may be able to rework the design in question sufficiently so as to avoid infringement. In addition, a company that has received an opinion letter to the effect that its proposed product is not infringing will stand in a better position should it be subsequently sued. At the very least, it generally will not be held to have infringed willfully or intentionally, which will reduce its legal exposure.

3.7.3. Copyright Disputes

Under the Copyright Act, a copyright owner is entitled to recover damages from an infringer in an amount equal to the copyright owner's lost profits (as proven by the copyright owner) plus the infringer's profits attributable to the infringement. Since these two damages components can sometimes be difficult to prove, statutory damages of up to $30,000 per infringed work (and $150,000 per infringed work in cases of willful infringement, which includes situations where the copyrights of another were recklessly disregarded) are available, but *only* if the copyright owner has registered the work with the Copyright Office prior to initiating an action. In addition to damages, attorneys' fees may also be awarded *if* the infringed work was timely registered with the Copyright Office.

3.8. Summary of Key Points

1. Copyright protects original, creative works that have been fixed in tangible form, such as literary works, drawings, paintings, sculptures, musical compositions, photographs, and computer software.
2. Under U.S. law, copyright protection does not extend to fashion designs because clothing is considered to be a utilitarian item. Although copyright cannot protect the utilitarian or functional aspects of apparel or other fashion items, it may protect those creative elements that are considered physically or conceptually "separable" from the item. It has been difficult for the courts to lay down a precise, consistent rule for determining whether a given aspect of a fashion item is separable.
3. In those cases where the criteria of creativity, originality, and separability are met, copyright may protect fabric prints, images on garments, embroidery, surface designs on textiles or apparel, jewelry, sculptural elements of accessories, and fashion photography.
4. The duration of copyright is from the moment of its creation until 70 years after the author's death (and 95 years after publication or 120 years after creation, whichever comes first, for works owned by a corporation). When the term of protection has expired, the original work is considered to be in the public domain.

5. Original works are not required to be registered with the U.S. Copyright Office or bear a copyright notice, as they are automatically granted copyright protection. However, registration is a prerequisite for obtaining statutory damages in a copyright infringement lawsuit.

Notes

1. The term "intellectual property" was unknown in the eighteenth century. Edward C. Walterscheid, *To Promote the Progress of Science and the Useful Arts: The Background and Origin of the Intellectual Property Clause of the United States Constitution*, 2 J. INTELL. PROP. L. 1 n.1 (1994). I will nevertheless use the term "Intellectual Property Clause" (or "IP Clause," for short) to refer to this constitutional provision addressing copyrights and patents.

2. Act of May 31, 1790, ch. 15, 1 Stat. 124.

3. See 17 U.S.C. § 302(a). But see 17 U.S.C. § 302(c) ("In the case of an anonymous work, a pseudonymous work, or a work made for hire, the copyright endures for a term of 95 years from the year of its first publication, or a term of 120 years from the year of its creation, whichever expires first.").

4. See 17 U.S.C. § 102(a) ("Works of authorship include the following categories: (1) literary works; (2) musical works, including any accompanying words; (3) dramatic works, including any accompanying music; (4) pantomimes and choreographic works; (5) pictorial, graphic, and sculptural works; (6) motion pictures and other audiovisual works; (7) sound recordings; and (8) architectural works.").

5. The copyrightability of certain two-dimensional fashion-related works, like patterns for apparel, cannot be used to circumvent the general non-copyrightability of three-dimensional fashion articles. See, e.g., *Varsity Brands, Inc. v. Star Athletica, LLC*, Case No. 10-02508, 2012 U.S. Dist. LEXIS 85836, at *21-*22 (W.D. Tenn. Jun. 21, 2012).

6. 17 U.S.C. § 101 (emphasis added).

7. *Jovani Fashion, Ltd. v. Fiesta Fashions*, No. 12-598-CV, 2012 U.S. App. LEXIS 21245, at *2 (2d Cir. Oct. 15, 2012).

8. See *Galiano v. Harrah's Operating Co.*, 416 F.3d 411, 419 (5th Cir. 2005) ("[the bulk of authority] does not conclude that clothing designs do not qualify for copyright protection *per se*, but it rather concludes that clothing designs rarely pass the 'separability' test").

9. *Chosun Int'l v. Chrisha Creations*, 413 F.3d 324, 329 (2d Cir. 2005).

10. *Eliya, Inc. v. Kohl's Department Stores*, 06 Civ. 195 (GEL), 2006 U.S. Dist. LEXIS 66637, at *30-*31 (S.D.N.Y. Sep. 13, 2006).

11. See *Folio Impressions Inc. v. Byer California*, 937 F.2d 759, 763 (2d Cir. 1991) ("Among those forms of 'writings' now recognized as entitled to copyright protection are fabric designs[.]").

12. See, e.g., *Eve of Milady v. Impression Bridal, Inc.*, 957 F. Supp. 484 (S.D.N.Y. 1997); *Imperial Laces v. Westchester Lace*, 95 Civ. 5353, 1998 WL 830630 (S.D.N.Y. Nov. 30, 1998); *Express, LLC v. Fetish Group Inc.*, 424 F. Supp. 2d 1211, 1224 (C.D. Cal. 2006).

13. See *Galiano v. Harrah's Operating Co.*, 416 F.3d 411, 419-420 (5th Cir. 2005) ("Design of sweaters is usually classified as 'fabric design' and is entitled to copyright protection."); *Segrets, Inc. v. Gillman Knitwear Co.*, 207 F.3d 56, 62 (1st Cir. 2000) (parties agreed sweater copyrights were valid, leaving only question of infringement for "knockoffs"). See also *C&F Enterprises v. Barringtons, Inc.*, Civ. No. 96-1108-A, 1997 U.S. Dist. LEXIS 14054 (E.D. Va. May 13, 1997) (needlepoint stockings held copyrightable and infringed by defendant).

14. *Feist Publ'ns, Inc. v. Rural Tel. Serv. Co.*, 499 U.S. 340, 345 (1991).

15. *Prince Group v. MTS Prods.*, 967 F. Supp. 121, 125 (S.D.N.Y. 1997).

16. *Folio Impressions, Inc. v. Byer California*, 937 F.2d 759, 764 (2d Cir. 1991).

17. 91 U.S.P.Q.2D 1439, No. CV 07-05395-VBK, 2009 U.S. Dist. LEXIS 60375, at *9-*10 (C.D. Cal. Jul. 8, 2009).

18. See, e.g., *Metal Morphosis, Inc. v. Acorn Media Publ., Inc.*, 639 F. Supp. 2d 1367, 1373 (N.D. Ga. 2009) ("[E]ven an unwitting purchaser who buys a copy in the secondary market can be held liable for infringement

if the copy was not the subject of a first sale by the copyright holder. Thus unless title to the copy passes through a first sale by the copyright holder, subsequent sales do not confer good title.") (citing *Am. Int'l Pictures, Inc. v. Foreman*, 576 F.2d 661, 664 (5th Cir. 1978)).

19. See, e.g., *L.A. Printex Indus., Inc. v. Aeropostale, Inc.*, 676 F.3d 841 (9th Cir. 2012) (ruling that fabric-pattern copyright infringement case could not be disposed of on summary judgment); *Star Fabrics, Inc. v. Target Corp.*, 2011 U.S. Dist. LEXIS 108846, 100 U.S.P.Q.2d (BNA) 1320 (C.D. Cal. Sept. 22, 2011) ("copyright misuse" defense raised and rejected by court).

20. See, e.g., *Dolori Fabrics, Inc. v. Limited, Inc.*, 662 F. Supp. 1347, 1349-50 (S.D.N.Y. 1987) (fabric-pattern infringement case involving cross-claims "to enforce an indemnification agreement and the warranty against infringement codified in N.Y. U.C.C. § 2-312").

21. 71 F.3d 996 (2d Cir. 1995).

22. 92 Civ. 3653 (PKL, 1992 U.S. Dist. LEXIS 8358 (S.D.N.Y. Jun. 8, 1992).

23. 165 F.3d 120, 132 (2d. Cir. 1998), abrogated on other grounds, 529 U.S. 205 (2000).

24. *Id.* at 132. The dissenting judge expressed his doubts that the majority's copyright ruling would realistically be "applied beyond the precise facts of this case." *Id.* at 133 (Newman, J.).

25. 292 F. Supp. 2d 535, 553-54 (S.D.N.Y. 2003).

26. 06 Civ. 195 (GEL), 2006 U.S. Dist. LEXIS 66637, at *34-*36 (S.D.N.Y. Sep. 13, 2006).

27. *Id.* at *34.

28. *Id.* at *36.

29. See *Vacheron & Constantin-Le Coultre Watches, Inc. v. Benrus Watch Co.*, 260 F.2d 637, 644 (2d Cir. 1958) (Clark, J., dissenting) (internal citations omitted). See also *Davis v. Gap Inc.*, 246 F.3d 152, 156 (2d Cir. 2001) (Leval, J.) (copyright available for "nonfunctional jewelry worn over the eyes in the manner of eyeglasses").

30. 262 F.3d 101, 109 (2d Cir. 2001).

31. *Herbert Rosenthal Jewelry Corp. v. Honora Jewelry Co.*, 509 F.2d 64, 65 (2d Cir. 1974) ("[B]eyond the initial observation that both pins are turtles and both are jeweled, we believe the average layman would indeed detect numerous differences [between the works.]").

32. 379 F. Supp. 2d 1110, 1114 (D. Colo. 2005).

33. *Id.*

34. 632 F.2d 989, 993 (2d Cir. 1980).

35. *Chosun Int'l v. Chrisha Creations*, 413 F.3d 324, 328-29 (2d Cir. 2005).

36. See, e.g., *Severin Montres, Ltd. v. Yidah Watch Co.*, 997 F. Supp. 1262, 1265 (C.D. Cal. 1997) ("[t]he frame around the face [the watch] which forms the letter 'G' in particular makes the [watch] unique and represents artistic design separable from the utilitarian aspects of the watch").

37. See, e.g., *Chosun Int'l v. Chrisha Creations*, 413 F.3d 324, 329-30 (2d Cir. 2005) ("elements of [the plaintiff's] plush sculpted animal costumes are [conceivably] separable from the overall design of the costume, and hence eligible for protection under the Copyright Act"); *Wildlife Express Corp. v. Carol Wright Sales, Inc.*, 18 F.3d 502, 507 n.3 (7th Cir. 1994) (affirming copyrightability of stuffed animal heads attached to an otherwise non-copyrightable duffel bag); *Animal Fair, Inc. v. AMFESCO Industries, Inc.*, 620 F. Supp. 175 (D. Minn. 1985), *aff'd mem.*, 794 F.2d 678 (8th Cir. 1986) (upholding copyrightability of a bear-paw design as "conceptually separable" from utilitarian features of slipper).

38. 11-CV-1649, 2011 U.S. Dist. LEXIS 80283 (E.D. Pa. 2011).

39. See, e.g., *Jovani Fashion v. Cinderella Divine Inc.*, 820 F. Supp. 2d 569, 546-47 (S.D.N.Y. 2011), *aff'd sub nom. Jovani Fashion Ltd. v. Fiesta Fashions*, No. 12-598-CV, 2012 U.S. App. LEXIS 21245 (2d Cir. Oct. 15, 2012), *cert. denied*, 12-863, 568 U.S. ___ (Mar. 13, 2013).

4

Design Patents, Utility Patents, and Trade Secrets

George Gottlieb

4.1. Introduction

In addition to the protection afforded by trademark and copyright law, fashion companies may wish to avail themselves of patent and/or trade secrets protection. In the United States, there are two types of patents: design patents and utility patents. Design patents protect the original and ornamental design of an article of manufacture. Utility patents protect new functionality and do not cover any of the aesthetic elements that design patents protect. Unlike other forms of IP, trade secrets cannot be registered. However, trade secrecy law can provide important protections under circumstances in which a company prefers to keep its proprietary information secret and confidential.

4.2. Design Patents

Design patents have been aptly called "picture patents," meaning that they are used to protect the ornamental appearance of an object or an object component. In most cases, companies seek design patents when copyright protection is not appropriate or helpful for some reason. Design patents are sometimes considered to be relatively expensive or slow to obtain, but experienced patent counsel can minimize these constraints. Once obtained, design patents yield quite strong protection over their 14-year term and consequently are widely used in the fashion world. *Fashion Law in Court: Design Patent Protection for Sneakers* provides an example of the protection of IP offered by a design patent for a sneaker.

4.2.1. The Scope of Design Patent Protection

Design patents protect the "ornamental" design of any product or component of a product. Design patents are available to any person who "invents a new, original and ornamental

> **Fashion Law *in Court***
>
> ### Design Patent Protection for Sneakers
>
> The U.S. Court of Appeals for the Federal Circuit in Washington, DC, had to decide whether L.A. Gear's design patent on its "Hot Shots" line of shoes was infringed by Melville Corporation's competing line of shoes. Melville argued that L.A. Gear's patent was invalid because all of the shoes' components were functional: the components served practical purposes (e.g., the mesh on the side of the shoe provided foot support) and were not used for ornamental purposes. The Court rejected this argument, stating that since the overall appearance of the patented shoe was ornamental, it made no difference whether individual components were functional. Next, Melville argued that the L.A. Gear design patent was invalid because it was "obvious" to an ordinary shoe designer, pointing to some 22 prior references where the components were shown. The court rejected this defense, stating that while the individual components might be known, there was no "teaching" in the prior art to combine them in the way shown in the design patent. The court ruled that Melville had infringed L.A. Gear's design patent, found that the infringement was willful, and suggested that L.A. Gear be awarded attorney's fees and damages.
>
> *Source: L.A. Gear, Inc. v. Thom McAn Shoe Co., 988 F.2d 1117 (Fed. Cir. 1993).*

design for an article of manufacture." Typical fashion objects that might be protected by a design patent are eyeglass frames; handbags; footwear; tabletop items, such as dishes, cutlery, and place mats; perfume bottles; and jewelry. A design patent can also protect a component of a product. For example, in the case of a watch, the watch face, the hour and minute hands, and the band might be protected by separate design patents. The advantage of such separate protection is that if a competitor copies one, but not all components, there is solid protection for that one component.

4.2.2. Procedure for Obtaining a Design Patent

Design patents are obtained by filing an application in the United States Patent and Trademark Office (PTO). The application must contain clear and complete drawings showing all views of the object. A design patent application must satisfy the following three basic requirements: (1) the design must be "new," (2) the design must be "nonobvious" compared to prior known designs in the marketplace or in prior patents, and (3) the design must be ornamental and not solely functional. A patent that has been officially issued by the PTO is not, however, immune from all subsequent challenge. Thus, for example, if the PTO has issued a design patent and the patent holder brings a lawsuit against an alleged infringer, the defendant can challenge the design patent for failure to satisfy one of the three required terms. If a court determines that one of those elements has not been satisfied, it can invalidate the patent, even though the PTO approved it.

4.2.3. "Inventors" of the Design in the Patent Application

The "inventors" of a design patent are always the individual or individuals who have made a material contribution to the design. Under U.S. patent law, a company or corporation cannot be an inventor. Thus, as a matter of procedure, it is always the inventors who must technically file the design patent application. However, the company involved can own the design by an assignment of invention document or under general "work for hire" principles of employment law. Failing these, the inventors own the design and application.

4.2.4. The Critical Importance of the Design Patent Drawings

The importance of the drawings that are included in a patent application cannot be overemphasized. The drawings not only picture the design; they define it. Upon issuance, the design patent covers the pictured design and nothing else. The drawings should be carefully discussed by the designer and the patent professional.[1]

4.2.5. What Product "Functionality" Cannot Be Protected?

Design patents may protect only the ornamental aspects of a design, not any of its functional aspects. For example, a design patent on jewelry or a handbag would generally not protect any functional elements of the clasps. If sufficiently innovative, such functional elements might be protected by utility patents. However, if the clasps possess both ornamental and functional aspects, the ornamental aspects might be protectable under a design patent.

4.2.6. How Long Does It Take to Get Design Patent Protection?

A design patent will generally issue 10 to 20 months after an application has been filed in the PTO. For the fast-moving fashion industry, driven by multiple seasons per year, this relatively lengthy period is the principal drawback of the design patent option. Thus, design patents are not useful for many trendy or seasonal fashion items because the items will be off the market before the patent is finally obtained. However, for certain kinds of designs that are likely to remain stable for several years (shoes, jewelry, accessories, etc.), a design patent makes sense, and many fashion companies do make use of design patents for such designs. The major athletic shoe companies, for example, routinely obtain design patent protection for their shoe models, which may remain in the market for several years. Moreover, for companies that rely heavily on design patents, it is important to note that experienced patent practitioners can obtain design patents on an expedited basis, minimizing this potential disadvantage.

4.2.7. Marking on the Product

While a patent application is pending in the PTO, a product should be marked "Patent Pending." Once a design patent has been issued, the product should be marked "Design Patent No.___." Failure to mark the product in that manner can negatively affect the ability to recover damages from an infringer.

4.2.8. Time Is of the Essence

Design patent applications *must* be filed in the PTO within one year of the object's first public availability. This deadline cannot be extended. A filing that does not observe this timeline will result in a finding of invalidity of the issued design patent, once a court learns about the missed deadline. The best practice is to file the application *before* the product hits the market.

4.2.9. Term of Design Patents

Design patent protection lasts 14 years from the date of issuance. Because design patents cannot be renewed, the design enters the "public domain" (is no longer protected) once the patent expires, unless the design is also protected by some other form of IP. Although limited, the 14-year term of design patent protection is often sufficient for a fashion company's purposes—by the time the design patent has expired, the company may have stopped using the given design and moved on to new designs.

4.2.10. Pros and Cons of Design Patents

Design patents are important in the fashion industry because they can be used to protect a wide variety of objects in the fashion industry. No actual model of the product is required (in contrast to trademark); if a designer can draw his or her design in two or three dimensions, it can be protected.

The protection provided by a design patent is not broad in scope. A design patent protects against only imitations that are quite similar to the patented design. Consequently, an

---

Fashion Law *in Court*

High-Profile Design Patent Disputes

Design patents are being used more and more frequently as a tool of fashion companies to protect their designs, including two recent cases involving fashion heavyweights. Shapewear brand Yummie Tummie recently sued the billion-dollar shapewear giant Spanx, asserting infringement of its design patents. Design patent protection is ideal for shapewear, as such products are extremely profitable (and therefore important to protect) and do not constantly shift from season to season. Second, Lululemon sued Calvin Klein for infringement of the design patents in its multi-waistband yoga pants. Lululemon alleged that the waistband of Calvin Klein's pants was an impermissible infringement of their own overlapping waistband.

Both cases settled quickly, as do the great majority of litigations. Yet these cases make it clear that design patents are no longer being overlooked as an effective tool to protect fashion products.

Sources: Complaint in *Times Three Clothier, LLC v. Spanx, Inc.*, 13 CV 2157 (S.D.N.Y. 2013). Complaint in *Lululemon Athletica Canada Inc. v. Calvin Klein, Inc. and G-III Apparel Group, Ltd.*, 12 CV 1034 (D. Del. 2012).

experienced designer for a rival firm can easily modify a design so as to avoid infringement. Moreover, protection does not begin until the patent is issued.

As a general rule, designers and fashion companies are well advised to consider copyright protection before initiating a design patent. Since copyright protection is easier to obtain and lasts much longer, it is a preferable form of IP. Thus, for example, a rug design might be equally protectable by copyright or a design patent, and in such cases copyright protection should be preferred. Certain fashion or apparel designs may not be copyrightable (i.e., because the design is not physically or conceptually separable from the item of fashion or apparel) but may nonetheless be protected by a design patent (i.e., because the design itself is not functional but only ornamental).

4.2.11. Costs

The legal fees for preparing and filing a design patent application are on the order of $1,500 to $2,000, plus a PTO fee of $380 (assuming the applicant is a "small entity" with fewer than 500 employees; fees for larger organizations are slightly higher). Additional communications with the PTO examiner, if needed, can cost $500 to $1,000. Paying the final issue fee (again, for a small entity), including the PTO fee of $510, will usually cost around $1,000.

4.2.12. Remedies for Design Patent Infringement

If a design patent holder wins an infringement lawsuit, possible remedies include a permanent injunction against future infringement, the profits earned by the infringer, the patent holder's damages, and in cases of willful infringement, attorneys' fees.

Practice Tip: Best Practice in Design Patents

- ▶ The design patent application must be filed within one year of public availability of the item; it is best to file before the product is marketed. A design patent is often the only way to protect a product if copyright protection is not available.
- ▶ Mark "Patent Pending" or "Design Patent No.___," as appropriate, to ensure that damages may be awarded in the event of an infringement.
- ▶ Understand that protection starts only when the PTO issues the design patent; there is no design patent protection prior to issuance.
- ▶ Promptly notify copiers of rights.

4.3. Utility Patent Protection

In contrast to design patents, utility patents protect innovations in product functionality. A utility patent could, for example, protect a new hinge mechanism on a pair of glasses or a new clasp device on a handbag. Utility patents can also protect processes and techniques, such as the making of a type of fabric. Chemical processes, such as new methods of washing jeans to achieve unusual effects, are a typical example of the application of utility patent protection in the fashion industry.

4.3.1. The Scope of Utility Patent Protection

Utility patents protect the functional or utilitarian aspects of a new product or method. The patented product or service must not only be new and original ("novel" in legal parlance); it must also be "nonobvious," which is to say, not trivial. If a fashion company or designer invents a new zipper or a new sneaker, a utility patent will protect only the "nonobvious" differences between the invention and prior zippers or sneakers. The historical record of technical knowledge, evidenced by all the patents and publications that have been granted or written in a particular category, is referred to as *prior art*. To be patentable, an innovation must represent a significant step beyond the prior art. Trivial differences between a new design and the prior art are not patentable.

4.3.2. Procedure for Obtaining a Utility Patent

A utility patent is obtained by filing an application in the PTO. The application must contain a full technical discussion of the product, including drawings showing the product or method. The application will include a number of *claims*, which are statements of the innovative features or aspects of the product.

The grant of a patent is always provisional in the sense that a patent right can be challenged. For example, if the requirements of novelty and nonobviousness have not been satisfied and a lawsuit is brought, the accused infringer can challenge the validity of the utility patent. If the court determines that one of those elements had not been satisfied, it will invalidate the patent.

4.3.3. Marking on a Product

While a patent application is pending in the PTO, a product should be marked "Patent Pending." Once the utility patent issues, the product should be marked "Patent No.___." Failure to mark the product appropriately can limit or preclude the recovery of damages from an infringer.

4.3.4. Time Is of the Essence

As with design patents, applications for utility patents must be filed in the PTO within one year of an invention's public availability. This is an absolute deadline. Ideally, the utility application should be filed before the product goes on sale. Should a challenge arise as to who was the first to invent a particular item, priority will be given to the first party to file a patent application.

Utility patent protection lasts a maximum of 20 years from the filing date of the application. A utility patent cannot be renewed beyond this 20-year term.

4.3.5. Provisional Patent Applications

A provisional application provides a one-year-only window to preserve the date of invention. Before the year is up, the applicant must file a nonprovisional application. The provisional application, which must describe the invention, establishes an early effective filing date and allows the term "Patent Pending" to be applied. This option is useful when an inventor or company is not ready to file a full utility application (e.g., the product is still being tested) but still wants to establish a date of invention. These types of applications are often used by individual inventors or by smaller companies who want a one-year testing period for their product. A provisional patent application cannot be filed for a design patent.

4.3.6. Costs

Legal fees for a prior art search range from $2,500 to $5,500. The cost for legal services for preparing and filing a utility patent application in the PTO range from $6,000 to $10,000, depending upon the complexity of the product, plus a PTO filing fee of at least $500 for a "small entity" (500 or fewer employees). "Prosecution" of the patent application, that is, communication with the PTO examiner, which is usually required, can cost an additional $2,500 to $7,500. Maintenance fees must be paid in the third, seventh, and eleventh years after the issuance of the patent in the amounts of $1,600, $3,600, and $7,400, respectively, and if they are not paid, the patent expires.

4.3.7. Pros and Cons of Utility Patents

The principal benefit of a utility patent is that it offers very powerful protection. Competitors are likely to accord great respect to this form of protection, in part because court battles over patents can prove very expensive. Competitors faced with a patent infringement suit therefore often choose to drop the competitive item or pay a royalty. However, this form of protection is difficult and costly to obtain and costly to maintain.

Practice Tip: Prior Art Search for a Patent

Conduct a careful prior art search to make certain that you do not infringe prior patents of others and to determine the state of the prior art generally so you can find out whether your proposal is nonobvious. This will enable you to anticipate whether, after examination, the PTO will grant a patent.

Copies of patents may be obtained via the PTO website and from Google Patents at no cost. You can also do your own simplified prior art searches via the PTO website and through an Internet search. Discuss these options and any results you find with your IP attorney before a patent application is filed because the results of these searches *must* be disclosed to the PTO.

4.3.8. Damages for Patent Infringement

In cases involving the infringement of a utility patent, a patent owner is entitled to recover damages "adequate to compensate for the infringement"; in no case will those damages be less than a "reasonable royalty" (the amount of the "reasonable royalty" will vary depending on the industry in which the infringer operates).

In exceptional cases, a court may award the prevailing party (which is not necessarily the patent owner) attorney's fees.

4.3.9. The Role of Declaratory Judgments

Protecting one's business from accusations of infringement of a competitor's protected IP rights can be as important as protecting the company's own IP. *Fashion Law in Court: Protecting a Method for Making Jeans with a Specific "Washed" Look* describes how Levi Strauss saved itself from serious problems by seeking a declaratory judgment. Declaratory judgments state the rights, duties, or obligations of each party involved in a legal issue. By filing a request for a declaratory judgment, a party seeks to determine in advance whether a given action is legal. Declaratory judgments are particularly common in patent law cases because they allow a competitor to "clear the air" with regard to potential infringement of another company's patented product or service. If it were not for the availability of declaratory judgments, patent owners could simply refrain from filing suit until the six-year statute of limitations had almost expired. During this time, monetary damages would continue to accrue. Declaratory judgments allow a company to ascertain its legal rights and liabilities regarding a given patent before beginning production of a potentially infringing product.

Fashion Law *in Court*

Protecting a Method for Making Jeans with a Specific "Washed" Look

A federal court in New York decided such a case, in which a patent had been granted for a method for stonewashing jeans to achieve an unusual "washed" effect, and a company using a similar product sought a declaratory judgment.

In 1988, an Italian inventor, Francesco Ricci, was issued a patent by the U.S. PTO for a method for producing a random fading effect on fabrics by bleaching them and for the products, for example, jeans, made by that method. Ricci assigned the patent to Golden Trade, S.r.L. of Bologna, Italy. Golden Trade attempted to license the patented invention to major jeans manufacturers, including Lee Jeans and Levi Strauss & Co., but only Greater Texas Finishing Corp. took a license. Soon after, Golden Trade filed a suit for infringement of its patent against Lee and Blue Bell (maker of Wrangler jeans) and then Jordache Enterprises, Inc.; Gitano Group, Inc.; Bugle Boy Industries, Inc.; Rio Sportswear, Inc.; and Bon jour International Ltd.

Levi Strauss filed a declaratory judgment action, in anticipation of Golden Trade's coming after it next, claiming that the Ricci patent was invalid and was not infringed. The Court found that Ricci's patent claims for the products with the random faded effects did not meet the requirements for a utility patent. The Court ruled that Ricci's patent was invalid for claiming nonpatentable subject matter.

Source: Levi Strauss & Co. v. Golden Trade, S.r.L., 1995 U.S. Dist. LEXIS 22145, 1995 WL 710822 (S.D.N.Y. Nov. 30 1995).

4.3.10. Recent Changes to U.S. Patent Law

A sweeping revision to existing American patent law, the America Invents Act (AIA) was signed into law in 2011 and took effect in 2013. Under the AIA, the U.S. patent system was changed from a "first-to-invent" system to a "first-inventor- to-file" system, meaning that patent protection is available only to the first party to file for a patent application. Under certain instances, however, the first party to use the subject of a patent can still gain priority over a party that filed first. The AIA also instituted a number of fee adjustments and created a new class of applicants: "micro-entities" (defined as entities meeting strict size requirements, including not exceeding a certain income level and not having filed more than four prior patent applications). Fees assessed to micro-entities are up to 75 percent less than those assessed to other entities.

4.4. Trade Secrets

A *trade secret* is defined as confidential business information that is kept private and guarded within the company.

4.4.1. What Trade Secrecy Law Protects

Trade secrets can include formulas and techniques, customer lists, computer software, and many other kinds of confidential business information. In the fashion world, formulas for perfumes, factory sources for the production of goods, special manufacturing techniques, and color blends for products may all be treated as trade secrets. Trade secrecy protection lasts indefinitely, so long as the information is kept confidential within the company and does not leak out.

4.4.2. How Is Trade Secrecy Protection Obtained?

Trade secrets must be protected by confidentiality agreements signed by all employees and vendors who may learn the company's trade secrets. Knowledge of trade secrets should be limited only to those who have a "need to know." Trade secret documentation should also be retained under secure conditions in the company.

4.4.3. Time Is of the Essence

New employees and new vendors should be required to sign trade secret agreements. When employees or vendors part ways with the company, they should be reminded that the trade secret agreement prohibits them from using specified trade secrets at their new place of employment or to benefit other customers.

4.4.4. Pros and Cons of Protecting Trade Secrets

Trade secrets can be retained forever, but only if they are carefully guarded by agreements and security. If the trade secret ever leaks out, or if a competitor can figure it out by careful "reverse engineering" analysis of a product, protection is lost.

Fashion Law *in Practice*

A Failed Marriage Leads to Fashion Trade Secret Case

In 2012, fashion designer Tory Burch alleged that her ex-husband, J. Christopher Burch, misappropriated trade secrets after he started the "C-Wonder" brand, which sold similar products to her own line. Despite the fact that Mr. Burch had been a consultant and co-chairperson of Tory Burch LLC, Ms. Burch alleged that Mr. Burch had misappropriated trade secrets that he was obligated to respect due to confidentiality agreements he had signed while holding those positions. The case ultimately settled, but it demonstrates that trade secret cases can arise from failed partnerships and not just from theft of confidential information.

Source: Burch v. Burch is Finally Over (January 2, 2013), http://fashionista.com/2013/01/burch-v-burch-is-finally-over/ (last visited June 17, 2013).

Practice Tip: Keep Your Secrets Secret

Trade secret protection requires rigorous confidentiality protocols. There must be confidentiality agreements with all connected employees and vendors and adequate security must be maintained. Protection fails if the item can be reverse-engineered.

4.5. International Protection

Patents and trade secrets are protected in some fashion in virtually all countries. In some countries the protection may be classified under "industrial design" law. As with other forms of IP, every country has its own rules and procedures governing each form of protection. The Patent Cooperation Treaty (PCT) makes securing patent protection in multiple countries somewhat easier.

As with other forms of IP, patent protection would ideally be sought in every country, but this is often not practical due to the expense involved. At a minimum, it is best to secure protection in those countries in which the company sells or plans to sell its products and in those countries in which the company's products are manufactured.

So long as a company has protection in those countries that are important to it, it can usually prevent infringing or counterfeit products from entering those countries or, if they have already entered a country in which the products are protected, from being sold. For example, a U.S. patent owner can prevent the sale in the United States of products that infringe its patent regardless of where those products were made.

4.5.1. Registered or "Industrial" Designs

A registered or "industrial" design is similar to, and in some countries equivalent to, a design patent, meaning it protects the "ornamental" design of any product or component of a product, such as handbags, shoes, eyewear, and perfume bottles. Most countries require a company or designer to apply to register a design *before* the associated product is introduced into the marketplace (although some countries have a "grace period," similar to that in the United States).

4.5.2. International Patent Procedures

The PCT offers a streamlined process for obtaining patent protection in member countries by filing only one patent application. As with a U.S. patent application, there are important deadlines by which a PCT application must be filed after an invention is introduced to the public. Note that each country has different rules for determining whether a particular invention is entitled to patent protection and a PCT application will have to be examined by each country's national patent office to obtain a patent in a particular country.

4.6. Summary of Key Points

1. Patents provide protection for fashion designs. Design patents protect the original and ornamental appearance of an article. Utility patents provide powerful protection for new functionality, such as processes for dying. Patent protection is obtained by filing an application with the USPTO. International protection may be secured via the Patent Cooperation Treaty.

2. The patent inventor and owner is the individual (or individuals) who made a material contribution to the design unless the invention is created as a "work for hire." Design patent protection lasts for 14 years from the date of issuance. Utility patent protection lasts up to 20 years from the application filing date.

3. As a result of the America Invents Act, the U.S. patent system is now a "first-inventor-to-file" system.

4. Trade secret law provides a form of protection for fashion if the designs or design processes involve information that the company prefers to keep secret and confidential, such as formulas for perfumes or factory sources for the production of goods.

5. Trade secrecy protection is granted automatically and lasts indefinitely, so long as the information is kept confidential.

Note

1. As differentiated from other forms of protection discussed in this chapter, design patents and utility patents can be filed only by attorneys who are registered in the PTO.

5

Design Piracy Legislation

Should the United States Protect Fashion Design?

Guillermo C. Jimenez, Joseph Murphy, and Julie Zerbo

5.1. Introduction

Over the past century, the U.S. Congress has been the scene of approximately 100 failed attempts to pass legislation introducing intellectual property protection for fashion designs. Currently, American law provides minimal legal protection for fashion designs *per se*. While original fabric prints and surface designs, creative jewelry and accessories designs, innovative sculptural or ornamental elements, and novel fabrics and fibers may be protectable under trademark, trade dress, copyright, design patent, and/or utility patent regimes, in most instances, the *design* of a garment (i.e., the cut and construction of a garment) is not protectable.

European Union law, by contrast, has long provided strong protection for fashion designs (design protection is also strong under Japanese law). A decision to follow the European model would fundamentally transform the U.S. fashion industry. For the foreseeable future, Congress is likely to continue to reintroduce and reconsider bills to adopt European-style protection for fashion designs (the most recent version was known as the Innovative Design Protection Act, or IDPA).

Although such legislation is supported by the Council of Fashion Designers of America (CFDA) and the American Apparel and Footwear Association (AAFA), prospects for passage remain daunting in light of entrenched resistance from certain sectors of the fashion industry, especially retailers. This clash of interests in the halls of Congress has generated a fascinating intellectual debate. On the one side, proponents—such as iconic fashion designer and CFDA President Diane Von Furstenberg, Harvard Law Professor Jeannie Suk, and fashion law scholar Professor Susan Scafidi—have argued that fashion designs are creative works meriting copyright-style protection. These proponents contend that such protection would not unduly hamper the fashion business, but would help put an end to the practice of producing near-identical knockoffs. On the other side, opponents—such as law professors Kal

Raustiala and Christopher Sprigman, media scholar Johanna Blakley, and the California Retailers Association—have argued that the American fashion industry is vibrant precisely because its weak legal regime forces fashion companies into perpetual creativity in order to stay ahead of knockoffs and imitators. Opponents maintain that fashion design protection would lead to a flood of frivolous litigation and raise the cost of apparel to the consumer.

Should the United States adopt such legislation? This chapter will review the arguments for and against the most recent proposals and compare the proposed American regime with the European system. As opposed to most of the other material in this book, this section does not deal with what the law is today, but what the law may become in the near future.

In the interest of full disclosure, let it be noted that although this chapter seeks to provide a fair analysis of the arguments put forward on both sides, it does not pretend to arrive at an impartial conclusion. After evaluating the relative cogency of the arguments on both sides, it seems here that the designers and their advocates have advanced the stronger case.

Most of the arguments against design piracy legislation are now outdated in light of adjustments made to the most recent legislative proposals, which removed some of the objectionable features of previous bills. Moreover, many of the arguments advanced against fashion design protection are specious in any case or, at the very least, unsubstantiated. One of the major factors behind the legislative impasse in the U.S. Congress is an economic calculus on the behalf of American retailers that passage of design piracy legislation would raise their legal risks and administrative costs. Does the perceived risk to retailers outweigh the interests of designers in protecting their creative designs? To some extent, the answer depends on one's perspective. To date, the retail lobby has been able to apply greater leverage. If the design groups, such as the CFDA, hope to tip the balance, they must recruit more support, both logical and logistical. For one thing, they will have to persuade independent designers and small fashion companies that design protection will benefit them as well and that it will not end up merely as another weapon in the legal arsenal of famous designers and large brands.

5.2. Summary of Recent U.S. Proposals

Fashion designers have successfully urged their legislative champions to regularly reintroduce legislation to protect fashion designs via an amendment to existing U.S. copyright statutes. Thus, on July 13, 2011, Congressional Representative Robert Goodlatte (Virginia) introduced H.R. 2511, the Innovative Design Protection and Piracy Prevention Act (IDPPPA), and on September 10, 2012, U.S. Senator Charles Schumer (New York) introduced a slightly different Senate version, S.3523, the Innovative Design Protection Act of 2012 (IDPA). The two proposals were very similar except that Senator Schumer's contained an additional modification aimed at mollifying the retail sector (which has long opposed fashion design protection) by reducing their potential legal exposure in infringement actions.

These two bills differed significantly from previous attempts to introduce legal protection for fashion designs. In order to overcome long-standing opposition from other sectors of the fashion industry, in particular from the American Apparel and Footwear Association (AAFA), the CFDA and its legislative supporters had agreed to submit a more narrowly focused bill. Most importantly, the new legislation would set a much higher standard for infringement, prohibiting

Fashion Law *in Practice*

The Absence of Legal Protection for Fashion Designs under U.S. Law

Foley + Corinna is a fashion company that was founded by the design team of Dana Foley and Anna Corinna, two women who had met and struck up a friendship at the 6th Avenue Flea Market in New York City. By 2008 the small company was doing over $20 million per year in business. In 2007 Foley + Corinna was the beneficiary of a public relations coup when celebrity Paris Hilton wore one of their dresses on the David Letterman show. However, it seemed that someone at the fast-fashion company Forever 21 had also been watching the same show, because Forever 21 soon began selling a $40 knockoff of the Foley + Corinna dress, which retailed at a much higher price point.

Anna Corinna's reaction was typical of fashion designers who discover that a replica of their creative designs is being sold in a cheap, knockoff version. She said: "It's awful. To me, the most awful part is that they're huge companies and they [employ] designers, and a designer's job is to design. . . . I totally understand being influenced by or inspired by, because everybody does that. But this obviously is neither. To me they should be embarrassed. They're not designing, they're stealing."[a] In another interview Corinna observed: "It's almost as if their people had told themselves, 'Mmm, this is good stuff. Let's forget product development and just do what they're doing.' This is just a blatant steal."[b]

Many other designers have been equally offended by Forever 21's knockoff practices, and quite a few have brought their complaints to court. Forever 21 was sued more than 50 times in one 5-year period, settling virtually every case out of court. A number of commentators have speculated that Forever 21 has simply incorporated the cost of legal settlements into their business model. In doing so, they have earned the wrath of those designers who they seem to knock off over and over again, such as Diane von Furstenberg and Anna Sui. Sui was so upset at these practices that at a runway show in 2007 she handed out T-shirts bearing photographs of the founders of Forever 21 next to the following printed injunction: "Thou shalt not steal."

One might assume from the above that the American fashion industry would overwhelmingly support a move to legally protect fashion designs. However, although many celebrated fashion designers have supported legislation to that effect, these efforts have not been supported by a clear industry consensus, and the topic remains a controversial one.

---

[a]Quoted in *The Knockoff Economy* by Kal Raustiala and Christopher Sprigman, Oxford University Press: New York (2012), p. 19.
[b]"Faster Fashion, Cheaper Chic" by Ruth La Ferla, *New York Times*, May 10, 2007.

---

only copies that were "substantially identical" to the originals. This is a much stricter standard than the "substantially similar" threshold for infringement in other copyrighted works. This concession would allow would-be imitators to avoid the risk of infringement simply by varying a design slightly; as Corinna stated in the box above, all designers accept the concepts of "influenced by" or "inspired by" versions. To run afoul of this new provision, a copycat company would have to produce an exact replica of a protected item.[1]

Under the IDPA, there is also a high threshold for obtaining protection in the first place: a protectable design must be the result of the designer's own creative endeavor and must provide a unique, distinguishable, nontrivial, and nonutilitarian variation over prior designs. Such protection would begin when a design is made public and would last for only a period of 3 years (extremely short compared to all other forms of copyright protection). Anything created prior to the enactment of this legislation would be considered to be in the public domain. The IDPA also provides a list of limitations to liability; for example, there is no liability for designs that are the work of a defendant's independent creation, and there is no liability for someone who copies the design for his or her personal home use.

These modifications were intended to overcome the objections of opponents, who had warned of dire consequences for the fashion industry if previous versions had passed. However, despite the substantial narrowing of the bill's focus, opponents continued to make the same arguments, in particular, that knocking off was an essential and beneficial aspect of the fashion industry that would be needlessly harmed by the proposed legislation. Neither bill was given much chance of success, given the long history of failed attempts to enact similar legislation over much of the previous century. In fact, neither of the bills made it out of committee and neither received a floor vote.

5.3. Arguments against Design Piracy Legislation: A Critical Review

Let us begin by analyzing the arguments against design piracy legislation.

5.3.1. The "Paradox" Argument: Piracy Is Good for the Fashion Business

Law professors Kal Raustiala (of UCLA) and Christopher Sprigman (of the University of Virginia) have argued that design piracy legislation would be counterproductive because design piracy and weak intellectual property protection are actually good for the fashion industry. Raustiala and Sprigman maintain that the American fashion industry actually owes much of its vibrancy to its penchant for knocking off designs. These authors look approvingly on the practice of prom dress and evening gown companies (such as Faviana, ABS, and Promgirl) that immediately copy the designs worn by celebrities on the red carpet at the Academy Awards. In their view, copycats force designers to come up with ever-new designs in an endless quest to stay ahead of the game, creating a virtuous cycle of innovation that benefits the consumer.

As indicated below, there are a number of problems with this argument and its corollaries.

5.3.2. Is the U.S. Fashion Sector More "Vibrant" Than the European or Japanese Fashion Sector?

Raustiala and Sprigman (and like-minded commentators) maintain that the economic vibrancy of the American fashion industry is due to its penchant for knockoffs, but they do not provide any comparative long-term economic evidence in support. In Europe, strong protection exists for fashion design, but the European fashion sector is certainly not lacking in vibrancy, neither artistic nor economic. Contrary to what one might expect from the "Piracy Paradox" argument, fashion is alive and well in Paris and Milan (not to mention,

London, Madrid, Berlin, Amsterdam, and Stockholm). In fact, 85 years of strong protection for fashion designs in France seem only to have cemented Paris's status as fashion capital of the world.

Indeed, the world's most successful high-fashion companies are located in Europe (e.g., Louis Vuitton, Chanel, Hermès, Yves Saint Laurent, Gucci, Armani, and Prada), as are the world's most successful fast-fashion companies (H&M, Mango, and Zara). Opponents of American design piracy fail to cite any convincing economic evidence that the American fashion sector earns a long-term higher return on investment, or is more productive, or is more profitable, than the European fashion sector. Even if they were able to do so, they would still have to establish that such an economic disparity was due to costs associated with legal protection.

The most well-known argument against design piracy legislation is thus an economic one, but it is based on assumptions unsubstantiated by convincing economic evidence and contradicted by the strong performance of the European fashion sector.

5.3.3. Failure to Address Strong American IP Protection for Fashion Elements and Failure to Proffer Evidence of Harm Caused by Said Protection

The "Paradox" argument described above is based on the corollary assumption that American fashion benefits from supposedly "weak" or nonexistent intellectual property protection. However, the assumption of weak IP protection is itself legally questionable. In actuality, American fashion companies have access to a broad range of extremely strong forms of IP protection—copyright (which extends to original prints and patterns that appear on garments, as well as to separable aspects of original accessories), trademarks, trade dress (which protects the appearance or packaging of a product), and design patents. If American fashion is vibrant because of weak IP protection, some explanation should be given as to why the strong protection already available does not do any damage (it clearly must not cause any serious damage, if the U.S. fashion industry is indeed "vibrant").

In 2008, Adidas obtained a $305 million judgment against Payless Shoes for selling athletic shoes with a striped design that was confusingly similar to Adidas's famous three-stripe pattern (the judgment was later reduced to a still-significant $50 million). It is difficult to conceive of stronger protection than a money judgment of that magnitude. Yet Payless was not forced to raise prices nor diminish the breadth of its product line, and its stock continued to climb in the year after the verdict was announced.[2] At a lesser but still impressive level, Gucci earned a $4.3 million judgment against Guess for a long history of what Gucci referred to as a massive infringement scheme, and thereafter Guess continued to offer a popular line of mid-priced, trendy apparel. Most recently, Yummie Tummie received a $6.75 million payment in settlement of its patent infringement claims against Maidenform. Maidenform remains a market leader in its sector. In none of these cases was the existence or long-term profitability of the losing company threatened, nor is there any evidence of harm to consumers, nor of a narrowing of the product line available to consumers.

5.3.4. Failure to Consider the Success of "Fast-Fashion" Companies

It is often argued that design piracy is beneficial because it "democratizes" fashion. Knock-offs, in this view, allow the middle class to afford the same styles worn by those who patronize haute couture and luxury designers. However, no company has been more successful in creating low-price couture imitations than Zara, a Spanish company that must contend with Europe's rigorous protection for fashion designs. Likewise, H&M, a fast-fashion company known for its extremely low price points and trend-forward apparel and accessories, is based in Sweden. These companies are able to offer trendy designs at "democratic" prices despite being based in Europe, where designs are strongly protected by law. How are they able to do so? Such companies simply employ designers who imitate trends rather than churn out "photocopies" of high-fashion designs (an accusation that has been leveled at American copycats such as Forever 21, Faviana, or ABS).

5.3.5. Failure to Consider Evidence That Low-Price Goods Persist Even in the Presence of Strong Design Protection

The cost-based argument is exemplified by the hyperbolic claims of California Fashion Association board member Stacy Riordan, who referred to one of the IDPA's predecessor bills as "The Destruction of Affordable Fashion Act." In Riordan's view, consumers would be forced to pay higher prices for fashion and apparel because low-cost competitors would be unable to get around the IP protection afforded to name brands.

However, there is evidence that a strong impact on prices would be unlikely. Consider the example of Crocs, a brand of low-cost foam footwear that experienced an extraordinary vogue beginning in 2005 (despite derision from fashion circles). Instantly, Crocs was faced with a host of identical knockoffs produced overseas and imported into the United States. However, Crocs was able to stop importation of the identical replicas by bringing an action for design patent infringement. This result did not stop Crocs's competitors from making slight adjustments to their shoes to avoid infringing Crocs's design patent; thereafter, they continued to offer rival products at extremely low price points. Today, a consumer can buy "real" Crocs at moderate price points (in the range of $20 to $50) or buy "imitation" Crocs for $10.

Similarly, a consumer can buy a Marc Jacobs jacket for $1,500 or a Marc Jacobs–influenced jacket at Zara for $150. There is no evidence that affordable fashion is threatened by design piracy legislation. The cost-based argument ignores the "Zara solution": a company can simply hire a designer to interpret or imitate a trend and thus can continue to produce trendy fashion items at low cost and sell them at low prices. Under the legislative proposals, one simply cannot sell identical replicas of particular branded goods.

5.3.6. The Absence of Creativity Argument: There Is No New Sleeve under the Sun

It is often argued that fashion is essentially repetitive and therefore devoid of creativity worthy of legal protection: a pocket is a pocket and a sleeve is a sleeve, and since these are old and well-known concepts, it is absurd to think that anyone should be allowed to "own" them. There is a germ of truth in this argument, but it is overstated and used to reach an illogical conclusion. Indeed, it is difficult to create an entirely new and original fashion design. However, there is no danger that classic designs would be protected in any event. Traditional design elements, from basic sleeves, hems, collars, buttons, and pockets to classic silhouettes and designs, including the pencil skirt, the button-down shirt, and the basic suit coat, are already in the public domain, exempt from protection.

However, it is also undeniably true that new aesthetic concepts are regularly developed in fashion. A simple image search on the Internet of the names Alexander McQueen or Rei Kawakubo yields evidence of prolific innovation. A popular footwear designer, Stuart Weitzman, has produced scores of shoe styles never before seen. Creative art in any domain will always represent the top of a pyramid, with the base of the pyramid composed of popular art (much of which is repetitive or imitative). The same dichotomy is already found in other fields that are fully copyrightable. Postcard photographs of the Statue of Liberty, birthday greeting cards, and melodic ballads conveying the message "I love you" can all be protected by copyright—provided that they contain some small measure of creative difference from previously existing works. In the landmark *Feist* decision,[3] the U.S. Supreme Court clarified the extremely low threshold for creativity under American copyright law: even a directory of telephone numbers could be copyrightable (provided it was not arranged mechanically in alphabetical order).

It is sometimes argued by analogy that fashion is like other creative areas that are not subject to copyright. Thus, culinary recipes are not copyrightable, nor are jokes. However, this argument ignores the marketplace reality that culinary recipes are not sold by the recipe but in the form of delicious food prepared by a master chef in a reputable restaurant (which is invariably trademarked) or in the form of a cookbook, which may be copyrighted. Similarly, no one goes to a comedy club to buy a joke. We watch famous comedians because of their masterful delivery of a comic routine, and the joke books and concert videos of such comedians are fully copyrighted. If, however, you were to make a cartoon that copied the entire routine of a famous comedian as featured in a television show or movie, you would soon find yourself in receipt of a very serious cease and desist letter from the comedian's attorney.

5.3.7. The Frivolous Litigation Argument: Failure to Address the "Forever 21 Problem"

Opponents of design piracy legislation argue that it would lead to a rash of costly, frivolous litigation. Such litigation would bully small designers, raise costs at large companies, and burden the courts. However, there is evidence that American fast-fashion companies already find themselves in court more often than their European counterparts. Thus, Harvard Law professor Jeannie Suk has pointed out that in one 5-year period the American company Forever 21 generated significantly more litigation than did its European counterparts Zara or H&M.[4] The low level of litigation in Europe is probably due in part to the context of highly protective design law, which acts as a deterrent.

Moreover, the IDPA (and many of the bills that preceded it) contains several features aimed at avoiding frivolous lawsuits, most importantly the exclusion from any protection of design staples (e.g., the white T-shirt or basic denim pants) that are commonplace, lacking in originality, and essentially part of the public domain. In addition, the IDPA featured a heightened standard for protecting designs, in that they must "provide a unique, distinguishable, non-trivial and non-utilitarian variation over prior designs for similar types of articles." As noted above, there is also a tightened standard of infringement that requires that the original design and the alleged copy be "substantially identical." Lastly, the bill puts a high burden on plaintiffs to bring a case to court, by requiring particularized pleadings, meaning that the plaintiff will have to plead facts clearly establishing a case, with penalties for misrepresentation.

5.3.8. Failure to Address Easy Solutions: Research, Imitative Design, and Licensing

It is often argued that copyright-style protection for fashion designs would grant a monopoly to a given designer for a sleeve—or some other such design element—and enable that designer to prevent the rest of the world from using it. Independent designers would become hesitant to follow trends, fearing litigation from large fashion houses, and retailers and distributors would fear becoming mired in such litigation and therefore refuse to carry items from certain designers.

However, these extreme consequences are not found in Europe, though European designers benefit from much stronger IP protection for fashion than that which has been proposed in the United States. Just as entrepreneurs are able to engage in trademark searches before risking funds on a new logo, and just as inventors must scan patent databases before seeking to patent a potentially novel invention, designers would be able to search copyright fashion registries for prior registration of designs they wish to employ. If challenged to cease and desist, they could, under the new legislative proposals, simply cease and desist without suffering damages. It is unlikely that this would bring fashion to a halt, as it is rare for any fashion house to stake its entire business on a single fashion item. Moreover, they could seek an amicable financial arrangement in the form of a license to continue to produce the disputed item.

It is a common fashion industry practice for large retailers to oblige their fashion vendors and suppliers to sign contracts that indemnify the retailer for losses suffered by IP litigation. In actual practice, retailers do not commonly challenge or even investigate allegations of IP infringement against vendors featured in their stores. The most usual practice is simply for the retailer to pull the challenged line and seek indemnification or chargeback compensation from the vendor. While this may be inconvenient for retailers, it is far from disastrous.

5.3.9. The Argument That Copyright Protection Is Inappropriate for Utilitarian Products

It is argued that copyright protection was developed for products that are principally creative, while clothing generally has a strong functional component. Therefore, courts would struggle to apply and adapt existing copyright law to this new context; design patent law, in this view, is more appropriate for the production of fashion items.

At an abstract level, this argument is hard to refute. However, in practice we see that similar legal expansions for copyright in the past have not produced catastrophic results. It used to be that ornamental architectural elements, vessel hulls, silicon chip designs, and computer software programs were not protected by copyright. Progressive expansion of the scope of copyright law brought these sectors within the copyright fold. Vessel hulls certainly have a utilitarian aspect since they allow ships to stay afloat on the water, and computer programs and silicon chip designs allow computers to operate. However, there are no reports of extreme inhibition of creativity in the markets for vessel hulls, silicon chips, or software as a result of this copyright protection, nor have the courts struggled to adapt copyright law to these contexts. Moreover, if we use Europe as a guide, the protection of fashion design in Europe has not resulted in creating uncertainty or in clogging the courts with a new wave of litigation.

5.4. Evaluation of Arguments in Favor of Design Piracy Legislation

5.4.1. The Fundamental Argument: Fashion Is Creative

At the broadest level, the push for design piracy legislation is a call for legal recognition of the creativity and artistic value inherent in original fashion designs. Any system of law that uses copyright law to protect vessel hulls and computer software but fails to extend this protection to fashion can be accused of inconsistency, as fashion is widely considered to be as artistically creative an industry as (if not more than) vessel hull design or computer programming.

To this basic argument is added the urgent need to react to technological developments: information technology has accelerated the speed, precision, and volume of design piracy. Perfect 360° photographic images can be instantly transmitted from a fashion show to factories in China and other places where they can be quickly copied, with knockoff garments shipped back into the United States within a short time frame. Knockoffs are sometimes available to the public even before the originals reach their legitimate distribution outlets.

5.4.2. The Value of Design Piracy Legislation Is Sometimes Overstated

In lobbying campaigns carried out on behalf of design piracy legislation, it is sometimes implied that design piracy protection would put an end to knockoffs. This seems unlikely, however, given the success of Zara and H&M in avoiding legal chastisement. Passage of design piracy legislation would not put Forever 21, Faviana, or NastyGal.com out of business; it would simply force them to hire more designers and do a more careful job in imitating fashion leaders. They would have to stop churning out near-perfect replicas, but they could continue to produce trendy items that were clearly inspired by market leaders.

Moreover, design piracy legislation would have little effect on true counterfeiters, who continue to ply their wares in the face of criminal penalties. Although the focus in anticounterfeiting is on trademark counterfeiting, many counterfeit items infringe both trademark and copyright protection in the same item. Thus, for example, an authentic Hermès or Louis Vuitton handbag may feature a copyrighted printed canvas or inner lining, and the counterfeit item will steal both the trademark (with false labels and logos) and the copyrighted material.

5.4.3. Many Popular Designs Will Be Ineligible for Copyright Protection

Opponents of piracy design legislation often point out that European fashion houses actually do not rely heavily on their availability to register fashion designs. Total fashion registrations can be measured in the thousands rather than in the hundreds of thousands or millions.

Many new items produced by fashion houses will always be composed of classic, non-copyrightable elements and therefore will be ineligible for protection. Thus, it is often pointed out that many "new" designs are simply reinterpretations of classic designs. Fashion houses will simply have to rely on existing trademark, trade dress, and design patent protection to protect elements of these designs, as is already possible. Design piracy legislation is certainly no panacea against knockoffs, nor is it intended to be. It is intended only to prevent companies from acting as "free riders" on the design innovations of fashion leaders by preventing them from commercializing exact copies of original designs. Moreover, what opponents fail to mention is that in Europe, registration is not necessarily a prerequisite for protection and, therefore, not an entirely valid measure of European enforcement of design protection.[5]

5.4.4. Compliance with International Treaties

Proponents argue that without protection for fashion designs, U.S. law is in violation of international treaty obligations. For example, passage of the IDPA would help bring U.S. law in line with the Berne Union and the Uruguay Round Agreement on Trade-Related Aspects of Intellectual Property Rights (TRIPS), which require members, such as the United States, to "provide for the protection of independently created industrial designs that are new or original."[6] Extending copyright protection to original fashion designs would enable the United States to meet these international norms.

5.5. Comparison: Fashion Design Protection in the European Union

5.5.1. European Community Design Protection Regulation

In stark contrast to American law, the European Union (EU) affords fashion designers an exclusive and independent right against design copying. On March 6, 2002, the European Community Design Protection Regulation (the "Regulation") came into force and was made applicable to all 27 EU Member States.[7] The Regulation provides designers with exclusive rights to use their designs in commerce, to enforce those rights against infringers, and to claim damages. Recognizing that the duration of protection may be less important for some designs than for others, the Regulation creates short-term protection for Unregistered Community Designs (UCD) and long-term protection for Registered Community Designs (RCD).[8] The Regulation was created to harmonize design laws within the EU community and does not override any national laws governing fashion design in individual EU countries.[9]

Regardless of registration, a design must be new and possess individual character in order to qualify for protection under the Regulation.[10] "Design" is defined as "the appearance of the whole or part of the product resulting from its features and, in particular, the lines, contours, colors, shape, texture and/or materials of the product itself and/or its ornamentation."[11] A design is considered new if no identical design has been made available to the public.[12] Individual character is assessed by whether the overall impression the design produces on the informed user differs from the overall impression produced by any publicly available design.[13] If a design is found to have infringed an RCD or UCD, the court[14] will issue an injunction prohibiting infringing acts, a seizure order for the infringing products or any materials used to manufacture such products, and any other sanctions deemed appropriate.

5.5.2. Registered Community Designs

Applications to register a design must be made to the Office for Harmonization in the Internal Market (OHIM). A designer need file only one application and make one fee payment in order to obtain protection across the EU. In addition, a single application can contain multiple designs.[15] Registered designs are protected for five years, renewable up to a maximum of 25 years (or an additional four times).[16] The RCD not only protects its owner against copying but also against the independent creation of an identical or similar design.[17]

The RCD permits designers to test their design in the marketplace by allowing a 12-month grace period between placing the design on the market and applying for registration. The public disclosure of the design during the 12-month period will not be considered in determining the novelty or individual character of a design.[18] Moreover, the RCD provides some insulation against competitors by permitting publication in the Community Design Bulletin to be deferred upon request so that the design may be kept secret until it is made publicly available.[19]

5.5.3. Unregistered Community Designs

UCD protection is automatic once a design is made available to the public and lasts for three years.[20] Public disclosure, however, is not the only means of making a design available. Disclosure may occur through designs going on sale, prior marketing, publicity, or exhibiting the design at a trade show.[21] Unlike an RCD, a UCD only protects its owner against deliberate copying of the owner's design.[22] The owner of a UCD is not protected against the independent creation of an identical or similar design. If there is proof that the alleged infringing design was created independently by a designer with no reason to know of the UCD, the UCD owner has no legal recourse.

The impact of the European scheme is difficult to measure due to the small number of cases disputing design protection. In one reported case, Jimmy Choo utilized the protection offered in suing a retailer for infringing its registered and unregistered design rights in a handbag.[23] The court ruled in favor of Jimmy Choo, finding that the handbags at issue were copies, which suggests that the European law can be very effective and beneficial to a high-end fashion designer. Despite the dearth of case law, it is possible that designers do indeed utilize the protection offered by the law to reach out-of-court resolutions that are not reported.

5.6. Summary of Key Points

1. Current and recent legislative proposals to protect fashion design in the United States have focused on the problem of companies that execute and sell near-exact replicas of existing designs. Given this limitation, warnings of major harm to the entire fashion industry are overstated and unsubstantiated.
2. Europe's continued fashion preeminence despite strong design protection provides an example of a thriving fashion sector that coexists with robust legal protection for fashion designs.
3. Knockoffs that are inspired by a design innovation but that do not copy it exactly are here to stay and must be accepted as a characteristic element of a trend-driven industry.

Notes

1. http://www.govtrack.us/congress/bills/112/s3523/text.

2. "*Adidas v. Payless:* 100 Million for Every Stripe," *Wall Street Journal*, May 8, 2008, http://blogs.wsj.com/law/2008/05/07/adidas-v-payless-100-million-for-every-stripe-payless-could-pay-more/ (last accessed August 29, 2013); on Adidas stock price, see http://www.advfn.com/nyse/StockChart.asp?stockchart=PSS.

3. *Feist Publications v. Rural Telephone Service Co.*, 499 U.S. 340 (1991).

4. See C. Scott Hemphill & Jeannie Suk, *The Law, Culture, and Economics of Fashion*, 61 STAN. L. REV. 1147, 1172-73 (2009).

5. Office for Harmonization in the Internal Market, "What Is a Community Design?," http://oami.europa.eu/ows/rw/pages/RCD/communityDesign.en.do (last accessed September 3, 2013).

6. Agreement on Trade-Related Aspects of Intellectual Property Rights art. 25, Annex 1C, Apr. 15, 1994, 33 I.L.M. 1197, 1207 (1994).

7. Council Regulation (EC) No. 6/2002 of 12 December 2001 O.J. (L 3, 1.2002, at. 1), amended by Council Regulation (EC) No. 1891/2006 of 18 December 2006 O.J. (L 386, 29.12.2006, at 14), available at http://oami.europa.eu/en/design/pdf/6-02-CV-en.pdf.

8. Office for Harmonization in the Internal Market, "What Is a Community Design?," http://oami.europa.eu/ows/rw/pages/RCD/communityDesign.en.do (last accessed September 3, 2013).

9. See Uma Suthersanen, *Design Law in Europe: An Analysis of the Protection of Artistic, Industrial, and Functional Designs in Europe, including a Review of the E.C. Design Regulation, the E.C. Design Directive, and International Design Protection* 13-010 (London: Sweet & Maxwell, 2000), for an analysis of national design laws in Europe.

10. Council Regulation (EC) No. 6/2002 of 12 December 2001 O.J. (L 3, 1.2002, at. 1), amended by Council Regulation (EC) No. 1891/2006 of 18 December 2006 O.J. (L 386, 29.12.2006, at.14), art. 4(1).

11. *Id.* art. 3(a).

12. *Id.* art. 5(2).

13. *Id.* art. 6(1).

14. Pursuant to the Regulation, each EU member is to designate a Community Design Court within their territory to hear infringement cases. Council Regulation (EC) No. 6/2002 of 12 December 2001 O.J. (L 3, 1.2002, at 1), amended by Council Regulation (EC) No. 1891/2006 of 18 December 2006 O.J. (L 386, 29.12.2006, at 14), art. 80(1).

15. *Id.* art. 37(1).

16. *Id.* art. 12.

17. *Id.* art. 19(1).

18. *Id.* art. 7(2)(b).

19. *Id.* art. 50(1).

20. *Id.* art. 11(1).

21. *Id.* art. 11(2).

22. *Id.* art. 19(2).

23. *J Choo (Jersey) Ltd. v. Towerstone Ltd.*, [2008] E.W.H.C. 346 (H.Ct., 16th January, 2008) (U.K.), available at http://www.bailii.org/ew/cases/EWHC/Ch/2008/346.html.

7

Fashion Licensing

Karen Artz Ash and Barbara Kolsun

7.1. Introduction

This chapter presents an overview of brand licensing and identifies the various issues that arise from these contractual arrangements in the fashion industry. License agreements are absolutely vital to the fashion industry, and it is no exaggeration to state that global fashion is built substantially on a foundation of brand licenses. As we will see, license agreements must be living instruments. As a result, the best ones are carefully designed to govern how people and companies work together over significant periods of time as true business partners, united in the mutual goal of exploiting a common intellectual property right (usually, a fashion brand's trademark).

7.2. What Is a License?

A license is an agreement under which one party grants to another the right to exploit certain intellectual property, subject to guidance, oversight, and other specific constraints. A licensor is the owner of the intellectual property (or, in some cases, a related party authorized by the owner to exploit its IP rights).[1] The licensor–licensee relationship should always be memorialized in a written contract. In the fashion industry, the principal asset of most fashion houses is their trademark (and associated logos). Accordingly, in addition to state law governing the formation and interpretation of the contract, the Lanham Act (i.e., Federal Trademark Act) is also applicable.

7.3. Why License?

The licensing relationship should be mutually advantageous to the parties involved. Licensing allows a brand owner to engage in controlled expansion without having to invest in costly infrastructure. Frequently, licensing facilitates expansion into new product categories, increases market penetration, expands distribution channels, and enhances brand awareness. For example, a clothing designer can seek brand extensions into fragrances, cosmetics, jewelry, shoes, eyewear, accessories such as handbags, home collections, and lower-priced apparel to create a complete "lifestyle brand." These complementary extensions can enhance brand awareness, supported by new points of sale in prime locations (e.g., accessories and perfumes, common objects of a licensing brand extension strategy, generally appear on the first floor of department stores) and different categories of stores (e.g., optical shops and home goods stores).

Licensees also benefit from licenses because they allow a party with infrastructure and expertise to market a well-known brand. In many instances, marketing of a famous brand can enhance the licensee's access to retailers for other brands—although most licenses prohibit a licensee from making or marketing brands and products that are directly competitive to the licensor's brands or products.

Licenses are also beneficial for licensors looking to enter international markets or for licensees looking to import foreign brands. Licensors may benefit from access to foreign distributors and retailers who have established local commercial relationships and expertise. Likewise, local retailers may benefit from introducing foreign brands and products to their home locations.

Strategic fashion licensing can be very profitable. Of the world's top five licensors in 2011, fashion companies were the second and third most profitable.[2] In 2011, retail sales of licensed fashion merchandise exceeded $18 billion in the United States and Canada alone.[3] The best licensors succeed through strategic license agreements that increase brand exposure while minimizing business risks and costs.

7.4. Finding Licensing Opportunities: Licensing Agents

7.4.1. Licensing Agents—How Can They Help?

Licensing agents can assist a brand owner in identifying and capitalizing on marketable opportunities via licensing.[4] In the law, an "agent" is one who is empowered to act on behalf of another person or entity.[5] In the context of licensing, agents may be called upon by licensors to:[6]

1. Develop a strategic licensing plan, including identifying promising retail channels and identifying target licensees capable of assisting in the execution of the licensing objectives.
2. Identify and pursue opportunities with potential partners who have the proper expertise and market positioning.
3. Provide guidelines on realistic financial goals.
4. Broker and negotiate licensing arrangements.
5. Monitor performance and assist in quality control.[7]

While agents are often called upon to help expand product scope and market penetration for young and rapidly growing brands, agents may also help identify "out-of-the-box opportunities" for developed or well-known brands. For example, a fine watch brand might

---

Fashion Law *in Practice*

Licensing by Entertainers and Celebrities

Entertainment personalities commonly lend their names to fashion accessories and clothes. Jennifer Lopez (J Lo) and Lauren Conrad are two notable examples of celebrities who lent their names and images to apparel and accessories marketed exclusively through a single retailer, such as Kohl's or JCPenney. Since celebrities are usually represented by agents in their entertainment lives, they turn to agents to identify licensing opportunities, to negotiate equitable terms, and to administer the day-to-day execution of licensing relationships. Agents will make sure that new licensing opportunities do not conflict with existing ones and that photographs or likenesses used to promote the products are commensurate with the star's image and persona.

---

be advised to target luxury automotive companies for prestige product placement through branded interior clocks.

Conversely, a prestige designer might be interested in exploiting down-market opportunities in the mass channel, an option fraught with risk (since brand integrity is at stake). A wrong move with a poor partner can compromise a prestige brand's exclusivity. A good licensing agent will have the know-how to match the licensor with the best possible licensee and thereafter assist with the negotiation of a successful license agreement.

In choosing an agent, the licensor should first carefully consider whether the agent's strategy is aligned with the licensor's. In many cases, the agent's relationship with the brand owner is short term. Since agents do not get paid until licenses are signed and revenue starts to flow, they have an incentive to quickly sign as many licenses as possible. This can result in contracts with inappropriate partners or with less advantageous terms. This approach raises the risk to the brand that the licensee may produce and sell substandard products that will damage the brand's image in the marketplace.

Business terms with a licensing agent vary according to the type of licensing arrangement that is ultimately concluded. Typically, agents receive some portion of the royalties or profits generated through the licensing facilitated by the agent. Since the agent's commissions are usually based upon the services provided by the agent, the licensor should clearly define the role and extent of the agent's services.

7.5. Negotiating a License

Key issues to keep in mind when negotiating a licensing contract are as follows.

7.5.1. Preparation

► Get to know your licensing partner. Allow sufficient time in the negotiation to really get to know the other party. Otherwise, after the contract is signed, you may find yourself locked into an underperforming partnership for years.

- ▸ Address brand goals, strategic vision, and readiness to expand into other product lines.
- ▸ Ascertain whether the licensing partner has the infrastructure to adequately support the license.
- ▸ Investigate the other party's financial situation to determine whether it has the resources to support the alliance.
- ▸ Research the other party's reputation and track record in the industry.
- ▸ Licensors should carefully investigate the market success of the candidate licensee's other licensed products.
- ▸ Licensees should carefully evaluate the licensor's brand strengths and potential weaknesses.

7.5.2. Post-Preparation, Pre-Negotiation

Since the typical licensing arrangement requires a multiyear commitment, any sign of antagonism in the initial negotiations is an ominous warning sign. If the negotiations are difficult from the start, it may be prudent to simply reevaluate the choice of licensing partner. As a general rule, neither party should seek a significant concession without granting an equivalent concession. Business executives often want to close the deal quickly, but it is important nonetheless to make every effort to ensure that the agreement clearly and precisely spells out the parties' mutual obligations and thereby protects each side's interests. When negotiations hit a roadblock, experienced professionals will calmly seek to discern the reasons underlying the other side's positions so as to identify a potential compromise that meets both sides' legitimate business requirements. Both sides should remain open to the need to modify terms in the proposed contract at the other side's request, subject to the caveat that the licensor should

---

Fashion Law *in Practice*

To Deal or Not to Deal?

Parties should be careful not to enter into unclear "deal memos" or letters of intent just to get things started. Such vehicles are best used to propose terms but should clearly state that they do not intend to constitute a final agreement. Used improperly, such agreements may be interpreted as binding and thereby ultimately harm brand reputation and relations between the parties. For example, in *World Championship Wrestling*, a deal memo did just that. While working on a complete marketing and distribution agreement, the parties entered into the deal memo. Relations broke down, however, and the parties never reached agreement on the full merchandising agreement. In the full agreement, the licensor wanted to limit distribution channels to department stores, specialty stores, and mid-tier stores. However, the court found the deal memo enforceable. Thus, sale of T-shirts bearing the licensor's marks at flea markets, a distribution channel harmful to the brand, was permissible. If the parties had taken the time to flesh out the agreement, the licensor could have avoided the detrimental sales or had adequate grounds to bring an action for breach of contract, trademark infringement, and other relevant claims.

Source: World Championship Wrestling, Inc. v. GJS Int'l, Inc., 13 F.Supp.2d 725 (N.D. Ill. 1998).

---

always maintain tight control over creative and distribution channels to protect the integrity of the brand.

Licensing agreements are too important and too constraining to be rushed (see *Fashion Law in Practice: To Deal or Not to Deal?*). A poorly drafted licensing agreement or a bad match can be detrimental in the long run to a company's brand image, sales, goodwill, and customer relations.

Negotiation Checklist

- ▶ Draft a term sheet with key goals and responsibilities (with the caveat that it clearly states that it does not represent the full or final agreement).
- ▶ Figure out how far you will bend to accommodate the other party if it does not agree to your proposed terms.
- ▶ Work with counsel to memorialize terms, understand the meaning of the terms, and help reach a final agreement for execution.

7.6. Key Terms and Sample Clauses

The key terms in a licensing agreement are as follows.

7.6.1. Definitions

The Definitions section sets forth the meaning of the terms within the agreement. This is important because parties may want to attribute specific meanings to terms that may otherwise be used differently in everyday language.

7.6.2. Grant of License/Rights Retained by Licensor

The Grant of License/Rights Retained by Licensor section sets forth exactly what intellectual property is being licensed. It should clearly define the rights granted, such as trademark, patent, copyright, trade secret, manufacturing, and technical know-how. Note that a copyright owner maintains a "bundle" of exclusive rights,[8] so any license concerning copyright should clearly define which rights are granted (these rights are separable).

The grant section should clearly state which rights are retained by the licensor and are *not* granted to licensee. The express reservation of specifically described rights will avoid disputes later. Some licensing agreements contain provisions stating that "all rights not granted to licensee are retained by licensor." Such broad provisions, however, often lead to disagreement over the scope of reserved rights. To avoid disputes, "catchall" provisions should complement an express reservation of specifically described rights.

The contract should specify when, where, and on what type of products the licensed intellectual property rights may be used. For example, a license may specify that a trademark may be used only on jeans, or that a copyrighted image may be reproduced and distributed only on T-shirts, or that a patented zipper may be used only on handbags. Limiting the scope of use helps licensors control who makes, uses, and sells their products, thereby creating a stable of licensed "experts." The licensee should review the grant terms to make sure that its terms are broad enough to support what the licensee wants to do. Conversely, the licensor must be vigilant that the rights granted are sufficiently well defined.

Rights granted under a license may be exclusive or nonexclusive. Under an exclusive license, the licensee is the only entity authorized to exploit (as defined by the contract) the licensed intellectual property in the designated "territory." Since fashion and apparel products are now often manufactured in Asia or other places where the licensee may not be authorized to sell, exclusivity is commonly limited to distribution and sale (and not manufacture) in a discrete territory. Exclusive licensed rights will command higher rates of compensation to the licensor by the licensee.

Licenses that do not confer manufacturing exclusivity can be beneficial for both the licensor and licensee, as for example when a mark is well known and product lines and brand extensions require multiple manufacturers. It is common for a fashion licensor to have separate licenses for different categories—for example, one for swimwear, one for shoes, one for jeans, and so on. Each licensee will possess specific expertise in the particular product category. It is rare for a licensee to be granted exclusivity for all categories of apparel. The extent of the territory should be carefully defined. Licensors should be careful not to grant an overly broad territory, which might limit the licensor's ability to profitably license to other parties, while overly narrow territories may stifle brand expansion. If the territory is too narrow, the licensor may fail to fully exploit an opportunity to expand brand recognition. As an essential part of their due diligence, both parties should assure themselves that an adequate consumer market exists in the territory for the licensed products.

While the licensing of proprietary brands and designs is perhaps the most common approach, many licenses also seek to exploit the popularity of a specific designer or celebrity. These licenses in particular should clearly define the scope of rights granted. For example, a popular couture designer may agree to design ready-to-wear tops, dresses, and scarves for the licensor only. The fashion house licensor must consider the types of products it wishes the designer or celebrity to design or promote, the cachet associated with the designer or celebrity, and any other information about the individual that may have an impact on the brand. On the other side, the designer or celebrity should consider the nature of the brand, whether its manufacturing practices are ethical, and how the designer or celebrity's name or likeness should be used in connection with the fashion company's products.

License agreements commonly prohibit licensees from manufacturing and selling competitive products under a competitive trademark. Thus, many well-known designers prohibit their licensees from acting as licensees for other designers. The license may also prohibit a licensee from selling similar products not bearing the licensor's mark.

Most agreements also contain a provision under which the licensee agrees not to cancel, oppose, or otherwise challenge the validity, enforceability, or ownership of licensor's mark (or the license granted by the agreement). However, broad language in provisions seeking to restrain the licensee's acts may run afoul of anticompetition law in some countries. It is advisable to consult local counsel with respect to these provisions.

```
┌──────────────────────────────────────────────────────────┐
│                                                            │
│            SAMPLE CLAUSE: GRANT OF LICENSE                 │
│                                                            │
│   Licensor grants to Licensee the right and license to use the [patents, trademarks,
│   copyrights, designs, information] on or in association with the Licensed Products.
│   Such grant conveys the [nonexclusive] right to manufacture, source, and have man-
│   ufactured the Licensed Products, and the [exclusive] right to sell, market, distribute,
│   promote and advertise the Licensed Products in [define territory: e.g., the United
│   States, Japan, worldwide]. Licensee may manufacture or source the manufacture of
│   the Licensed Products outside of the Territory in which the Licensed Products may
│   be sold, provided that Licensor consents in writing.
│
│   Licensee shall not at any time during or after the effective term of the Agreement
│   dispute or contest licensor's exclusive right and title to the licensed intellectual prop-
│   erty or the validity thereof, and shall not seek to oppose or cancel any of Licensor's
│   pending or registered marks, or invalidate or render unenforceable any of Licensor's
│   [patents, trademarks, or copyrights].
│                                                            │
└──────────────────────────────────────────────────────────┘
```

7.6.3. Additional Trademark Considerations

Trademark license contracts should feature an attached schedule listing the licensed marks and their registration numbers. The schedule can be amended if new marks are registered. In the event that new trademarks are added by the licensor (for use with the licensed mark), the license should specify responsibility for clearance and filing of additional registrations and should confirm that ownership is retained by the licensor. The agreement should also include a provision requiring the licensee to cooperate in the process of obtaining and maintaining the registrations.

Since a licensor must always protect its licensed marks, the license should include a provision stating that the licensee will not challenge or oppose the marks.[9] The agreement should also specify who will enforce the marks and who will bear the expense of enforcement if there is third-party infringement. The parties should be required to notify each other if either is aware of third-party infringement. In some countries only an exclusive licensee will be able to enforce the marks. In the United States, trademark owners must "police" their marks in order to maintain strong rights in the mark. A failure to police may result in loss of a mark or decreased strength of a mark. A weak mark can be more difficult to enforce.

In some countries, trademark licenses must be recorded, and the trademark must first be registered in order to permit recordation. In such countries, licensing agreements that are not recorded may not be enforceable. It is therefore imperative to update the recordation each time a new mark becomes subject to the license. Foreign laws may prohibit the licensee from registering the license with the trademark office without prior written authorization of the licensor.

SAMPLE CLAUSES: PROTECTION AND OWNERSHIP OF LICENSED TRADEMARKS

Licensor shall seek, obtain, and, during the term of this Agreement, maintain at its own expense, appropriate protection for the licensed trademarks ("Trademarks"), and shall retain all right, title, and interest in the Trademarks as well as any modifications used by Licensee.

If Licensee requests that Licensor obtain trademark protection for a particular item, Licensor agrees to take reasonable steps to obtain such protection, and Licensee shall reimburse Licensor for all costs associated with filing, prosecuting, and maintaining the mark. The parties agree to execute any documents and assist the other to achieve any of the trademark protection provisions.

Licensee acknowledges Licensor's ownership, exclusive rights, value, and goodwill in the Trademarks; that the Trademarks are unique and associated with Licensor; that Licensee's use of the Trademarks inures to the benefit of Licensor; and that Licensee shall not acquire any rights in the Trademarks.

Licensee shall not, at any time during or after the effective term of the Agreement, dispute or contest Licensor's exclusive right and title to the Trademarks or the validity thereof and shall not seek to oppose or cancel any of Licensor's pending or registered marks.

7.6.4. Term and Termination

All agreements should specify the term (i.e., duration of the license) and what happens upon termination or expiration. Licensors commonly seek a short initial term to give the licensee an introductory period of performance. Conversely, a licensee may want a very long term if it is making a substantial investment in infrastructure or personnel. The term may be renewed upon written notice or may be automatic. Ideally, renewal should require affirmative measures and should not be self-effecting. Occasionally, the parties may negotiate roll-over provisions that automatically extend the length of the agreement, but this is not advisable for a first agreement, as the parties may wish to renegotiate terms at the conclusion of the initial term.

The licensor should always retain the ability to terminate upon a material breach of the agreement, for instance, failure to pay royalties, failure to satisfy quality obligations, failure to meet sales minimums, or unauthorized sale of products. Upon termination, the parties may want certain obligations to remain in force, such as the obligations to pay royalties, to refrain from challenging the trademark registration, or to maintain the confidentiality of business information. The license should thus define the post-termination rights of the parties as regards the disposition of product or the use of licensed intellectual property. The agreement should include applicable wind-down terms, disposition of inventory, buy-back options, and royalty obligations during the disposition period, among other terms. Agreements commonly require that upon termination in advance of natural expiration, the payment of minimum royalties for the balance of the licensed term is accelerated and payment is due immediately.

SAMPLE CLAUSES: TERMINATION OF THE LICENSING AGREEMENT

Upon termination, all royalty obligations shall become immediately due and shall continue for any post-termination cure periods.

Licensor may terminate the Agreement by giving written notice to Licensee in the event Licensee fails to meet any of the deadlines set for product launch, fails to sell any Licensed Products for two consecutive royalty periods, fails to make three or more timely royalty payments during any twelve (12) month period, fails to maintain product liability insurance as required by the Agreement, files a petition in bankruptcy, is found to be bankrupt or insolvent, or fails to comply with the provisions of the Agreement regarding patents, trademarks, or copyrights.

Either party may terminate upon sixty (60) days written notice to the other party upon a breach of a material provision of the Agreement, provided that the breaching party fails to cure within the specified cure period.

Licensee shall be entitled to a six (6) month sell-off period of all inventory existing upon expiration or termination of this Agreement, except where termination is based upon Licensee's material breach (for which Licensee must immediately cease all sales of Licensed Products). All sales during the sell-off period are subject to the terms of the Agreement, including the payment of royalties, which shall be due within thirty (30) days after the close of the sell off period.

Upon expiration or termination of the Agreement, all of the rights of Licensee under this Agreement shall terminate and immediately revert to Licensor, and Licensee shall immediately discontinue all use of the patents, trademarks, copyrights, designs, or information licensed and return any materials provided by Licensor at no cost whatsoever to Licensor.

7.6.5. Compensation

The licensee usually pays the licensor a royalty, which may come in the form of a flat fee, a percentage of net sales, or some combination thereof. It is important at the outset to distinguish between wholesale licenses and retail licenses (sometimes called "territorial licenses"). In a wholesale license, the licensee is granted the right to manufacture (or source) the product and to sell it at wholesale to others who will then sell to the retail consumer. In a retail license, the licensor grants to the licensee the right to operate retail stores identified by the trademark and sell licensed products only in the retail store space. We will first discuss compensation in wholesale licenses.

Royalty rates in fashion licenses commonly range from 5 to 15 percent of a revenue stream, which may be defined as "wholesale sales," "gross sales," or, more typically in a wholesale license, "net sales." Generally, royalties on wholesale sales generate the greatest income to the licensor. In any case, the agreement should clearly define the given term. For example, net sales are commonly calculated as gross sales less specified discounts and returns. Higher royalties may be commanded by more well-known brands and by agreements that may also contemplate separate advertising contributions. The agreement should also state the exclusions or deductions that are not allowed. For example, foreign withholding taxes on royalty income in certain countries can be as high as 30 percent and can be excluded from the net sales calculation.

Some agreements set guaranteed minimum royalty payments per a given time period based upon earned royalties only. Well-drafted licenses for mature brands generally include both guaranteed minimum annual royalty payments (generally paid in advance and prorated on a quarterly basis) and minimum annual net sales obligations. The use of guaranteed minimum obligations avoids the "warehousing" of brands and compels actual business development commensurate with royalties. Guaranteed royalty payments alone cannot assure the licensor of reaching objectives as regards expansion of the brand, its goodwill, and its reputation. The inclusion of minimum sales requirements also enables the licensor to terminate the agreement if such objectives are not being met. The licensor is thus able to seek out another licensee if sales fall below expectations.

Licensors commonly seek bifurcated agreements that separate design fees and royalty fees. In such contracts, royalties are calculated only on net sales, and deductions from royalties for design costs by the licensee are not allowed. Licensees, conversely, prefer as many exclusions or deductions as possible to cover their expenses and lower royalty payments. Other common exclusions include sales from licensee to licensor when the agreement permits licensor to buy products from licensee at a discount.

Royalties may be set on an escalating (or descending) basis. The agreement should require that royalty payments be accompanied by a detailed statement of sales, credits, discounts, and exclusions from sales if the royalty is based upon net sales. The licensor should include a provision permitting termination for nonpayment or chronic late payment. Penalty provisions for late payments are also common. The license should precisely specify the mode and currency payment (for example, U.S. currency by wire transfer) and provide for a right to audit the licensees, records for up to three years following the expiration or termination of a license.

In retail licenses, royalties are calculated on sales at retail, as opposed to sales made at wholesale. Retail licenses provide for either (i) an attributed arm's-length wholesale amount for which the full royalty rate will apply or (ii) a reduced royalty rate (usually reduced by 50 percent) applied to retail sales at the retail selling price. Often, where there is an accompanying distribution arrangement (as opposed to a manufacturer's license), the company must purchase all products from the licensor subject to "minimum purchase" requirements. The location, design, appearance, style, layout, and all other aspects relating to the operation and appearance of the retail store must be approved by licensor.

Key terms in retail licenses include the following:

- Location of retail spaces
- Appearance of retail spaces (inside and out)
- Display and signage
- Indemnification in favor of licensor
- Liability for employees to be borne by the licensee
- Maintenance of the premises at the licensee's expense

- ▶ Termination and requirements that store signage be removed and/or possible option by the licensor to obtain assignment of the leases
- ▶ Product supply to stores

SAMPLE CLAUSES: ROYALTY TERMS

Licensee shall pay Licensor a Royalty of [3 to 15 percent] of Net Sales (as defined herein). Licensee agrees to pay Licensor a minimum royalty of [value] per year commencing on the first day of January, which shall be payable as an advance against the royalty owed.

The royalty owed Licensor shall be calculated on a quarterly basis and shall be payable no later than thirty (30) days after the end of the preceding full calendar quarter, i.e., commencing on the first day of January, April, July, and October [with the exception of the first and last calendar quarters, which may be "short" depending upon the effective date of this Agreement].

With each Royalty Payment, Licensee shall provide Licensor with a written royalty statement in a form acceptable to Licensor and shall include information such as stock number, product description, units sold, quantity shipped, gross invoice, amount billed customers less discounts, returns, and/or sales for each Licensed Product. Also, the statement shall be provided even where no Licensed Products were sold during the Royalty Period.

"Net Sales" means Licensee's gross sales (the gross invoice amount billed customers) of Licensed Products, less discounts and allowances actually shown on the invoice (except cash discounts or discounts granted to a party affiliated with Licensee), less any bona fide returns (i.e., returns actually made or allowed as supported by credit actually issued to customers). No other costs incurred in the manufacturing, selling, advertising, and distribution of the Licensed Products shall be deducted nor shall any deduction be allowed for any uncollectible accounts or allowances. If Licensed Products are sold at a discount to a party affiliated with Licensee, the Royalty shall be calculated on the basis of the regular price charged other parties.

A royalty obligation shall accrue upon the sale of Licensed Products regardless of the time of collection by Licensee, and a Licensed Product shall be considered "sold" when the Licensed Product is billed, invoiced, shipped, or paid for, whichever is first.

Late payments shall incur interest at the rate of one (1) percent per month from the date such payments were originally due.

7.6.6. Currency/Audit

The Currency/Audit section of the agreement sets forth the exact manner of payment to the licensor and further specifies the licensor's rights to inspect the licensee's accounting books and records. Audits and inspections can be crucial tools for a licensor wishing to observe and verify the actual business practices supporting the payment of royalties.

Licenses commonly require the licensee to pay for the audit if the licensee is found to owe a specified amount (usually a percentage) in excess of the royalties actually reported and paid. Also, the license may specify that the licensor's acceptance of the royalty does not constitute agreement to the amount paid, thereby permitting the licensor to challenge payments already made and accepted.

An audit will require access to confidential information, and the agreement may place restrictions on the use of such confidential information.

SAMPLE CLAUSES: ROYALTY AUDITS

Licensor shall have the right, upon at least five (5) days written notice to inspect Licensee's books and records with respect to the subject matter of this Agreement. In the event that the inspection reveals a discrepancy in the amount of Royalty owed Licensor from what was actually paid, Licensee shall pay such discrepancy plus interest, calculated at the rate of two (2) percent per month. If the discrepancy is greater than [one thousand dollars ($1,000)], Licensee shall reimburse Licensor for the cost of the audit including any attorney's fees incurred in connection therewith.

In an investigation, any confidential and proprietary business information made available to Licensor or a third party acting on its behalf shall be retained in confidence and not disclosed to any non-interested third party for a period of two (2) years from the date of disclosure, except where required by law or where written permission is granted by Licensee. Any such information may be used in any proceeding based on Licensee's failure to pay its actual Royalty obligation.

7.6.7. Design

Design sections in license agreements explicitly provide for how the licensed products will be designed, the approval process, the creation of prototypes, and schedules relating to production, delivery, promotion, and market delivery of the goods. This section should state whether third-party contractors are permitted, and the extent to which such parties are governed by the terms of the agreement, proper indemnities, and ethical compliance guidelines.

7.6.8. Quality Control, Advertising, and Promotion Minimums

Quality control of the licensed product is imperative, as lack of control may weaken or destroy a brand and its reputation. Thus, the licensor should retain the right to control the design of the licensed product, including materials used, overall quality, and manufacturing processes. These quality controls should include the right to inspect manufacturing plants and review and comment on samples and prototypes throughout the manufacturing process.

The level of quality control will vary depending upon the product being licensed and the licensor's relationships with the licensee. In some instances, as for example where the licensor and licensee have enjoyed a long, cooperative relationship, the licensor may accept a less active role in supervising quality. The licensor's level of control, however, should never be so lax as to jeopardize the licensor's marks.

The licensor should specify the appropriate channels of distribution for sale of the products. For example, if the license grants rights to designer names or marks associated with luxury goods, the licensor should prohibit inappropriate distribution, as by stating: "Licensee may not distribute Articles bearing the Licensed Marks to discount outlets, mass market discounters, and warehouse stores." Such sales could "cheapen" brand reputation and weaken the licensor's marks. If the parties insert language requiring the licensee to engage in distribution patterns "consistent with Licensor's past practice," the license should clearly define these past practices as by stating that they included distribution through "reputable retail outlets, including department stores and specialty stores." Failure to define past practices opens the door to questions of fact and may allow quirks in earlier distribution patterns to be included in the permitted regular channels of distribution.

Licensors should maintain control over manufacturing by requiring the licensee to identify its manufacturers by name and address, and by reserving the right to inspect the manufacturers' premises for human rights compliance and quality control. The license should permit the licensor to conduct sample inspections and spot visits to the licensee's facilities. The licensor should avoid any restriction on the number of inspections permitted. In addition, where the licensee is responsible for sales and customer interaction, the licensor should have the ability to review customer service complaints and responses.

The license should specify where and when the licensee may advertise and promote the licensed products and should require the licensee to submit advertisements or promotions to the licensor for prior review and approval. Such controls help maintain brand integrity and can prevent an association with a person or campaign contrary to the goals of the brand, and will give the licensor an opportunity to supervise the licensee's marketing efforts. The agreement should require the licensee to abide by all international, national, and local laws. At a minimum, compliance should meet human rights laws and operational safety requirements.

SAMPLE CLAUSES: QUALITY CONTROL

The Licensed Products shall be of a high quality and in conformity with a standard sample approved by Licensor. Prior to the manufacture of the Licensed Products, and on a yearly basis thereafter, or more frequently as required by Licensor, Licensee shall submit to Licensor for approval, at no cost to Licensor, samples of all Licensed products that Licensee intends to manufacture or is manufacturing and all samples of all promotional and advertising material. Licensor shall approve or disapprove within thirty (30) days after receipt. Once the samples are approved, Licensee shall not materially depart from the sample without Licensor's written consent.

If quality falls below the approved standard sample, Licensee shall have thirty (30) days after notification by Licensor to use its best efforts to restore such quality. Upon a failure to cure, the Licensor may terminate the Agreement and require that the Licensee cease using the patents, trademarks, copyrights, designs, or information licensed.

Licensor may inspect the facilities where the Licensed Products are being manufactured and packaged.

Fashion Law *in Practice*

Is Costco Prestigious Enough?

Licensing conflicts can arise even between sophisticated parties. In 2000, one of the United States' most famous fashion designers brought suit against his leading licensee (which itself was one of the country's largest fashion companies). The famous designer objected, above all, to the licensee's distribution of licensed products to "warehouse clubs" such as Costco, Sam's Club, and BJ's. The designer claimed that the high reputation of his brand was being degraded by licensee's distribution through warehouse club channels. In response, the licensee argued that such distribution channels were not prohibited under the licensing contract, and that in any event, these types of retailers had become known for selling prestige brands to the same target customer coveted by the licensor.

A key provision in the license agreement set forth distribution obligations as follows:

In order to maintain the reputation, image and prestige of the Licensed Marks, Licensee's distribution patterns (a) *shall consist of those retail outlets whose location, merchandising and overall operations are consistent with the quality of Articles and the reputation, image and prestige of the Licensed Marks*, and/or (b) shall be consistent with Licensor's past practice, and (c) may include those authorized distribution channels in which apparel products manufactured by Licensor and its licensees and sub-licensees bearing the [licensed] mark have been or are being sold and such other distribution channels as licensor shall approve. [italics added]

Note the ambiguity of the contract language. Is Costco a retail outlet whose operations are "consistent with the quality" of a prestige fashion designer? There are strong arguments on either side. Faced with the disconcerting possibility of having a court of jury decide this difficult question, the parties settled the dispute. Clearly, the legal uncertainty would have been avoided if the contract had clearly stated whether distribution through warehouse clubs would be acceptable.

7.6.9. Sales and Product Delivery Deadlines and Schedules

The parties should agree upon sales guidelines, such as the size and nature of the sales staff that the licensee must employ (for example, the agreement may require the assignment of a global brand manager). The parties may also specify a schedule for regular licensing meetings and stipulate who will pay for travel expenses to these meetings. Product distribution guidelines may also be set, including standards for marketing and retailing, cost of products, whether approval is required for changes in cost, and how and where the product will be distributed. If the products will be sold in retail outlets, the agreement may specify requirements for the location of the licensed product within the store, the type of display, and the number of sales staff or expertise of the sales staff on location. Product placement in showrooms and at trade shows may also be specified.

If the products are to be sold over the Internet, the agreement may specify the website format or placement of the products on the website, the pictures to be used, the placement of promotional pictures, unique brand subpages or sites within a larger retail website, use of social media and mobile platforms, and the geographical territory in which the products may be sold and delivered to customers.

Delivery of designs, prototypes, and/or product samples may be specified on a production schedule. Delivery of product samples may also be required on a continuing basis to ensure quality control. Structured deadlines will help keep production on schedule and avoid delays. A complete agreement will also include a structure or calendar for product development that includes product launch dates.

SAMPLE CLAUSES: PRODUCTION SCHEDULES

Licensee shall launch the Licensed Products in [territory] on or before [date].

Licensee's failure to meet the deadline(s) shall constitute a material breach of the Agreement. Licensee shall have sixty (60) days to cure, and failure to cure will result in termination of the Agreement upon Licensor's notice of termination.

7.6.10. Representations and Warranties and Risk Controls

Both parties commonly provide assurances in the form of representations and warranties. These include, for example, assurances that the licensor actually owns the marks or has the right to exploit and grant rights to use the mark; that licensor is not involved in any disputes challenging such rights; that the licensor has the authority to enter into the licensing agreement; and that the licensor will maintain the validity of the marks. Likewise, licensors should seek assurances that the licensee has the requisite financial status and staffing to produce and market the licensed products; that the licensee will use its best efforts to promote and sell the licensed products; and that licensee does not and will not sell directly competing products.

7.6.11. Indemnification/Insurance

An indemnification clause sets forth the parties' respective responsibility for legal claims or lawsuits brought in connection with the products and trademarks (or other licensed rights) under the agreement. The license agreement should include indemnification from the licensee in favor of the licensor—and its affiliates, parents, subsidiaries, officers, directors, employees, and customers—for licensed products that are manufactured by or for the licensee. The exceptions to such indemnity are usually narrow and limited to (a) use of the licensed trademark in an approved manner; (b) contractually required use by the licensee of business and advertising materials provided by licensor; and (c) product specifications established and required by the licensor.

Insurance requirements support the indemnification obligation and ensure that the party charged with indemnifying the other will have insurance to support the representation. The licensee, as manufacturer of the product, is in the best position to be aware of the risks, safety issues, and potential pitfalls in manufacturing. Thus, the licensing agreement should require the licensee to name the licensor as an "additional insured," thereby obligating the licensee's insurer to provide coverage directly to the licensor.

The licensor will also want the licensee to indemnify it against lawsuits arising out of injury caused by the product. Although personal injury actions involving apparel or accessories are not extremely common, it does happen that consumers sue companies for injuries caused by serious product defects such as flammable fabrics or even by such seemingly minor product flaws as broken heels on shoes, lack of shoe traction, damage to a white couch caused by jeans "bleeding" onto the couch, punctures from underwire foundation garments, and so on.

The licensee will want the licensor to indemnify it for claims made against the licensee for trademark, copyright, or patent infringement when such property was used by the licensee in conformity with the scope and conditions of the license agreement.

SAMPLE CLAUSES: INDEMNIFICATION

Licensee agrees to defend, indemnify, and hold harmless Licensor, its officers, directors, agents, attorneys, employees, licensees, parents, subsidiaries, affiliates and all those in privity with one or more of them, against all costs, expenses, and losses (including reasonable attorneys' fees and costs) incurred through, as a result of, or relating to claims of third parties against Licensor based on the manufacture, distribution, advertising, promotion or sale of the Licensed Products, including, but not limited to, actions founded on product liability.

SAMPLE CLAUSES: INSURANCE

Licensee shall obtain and maintain at its own cost and expense standard Product Liability Insurance and General Business coverage naming Licensor as an additional insured from a qualified insurance company licensed to do business in [State] with coverage in an amount in excess of _____. Licensee agrees to furnish Licensor a certificate of insurance upon execution of this Agreement. Licensee shall not manufacture, distribute or sell the Licensed Products prior to receipt by Licensor of evidence of insurance.

7.6.12. Miscellaneous Terms

(a) Confidentiality

The parties should agree to keep the terms of the license agreement confidential or at least to keep certain sensitive information confidential for a period of time. If financial or other terms are agreed to be kept confidential, but recordation is required, companies may block out the confidential terms or execute a short form license for recordation that excludes the confidential terms. Local trademark counsel should be consulted to determine the applicable recordation requirements.

(b) Personnel and Third Parties

The individuals, representatives, or officers designated to receive notices under the agreement should be clearly identified, including the party's name and contact information and the name and contact information of outside counsel. Often a principal officer's title or position is more appropriate than an individual's name because the individuals employed by the principal may change over time. All agreements with international parties should require overnight delivery by a recognized courier with confirmation of receipt, which may be supplemented with email delivery.

If a particular individual is vital to the success of the license—for example, a famous designer—the agreement should address what happens if such person ceases his or her association with the company. Similarly, licenses should address what will happen if there is a change of control or a change in key personnel of the licensee.

(c) Sublicensing; Change of Control

The agreement should indicate whether the licensee may grant sublicenses. Granting sublicenses may be necessary for manufacturing certain products or to allow affiliates of the licensee to use the marks or sell the licensed products. As a general rule, licensors should restrict the right to sublicense and require prior written approval. The license agreement should provide that it will remain binding on all permitted successors of the parties and permitted sublicensees. The licensor should also restrict the licensee's ability to freely assign the agreement to third parties. If a licensee is free to do so, it may assign to a third party who is unacceptable to the licensor. The licensor may not want to do business with a given third party for a number of reasons—for example, the third party may have a poor track record or may distribute products that compete with those of the licensor.

SAMPLE CLAUSES: SUBLICENSING RESTRICTIONS

Licensee may not grant any sublicenses to any third party without the prior express written consent of the licensor, which may be withheld for any reason.

(d) Restrictions on Customers for Licensed Products

A licensor may wish to limit the types of customers to whom a licensee may sell licensed products. One motivation for such a limitation is the desire to minimize "parallel importing." Parallel importing arises when goods bearing valid trademarks are manufactured abroad but are then imported into the United States without the trademark owner's authorization. In such cases, the unwelcome parallel imports may end up competing with the licensor's goods intended for domestic sale. Confusion can arise because the parallel imports may bear the same valid trademarks as those on the goods intended for domestic sale. Provisions restricting distribution should nonetheless be worded carefully because some restrictions may not be enforceable as contrary to antitrust law.

(e) Controlling Law and Resolution of Disputes

If the parties are located in different countries and do business in different languages, the agreement should be translated into each party's language but should also clearly indicate which language version will control in the event of questions of interpretation and performance. The agreement should define which laws are to be applied in resolving disputes and in which jurisdiction actions can be brought and tried. The agreement should provide that any amendments to the agreement must be mutually signed and agreed upon.

Disputes concerning a license agreement may be resolved via the court system, mediation, or arbitration. If all parties to the agreement are based in the United States, it may be acceptable for disputes to be resolved via the court system. In an international context, arbitration is often preferable, and in such cases the arbitration clause should specify a local site for the arbitration. The agreement may also provide for recovery of damages, attorneys' fees, and equitable relief.

A severability clause should also be included, which provides that the legal invalidity of one or more of the agreement's provisions will not impact the validity of the remaining provisions.

SAMPLE CLAUSES: DISPUTE RESOLUTION

This Agreement shall be governed by the laws of the State of [insert] and all disputes shall be resolved in accordance with the laws of this State.

Any dispute, claim or controversy arising out of or relating to this Agreement or the breach, termination, enforcement, interpretation or validity thereof, including the determination of the scope or applicability of this agreement to arbitrate, [may or shall] be determined by arbitration in [insert the desired place of arbitration], before [one] [three] arbitrator(s). At the option of the first to commence an arbitration, the arbitration shall be administered either by Judicial Arbitration and Mediation Services (JAMS) pursuant to its [Comprehensive Arbitration Rules and Procedures] [Streamlined Arbitration Rules and Procedures] [International Arbitration Rules], or by [name an alternative provider] pursuant to its [identify the rules that will govern]. Judgment on the Award may be entered in any court having jurisdiction. This clause shall not preclude parties from seeking provisional remedies in aid of arbitration from a court of appropriate jurisdiction.

Allocation of Fees and Costs: The arbitrator may, in the Award, allocate all or part of the costs of the arbitration, including the fees of the arbitrator and the reasonable attorneys' fees of the prevailing party.

SAMPLE CLAUSES: SEVERABILITY

Invalidity of any term of this Agreement shall not affect the validity or operation of any other term, and the invalid term shall be deemed severed from the Agreement.

7.7. Negotiation and Drafting Tips

- When executing a term sheet, letter of intent or deal memo, be clear as regards what effect the document is intended to have and how binding it will be.
- Always use consistent language within a clause or section if the same thing is intended in each section.
- Avoid the use of "and/or," as this creates a built-in ambiguity susceptible of multiple interpretations.
- Either define the prestige, reputation, or identity of a trademark carefully or specifically allow for it to adapt and change. If acceptable channels of distribution define the brand's integrity, then those channels should be carefully and precisely defined.
- Allow for changed circumstances in the agreement. If a license is very long in duration, make certain that it accommodates a potentially changing marketplace. Licensors should seek prior approval over new retail channels in agreements. Licensees should opt for maximum flexibility. Additionally, if a retail price criterion defines a product or its market positioning, possible future price inflation should be anticipated.
- Amendments to the agreement should always be properly integrated. It is crucial that the single modifications made to one provision are carried through as reflected in necessary changes to other clauses. A fresh rereading of the entire agreement will highlight interdependent clauses and definitions.
- A merger clause should be included, declaring the contract to be the complete and final agreement between the parties.[10] If a contract contains a standard merger clause, the contract will not be affected by the parties' conduct or any other circumstances outside of the written agreement. If the parties intend for the contract to embody all circumstances and practices, including those outside of the written agreement, make certain that the merger clause is sufficiently comprehensive to cover such circumstances.
- If the parties intend for there to be a fiduciary or other special relationship between them, they must expressly provide for it in the agreement. For example, if the license agreement provided that it contained "the entire understanding and agreement between the parties concerning its subject matter," one party is barred from claiming that the other party breached a fiduciary or other role imposing special duties based on the "close business relationship" between the parties.
- Parties should take care to draft liquidated damages provisions that predetermine the measure of damages if a party breaches the agreement.[11] These provisions are likely to be upheld by the court so long as they are not grossly out of scale with foreseeable losses.
- Licensees should ensure that their business is not undercut by the actions of the licensor. Licensees should consider negotiating for exclusive licenses with regard to certain marks or certain geographic regions. Additionally, they should ensure that the quality of the marks will be maintained by the licensor.
- Contract language stating that acceptance of payment or performance does not waive the right to raise objections may be insufficient to preserve all possible legal causes of action. Typically, license agreements include provisions stating that acceptance by the licensor of royalty (and other) payments does not constitute an acknowledgment that payments are adequate or that there are no outstanding breaches. Such provisions also commonly provide that acceptance of payments does not foreclose the availability of

---

Fashion Law *in Court*

Gucci v. Guess

In *Gucci Am., Inc. v. Guess?, Inc.*, Guess had licensed various shoe designs to Marc Fisher Footwear LLC ("MFF") for manufacturing. When Guess's legal department became aware that some of the licensed material may have infringed Gucci's trademarks, it notified MFF and ordered it to cease using the design. Gucci sued Guess for trademark infringement, and the court held that Guess had indeed infringed some of Gucci's trademarks.

Gaps in the Licensing Agreement: A few prudent revisions to the license agreement would have limited Guess's exposure to liability for infringement of Gucci's marks. For example, an emergency provision allowing Guess to order MFF to cease use of the designs under certain circumstances would have limited Guess's exposure to infringement liability. Additionally, Guess might have sought better control over MFF's third-party retailers and distribution channels.

Problems with Guess's Design and Licensing Process: As a self-described "trend follower," Guess and its licensees researched fashion industry trends, created designs consistent with its brand, and checked compliance with intellectual property laws. It then provided its licensees with "trend inspiration" (in the form of magazine clippings, trend-watch services, etc.), which the licensees used to produce products that Guess reviewed and approved for aesthetics and brand cohesion. Guess's licensing department monitored the products and the licensees' use and modifications of Guess's intellectual property and worked with the licensees to achieve a consistent and coherent style for each season. Once the designs were approved, the licensees produced samples for physical review and brand cohesion. The language in the final court judgment suggests that Guess would have been well advised to take a more active role in clearing products for intellectual property conflicts.

Lesson: Licensors must insist upon effective intellectual property clearance procedures with their licensees.

---

other legal and equitable remedies, whenever asserted. Despite such provisions, the continued acceptance of payment or conduct by the other party may still foreclose legal and equitable remedies. Continued acceptance may bar later demands for termination.

► It is important to understand the difference between a provision that says the license may not be assigned and a provision that allows the other party to terminate if there is a "change of control." A provision prohibiting assignment forbids the licensee (typically) from transferring its licensed rights to someone else. A provision addressing change of control, however, protects a party against a change in ownership, management control, or leadership of its counterparty. Typically, this provision may be triggered upon the transfer of property, assets, or stock ownership. When drafting a license agreement, the drafter should focus on the entity he or she is representing and the corporate structure of that entity, and then include these provisions in the manner most suitable for the client's interests. Usually, a licensor wants to control who has the right to exploit its property. A contract that is silent on assignment is generally freely transferable. Drafters should contemplate this and realize its implications, including a future sale of the business. When third parties evaluate an acquisition or an investment in a corporation, the company's value to the acquirer may be significantly diminished if a potentially lucrative license may be terminated based on a change of control.

▶ The licensor should carefully negotiate the extent to which it can control the actions of the licensee with regard to the licensed property. The licensor should continually have oversight of the licensee's actions with respect to the licensed property throughout the life of the agreement.

▶ It is important to know the financial health of the other party to a trademark license. If there is an imminent potential for bankruptcy, efforts should be made to have additional safeguards in place. The effect of bankruptcy (itself the subject of court proceedings during the pendency of the dissolution or reorganization) is discussed in more detail below.

7.8. The Bankruptcy Code and Trademarks

Traditionally, trademarks have not been accorded the same protection as patents and copyrights in bankruptcy. In its definition of intellectual property, the U.S. Bankruptcy Code (the "Code") includes patents and copyrights but does not mention trademarks.[12] Presumably, this was because trademark licenses are unique in requiring ongoing quality control and oversight by the licensor. The affirmative duty of the licensor to approve the quality of products bearing the licensed mark conflicts with provisions of the Bankruptcy Code, which allows licensees to choose whether they will continue using the licensed property post-bankruptcy.

Consequently, the impact of bankruptcy on parties to a trademark license agreement is distinct from the impact on parties to a copyright or patent agreement. When a trademark licensor is in bankruptcy, it may reject the entire trademark license agreement, thereby terminating the licensee's right to use the licensed name and mark.[13] Similarly, when a licensee is in bankruptcy, it may reject the license agreement. In both cases, the non-debtor party is left in a difficult position whereby the only recourse might be to bring a pre-petition unsecured claim for damages. Since such claims may fall short of the actual financial damage, the termination of the license may have a drastic economic effect on the non-debtor party.

Licensors and licensees can take precautions to minimize risks should the other party go bankrupt:[14]

1. License agreements should provide for required prior written notice of bankruptcy filing. With such notice, the non-debtor may have an opportunity to get involved in the proceedings early.[15]
2. License agreements should provide guidance to the bankruptcy court or trustee about how to treat the license agreement. Thus, the license agreement may provide that the parties mutually acknowledge that the licensed property constitutes "intellectual property" under the Code, and that the agreement should be governed by the Code in the event of bankruptcy.[16]
3. The Code requires the non-debtor licensee electing to retain its rights in the license agreement to continue to make all royalty payments under the contract. Therefore, to minimize the risk of paying for services it will no longer receive, licensees should either

structure agreements so that payment for licensor's services are treated separately from the payment of royalties from use of the trademark or set forth those services in a separate agreement.

4. A licensee should ensure that the agreement allows the licensee, in the event of a licensor's bankruptcy, to secure any third-party support necessary to develop the licensed products without violating the agreement's exclusivity or confidentiality provisions.

5. *Ipso facto* clauses in license agreements state that the agreement is automatically terminated, or some other consequence occurs, when a certain event—often the filing for bankruptcy—occurs. Although most standard form agreements include such clauses, a provision that ties default to termination of the agreement is unenforceable under the Bankruptcy Code.[17]

6. License agreements should tie termination to financial condition, not bankruptcy. A bankrupt licensee could cost a licensor significant income from reduced sales and royalties, damage to its brand, and the possibility that its licensed rights will be assigned to a third party during the bankruptcy proceedings.[18] Therefore, a licensor is well advised to include independent financial obligations in the license. One such provision would be a clause allowing the licensor to terminate for nonpayment or chronic late payment, thereby allowing a financially troubled licensee to be terminated long before it declares bankruptcy.

7. Licensees should seek to obtain a security interest in the licensor's trademark, goodwill, or other property.

8. A liquidated damages provision, triggered by the bankrupt party's breach or failure to perform services, provides a definite amount for the court to find as to damages for the non-debtor party.

9. License agreements should provide a right of first refusal to the licensor. Where a licensee is the debtor, the trustee or debtor-in-possession may have the right to transfer, sell, or assign the agreement to a third party. Therefore, a non-debtor licensor should ensure that the assignment language used in the agreement does not impair any rights it has as a creditor or its rights to object to any assumption or assignment.

7.9. Product Liability Issues in Fashion Licenses

With fashion and apparel products—as with all consumer products—there is some potential exposure for legal actions based on the sale of dangerous or defective products. Accordingly, it is prudent to have an understanding of this product-liability exposure and to confer with insurance agents—at least so as to be able to evaluate the level of risk and obtain proper insurance coverage.

From a licensor's perspective, the licensee should assume all responsibility for manufacturing. Since a licensor must exercise approvals and quality control, it is best protected by:

▶ Using strong indemnification language, including language that states that the indemnity prevails even if the licensor approves the design or product

▶ Making sure the licensee is adequately insured and provides proof of insurance (and renewal notices)

- Making sure licensor is added to all insurance policies as an "additional insured"
- Making sure licensee and its vendors (if contractors are permitted) comply with CPSIA and all Consumer Product Safety legislation, including the proper issuance of all GCC documents and modifications
- Making sure the licensee and all vendors indemnify the licensor for product defects, and inaccuracies or misrepresentation in the GCC documents
- Requiring product testing by the licensee with no directions or specific requirements (other than of adequacy) on the type of testing

7.10. Summary of Key Points

1. A license is an agreement under which one party grants to another the right to exploit certain intellectual property, subject to guidance, oversight, and other specific constraints. The licensor is the owner of the intellectual property. In fashion, the most common arrangement is for a famous brand to license its trademark to a licensee who has expertise in manufacturing and/or distribution of a particular type of goods.
2. Licensing allows fashion companies to expand rapidly into sectors or geographic areas where they would otherwise lack the capital or expertise to operate. Licensing allows a brand owner to engage in controlled expansion without having to invest in costly infrastructure, and it can generate immediate revenue to finance current operations.
3. Licensing agents may provide licensors with a number of services, including identifying marketable opportunities and reliable licensees.
4. Negotiating a license requires careful pre-negotiation preparation to ensure that the agreement clearly and precisely spells out the parties' mutual obligations and protects each side's interest.
5. Key terms to an agreement should include definitions, grant of license/rights retained by licensor, protection and ownership of licensed trademarks, term and termination, compensation or royalty terms, currency/audit, design, quality control, advertising and promotion minimums, sales and product delivery deadlines and schedules, representations and warranties and risk controls, indemnification/insurance, sublicensing, change of control, and dispute resolution.
6. Bankruptcy Code and trademarks—Trademarks traditionally have not been accorded the same protection as have patents and copyrights in the U.S. Bankruptcy Code.
7. Product liability issues in fashion licensing—From a licensor's perspective, the licensee should assume all responsibility for manufacturing, since there is some potential for legal actions based on the sale of dangerous or defective products.

Notes

1. It is common for a brand or intellectual property holding company to hold title ownership of marks and other intellectual property, and for such an entity to allow exploitation of the property by or through a related entity. This is typically accomplished by an underlying license agreement. Such exploiting entity then enters into licenses with third parties and represents that it has the right to do so.

2. The rankings are based on worldwide sales of licensed merchandise at retail. Tony Lisanti, "Top 125 Global Licensors," *License! Global Magazine,* May 2012, at T3, T3-T5, available at http://www.rankingthebrands.com/ PDF/Top%20125%20Global%20Licensors%202012,%20License%20Global.pdf.

3. *Fashion Licensing Shows Strongest Growth of Any Property Type,* EPM Commc'n (June 1, 2012), http:// www.epmcom.com/public/Fashion_Licensing_Shows_Strongest_Growth_of_Any_Property_Type.cfm.

4. Information on licensing agent is available at the following URLs: http://www.licensingpages.com/ aboutlicensing/licensing-terminology/, http://www.partnershipmarketing.com/hm%E2%80%99s-promiscu- ous-brand-partnerships-leave-them-looking-empty/, http://www.businessfinventing.com/ar ticles/licensing_ can_somebody_do_this_for_me.html, http://www.jjkaufman.com/articles/ArtistAgentRelationship.htm, http:// www.breitlingforbentley.com/en/bfb/breitling-for-bentley-0-0, http://www.mediaweek.co.uk/news/205807/, http://www.licensing.cc/NewsDetail1.asp?id=520.

5. Definition of "Licensing Agent," US Legal, http://definitions.uslegal.com (search "Licensing Agent").

6. "Licensing Definitions," Purdue Univ. Office of Marketing and Media, https://marketing.purdue.edu/ Toolkit/Trademarks/Policy/Definitions (last accessed November 13, 2012).

7. Comparatively, brand strategists assist brand owners by identifying and honing the DNA or equity of a brand to deliver a clear and consistent product message and then directing brand owners to appropriate new product categories and partners. Unlike agents, brand strategists are paid through fees or retainers and not through a percentage of royalties. That said, brand strategy consultants that are retained to develop new mar- kets can also be compensated (similar to sales teams) through a percentage of sales or purchases of product within the markets they develop. The authors wish to thank Sam Wilson of CRG Licensing for her contribu- tion to this section.

8. The bundle of exclusive rights includes the right to reproduce the work, prepare derivative works, distrib- ute copies to the public, perform the work, and display the work publicly. 17 U.S.C. §106.

9. In the United States, a party may seek to "oppose" a trademark application to halt registration of a mark if it believes that it would be injured by the registration of the mark. A party may also petition to "cancel" a registered mark. A successful opposition or cancellation of a mark will result in a failed attempt to register or removal of a mark from the trademark registry. 15 U.S.C. §§ 1063, 1064.

10. Definition of "Merger Clause," US Legal, http://definitions.uslegal.com (search "Merger Clause").

11. Definition of "Liquidated Damages Clause," US Legal, http://definitions.uslegal.com (search "Liqui- dated Damages Clause").

12. 11 U.S.C. § 101 (2012).

13. License agreements are generally executory contracts that the bankruptcy trustee may assume or reject, pursuant to § 356(a). 11 U.S.C. § 365(a) (2012).

14. For an extensive elaboration of these ten points, see Carroll, Schuyler G., and Blankley, Adrienne Woods, of Arent Fox LLP, *Court Ruling Questions Assignability of Trademark Licenses in Bankruptcies* (March 17, 2006); Bob Eisenbach, *Trademark Licensor In Bankruptcy: Special Risk for Licensees* (September 4, 2006), http://bankruptcy.cooley.com; and Ash, Karen Artz, and Danow, Bret J., of Katten Muchin Rosenman LLP, "Reducing the Effects of Licensing Bankruptcy," *Managing Intellectual Property* (July/August 2004). See also Ash, Karen Artz, "Fashion Licensing, Bankruptcy in Fashion Licensing," *The Licensing Journal* (August 2012).

15. 11 U.S.C. § 365.

16. See § 365(n).

17. See § 365(b)(2).

18. See § 365(n).

8

Counterfeiting

Barbara Kolsun and Heather J. McDonald

8.1. Introduction

Trademarks stimulate global consumer demand for products by increasing the recognition and popularity of certain providers of goods and services.[1] Trademarks create an association between a product or service and a particular brand's name and reputation for quality. Since consumers cannot always inspect the quality of every product they buy or service they use, trademarks provide them with an easy and dependable source of information about potential purchases.[2] Trademarks thus provide great value both for consumers and for the suppliers of branded products and services. Regrettably, however, counterfeiters have learned to misappropriate the value of popular trademarks by creating illicit and low-quality copies of apparel and luxury goods, thereby earning large (though illegal) profits (see Figure 8.1).

8.1.1. What Is Trademark Counterfeiting?

Trademark counterfeiting is the act of manufacturing or distributing a product or service bearing a mark that is identical to or substantially indistinguishable from a registered trademark.[3] In effect, trademark counterfeiting is the theft of valuable intellectual property. Counterfeiters not only steal the trademark owner's intellectual property, they also decrease the value of authentic products in the marketplace by making otherwise exclusive products appear to be available at mass-market prices. The following federal criminal statutes are especially helpful in combating counterfeiting:

> ▸ *The Stop Counterfeiting in Manufactured Goods Act, 18 U.S.C. § 2320.* This law establishes prison terms up to 20 years and fines up to $15 million for the trafficking and sale

Julie Zerbo, The Catholic University of American Columbus School of Law, Class of 2013; Aubrie Brake, Florida International University College of Law, Class of 2013; and Morgan Elam, University of Pennsylvania Law School, Class of 2013, provided additional research.

Fig. 8.1. These counterfeit handbags were seized from a New York City warehouse before they could be sold on the streets as designer merchandise. (*Courtesy of Fairchild Publications, Inc.*)

of counterfeit goods. It strengthened anticounterfeiting enforcement by adding mandatory forfeiture, destruction, and restitution provisions. Further, the law tightened U.S. laws against counterfeit labels and packaging. While it was already illegal to manufacture, ship, or sell counterfeit products, this legislation closed a loophole allowing the shipment of falsified labels or packaging, which counterfeiters previously were able to attach to fake products in order to cheat consumers by passing off poorly made items as brand-name goods. Those convicted of counterfeiting are now also required to reimburse the legitimate business they harmed.

▶ *Trafficking in Counterfeit Goods or Services Anticounterfeiting Consumer Protection Act of 1996, 18 U.S.C. § 2320.* The core provision of this statute reads as follows:

> Whoever intentionally traffics or attempts to traffic in goods or services and knowingly uses a counterfeit mark on or in connection with such goods or services shall, if an individual, be fined not more than $2,000,000 or imprisoned not more than 10 years, or both, and, if a person other than an individual, be fined not more than $5,000,000. In the case of an offense by a person under this section that occurs after that person is convicted of another offense under this section, that person convicted, if an individual, shall be fined not more than $5,000,000 or imprisoned not more than 20 years, or both, and if other than an individual, shall be fined not more than $15,000,000.

A number of other federal statutes can be used to prosecute counterfeiters, such as:

- 18 U.S.C. § 2319—Criminal Infringement of a Copyright
- 18 U.S.C. § 1961 et seq.— Racketeer Influenced Corrupt Organizations (RICO) Act
- 18 U.S.C. § 371—Criminal Conspiracy
- 18 U.S.C. §§ 1956, 1957—Money Laundering
- 18 U.S.C. § 542—Entry of Goods by Means of False Statements
- 18 U.S.C. § 545—Smuggling Goods into the United States

8.1.2. The Development of U.S. Anticounterfeiting Legislation

In 1946, Congress enacted early legislation to protect trademarks that enabled trademark owners to enforce and protect their trademarks through civil litigation.[4] However, these early laws did little to protect trademark owners against counterfeiting.[5] In 1982, brand owners lobbied for Congress to establish criminal penalties against trademark counterfeiting.[6] By then, the problem was reaching crisis proportions.[7] The legislature amended the 1946 statute in 1984 to criminalize trademark counterfeiting and included stiffer penalties for counterfeiters.[8]

8.1.3. "The Crime of the Twenty-First Century"

Theft of IP through trademark counterfeiting is often referred to as "the crime of the twenty-first century."[9] As technology advances, criminals and infringers are able to copy trademarks more quickly and cheaply and with increased accuracy, allowing for larger profits. The growth of worldwide communications and formation of multinational corporations has increased the international recognition of and desire for specific brand names, creating an international market for counterfeit goods. Much of today's counterfeiting problem is linked to China,[10] although various other nations represent threats to U.S. intellectual property rights (IPR).

The Office of the United States Trade Representative issues a yearly Special 301 Report that aims to encourage and maintain international IPR protection and enforcement. The report identifies a wide array of concerns, including the policies that may unfairly disadvantage U.S. IPR holders and the continuing challenges of piracy over the Internet. Further, the Special 301 Report identifies countries that do not provide adequate IPR protection for its citizens and to the citizens of the United States and thus are often key manufacturers and exporters of counterfeit goods. These nations are referred to as Priority Watch List and Watch List countries. In 2012 the Priority Watch List included Algeria, Argentina, Canada, China, Chile, India, Indonesia, Israel, Pakistan, Russia, Thailand, Ukraine, and Venezuela.[11] In Latin American countries the biggest problems arose from domain name pirates and counterfeiters who presented themselves as authorized distributors for legitimate U.S. companies.

China has been a constant presence in the Special 301 Report, as China's unprecedented economic growth has been accompanied, unfortunately, by rampant counterfeiting.[12] Some legal scholars have argued that China does not encourage individual creativity or intellectual curiosity because the resulting ideas and innovations may disrupt China's economic and bureaucratic model. According to this view, China promotes a copycat-driven culture. Professor Peter Yu, who has written extensively on the subject, states:

[T]he culprit behind the Chinese piracy problem is the Confucian beliefs ingrained in the Chinese culture, the country's socialist economic system, the leaders' skepticism toward Western institutions, the xenophobic and nationalist sentiments of the populace, the government's censorship and information control policy, and the significantly different Chinese legal culture and judicial system.[13]

Professor Yu suggests that China's reluctance to embrace IP laws is due to the perception that such laws protect only foreigners and not Chinese citizens, and also due to the impression that such laws were adopted as the result of foreign pressure to comply with Western IP laws, which created further hostility and resistance.[14]

The United States and its trading partners have formed various alliances to combat international IP violations. In 2006, European and U.S. officials joined forces to fight counterfeiting by creating the EU-US Action Strategy for the Enforcement of Intellectual Property Rights, which sought to identify worldwide IP issues and marshal industry support to resolve them. The organization's first project focused on key priorities, in particular bilateral efforts to encourage respect for IPR in China and Russia.[15]

In 2011, the U.S. joined Australia, Canada, Japan, Morocco, New Zealand, Singapore, and South Korea in signing the Anti-Counterfeiting Trade Agreement (ACTA).[16] This treaty aims to combat cross-border counterfeiting by establishing global standards for the enforcement of intellectual property rights. However, because ACTA has not yet been ratified by those countries that are leading exporters of counterfeit goods and that have the lowest amount of protection for intellectual property rights,[17] its effectiveness remains questionable at this point. Of the 2012 Priority Watch List countries, only Canada has ratified ACTA.[18]

8.1.4. Identifying a Counterfeit: An Overview

Some counterfeits are easier to spot than others. Counterfeit handbags purchased at flea markets are often of very poor quality (e.g., imitation leather, with loose seams and stitching). Frequently, the difference in quality between a counterfeit and the authentic product is readily apparent to the ordinary consumer. However, many counterfeiters today are capable of producing extremely accurate imitations of famous branded products. Due to technological advances, counterfeiters can mimic everything from particular stitching methods to precise thread coloring, which makes it more difficult for consumers to distinguish between authentic goods and counterfeits.

Because of the difficulty in identifying these higher-quality counterfeits, companies are developing new methods to spot fakes. Some companies have incorporated innovative product security devices in packaging or inside a product itself, such as holograms in hang tags. Others label their products with security codes that allow the company to detect and track authentic versus imitation goods.

Brand owners must be prepared to train investigators and law enforcement officials, such as Customs officers, on how to accurately identify counterfeits. Also, trademark owners should update their counterfeiting prevention measures periodically to ensure that adequate provisions are in place, as counterfeiters' methods are constantly evolving and increasing in sophistication.

8.1.5. A Growing Problem and the Governmental Response

Counterfeiting is approximately a $600 billion per year international industry.[19] The International AntiCounterfeiting Coalition (IACC) estimates that in 2011, losses to U.S. companies from trademark counterfeiting amounted to between $200 billion and $250 billion.[20] Further, more than 750,000 Americans have lost their jobs due to the manufacture and sale of counterfeit merchandise.[21] Congress noted that counterfeiting costs legitimate employers thousands of potential job opportunities, owing in part to lost profits and in part to competition from illegal operations that do not comply with national employment standards.[22] In addition, a recent IACC survey reported that Fortune 500 companies commonly spend as much as $2 to $4 million per year to combat counterfeiting, with some reporting spending up to $10 million annually.[23]

U.S. Customs & Border Protection (CBP) and Immigration & Customs Enforcement (ICE) seized nearly $200 million worth of counterfeit goods intended for sale in the United States in 2011.[24] Seizures at express courier and mail facilities have increased recently, as many counterfeit companies now sell directly to consumers via the Internet.[25]

According to a 2004 New York City Comptroller's report,[26] counterfeiting cost New York City $380 million in lost sales taxes, $290 million in lost business income taxes, and $360 million in lost personal income taxes.[27] The Los Angeles County Development Corporation reported that counterfeiting costs the Los Angeles economy 106,000 jobs and $4.4 billion in lost wages each year.[28] In 2011 alone, the New York and New Jersey seaports seized more than 400 shipments of counterfeit goods valued at about $100 million, a 53 percent increase over the previous year.[29] In recent years, Congress has taken a more proactive approach to the fight against counterfeiting. New federal and state anticounterfeiting laws have been passed to help trademark owners enforce their rights and allow federal and state authorities to protect the consuming public (see *Fashion Law in Practice: The Local Level: Counterfeiting and State Law Enforcement* on page 153). Government agencies, such as the Federal Bureau of Investigation, Secret Service, and Customs Service (now part of the Department of Homeland Security), now monitor and establish trade regulations, patrol the borders, and monitor the Internet in order to locate and prosecute counterfeiters. Approximately two-thirds of U.S. states have gone further in adopting specific new laws criminalizing trademark counterfeiting. These laws generally include felony penalties, prison terms, and fines for those convicted of crimes associated with trademark counterfeiting.[30]

Trademark owners also have various civil remedies at their disposal to protect their trademarks. Under existing laws, companies can seize counterfeit products, permanently enjoin the manufacture and sale of those products both in stores and flea markets and online and seek monetary damages.[31]

8.1.6. Not a Victimless Crime

A common misconception is that counterfeiting is a "victimless crime." While the most obvious victims might be the large corporations that lose sales, those that are most grievously harmed include the low-wage workers who toil in grim sweatshops (counterfeiters do not invest in humane factories) and the unwitting consumers of counterfeit products who are not only defrauded but often put into physical danger (counterfeiters are known to sell counterfeit medicines and even airplane parts). Many people who purchase counterfeits do not realize the pervasive social harms associated with these products. Government reports indicate that counterfeiting also provides substantial funding for organized crime and terrorist organizations.

8.1.6.1. Harm to Trademark Owners

The most obvious harm created by counterfeiting is in lost sales for the trademark owner. While customers who purchase counterfeits at flea markets or on the street may be well aware that they are purchasing illicit products, online shoppers (even those who are willing to purchase the authentic product at a higher price) can be tricked into purchasing counterfeits through the use of sophisticated websites that appear to be legitimate and contain authentic photographs of the goods (such photographs are often simply poached from websites of the trademark owner). Internet-based counterfeiting sales can be particularly harmful to trademark owners. If an innocent purchaser of a counterfeit believes that the product is authentic, he or she will likely associate the inferior quality of the counterfeit with the trademark owner's brand. Accordingly, he or she may have reservations about purchasing the mark owner's products in the future.

8.1.6.2. Harm to Consumers

Consumers are also placed at serious risk from the purchase of nongenuine products. Counterfeiting is profitable because counterfeiters make inexpensive products by taking shortcuts in manufacturing and quality control. Counterfeiting factories operate beneath the radar of international standards and thus do not comply with minimum public safety requirements, thereby posing a substantial threat to the health and safety of consumers. Counterfeit garments may be washed or dyed with toxic substances or skin irritants or made of cheaper materials that may be more flammable than higher-quality fabrics. Counterfeit sunglasses may not be shatterproof or provide protection from ultraviolet rays. Counterfeit designer fragrances may contain harmful bacteria or ingredients that cause allergic reactions.

8.1.6.3. Consumer Education

An essential component of the fight against counterfeits is consumer education. In addition to policing their trademarks and preventing the trafficking and sale of counterfeit goods, companies must educate consumers about the dangers associated with counterfeit goods. One highly effective public relations strategy that fashion companies have utilized is to launch a major public awareness campaign. For instance, the Paul Mitchell hair company has run television commercials stating that its products are sold only in salons and that products purchased elsewhere are not guaranteed by the company and may be dangerous. British outerwear brand Barbour has taken to the Internet to inform consumers about counterfeits. The company purchased Google ads that appear each time someone types the words "fake Barbour" into the search engine. The company's "Counterfeit Education" page contains a history of the luxury brand, information about the downsides of counterfeiting, and an e-mail address to report suspicious and/or counterfeit goods. The page also includes a list of known counterfeit websites that purport to sell "Barbour" goods.[32]

Consumer education campaigns also appear in print publications. *Harper's Bazaar*, for example, devotes one issue every year to its "Fakes Are Never in Fashion" campaign in order to "expose the atrocities of the fake trade and focus on the significance of purchasing authentic luxury goods." This issue has become a popular venue for fashion companies to place anticounterfeiting ads.

A useful, lower-cost alternative is to use the company's website to describe its problems with counterfeiting, identify legitimate retail outlets, and enable consumers to report counterfeiters. Given the increase in online shopping and the prevalence of fakes online, this should be an essential feature of fashion company websites. For instance, Chanel has a page dedicated to identifying its authorized retailers, as well as its counterfeit policy. Christian Louboutin's website has a "Stop Fake" page that lists licensed retailers and warns shoppers, "When something is too good to be true, that's usually what it is worth. Websites selling low, low priced Louboutin looking shoes are probably not selling the real thing." The site also warns fashion buyers: "We make no shoes in Asia. There is no factory in China that can sell legitimate shoes to anyone as we do not use any factories in China."[33]

In addition to local and state law enforcement efforts, various industry and international organizations educate consumers about the ill effects of piracy and counterfeiting. The French luxury goods association Comité Colbert sponsors a campaign against counterfeiting to raise awareness among travelers in French airports. One of their airport ads bears an image of a Christian Dior handbag and reads "Real Ladies Don't Like Fake." Similarly, Thailand's Ministry of Commerce Intellectual Property Department has launched a campaign to educate young adults of the dangers associated with counterfeit goods.

8.1.6.4. A Drain on Law Enforcement

Counterfeiters generally run all-cash businesses and avoid keeping records or paying taxes. Cash-only operations do not leave a paper trail, which can make large-scale counterfeiting operations difficult to investigate and allows counterfeiters to hide assets from law enforcement. Without records, it is impossible to verify whether counterfeiters are complying with human rights laws and health or safety standards in their factories. It is likely that most of them are not in compliance, as it is expensive and time consuming to comply with such standards.

Organized crime and terrorist organizations have become increasingly involved in counterfeiting operations.[34] Organized crime groups distribute counterfeit products through the same sophisticated routes that they use for narcotics trade.[35] Legislators have recognized the relationship of counterfeiting to organized crime and terrorism. In 2005, the U.S. Senate Homeland Security and Governmental Affairs Committee held hearings on the links between counterfeiting and terrorist activities.[36] The U.S. government has established that al Qaeda, Hezbollah, and the Irish Republican Army have made use of funds derived from counterfeiting operations.[37] Further, the FBI uncovered evidence linking the street sales of counterfeit merchandise in New York to the terrorist bombing of the World Trade Center in 1993.[38]

Interpol as well has investigated the relationship between counterfeiting and terrorist funding.[39] In fact, Interpol reports that counterfeiting is not merely a single source of funding for such organizations but that it is becoming the preferred method of funding for these groups.[40]

8.1.7. Anticounterfeiting Today

As Customs agencies respond more effectively to imports of counterfeits, these operations evolve in complexity. To avoid seizure at U.S. borders, counterfeiters now routinely disguise illegal products. Some ship unlabeled clothing and accessories to the United States and then ship the trademark-infringing labels separately. When the unlabeled (and otherwise legal) products[41] make it past Customs, the false brand labels are attached and sold to U.S. buyers. In 2001 U.S. legislators responded with 18 U.S.C. § 2320, a law prohibiting trafficking in counterfeit labels, emblems, hardware, and packaging that is not attached to any goods. Mark owners have pushed for further legislation in the case of "famous" marks, which would remove the burdensome requirement that spurious marks must be used in connection with goods or services identical to those for which the genuine mark is already registered in order to be considered counterfeit.[42]

8.2. Nature of the Counterfeiting Problem

The United States Code defines a counterfeit as "a spurious mark that is identical with or substantially indistinguishable from the original registered mark."[43] Under 19 C.F.R. § 133.21(a), this standard is reached when the "copying or simulating mark or name" is either "an actual counterfeit of the recorded mark" or "is one which so resembles it as to be likely to cause the public to associate the copying or simulating mark with the registered mark or name."[44]

All counterfeits are infringements, but not all infringements are counterfeits. Counterfeiting is a particularly egregious form of trademark infringement, but it is narrower in scope than other trademark infringement in that it applies only to marks that are identical to or substantially indistinguishable from the actual mark and that are intended to deceive the consumer.[45]

If Company X makes shoes that look exactly like Company Y's shoes and also bear Company Y's trademark, Company X is engaging in counterfeiting, the unauthorized exploitation of Company Y's name and brand. However, if Company X creates shoes with a pattern and trademark that are very similar to Company Y's but not identical, then there is less likelihood that this product will be considered counterfeit. Such usage, however, may be found to infringe Company Y's trademark if consumers find the products "confusingly similar."

The distinction between counterfeiting and other trademark infringement is important because it can result in drastically different consequences for the wrongdoer. Ordinary infringement may be countered with an injunction prohibiting the defendant from manufacturing and selling the product, and monetary damages may be available as well. Counterfeiting, on the other hand, also exposes the wrongdoer to seizure and destruction of the counterfeit goods and stiff criminal penalties, including large fines and even imprisonment.

A further defining characteristic of trademark counterfeiting is that in order to constitute a counterfeit, the offending usage must be on the same type of goods or services as those that are covered by the mark owner's registrations.[46] Generally, branded manufacturers must file trademark registrations specifically defining which classes of products their marks will be used on. Most countries use the International Classification of Goods and Services. Under this system, "Class 25" covers clothing, which includes apparel, footwear, and headgear.[47] If Company X has a valid trademark registration for Class 25 products, then it has the exclusive right to place its mark on such products. However, a person who wishes to put Company X's mark on sunglasses, which is covered by Class 9,[48] may not be guilty of trademark counterfeiting, although there may be a trademark infringement or copyright infringement issue in doing so under the doctrine of related use.[49]

Ownership of the trademark in question plays a critical role in counterfeit cases, and the way in which ownership is gained varies depending on the jurisdiction. The United States is a first-to-use jurisdiction,[50] which means that ownership goes to the first party to use the mark in commerce, not to the first party to file for registration of the mark.[51] In comparison, China is a first-to-file jurisdiction.[52] Well-known brands are often the victims of Chinese trademark "pirates," who register a brand name in a class not yet utilized by the brand owner. Stuart Weitzman had not yet utilized its well-known name for fragrance when it discovered that a Chinese "pirate" had registered "Stuart Weitzman" in class 3. After a lengthy and expensive battle before the Chinese Trademark Review and Adjudication Board, Stuart Weitzman IP, LLC was able to successfully oppose the unauthorized registration of the mark Stuart Weitzman in Class 3, which could have interfered with licensing rights rightfully owned by Weitzman. Similarly, Calvin Klein was forced to litigate in Chile to wrest its name back from a trademark "pirate" who had registered the Calvin Klein mark for apparel and opened local Calvin Klein retail stores.

"Use" within the context of the Trademark Counterfeiting Act of 1984[53] is defined very broadly. Thus, "use" may include the transportation of counterfeit handbags in a van and not just displaying or offering the bags for sale. This reflects Congress's intention to broadly "control and prevent commercial counterfeiting."[54] This enables mark owners and law enforcement to target illegal goods in various stages of the stream of commerce and not merely at the point of sale.

8.3. Agents in the Effort

It is the responsibility of trademark owners to take the initiative to police and protect their trademarks against unauthorized use.

8.3.1. Management

Effective trademark enforcement begins at the top. Management must be aware of the nature and scope of the counterfeiting problem and drive the company's enforcement efforts. Management should facilitate cooperation between in-house and outside counsel and law enforcement by designating contacts for specific anticounterfeiting operations, such as producing affidavits of authenticity, identifying counterfeit goods, providing testimony when necessary, and supporting civil litigation.

Not only is senior management integral in the fight against counterfeits, business and sales personnel must also be involved. Sales personnel are closest to consumers in the marketplace and thus often best suited to see or hear about counterfeit products. Other business personnel may be particularly well equipped to identify differences in importation patterns and can help the legal team determine where to direct its efforts. Typically, investigations are international in nature. Therefore, it is essential that the internal teams work closely between regions and territories.

8.3.2. Preliminary Action Plan

Trademarks and domain names should be registered in all countries where the trademark owner sells goods or services or manufactures or distributes products or components. In addition, it is important to register trademarks in advance of actual use in large markets like China and India, in order to avoid problems when the brand becomes well known. As previously discussed, first-to-file countries, such as China, create significant piracy problems for brand owners, which could be lessened by brand owners' expedient registration of trademarks.

8.3.3. In-House Counsel

In-house counsel plays an important role in the battle against counterfeiting. In-house counsel should determine the appropriate anticounterfeiting strategy and maintain close contact with outside counsel and investigators hired to conduct anticounterfeiting operations and monitor anticounterfeiting progress. In very large companies, a specific in-house counsel may be assigned to work solely on combating counterfeiting operations.[55] However, in most corporations, anticounterfeiting is usually only part of in-house counsel's broad responsibilities.[56]

Experienced in-house counsel may assist investigators in formulating procedures to conduct local sweeps in targeted locations.[57] A program administrator (often a paralegal or in-house investigator) may also be instrumental.[58] It is important for that person to cooperate effectively with law enforcement to determine the authenticity of products and to track the chain of custody of counterfeits.[59] As such, this person should be routinely trained to identify counterfeit products.[60]

One of the most important functions of in-house staff is to maintain an evidentiary chain of custody. It is imperative to maintain files on each civil and criminal action related to the maintenance of a brand's trademarks. Such files should include a chain of custody form and the affidavit discussing the counterfeit product in question, with details about how it was discovered and how it differs from the authentic product. If all of the necessary documentation is in one place, it can be easily accessed by or forwarded to the party dealing with enforcement.[61]

8.3.4. Outside Counsel

In-house counsel must often seek the assistance of outside counsel in fighting counterfeiting. Outside counsel often becomes essential when civil litigation is involved because in many states corporations cannot represent themselves in court.[62]

As a general rule, in-house counsel should control and supervise the anticounterfeiting program because they are best situated to set the parameters of the program and shape its overall strategy.[63] Experienced anticounterfeiting attorneys can help in-house counsel develop and implement anticounterfeiting programs and also help coordinate the efforts of law enforcement, Customs, private investigators, and counsel for other brand owners. In-house counsel should seek specific anticounterfeiting experience in any outside counsel chosen to represent the company.[64] Many law firms working in the area of copyright and trademark registration and licensing lack specific expertise in successfully combating counterfeiting. Further, pricing should be carefully reviewed and negotiated because enforcement can become extremely expensive. Although many law firms will quote hourly rates, it may be more cost effective to establish a flat fee for cease and desist letters, affidavits, and other matters preliminary to litigation.

8.3.5. Federal Law Enforcement

U.S. Customs and Border Protection (CBP)[65] and Immigration and Customs Enforcement (ICE)[66] are powerful allies in anticounterfeiting enforcement. CPB and ICE conduct investigations at the borders; at major international ports, such as Los Angeles and Newark; and at various other ports throughout the country.

ICE (Figure 8.2) is the U.S. government's second-largest investigatory agency.[67] ICE agents use a variety of tactics to combat counterfeiting and work in conjunction with similarly oriented organizations, including the National Intellectual Property Rights Coordination Center, ICE Cyber Crimes Center, and ICE Attaché Offices overseas. In 2011, ICE and CBP confiscated nearly $200 million worth of counterfeit goods intended for sale in the United States.[68]

The FBI also serves an essential role in investigating counterfeiters. Because of the established links between counterfeiting and organized crime, money laundering, and terrorism, counterfeiting has received increased attention from the FBI's Computer Crimes division.

8.3.6. Border Enforcement, the U.S. International Trade Commission, and ACTA

U.S. Customs and Border Protection (CBP) is the federal law enforcement agency charged with regulating international trade and combating terrorism and importation of counterfeits. CBP has a track record of effectively seizing counterfeit goods at U.S. borders. For instance, in 2012 CBP seized over 20,000 pairs of counterfeit Christian Louboutin shoes that had been

Fig. 8.2. Smuggling or dealing in counterfeit goods is a serious violation of the law. Criminal penalties may include large fines and prison sentences. (*Photo courtesy of ICE.*)

exported from China. However, mark owners must understand that CBP can confiscate only products that it knows to be counterfeit. Consequently, trademark owners must record their registered marks with U.S. Customs and other relevant Customs organizations throughout the world. This recordation enables Customs to seize counterfeit goods at the borders and stop their entry into commerce. Recordation in the United States is simple and relatively inexpensive and can be done online.

In order to maximize the benefits of recordation, trademark owners should provide brand-specific training for Customs agents and inspectors at key ports of entry. The IACC Foundation[69] has an active training program through which trademark owners can participate in the training of Customs and other law enforcement entities. These programs are effective and relatively inexpensive (free for members in the United States and about $400 for nonmembers per session; the cost of travel is additional for both members and nonmembers). Training materials should be concise (no more than a page or two) and up to date. They should identify a contact that is current, reliable, and expert in identifying counterfeits of the brand's merchandise and provide his or her name, address, phone number, and e-mail. Pictures of registered marks and authentic labels and hardware should also be included in this material. Customs officials should be given instructions about only what the trademark holder knows the officials can seize. Thus, only clear-cut counterfeit goods (as opposed to mere infringements or knockoffs)[70] should be identified in such materials. Recordation should be routinely updated, as the countries where authentic goods are manufactured often change, as do company personnel and product styles.[71]

Trademark and other IPR holders are increasingly turning to the U.S. International Trade Commission (ITC) to combat piracy. Mark owners may file a complaint with the ITC under Section 337 of the Tariff Act of 1930, which prohibits "unfair acts in the importation of articles into the United States" and also prohibits the importation of articles that infringe valid U.S. patents, copyrights, and trademarks.[72] Thus, French luxury brand Louis Vuitton filed an ITC complaint in 2010 alleging that Chinese counterfeiters were infringing its famous Toile Monogram trademark and seeking to block imports of infringing goods from China. The ITC ruled in Louis Vuitton's favor and issued a general exclusion order (GEO) prohibiting the unlicensed entry of infringing products. Louis Vuitton's favorable ruling will likely encourage other fashion companies to utilize ITC actions in the future.[73]

8.3.7. Private Investigators

Trademark owners often enlist private investigators to help build cases against counterfeiters.[74] To do so, private investigators often make undercover purchases from manufacturers and sellers of counterfeits.[75] Ethical rules prohibiting attorneys from engaging in deceitful, fraudulent, or dishonest conduct do not restrict them from hiring private investigators to assist in the legitimate investigation of potential counterfeiting practices.[76] Courts have approved the use of a private investigator when "1) the investigation relates to violations of civil or constitutional rights; 2) the investigation is done explicitly to determine whether such rights have been violated; 3) the evidence is not reasonably available through other means; 4) the conduct engaged in by the target of the investigation with the [private investigators] would have been engaged in with a member of the public; and 5) the [private investigators] are not seeking to elicit statements about past conduct for use in the litigation."[77]

Private investigators can serve as valuable intermediaries between trademark owners and their lawyers and law enforcement agencies. It is preferable to hire a private investigator from the jurisdiction in which the counterfeiting operation is taking place. This ensures that the investigator is familiar with local law enforcement networks (many private investigators have backgrounds in federal and state law enforcement).

Further, private investigators often have resources to track counterfeiting operations to their source in larger operations, which is preferable when bringing suits (as discussed below). They can effectively identify bargains that seem to be "too good to be true" and pose as purchasers at brick-and-mortar retailers and through e-commerce websites, and they can also authenticate counterfeit products on behalf of the trademark owner. Private investigators can also help educate law enforcement and assist them in building their case.

In *Rolex Watch U.S.A., Inc. v. Michel Co.*, Rolex's counsel hired a private investigator to observe defendant Micha Mottale ("Mottale") and purchase items from him. Rolex suspected that Mottale was selling used Rolex watches that contained parts that were not supplied or authorized by Rolex, and generic replacement parts that were designed to fit authentic Rolex watches to certain retail jewelers and jewelry dealers.[78] Mottale sold the plaintiff's private investigator unauthorized replacement parts bearing the Rolex trademark.[79] The Court held that Rolex's use of a private investigator did not violate the "no contact" rule of attorney professional conduct because the private investigator's "interaction with Mottale was no different than the contact that Mottale has had with other customers."[80]

Similarly, Cartier deployed a private investigator to conduct an investigation into Park Cities Jewelers ("Park Cities") when Cartier suspected that Park Cities was altering genuine Cartier watches to simulate more expensive Cartier watches and thereafter selling them. In developing its case, Cartier's private investigator purchased a watch from Park Cities. The Court held that Cartier's use of a private investigator did not amount to "unclean hands." The Court further held that "[t]he prevailing understanding in the legal profession is that a public or private lawyer's use of an undercover investigator to detect ongoing violations of the law is not ethically proscribed, especially where it would be difficult to discover the violations by other means."[81]

Competent investigators usually have law enforcement contacts in multiple jurisdictions. A well-chosen investigator can relieve some of the burden of investigation from law enforcement officials, who are often involved in numerous cases at a time. While private investigators can be expensive, the benefits they offer can be immediate. As with outside counsel, investigators should possess specific expertise in anticounterfeiting cases. The best sources of referrals are other brand owners and the IACC. It is prudent to use a relatively small number of good and cost-effective private investigators to assist with criminal actions.

8.3.8. Trade Organizations

There are various trade organizations that unite trademark holders and support the fight against counterfeits. These include the IACC,[82] the International Trademark Association,[83] the Recording Industry Association of America,[84] the Motion Picture Association of America,[85] the American Apparel and Footwear Association,[86] and the Council of Fashion Designers of America.[87] While this list is not exhaustive, each of these organizations can assist trademark holders in developing and implementing anticounterfeiting strategies and programs.

8.4. Criminal Enforcement

Both federal and state criminal statutes are available to support owners in their battle against counterfeiting.

8.4.1. Enforcement under Federal Criminal Statutes

Criminal penalties for counterfeiting can be severe. Due to the size and complexity of large-scale operations, counterfeiters may commit a number of federal crimes within a single enterprise. These federal crimes may include money laundering[88] and mail and wire fraud[89] as well as conspiracy to commit such offenses. Counterfeiters may also be charged with tax evasion and human rights violations. In addition to the CBP, ICE, and FBI, a number of other federal agencies can play a useful role in supporting anticounterfeiting efforts, including the U.S. Postal Service, the Secret Service, the Internal Revenue Service, and the Bureau of Alcohol, Tobacco, and Firearms.

It can be difficult to persuade federal prosecutors to investigate and prosecute a counterfeiting case, as the federal dockets are full of other cases involving crimes that are a greater public threat than counterfeiting. However, in recent years, there have been significant federal counterfeiting cases. For instance, in *U.S. v. Chong Lam*, two individuals were indicted in the U.S. District Court for the Eastern District of Virginia for conspiracy to traffic in counterfeit goods, trafficking in counterfeit goods, and smuggling goods into the United States.[90] On several occasions, the U.S. Customs and Border Patrol has seized goods bearing counterfeit Burberry marks.[91]

The perpetrators in these cases were convicted and sentenced to time in prison.[92]

8.4.2. Enforcement by State Criminal Statutes

In addition to federal criminal statutes, most states in the United States have criminal counterfeiting statutes.[93] New York, California, and Florida, leaders in the movement against counterfeiters, have enacted severe criminal state law penalties for counterfeiting.[94]

8.5. Civil Enforcement

Civil enforcement of IPR has advantages and disadvantages. For instance, in addition to the seizure of the counterfeit goods, a civil suit can result in a monetary settlement in the trademark owner's favor. Unfortunately, counterfeiters have discovered sophisticated ways to hide their assets.

8.5.1. Civil Seizure Actions

In cases in which counterfeit goods are being sold, trademark owners can seek recourse by filing a civil action and seeking an ex parte seizure order, allowing for the seizure of goods.[95] Ex parte seizure proceedings are brought in the absence of, and usually without notice to, the opposing party (i.e., the trademark owner does not inform the alleged counterfeiter in advance that a judge is being requested to order a seizure of the goods). The party seeking ex

---

Fashion Law *in Practice*

The Local Level: Counterfeiting and State Law Enforcement

Counterfeiting is rampant in many U.S. metropolitan areas and around the world. In 2011, the New York Police Department busted a local handbag dealer with $3.5 million worth of counterfeit purses and wallets. That same year, law enforcement agencies seized nearly $3 million in counterfeit goods from a Washington, DC, farmer's market. As federal priorities shift, many domestic police departments have begun to focus on breaking up local counterfeit rings, which commonly consist of local manufacturers, distributors, vendors, and retailers. The NYPD, in particular, has undertaken many investigations in connection with a larger anticounterfeiting plan initiated by Mayor Michael Bloomberg.

New York City's Office of Special Enforcement has sought to cut down on counterfeit operations by engaging multiple city agencies—including the Building Department, Police and Fire Departments, Department of Consumer Affairs, District Attorney's Office, and the local tax authorities—to combat landlords who knowingly rent to counterfeiters. In one raid, the Office of Special Enforcement seized over $1 million in counterfeit products, including counterfeit watches, jewelry, and handbags purporting to be from Rolex, Tiffany, Coach, Gucci, Chanel, and others. In addition to recovering from the individual merchants, the city authorities sought payment from the owners of buildings on a block of New York's Canal Street that was notorious for counterfeit. "Property owners should know that they are responsible for what goes on in their buildings and that hosting illegal activity like counterfeiting is a losing proposition," said Mayor Bloomberg.

Similar law enforcement agencies around the world are also fighting counterfeit activity. In June 2012, the French national police dismantled an international crime ring responsible for producing counterfeit Hermès bags with the help of several of the luxury house's employees. The value of counterfeits stemming from one single branch of the large ring was estimated at 18 million euros (approximately $22 million).

Sources: "$3.5 Million in Fake Designer Goods Seized from NYC Store," *NBC New York*, Nov. 9, 2011, http://www.nbcnewyork.com/local/6-Arrests-NYC-Counterfeit-Fake-Designer-Purses-Wallets-Investigation-133583608.html (last accessed Sept. 25, 2012); Press Release, Immigration and Customs Enforcement, *ICE HSI Seizes $3 Million Worth of Counterfeit Items at D.C.-Area Flea Market* (Oct. 17, 2011), available at http://www.ice.gov/news/releases/1110/111017washingtondc.htm (last accessed Sept. 25, 2012); Joelle Diderich, "Hermès Hails Break Up of Fake Bag Ring," *Women's Wear Daily*, June 17, 2012; Press Release, New York City, *Mayor Bloomberg Announces Cash Payment that Settles "Counterfeit Triangle" Case Brought by the Office of Special Enforcement* (April 6, 2010).

parte relief must establish that the defendant counterfeiter would be likely—if given advance notice of court proceedings—to flee or destroy the illegal goods. In addition to permanent injunctive relief from the counterfeiting at issue, plaintiffs can also recover profits, damages, costs, and attorney's fees.

There are currently near-mandatory treble damages in civil counterfeiting cases.[96] As actual damages are often difficult to prove, plaintiffs may instead request statutory damages,[97] ranging from $1,000 to $200,000 per infringing mark and up to $2 million per mark if the conduct is willful.[98] In addition to statutory damages, trademark owners can recover attorneys' fees and costs.[99] However, the rights holder has the burden of showing that the infringement warrants increased damages.[100]

8.5.2. Third-Party Liability Actions

Retailers and vendors of counterfeits are generally the most accessible targets of a lawsuit by a rights owner. However, because retailers may earn only a small portion of the overall proceeds from a counterfeiting scheme, the money damages that can be recovered may be minimal. Despite this limitation, lawsuits against vendors can be an effective deterrence against counterfeiters and may result in admissions that can lead to sources and locations of counterfeit goods.

In recent years, courts have increasingly allowed trademark owners to bring lawsuits against a larger pool of third parties. Such third parties may have deeper pockets (financial assets) than retailers and vendors and accordingly are attractive candidates for lawsuits. Thus, trademark owners now often choose to file lawsuits against landlords, flea market owners, and online marketplace owners that rent space to counterfeiters, search engine optimization companies, registrars, Internet service providers (ISPs), and payment processing companies that enable online money transfers between buyers and sellers. Such suits have resulted in greater financial settlements for trademark owners.[101]

Trademark owners may sue third parties under theories of contributory[102] and vicarious liability.[103] Thus, case law has recognized that the owner of a flea market or swap meet may be liable in a trademark infringement suit stemming from a vendor's sale of counterfeit goods. A flea market or swap meet owner may be deemed contributorily liable if it knows or "has reason to know" that a vendor is selling counterfeit goods[104] or knowingly provides a vendor with space to sell counterfeit goods.[105] "Contributory" liability also applies when one party induces another to infringe a trademark, as by supplying a product that the party knows will subsequently be sold as a counterfeit.[106]

Simultaneously, the owner of a flea market or swap meet may be held vicariously liable. For vicarious liability to apply, the flea market owner does not need to have actual knowledge that its vendor is selling counterfeits, but it must have control over the individual vendors and receive a direct financial benefit.[107] Courts have held that a market owner may be deemed "in control" of the vendors if it has the right "to terminate vendors for any reason."[108] Direct financial benefit may be established if the flea market owner profits, for instance, by collecting admission at the door, charging customers for parking, or charging vendors to participate in the market.[109]

The landlord–tenant relationship may also give rise to third-party liability in connection with the sale of counterfeits. Similar to the standard established for flea market owners, courts have held that a landlord must have knowledge of the infringing acts of its tenant or exercise control over the leased premises to be held liable.[110] Landlords may also be held liable under state statutes similar to the contributory infringement laws. For example, New York landlords can be held responsible for the illegal conduct of their tenants if they fail to take appropriate action after being put on notice.[111] ISPs that knowingly host websites that offer counterfeit goods for sale can be held contributorily liable on the same grounds as physical property owners (see *Fashion Law in Court: Internet Service Providers Subject to Liability*).

8.5.3. Cease and Desist Letters

In combating counterfeiters, the most practical first step is often to send a cease and desist letter to the infringing individual or entity. Such letters provide notice that the trademark owner is aware of the counterfeiting activities and demand that they cease immediately. These letters may be sufficient to solve the problem in cases where the infringing party did not know that the product was counterfeit or where the infringer sells from a fixed location like a retail store that can be easily monitored. At a minimum, such letters put the counterfeiter on notice, which helps establish proof of willfulness if the conduct continues, which may result in greater damages awards for the trademark owner. A company should have a standard cease and desist letter on file that can be customized for each individual situation (see, e.g., Figure 8.3 on page 156). Trademark owners should reply to counterfeiters' responses immediately in writing, and the mark owner should follow up by visiting the counterfeiters' store or website to confirm compliance.

8.5.4. Foreign Enforcement

Effective anticounterfeiting outside of the United States requires the assistance of local experts who understand the language, laws, and legal system of the particular country. In countries where enforcement is difficult, foreign investigators and counsel are best placed to advise on the most practical ways to proceed (see Chapter 18).

8.6. Enforcement on the Internet

In recent years, counterfeiters have turned to the Internet as their primary method for selling goods. They market counterfeits on their own websites, on auction sites, and on social network sites like Facebook and Twitter.[112] Counterfeiting websites on the Internet have proven to be a problem of unprecedented proportions for trademark owners and consumers alike. For trademark owners, this is because information is transmitted so quickly and relatively anonymously to a large number of people that it can be difficult to trace counterfeiters or track the extent of the problem. Since it is difficult to verify the authenticity of products until consumers receive them, buyers are often duped.

8.6.1. Websites

Complex issues arise from the operation of rogue websites on "cybersquatted" domains (domains with addresses that are identical or confusingly similar to the mark owner's brand name).[113] Such sites appear to sell authentic goods, but the operators of these sites are not authorized to sell authentic products and are selling counterfeits. Consumers, believing they are ordering from legitimate sites, may share sensitive personal and financial information.

For instance, a website purporting to sell authentic Christian Louboutin pumps may feature the same images and information used on the website of an authorized retailer of authentic Louboutin shoes, such as Neiman Marcus. The high-quality pictures and detailed information on the site selling counterfeit shoes gives it the appearance of an authorized retailer. When consumers receive the counterfeit shoes, they are often without remedy, as most counterfeit sites do not provide legitimate contact information.

VIA FEDERAL EXPRESS

Manager
Fashion Jewelry
4321 86th Ave.
Brooklyn, NY 10000

Re: [Trademark/Copyright]
Our File: NY/97-004

Dear Sir/Madam:

We are writing on behalf of John Doe Jeanswear Company ("JDJC"), owner of the JOHN DOE trademarks (the "Trademarks"), regarding your sale of garments bearing counterfeits of the trademarks described below.

You are hereby advised that under federal law, only John Doe has the right to use the "JOHN DOE" name and trademarks on a wide variety of products, including jeans and T-shirts. These rights are evidenced in the trademark registrations owned by JDJC and granted by the U.S. Patent and Trademark Office, including Registration Number for the trademark JOHN DOE.

Use of the Trademarks on merchandise, labels, or tags without the express written consent of JDJC is a violation of both federal and state law. Both making such merchandise and selling it is illegal. Violators of these laws not only face criminal prosecution, but may have their illegal goods, as well as the means of making or selling the goods, and their business records seized. Infringers may also be required to pay damages up to three times their profits or three times JDJC's damages, as well as having to pay our legal fees if we must go to court to stop the illegal use.

You should know that JDJC does everything possible to protect its interests in its name and marks, and seeks all the penalties listed above if we do not receive cooperation from an unauthorized user. You should also know that no one is authorized to manufacture, advertise, offer for sale or sell any products utilizing the Trademarks without the express written permission from JDJC. Any merchandise you may obtain from, or which is offered to you by anyone other than JDJC is most likely to be counterfeit or stolen property.

Our investigator recently purchased from your store merchandise that bears counterfeits of the Trademarks. We hereby demand that you:

1. Immediately cease and desist from further distributing, and/or selling this infringing merchandise bearing the Trademarks; and

2. Remove from sale all infringing items in your possession or under your control which bear the Trademarks including jeans, T-shirts, silk screens, promotional items or merchandise of any kind or nature bearing, or items used to manufacture or reproduce the Trademarks. Any sales to the public taking place after your receipt of this letter will constitute intentional and willful violations of our company's rights. Moreover, each unit of counterfeit or infringing merchandise in your possession or control constitutes evidence of our company's claims, and serious legal consequences would result from any failure by you to preserve all such evidence. You may not contact your vendors in writing or orally to return this evidence to your vendors or otherwise dispose of it or inject it back into the stream of commerce.

We also demand:

1. That within 24 hours of our delivery of this letter to you, you provide your written commitment that you have ceased all sales of counterfeit garments bearing the Trademarks or infringing versions thereof, your store and every other wholesale or retail location owned or controlled by you;

2. That within five (5) days of our delivery of this letter to you, you provide us with copies of all documents, correspondence, purchase orders, pro forma invoices, correspondence and all other records of every kind relating to your manufacture, purchase, distribution, sale and marketing activity with respect to all merchandise bearing counterfeits or infringements of the Trademarks. Such records should include, without limitation, documents reflecting the purchase price or factory price of all counterfeit products sold by you;

3. That within five (5) days of our delivery of this letter to you, you provide us with a list of every other wholesale or retail location owned or controlled by you in which the counterfeit garments are or have been sold, and list of sources from which the counterfeit goods were obtained; and

4. That within five (5) days of our delivery of this letter to you, you provide to us all information and documentation relating to the number of units of counterfeit merchandise within your possession and control, including any outstanding orders of the counterfeit merchandise, the number of units of such merchandise heretofore sold by you, whether sold at your store or any other wholesale or retail location owned or controlled by you, or to any other person or entity, and the sales price for each unit sold.

If you do not agree to these demands, JDJC will take the strongest possible legal action. Having received this letter, you now have actual notice of JDJC's exclusive rights to the use of the Trademarks. Any continued sale of such items would constitute a willful infringement of JDJC's rights.

Nothing in this letter shall be construed as a waiver or relinquishment of any rights or remedies of JDJC.

Very truly yours,

Fig. 8.3. Model cease and desist letter. (*Source: Barbara Kolsun & Nils Victor Montan, "Building a Comprehensive Counterfeiting Program," in* Trademark Counterfeiting in the United States, *at 7-62 [Brian W. Brokate & Dawn Atlas, eds., 2008]*).

Fashion Law *in Court*

Internet Service Providers Subject to Liability

Gucci America v. Frontline Processing established the potential liability faced by third-party companies that provide payment processing for online counterfeit merchants. Gucci America, the U.S. division of the Italian luxury goods company, successfully sued an individual merchant for trademark infringement stemming from his sale of counterfeit Gucci bags on TheBagAddiction.com. Based on evidence collected in that case, Gucci filed a subsequent suit against two credit card processing companies for contributory trademark infringement.

In the *Frontline* case, Judge Baer of the Southern District of New York held that a third party may be liable for contributory trademark infringement if it "intentionally induces another to infringe a trademark, or if it continues to supply its product to one whom it knows or has reason to know is engaging in trademark infringement."[a] The court further distinguished the requirements for liability, stating that a service provider "must have more than a general knowledge or reason to know that its service is being used to sell counterfeit goods."[b] Even if the third party did not intentionally induce the merchant, it may still be held liable for infringement if it supplied services with knowledge or deliberate ignorance of the infringing conduct and these services are a "necessary element" of the merchant's operation.[c] The court ruled that if the merchant's business was "functionally dependent" on the credit card processing, they either knew or should have known that they were servicing an infringing site.[d] The holding in *Gucci v. Frontline* helps trademark owners expand their reach beyond online merchants of counterfeits and their web hosts, allowing them to sue payment processing and merchant services companies.

---

[a]*Gucci America, Inc v. Frontline Processing Corp.*, 721 F.Supp.2d 228 (2010); see also *Inwood Laboratories, supra* note 114. Since *Inwood*, courts have extended the logic of the decision to impose liability on providers of goods and services. See *RFMAS, INC. v. Mimi So*, 619 F.Supp.2d 39 (S.D.N.Y. 2009).
[b]*Gucci America, supra* note 138.
[c]*Perfect 10, Inc. v. Visa Int'l Serv. Ass'n*, 494 F.3d 788 (9th Cir. 2007); *Tiffany Inc. v. eBay Inc.*, 600 F.3d 93 (2d Cir. 2010).
[d]*Gucci America, supra* note 138.

A trademark owner's tactics to fight these types of sites include sending cease and desist letters to the site, as well as to the ISP hosting the site. Such letters should point out the penalties of contributory infringement and request removal of the site. Some counterfeiters may use advanced techniques to shield their actual identities by relying on false names and addresses in countries that do not comply with U.S. IPR standards. In such cases the most effective remedies include filing civil lawsuits against the web host and law enforcement. The Online Protection and Enforcement of Digital Trade Act (OPEN) was formally introduced in the U.S. House of Representatives on January 18, 2012. OPEN seeks to cut off monetary transfers to foreign websites whose primary purpose is piracy or counterfeiting by allowing intellectual property owners to petition the ITC to launch investigations.[114]

When counterfeit goods are sold on the Internet, trademark owners may also seek recourse by filing suits based on claims of trademark infringement, counterfeiting, and dilution under the Lanham Act.[115] Mark owners may also rely on the Anticybersquatting Consumer Protection Act, which prohibits registering, trafficking in, or using a domain name with bad faith to profit from the goodwill of a trademark belonging to someone else.[116]

In 2012 several major fashion brands, including Burberry, Michael Kors, True Religion, and Hermès, successfully brought suits based on violations of the Anticybersquatting Consumer Protection Act and the Lanham Act against online counterfeiters operating rogue websites with domain names similar to the trademarked names. In such suits, trademark owners have not only been awarded damages stemming from the sale of counterfeit goods; they have also been awarded permanent injunctions, forcing the website operators to immediately and permanently discontinue use of the unauthorized domain names.[117] For example, Hermès enjoined over 30 rogue websites, including Hermes-BagsOutlets.com, HermesOutletMall.com, and eHermes.com. Even more recently, MAC Cosmetics' parent company, Estée Lauder Cos. Inc., was awarded $90 million stemming from the sale of counterfeit MAC products. The defendants, a group of Chinese cybersquatters and pirates, were operating 112 websites, including themaccosmetics.com and maccosmeticworld.com. Defendants were ordered to immediately and permanently halt operation of the sites. Judge Ronnie Abrams of the Southern District of New York Court ordered that any funds extracted from the PayPal accounts associated with these sites be applied to the plaintiffs' $90 million judgment award.[118]

8.6.2. Auction and "Listings" Sites

Online auction websites are notorious for their popularity with counterfeiters. Two of the largest are eBay and Yahoo!, but there are dozens of others. Due to the sheer size of these sites and the resulting difficulty in monitoring them for counterfeit goods, such sites have essentially become digital flea markets for the sale of counterfeit merchandise, and in consequence site owners can be held liable under the same approach as for owners of ordinary flea markets and stores.

Under current law, the burden is on mark owners to police the unauthorized use of their trademarks. In order to fight auction and listing sites effectively, trademark owners must monitor sites and contact them to terminate counterfeit auctions ("Notice and Take Down"). Trademark owners can make use of special utilities provided by the sites to authorized mark owners, such as eBay's Verified Rights Owner (VeRO) Program, which allows IP owners to quickly report listings that they believe infringe their property rights. Mark owners may need to designate an in-house employee, investigator, or outside counsel to manage this aspect of an anticounterfeiting program. Unfortunately, the anonymity provided by ineffective Internet governance and third-party services (proxy servers, broker sites, etc.) makes investigation difficult and time consuming.

As noted in the MAC Cosmetics case above, trademark holders have been increasingly able to recover damages from defendants' PayPal accounts and from bank accounts to which funds have been transferred from PayPal accounts. This tactic was facilitated by Operation In Our Sites, a 2010 initiative of the U.S. Immigration and Customs Enforcement's Homeland Security Investigations and National Intellectual Property Rights Coordination Center. In 2010, the Department of Justice and Immigration and Customs Enforcement executed

---

Fashion Law *in Court*

eBay: Limited Gains against a Major Counterfeiting Problem

With the emergence of large online marketplaces selling counterfeits, it has become crucial for ISPs and trademark owners to protect intellectual property on the Internet and promote secure online shopping. Thus, in 2004 Tiffany brought suit against eBay for contributory trademark infringement stemming from the sale of counterfeit Tiffany products on its site.[a] In line with the long-standing U.S. legal position that it is the trademark owner's responsibility to police its mark, the United States District Court ruled against Tiffany & Co. on all claims. The court held that the test for contributory trademark infringement by an online marketplace is that the ISP must have "more than a general knowledge or reason to know that its service is being used to sell counterfeits."[b] The court was influenced by eBay's extensive efforts to prevent the sale of counterfeits: eBay maintained a $20 million/year program to promote trust and safety, which included a buyer protection program, a fraud engine, a "Notice and Takedown" system (VeRO), and measures specifically intended to prevent the sale of Tiffany counterfeits (which included earrings, necklaces, bracelets, pendants, cufflinks, brooches, and rings). The court also noted that Tiffany failed to produce concrete evidence that any consumer was actually misled by any of eBay's advertising, a necessary element in establishing both false advertising and trademark infringement claims.

Outside of the United States, courts take a different stance. Weeks prior to the July 2008 *Tiffany & Co.* decision, a French court ruled against eBay in a similar suit brought by LVMH and Christian Dior, awarding the luxury houses a total of $63.2 million.[c] More recently, the European Court of Justice ruled in favor of L'Oreal in a suit against eBay. Here, the court held that an ISP, whether or not it plays an active role by advertising or promoting the sale of infringing goods, may not rely on an exemption from liability, especially if it has not acted as a diligent online service provider should.[d] Both ISPs and trademark holders can take lessons away from these cases. ISPs must implement anticounterfeit efforts on their sites generally and also, specifically for brands that are well known and frequently counterfeited. Trademark holders, similarly, must police their trademarks to prevent counterfeiting and should not rely on ISPs to do this work for them.

---

[a]*Tiffany, supra* note 140.
[b]*Id.*
[c]*Louis Vuitton Malleteir v. eBay, Inc.*, Tribunal de Commerce, Paris, June 30, 2008; *Christian Dior Couture, SA v. eBay Inc.*, Tribunal de commerce, Paris, June 30, 2008.
[d]Case C-324/09, *L'Oreal SA & Ors v. EBay Intl AG & Ors*, 2009 E.C.R. 1094 (U.K.).

---

seizure orders against 82 websites engaged in the illegal sale and distribution of counterfeit goods and copyrighted works. This initiative led to the recovery of funds that otherwise would have been extremely difficult to collect since the defendant counterfeiters were located in other countries, usually China.

8.7. The Gray Market and the First-Sale Doctrine

Authentic products that are sold through unauthorized channels of distribution are commonly referred to as *gray market products* and often blur the line between counterfeits and authentic items. Because prices for products often vary substantially from country to country, intermediaries will purchase products legally from authorized dealers in countries where the products are less expensive and sell them to unauthorized retailers in countries where the products are more expensive. Such gray market transactions enable these retailers to sell the goods at lower prices than authorized retailers.

In a recent case, Zino Davidoff, the owner of the COOL WATER fragrance that is manufactured and marketed by Coty, Inc., brought a suit against CVS Pharmacy, alleging various trademark claims. Davidoff moved to enjoin CVS from selling the gray market COOL WATER perfumes it had purchased from authorized dealers. The U.S. Court of Appeals for the Second Circuit found CVS liable for trademark infringement. Because CVS had removed the production codes that Davidoff used to guard against counterfeits and protect the trademark from "quality slippage," the goods were no longer deemed authentic.[119] Products are not considered authentic if they do not conform to the trademark holder's quality control standards or if they materially differ from the products authorized by the trademark holder for sale. As such, the Second Circuit affirmed the lower court's finding and ruled in Davidoff's favor. The Court noted the importance of the "comprehensive quality assurance and anticounterfeiting program" that Davidoff and Coty had established.[120] The use of the UPC enables the Davidoff to compare its codes with those known to be used by counterfeits and recall any infringing products. By removing the codes, CVS prevented Davidoff from identifying and recalling potential counterfeit products.

The distinction between the authorized and unauthorized sale of goods is often insignificant if the goods being offered for sale are authentic. Trademark liability is not imposed for the sale of authentic goods even if the trademark owner does not authorize the sale. This is because the goal of trademark law is largely to prevent consumer confusion, and the unauthorized sale of authentic goods does not inherently cause confusion or dilution.[121] Thus, the Davidoff case turned on the fact that CVS removed the production codes, materially altering the Plaintiff's product. In contrast, if Costco is selling authentic 7 For All Mankind jeans manufactured in the United States, 7 For All Mankind has no recourse against the discount retailer even though Costco is not one of its authorized retailers.

The first-sale doctrine plays a large role in the realm of IP rights by limiting certain rights of a copyright or trademark owner, and often arises in the context of the gray market and subsequent, unauthorized sales. In accordance with the Copyright Act of 1976, "the owner of a particular copy [...] lawfully made under this title [...] is entitled, without the authority of the copyright owner, to sell [...] that copy."[122] Although the Copyright Act codifies the first-sale doctrine as relates to copyright, there is no equivalent federal trademark statute. Consequently, as regards trademarks the doctrine is based purely on case law. It was first acknowledged by the Supreme Court in 1924[123] and clarified by the Ninth Circuit in 1995.[124]

In order for the first-sale doctrine to apply, the goods at issue may be manufactured in the United States or lawfully made abroad. In 2013, the Supreme Court in *Kirtsaeng v. John Wiley & Sons, Inc.* held that the words "lawfully made under this title," i.e., Section 109 (a) of the Copyright Act, "favor a non-geographic interpretation." Prior to Kirtsaeng, the Ninth

Circuit's decision in *Omega S.A. v. Costco Wholesale Corp.*, upheld by the Supreme Court in a 2010 unsigned per curium opinion, held that in order for the first-sale doctrine to apply, the goods at issue must be manufactured in the United States. Omega had brought suit against Costco for its unauthorized sale of authentic Omega watches that Costco obtained through the gray market and sold at a discount. Each of Omega's watches bore a copyrighted symbol to signify its authenticity, which enabled Omega to bring copyright infringement claims against Costco for violating its exclusive right to distribute and for importing goods into the United States without its authorization.

Costco argued that its sale of the watches was permissible under the first sale doctrine. The court ruled in Omega's favor, holding that the language "lawfully made under this title" did not extend to goods made outside of the United States. Therefore, Costco could not sell the Swiss-made watches without authorization from Omega. The court distinguished this case from *Quality King v. L'Anza*, in which the first-sale doctrine had permitted the unauthorized resale of shampoo that was manufactured in the United States, exported, and then sold back into the United States.

In *Kirtsaeng*, a Thai student studying in the United States purchased copies of foreign edition English-language textbooks at Thai bookstores, where they sold at low prices; the student asked his family members to mail the books to him in the United States, where he resold the textbooks at a profit.

The *Kirtsaeng* decision is a win for consumers and discount retails and off-price merchants who tend to purchase imported goods from middlemen and distributors at a lower price instead of buying directly from authorized U.S. distributors, effectively overruling *Omega v. Costco*.

8.8. Summary of Key Points

1. Counterfeiting is not a victimless crime: it is a significant global problem, costing legitimate employers countless opportunities to create jobs, while putting consumers at risk of purchasing products beneath international standards that pose a risk of harm, generating funding for criminal enterprises and terrorist organizations, and placing workers in environments where there is no incentive to avoid sweatshop conditions.

2. All counterfeits are infringements, but not all infringements are counterfeits. Counterfeiting is narrower in scope than other trademark infringement (applying to only identical or indistinguishable marks) and can lead to drastically different consequences. Ordinary infringement can result in injunctions or money judgments, whereas counterfeiting can result in seizure and destruction of goods, large criminal fines, and even incarceration.

3. Anticounterfeiting measures can be two-pronged: criminal enforcement (with the collaboration of federal, state, or local law enforcement) and/or civil enforcement. Civil enforcement remedies can include cease and desist letters, civil seizure actions, third-party liability actions, and money judgments, which can include treble damages.

4. Civil seizure actions are generally based on obtaining an ex parte seizure order, which requires the brand owner to post a bond and establish through assertions of evidence a high likelihood of success on the merits.

5. Third-party liability actions may be pursued under theories of contributory liability or vicarious liability. Landlords may be held liable under state statutes for contributory

infringement. Internet service providers that knowingly host websites that offer counterfeit goods for sale can be held contributorily liable.

6. When counterfeit goods are sold on the Internet, trademark owners can seek recourse by filing suits for trademark infringement, counterfeiting, and/or trademark dilution under the Lanham Act. The burden is on mark owners to police auction websites and contact them to remove counterfeit product listings.

7. Authentic products sold through unauthorized channels of distribution are known as "gray market products" or "parallel imports." While such distribution is difficult to stop, because the goods are authentic, the brand owner may be able to stop sales when the gray market goods are materially different from other branded goods sold in the domestic market.

Notes

1. Curtis Krechevsky, *INTA and the Battle Against Counterfeiting*, 93 TRADEMARK REP. 145 (2003).

2. David J. Goldstone and Peter J. Toren, *The Criminalization of Trademark Counterfeiting*, 31 CONN L. REV. 1 (1998).

3. 15 U.S.C. §§ 1116(d)(1)(B)(II), 1127 (2008).

4. Lanham Act, 15 U.S.C. § 1051.

5. Krechevsky, *supra* note 1.

6. Rakoff & Wolff, *supra* note 4, at 494-96.

7. *Id.*

8. Trademark Counterfeiting Act of 1984, 18 U.S.C. § 2320 (2008).

9. *See* International AntiCounterfeiting Coalition, *The International Anti-Counterfeiting Coalition Facts on Fakes*, available at http://counterfeiting.unicri.it/docs/The%20International%20Anti-Counterfeiting%20Coalition.Facts%20on%20Fakes.pdf (last accessed Nov. 7, 2012), citing George W. Abbott, Jr. and Lee S. Sporn, *Trademark Counterfeiting* § 1.01 (2001).

10. See William O. Hennessey, "Protection of Intellectual Property in China (30 Years and More): A Personal Reflection," Sixth Annual Baker Botts Lecture (Dec. 17, 2009) available at http://www.law.gwu.edu/News/20112012events/Documents/Hennessey.pdf. See also Daniel C. K. Chow, *Counterfeiting in the People's Republic of China*, 78 WASH. U. L. Q 1 (2000), available at http://digitalcommons.law.wustl.edu/lawreview/vol78/iss1/1 (last visited Sept. 25, 2012).

11. Ambassador Ronald Kirk, Office of the United States Trade Representative, 2012 SPECIAL 301 REPORT (2012), available at http://www.ustr.gov/sites/default/files/2012%20Special%20301%20Report_0.pdf (last accessed Sept. 25, 2012).

12. *Id.*

13. Peter K. Yu, *From Pirates to Partners: Protecting Intellectual Property in China in the Twenty-First Century*, 50 AM. U. L. REV. 131, 165 (2000).

14. *Id.*, at 207.

15. *EU–US Action Strategy for the Enforcement of Intellectual Property Rights*, available at http://www.eurunion.org/partner/summit/summit06212006/2006euussummitintellprop.pdf (last accessed Sept. 25, 2012).

16. In 2012, Mexico, the European Union and 22 countries, which are member states of the European Union, finalized the ACTA. Press Release, Office of the United States Trade Representative, *U.S. Participants Finalize Anti-Counterfeiting Trade Agreement Text* (Nov. 15, 2010) available at http://www.ustr.gov/about-us/press-office/press-releases/2010/november/us-participants-finalize-anti-counterfeiting-trad (last accessed Sept. 25, 2012); Jason Walsh, "Europe's Internet Revolt: Protesters See Threats in Antipiracy Treaty," *The Christian Science Monitor*, Feb. 11, 2012, available at http://www.csmonitor.com/World/Europe/2012/0211/Europe-s-Internet-revolt-protesters-see-threats-in-antipiracy-treaty (last accessed Sept. 25, 2012); Olivia Solon, "The EU Signs Up to ACTA, but French MEP Quits in Protest," *Wired*, Jan 26, 2012, available at http://www.wired.co.uk/news/archive/2012-01/26/eu-signs-up-to-acta (last accessed Sept. 25, 2012).

17. Kirk, *supra* note 16.

18. *Id.*

19. It is important to note that it is difficult to come up with a precise figure because so much of the counterfeiting industry is below the economic radar. See International AntiCounterfeiting Coalition, *About Counterfeiting*, available at http://www.iacc.org/about-counterfeiting/ (last accessed Sept. 25, 2012).

20. *Id.*

21. *Id.*

22. *Id.*; S. 1984, 109th Cong. § 1 (2005).

23. Laurie Sullivan, "HP Cracks Down on Counterfeit PC Parts in China," *Electronic Business News*, June 26 2002, available at http://www.eetimes.com/electronics-news/4027805/HP-cracks-down-on-counterfeit-PC-parts-in-China (last visited Nov. 7, 2012).

24. International AntiCounterfeiting Coalition, *The Truth about Counterfeiting*, http://www.iacc.org/about-counterfeiting/the-truth-about-counterfeiting.php (last visited Sept. 25, 2012).

25. Press Release, Customs and Border Patrol, CBP, *ICE Release Report on 2011 Counterfeit Seizure* (January 9, 2012), available at http://www.cbp.gov/xp/cgov/newsroom/news_releases/national/01092012.xml (last accessed Sept. 25, 2012).

26. *Bootleg Billions: The Impact of the Counterfeit Goods Trade in New York City* is the only available study of its kind.

27. William C. Thompson, Jr., *Bootleg Billions: The Impact of the Counterfeit Goods Trade in New York City* 4 (Nov. 2004), available at http://www.comptroller.nyc.gov/bureaus/bud/04reports/Bootleg-Billions.pdf (last accessed Sept. 25, 2012).

28. Press Release, Office of City Attorney Carmen A. Trutanich, *City Attorney Gathers with Law Enforcement Partners to Discuss Continued Efforts to Combat Counterfeit and Piracy Crimes During Holiday Season* (Dec. 6, 2011), available at http://atty.lacity.org/stellent/groups/electedofficials/@atty_contributor/documents/contributor_web_content/lacityp_019129.pdf (last visited Sept. 25, 2012).

29. "Counterfeit Seizures Up but Value Down in '10," *Women's Wear Daily*, March 17, 2011.

30. *Id.*, at Chapter 4 and Appendix 4-2.

31. *Id.* at Chapter 4; see also 15 U.S.C. § 1116-1118.

32. Barbour, *Counterfeit Education*, http://www.barbour.com/counterfeit-education (last accessed Sept. 25, 2012).

33. *Stop Fake: Christian Louboutin, About Our Actions*, http://www.stopfakelouboutin.com/en (last accessed September 25, 2012).

34. See generally Maureen Walterbach, *International Illicit Convergence: The Growing Problem of Transnational Organized Crime Groups' Involvement in Intellectual Property Rights Violations*, 34 FLA. ST. U. L. REV. 591 (2007).

35. Anna-Lisa Jacobson, *The New Chinese Dynasty: How the United States and International Intellectual Property Laws Are Failing to Protect Consumers and Inventors from Counterfeiting*, 7 RICH J. GLOBAL L. & BUS. 45, 58 (2008).

36. *Counterfeit Goods: Easy Cash for Criminals and Terrorists: Hearing Before the Committee on Homeland Security and Governmental Affairs*, 109th Cong. (May 25, 2005), available at http://www.gpo.gov/fdsys/pkg/CHRG-109shrg21823/pdf/CHRG-109shrg21823.pdf (last accessed Sept. 25, 2012).

37. *The Links between Intellectual Property Crime and Terrorist Financing: Hearing Before the H. Committee on International Relations*, 108th Cong. (July 16, 2003) (Public Testimony of Ronald K. Noble), available at http://www.interpol.int/News-and-media/Speeches#n5884 (last accessed Nov. 7, 2012).

38. Willy Stern, "Why Counterfeit Goods May Kill," *Business Week*, Sept. 2, 1996.

39. Kathleen Millar, "Financing Terror: Profits from Counterfeit Goods Pay for Attacks," *U.S. Customs Today* (Nov. 2002), available at http://cbp.gov/xp/CustomsToday/2002/November/interpol.xml (last accessed Sept. 25, 2012).

40. *The Links between Intellectual Property Crime and Terrorist Financing*, *supra* note 44.

41. According to U.S. law, it is generally legal to make copies of clothing and accessories as long as these products do not bear misappropriated trademarks. As such, a large amount of counterfeiters ship the clothing and accessories and the labels separately. The labels, which bear misappropriated trademarks, are then attached to the clothing and accessories at factories in the United States and then sent to the U.S. buyers. This allows the counterfeiters to avoid seizure at the borders.

42. Trademark Dilution Revision Act of 2006, Pub. L. 109-312, 120 Stat. 1730 (2006).

43. 15 U.S.C. § 1127, 15 U.S.C. § 1116(d)(1)(B)(i), and 18 U.S.C. § 2320(e)(1).

44. See *Montres Rolex, S.A. v. Snyder*, 718 F.2d 524, 527 (2d Cir. 1983); see also Robert J. Abalos, *Commercial Trademark Counterfeiting in the United States, the Third World and Beyond: American and International Attempts to Stem the Tide*, 5 B.C. Third World L.J. 151 n.3 (1985), available at http://lawdigitalcommons. bc.edu/cgi/viewcontent.cgi?article=1395&context=twlj (last accessed Sept. 25, 2012).

45. The "confusingly similar" standard for infringement is a lower threshold to reach.

46. 15 U.S.C. § 1116(d)(1)(B).

47. United States Patent and Trademark Office, *Nice Agreement Tenth Edition—General Remarks, Class Headings, and Explanatory Notes*, http://www.uspto.gov/trademarks/notices/international.jsp (last accessed Sept. 25, 2012).

48. *Id.*

49. J. Thomas McCarthy, *McCarthy on Trademarks and Unfair Comp.* § 24:6 (4th ed. 2008).

50. *Id.* at § 16:18.

51. *Id.*; see also *Sengoku Works Ltd. v. RMC Int'l, Ltd.*, 96 F.3d 1217, 1219 (9th Cir. 1996) (noting that "To acquire ownership of a trademark is not enough to have invented the mark first or even to have registered it first; the party claiming ownership must have been the first to actually use the mark in the sale of goods or services").

52. Stephanie M. Greene, *Protecting Well-Known Marks in China: Challenges for Foreign Mark Holders*, 45 Am. Bus. L.J. 371, 375 (2008).

53. 18 U.S.C. § 2320 (2008).

54. *United States v. Diallo*, 476 F.Supp.2d 497 (3rd Cir. 2007) (suggesting that the Third Circuit defines "use" in the context of counterfeiting statute).

55. Barbara Kolsun & Nils Victor Montan, "Building a Comprehensive Counterfeiting Program" in *Trademark Counterfeiting in the United States*, at 7–6 (Brian W. Brokate & Dawn Atlas, eds., 2008).

56. *Id.*

57. *Id.*

58. *Id.*

59. *Id.*

60. *Id.*

61. *Id.*

62. N.Y. C.P.L.R. § 321(a).

63. Kolsun & Montan, *supra* note 64, at 7–9.

64. *Id.*

65. U.S. Customs and Border Protection Home Page, http://www.cbp.gov (last accessed Sept. 25, 2012).

66. U.S. Immigration and Customs Enforcement Home Page, http://www.ice.gov (last accessed Sept. 25, 2012).

67. U.S. Immigration and Customs Enforcement, *Overview*, http://www.ice.gov/about/overview/ (last accessed Sept. 25, 2012).

68. Press Release, U.S. Immigration and Customs Enforcement, *ICE Arrests 4 Illegal Aliens, Seizes $5 Million in Counterfeit Merchandise in Alabama* (May 2, 2008), available at http://www.ice.gov/news/releases/0805/080502montgomery.htm (last accessed Sept. 25, 2012).

69. The International AntiCounterfeiting Coalition Inc. Foundation Training Site, http://www.iaccfoundation.org/ (last accessed Sept. 25, 2012).

70. CBP is only authorized to seize blatantly counterfeit goods. As such, CBP may not seize mere knockoffs (copies of designer clothing or accessories that do not bear a misappropriated trademark) or goods that bear marks that amount to trademark infringement (goods that bear a mark similar to the trademark owner's but that is "not identical to or substantially indistinguishable from the original registered mark").

71. A trademark recordation with the CPB expires after 20 years. To continue uninterrupted CBP protection for trademarks, the trademark owner must submit a written application to renew CBP recordation to the IPR & Restricted Merchandise Branch not later than 3 months after the date of expiration. Renewal of Trademark Recordation, 19 CFR § 133.7.

72. 19 U.S.C. § 1337.

73. *In the Matter of Certain Handbags, Luggage, Accessories and Packaging Thereof*, ITC Inv. No. 337-TA-754 (U.S. Int'l Trade Comm'n May 30, 2012), available at http://www.usitc.gov/secretary/fed_reg_notices/337/337_754_notice05302012sgl.pdf (last accessed Oct. 23, 2012).

74. John K. Villa, *The Ethics of Using Undercover Investigators*, 28 ACC Docket 9, Nov. 2011, at 86.

75. *Id.*

76. *Id.*

77. *Id.* at 90.

78. See *Rolex Watch, U.S.A., Inc. v. Michel Co.*, 179 F.3d 704 (9th Cir. 1999).

79. *Id.*

80. *Id.*

81. See *Cartier, a division of Richemont N. Am., Inc. v. Symbolix, Inc.*, 386 F. Supp. 2d 354, 362 (S.D.N.Y. 2005).

82. International AntiCounterfeiting Coalition, *supra* note 26.

83. International Trademark Association Home Page, http://www.inta.org (last accessed Sept. 25, 2012).

84. Recording Industry Association of America Home Page, http://www.riaa.com (last accessed Sept. 25, 2012).

85. Motion Picture Association of America Home Page, http://www.mpaa.org (last accessed Sept. 25, 2012).

86. American Apparel and Footwear Association Home Page, http://www.apparelandfootwear.org (last accessed Sept. 25, 2012).

87. Council of Fashion Designers of America Home Page, http://www.cfda.com (last accessed Sept. 25, 2012).

88. Department of Homeland Security, *Money Laundering*, http://www.ice.gov/money-laundering/ (last accessed Sept. 25, 2012).

89. 18 USC § 1343 (Wire fraud); 18 USC § 1341 – (Frauds and Swindles).

90. *United States v. Chong Lam*, No. 3:07-CR-374, 2011 WL 1167208 (E.D. Va. Mar. 28, 2011). Defendants were charged under 18 U.S.C. § 371 for conspiracy to traffic counterfeit goods, 18 U.S.C. § 2320(a) for trafficking in counterfeit goods, and 18 U.S.C. § 545 for smuggling.

91. *Id.*; see also Shaun Tolson, "Prison Time for Peddlers of Phony Purses," *The Boston Herald*, Apr. 10, 2007, at 4; Shelley Murphy, "Cache of Knockoff Bags Triggers Federal Case," *The Boston Globe*, Nov. 4, 2005, at A1 (hearing the counterfeit case in federal court enabled pursuit of more serious criminal penalties when four individuals were arrested for the seizure of 20,000 counterfeit products).

92. *United States v. Chong Lam, supra* note 98.

93. See *Trademark Counterfeiting in the United States, supra* note 14, at Chapter 4 and Appendix 4-2.

94. N.Y. Penal Law § 165.70 *et. seq.* (2008); Cal. Penal Code § 350(a)-(g) (2008); Fla. Stat. §§ 831.032 (2007).

95. 15 U.S.C. § 1116.

96. 15 U.S.C. § 1117(b); see also *Koon Chun Hing Kee Soy & Sauce Factory, Ltd. v. Star Mark Management, Inc.*, 628 F.Supp.2d 312 (E.D.N.Y. 2009) (finding that an award of treble damages and attorneys' fees is mandatory when there are no exceptional circumstances surrounding the counterfeiting and the counterfeiting is willful); *Coach, Inc. v. 3rd Street Flea Market*, No. 2:10-cv-2410 (W.D. Tenn. Mar. 20, 2012) (awarded $5 million in jury verdict against the flea market owner for willful trademark infringement and $185,000 in attorneys' fees and costs).

97. 15 U.S.C. § 1117(c).

98. 15 U.S.C. § 1117(c)(2); see also *Burberry Ltd. v. John Doe 1*, No. 1:11-cv-830 (S.D.N.Y. May 18, 2012) (awarding $180 million in damages); *Hermes Int'l v. John Doe*, No. 12-cv-1623 (S.D.N.Y. Apr. 11, 2012) (awarding $100 million in damages); *Deckers Outdoor Corp. v. Does 1–101*, 11-cv-7970 and 12-cv-377 (N.D. Ill. Apr. 11, 2012) (awarding $363.2 million in damages); *Fendi Adele SRL v. Burlington Coat Factory Warehouse Corp.*, 2012 WL 1097338 (S.D.N.Y. Apr. 2, 2012) (Burlington's vendor is not required to indemnify Burlington for treble damages because of Burlington's willful infringement of Fendi's trademarks); *True Religion Apparel, Inc. v. Xiaokang Lee*, No. 1:11-cv-08242 (S.D.N.Y. Mar. 2012) (awarding $864 million in damages); *Tory Burch, LLC v. Yong Shen Int'l Trade Co.*, No. 1:10-cv-9336 (S.D.N.Y. May 13, 2011) (awarding $164 million in damages); *The North Face Apparel Corp. v. Fujian Sharing Import & Export Ltd.*, 10-civ-1630 (S.D.N.Y. Dec. 21, 2010) (awarding $78 million in damages).

99. *Fendi Adele, supra* note 107 (awarding Burlington $248,257.14, a portion of damages, attorney's fees, and prejudgment interest, against its vendor of counterfeit merchandise under indemnification); see also *Louis Vuitton Malletier, S.A. v. LY USA, Inc.*, 2012 WL 1034900 (2d Cir. Mar. 29, 2012) (holding that, in counterfeiting cases, Plaintiffs can recover attorney's fees *in addition to* statutory damages); *Coach Inc. v. Sassy Couture*, 2012 WL 162366 (W.D. Tex. Jan. 19, 2012) (awarding Coach $60,000 in damages and $52,490.50 in attorney's fees).

100. *Phillip Morris USA, Inc. v. Lee*, 547 F.Supp.2d 685 (W.D. Tex. 2008).

101. See also *Roger Cleveland Golf Co., Inc. v. Prince*, 2012 WL 1106775 (D.S.C. Mar. 30, 2012) (court denied search engine optimization company motion for relief from judgment and motion for remittitur; awarding Roger Cleveland Golf Company $70,000 per infringing mark); *Louis Vuitton Malletier, S.A. v. Akanoc*

Solutions, Inc., 658 F.3d 936 (9th Cir. 2011) (awarded $10,500,000 for contributory trademark infringement and $300,000 for contributory copyright infringement against ISPs).

102. Contributory liability occurs when a third-party defendant "directly contributes to another's infringement" in the absence of direct control. *Fonovisa, Inc. v. Cherry Auction, Inc.*, 76 F.3d 259, 264 (9th Cir. 1996).

103. *Id.* (Vicarious infringement is slightly different from contributory infringement in that the seller of counterfeit product is said to be acting as an agent of the principal. This infringement is the kind of liability that typically arises in flea markets, where the market owner can be held liable for the fact that a seller on his or her property is selling infringing content, regardless of whether the owner knows the content to be infringing.)

104. *Coach, Inc. v. Gata Corp.*, 2011 WL 2358671 (D.N.H. Jun 9, 2011) (Coach is entitled to summary judgment on its claim for contributory trademark infringement from flea market owner); *UMG Recordings, Inc. v. Bertelsmann AG*, 222 F.R.D. 408 (N.D. Cal. 2004); *Getty Petroleum Corp. v. Aris Getty, Inc.*, 55 F.3d 718, 719 (1st Cir. 1995).

105. The theory behind contributory liability is that "one who directly contributes to another's infringement should be held accountable"; *Fonovisa, supra* note 111 at 264. See also *Malletier v. Eisenhauer Road Flea Market, Inc.*, 2012 WL 457866 (W.D. Tex. Jan. 12, 2012) (flea market owner awarded $3.6 million in compensatory damages plus interest after jury trial and ordered to periodically inspect flea market booths on its property to determine whether counterfeit goods were sold and to promptly terminate leases of infringing tenants).

106. Heather J. McDonald, *Counterfeit Goods on Premises: Third Party Liability Actions Target Owners of Property Where Business Is Conducted*, N.Y.L.J., Oct. 29, 2007, at S2; see also *Inwood Laboratories, supra* note 114.

107. "Even in the absence of an employer-employee relationship, one may be [held] vicariously liable if he has the right and ability to supervise the infringing activity and also has a direct financial interest in such activities." *Fonovisa, supra* note 111.

108. *Fonovisa, supra* note 111 at 262.

109. *Id.* at 263.

110. *Id.* at 262; see also *Polo Ralph Lauren Corp. v. Chinatown Gift Shop*, 855 F.Supp. 648 (S.D.N.Y. 1994); 15 U.S.C. §1501.

111. N.Y. Real Prop. § 231 (2008).

112. Alexandra Steigrad, "Michael Kors Latest to Take on Cybersquatters," *Women's Wear Daily*, June 29, 2012, available at http://www.wwd.com/business-news/legal/kors-latest-to-take-on-cybersquatters-6018420 (last accessed Sept 25, 2012).

113. Rogue websites are those that are primarily dedicated to the illegal sale and distribution of counterfeit or pirated goods. Press Release, United States House of Representative Committee on the Judiciary, *Statement on Judiciary Chairman Lamar Smith, Hearing on H.R. 3261, the "Stop Online Piracy Act"* (November 16, 2011), available at http://judiciary.house.gov/news/Statement%20HR%203261.html (last accessed Sept 25, 2012).

114. Online Protection and Enforcement of Digital Trade Act, H.R. 3782, 112th Cong. (2012).

115. 15 U.S.C. § 1051 et. seq.

116. Anticybersquatting Consumer Protection Act, 15 U.S.C. § 1125(d).

117. *Burberry Limited, supra* note 107; *Hermès of Paris Inc., supra* note 107; *Michael Kors L.L.C. v. John Doe 1 a/k/a Zheng Little, et al.*, 1:11-cv-08653-SAS (S.D.N.Y. 2012); *True Religion Apparel, Inc., supra* note 107.

118. Alexandra Steigrad, "Lauder Wins MAC Cybersquatter Case," *Women's Wear Daily*, August 1, 2012, available at http://www.wwd.com/business-news/legal/mac-este-lauder-score-90-million-judgment-6131940 (last accessed Sept. 25, 2012).

119. *Zino Davidoff SA v. CVS Corp.*, 571 F.3d 238 (2nd Cir. 2007).

120. *Id.*

121. The Lanham Act does not impose liability for "the sale of genuine goods bearing a true mark even though the sale is not authorized by the mark owner" because such a sale does not inherently cause confusion or dilution. *Polymer Tech. Corp. v. Mimran*, 975 F.2d 58, 61 (2d Cir. 1992).

122. 17 U.S.C. 109(a).

123. "[A trademark] only gives the right to prohibit the use of it so far as to protect the owner's good will against the sale of another's product as his." *Prestonettes, Inc. v. Coty*, 264 U.S. 359, 368 (1924).

124. "[T]he right of a producer to control distribution of its trademarked product does not extend beyond the first sale of the product." *Sebastian Int'l, Inc. v. Long's Drugs Stores Corp.*, 53 F.3d 1073, 1074 (9th Cir. 1995).